CONTENDING IMAGES OF WORLD POLITICS

Contending Images of World Politics

Edited by

Greg Fry

and

Jacinta O'Hagan

First published in Great Britain 2000 by
MACMILLAN PRESS LTD
Houndmills, Basingstoke, Hampshire RG21 6XS and London
Companies and representatives throughout the world

A catalogue record for this book is available from the British Library.

ISBN 0–333–91375–2 hardcover
ISBN 0–333–91376–0 paperback

 First published in the United States of America 2000 by
ST. MARTIN'S PRESS, LLC.,
Scholarly and Reference Division
175 Fifth Avenue, New York, N.Y. 10010

ISBN 0–333–91375–2 (cloth)
ISBN 0–333–91376–0 (paper)

Library of Congress Cataloging-in-Publication Data

Contending images of world politics / edited by Greg Fry and Jacinta O'Hagan.
     p. cm.
     Includes bibliographical references and index.
     ISBN 0–333–91375–2 (cloth) — ISBN 0–333–91376–0 (pbk.)
        1. International relations. 2. Globalization. 3. World politics–1989–
           I. Fry, Greg.   II. O' Hagan, Jacinta.

JZ1310 .C66 2000
327.1—dc21
                                                            00–042065

This book is printed on paper suitable for recycling and made from
fully managed and sustained forest sources.

10   9   8   7   6   5   4   3   2   1
09 08 07 06 05 04 03 02 01 00

Copy-edited and typeset by Povey-Edmondson
Tavistock and Rochdale, England

Printed and bound in Great Britain by
Creative Print & Design (Wales), Ebbw Vale

For
Jim Richardson
gifted scholar and teacher of international relations

Contents

Acknowledgements

The approach to the study of world politics put forward in this book was first developed as a way of interesting our students in the theory of international relations. It was an attempt to show the relevance of theory in making intellectual, moral and political judgements about the major characterizations of world politics that students had heard about such as 'globalization', 'fragmentation', the 'end of history', the 'coming anarchy', or the 'clash of civilizations'.

Our first acknowledgement is to those students in the international relations theory class of the MA program in international relations at the Australian National University who found the standard presentation of the international relations theory perspectives rather boring and irrelevant to their real-world concerns, and who set us a challenge. And then were those students in subsequent years who tried out our new approach and unknowingly contributed to its development. To them all, our hearty thanks.

The idea was taken further in a workshop on *Metaphors for our Time* held in April 1999 at the ANU. It brought together many of the contributors to this volume and subjected our efforts to critical review. We are immensely grateful to Lorraine Elliott, Jan Jindy Pettman, Chris Reus-Smit, John Ravenhill, Wynne Russell and Peter Van Ness who acted as very effective critics of our work-in-progress – and to Amy Chen, who organized the workshop. We would also like to thank the Department of International Relations at the ANU for its financial support for the workshop, and in particular, John Ravenhill, head of department, for his encouragement at every stage of the process.

We would also like to acknowledge the support of the Center for International Studies at the University of Southern California where Jacinta has been a Visiting Scholar 1999–2000.

We are extremely appreciative of the hard work that Robin Ward of the Department of International Relations put into the copy-editing and indexing of the work. We would also like to thank Steven Kennedy, our publishing editor, for his patience and encouragement, and his occasional 'move it along' e-mail.

Finally we would like to thank Annie Bartlett, Nicky Bartlett-Fry, and Gary Frontin, for their incredible patience and support during the making of this volume.

We wish to dedicate the book to Professor Jim Richardson, who has recently retired from the Department of International Relations at the ANU after a long career as a teacher and researcher of international relations. Jim supervised the work of many contributors to this volume; others are colleagues and friends. Educated at University of Sydney under the philosopher John Anderson and then at Oxford, followed by a stint in the British Arms Control with his friend Hedley Bull, Jim then returned to Sydney University where he became a Reader in Political Science. He shifted to the ANU as Head of the Department of Political Science in 1975 before moving to the Department of International Relations as Professorial Fellow and later Head of Department.

Jim has had a major impact on the study of international relations in Australia. His writing has touched on all areas of the subject from foreign policy analysis, ethics, international relations theory, development studies, crisis diplomacy, Australian foreign policy, security studies, nuclear issues, and international history. His sharp, spare prose, full of insight and critique, is always an inspiration. He has imparted a spirit of genuine critical inquiry and open-mindedness to generations of scholars. We wish him well in retirement in Germany.

GREG FRY
JACINTA O'HAGAN

Notes on the Contributors

Roland Bleiker is Senior Lecturer, Peace and Conflict Studies, in the Department of Government at the University of Queensland.

Ian Clark is Professor of International Politics at the University of Wales, Aberystwyth.

Richard Falk is Albert G. Milbank Professor of International Law and Practice at Princeton University.

Greg Fry is Hedley Bull Fellow and Director of Studies, MA in International Relations, in the Department of International Relations, at the Australian National University.

Jim George is Senior Lecturer in Global Politics, in the Department of Political Science, at the Australian National University.

Paul Keal is Senior Lecturer in the School of Politics, University College of the University of New South Wales at the Australian Defence Force Academy.

Richard Little is Professor of International Politics at the University of Bristol.

Gavin Mount is a Research Scholar in the Department of International Relations at the Australian National University.

Jacinta O'Hagan is Lecturer in International Relations, in the Department of Government, University of Queensland.

Jo-Anne Pemberton is Lecturer in International Relations in the School of Political Science at the University of New South Wales.

V. Spike Peterson is Associate Professor of Political Science at the University of Arizona.

Jim Richardson has just retired as Professor of International Relations, Department of International Relations at the Australian National University.

Amin Saikal is Director of the Centre for Arab and Islamic Studies (the Middle East and Central Asia) and Professor of Political Science at the Australian National University.

Sanjay Seth is Senior Lecturer in the School of Sociology, Politics and Anthropology at La Trobe University.

Johanna Sutherland is a Research Scholar, Department of International Relations, at the Australian National University.

CHAPTER 1

Contending Images of World Politics: An Introduction

Greg Fry and Jacinta O'Hagan

In 1989, just prior to the fall of the Berlin Wall, Francis Fukuyama penned his famous essay, 'The End of History?'. His dramatic image of a new world in which ideological struggle was coming to an end, and in which perpetual peace among the liberal democracies was in prospect, was the opening gambit in a debate about the essential features of the post-Cold War world that continued throughout the 1990s and is still with us as we contemplate the nature of world politics at the beginning of the twenty-first century. It is a debate about what John Lewis Gaddis (1999) has appropriately called the 'geology' of the international system, a concern with the 'tectonic shifts' and 'seismic eruptions' emanating from the underlying processes of history, rather than with the surface changes in geopolitics. This focus on fundamentals is fuelled by the perception on the part of many commentators that the developments of the closing decade of the twentieth century were momentous, indicating a transformation rather akin to the shift from the medieval system to the modern states system in the mid-seventeenth century.

These commentators have, however, given very different accounts of the nature of this transformation and divergent characterizations of the emergent world order. The liberal triumphalism of Fukuyama's 'end of history' image, and of others suggesting the 'obsolescence of war' (Mueller, 1989) and the prospects of a 'democratic peace' (Russett, 1993), contrasts dramatically with Samuel Huntington's picture of a 'clash of civilisations' (1993a) and portrayals of a world in which 'the West and the rest' (Mahbubani, 1992, 1993) or 'Islam and the West' are seen as the main protagonists. The cluster of perspectives emphasizing 'the end of sovereignty' (Camilleri and Falk, 1992) and the move to a 'borderless world' (Ohmae, 1990) under the forces of 'globalization' (Friedman, 1999) provide a third very influential reading of the fundamental forces at work, while a fourth grouping emphasizes a

1

process of fragmentation and the breakdown of states, taking us towards a 'world of tribes', and even towards a 'coming anarchy' (Kaplan, 1994; Horsman and Marshall, 1994), or 'pandemonium' (Moynihan, 1993). Finally, there are those who characterize the transformation as a move from a world of states to one of regions, as in Walt Rostow's idea of 'the coming age of regionalism' (1990), or to one of 'global governance' in which 'a new medievalism' of overlapping jurisdictions and identities operates within a democratic structure (Held, 1995; Linklater, 1998).

There are also those who dispute the premise of fundamental transformation, offering instead a 'business as usual' characterization of contemporary world politics. These commentators concede that there is a dramatic change in the players in this political process but claim that the game remains essentially the same. Prominently represented in John Mearsheimer's 'back to the future' image (1990a), this is a world still in the grip of a political logic established by the Peace of Westphalia in 1648. It is a world of states in which war and conflict is possible and in which the balance of power remains the only reliable basis of order. In such a system the state is the only form of community and the only significant location of rights and responsibilities. But there are differences within this camp, some holding that we are in a sustained 'unipolar moment' (Krauthammer, 1990/91), and even a 'second American century', where a benign US hegemony remains the essential determinant of world order, while others suggest the inevitable operation of 'the balance of power' that will produce a multipolar order through the balancing behaviour of emergent great powers (Waltz, 1993).

Francis Fukuyama set the tone for this debate not only in terms of its focus on first order questions to do with the geological forces underlying world politics, but also in terms of the way in which it has been conducted. Fukuyama's perspective was presented as a provocative image of sound-bite length. 'The end of history' was joined, as we have seen, by a series of equally arresting images each seeking to capture, in Thomas Friedman's (1999: xviii) words, the 'one big thing' about the changing world order ushered in by the dramatic developments of the 1990s. Alongside these new prominent sound-bite images there are more subtle characterizations of world politics inherited from an earlier era which have also featured in this debate. These images have become such an unquestioned part of public policy and academic discourse that they are no longer seen as assumed pictures of reality, but as facts about the international system. We have in mind here such images as 'the international community', 'international society', the 'balance of power' and 'globalization'.

Together, these images represent the prominent options before us in understanding world politics at the beginning of the twenty-first century. Each represents a different position on the issue of what entities and forces matter in world politics, on the possibilities of peace and war, about the moral basis of global order, about how 'security' is to be viewed, and about whether the world should be seen as one polity, or two, or many. They also represent a view on whether the international system is fragmenting or integrating, and on what meaning we should attach to either process, and about the location of community, rights, and responsibilities in the world polity. Each has different normative underpinnings and poses different ethical questions. They therefore suggest very different understandings and very different implications for policy.

The purpose of this book is to critically examine the theoretical assumptions underpinning these prominent images in order that we might make more informed intellectual, political and moral judgements about what they represent as positions on the shape, and possibilities, of world politics at the beginning of the twenty-first century. The study begins where 'the public mind' begins, with the prominent images that feature in academic and policy debates, and in media commentary. It looks behind these images to examine the theoretical lenses that produce them. To continue the metaphor, we are also interested in the photographers and their predisposition to creating these particular images. In particular, we are interested in the normative commitments of the image-makers and the interests they represent. The volume is accordingly organized around these images, with each chapter devoted to a critical review of a particular characterization.

In this introductory chapter we first explain what we mean by 'world politics' and explain why we think it is an appropriate focus for international relations theory. We also propose some fundamental questions that guide this study of world politics. Second, we explain what we mean by 'image' and how we distinguish it from related concepts such as 'metaphor' and 'theory'. Third, we consider a major assumption of the approach we adopt to these questions; namely, that these images matter politically, and should therefore be regarded as much a part of political practice as part of the understanding of it. Fourth, we develop a claim about the contribution that the 'contending images' approach makes to the theory of world politics (or to International Relations theory as it is more usually known). Finally, we introduce the images we have selected for review in this volume and say something about why they have been chosen.

'World Politics'?

'World politics', the focus of this study, is still a controversial concept, and label, despite the increasing recognition it has received in the 1990s. During the Cold War, there was a tendency in the academic study of international relations to dismiss as utopian or Marxist those who spoke of 'world politics', 'world order' (Falk, 1987), 'world society' (Burton, 1972), or the 'world system' (Wallerstein, 1974). For mainstream scholars, it was the relations among states, or the *international* order, that formed the only real focus of study.[1] Since the end of the Cold War, however, a number of influences have come together to make 'world politics', or 'global politics', a more acceptable focus. Indeed the terms 'international politics' and 'world politics' are now more often used interchangably. First, as we have seen, the end of the Cold War, and the subsequent dramatic developments of the 1990s, created an interest in the 'geological' forces underlying the international system and in questions of the longue durée. The interest in the nature of change and the uncertainty about the fundamentals of the international system that has been driving this focus has inevitably broadened mainstream international relations thought beyond a state-centric focus or at the very least made such thinkers more conscious of the historical and social construction of state interests, a construction which depends on transnational ideas and processes. At the end of the Cold War, reflections on the nature of the 'new world order' by political leaders, media commentators and academics translated into an easier acceptance of the idea of 'world politics' to embrace something broader than inter-state politics.

This acceptance was also stimulated by a growing perception in the 1990s that the role of the state was diminishing. New developments in global governance, the increasing role of global financial markets, the vastly expanded global reach of capitalism, and the development of global communications all contributed to this view. The perception that a fundamental change in the organization of political community is taking place has prompted not only International Relations theorists, but also international lawyers, and political and social theorists, to shift their focus to a more complex global political system that still has states as primary players but also has other actors. Furthermore, the increased interest in the 1990s in normative and ethical questions in the study of international affairs has inevitably led to a broadening of focus. This shift represents a return to the nineteenth-century focus of International Relations thought when the nature of the existing and desirable global order was debated by Marxists, liberals, cosmopolitans and advocates of *realpolitik* (Knutsen, 1992; Wight, 1991).

Reflecting this broader canvas, the following chapters recognize a broad range of entities and actors including multinational corporations, non-government organizations, 'the international community', financial market brokers, civilizations, nations, ethnic groups and tribes, regions, global institutions, scholars, media networks, and regimes. There is also a more pronounced concern with large historical forces - technology, democratization, modernity, civilizational identity, globalization, knowledge, cyberspace, grand ideas - that further takes International Relations thought beyond a narrow understanding of world order focused on inter-state politics.

The questions that we would like readers to keep in mind as they progress through these reviews, and to which we will return in the concluding chapter, also reflect this broader understanding of international relations.

The first concerns the nature of change in world politics. Are we seeing a transformation of the world polity or simply surface change? And what is driving this change? Secondly, how should the broad framework of world order be envisaged? In political terms, 'Is the world to be seen as one world, two worlds or many'? In the recent past, when the world was imagined as two worlds, (reflected simultaneously in the East–West framework and the North–South division), or as comprising 'first', 'second', 'third', and 'fourth' worlds, this mattered greatly for political practice. What then are the political and ethical implications of such characterizations in current framings of the global polity? On this hinges the answer to other political and ethical questions – how the reach of justice, of inequality, and the democratic peace is viewed, and how hierarchy, inclusion and difference are imagined in the global polity.

A third question concerns the location of political community, identity and agency in world politics. Do they still remain with the state or are we moving beyond state sovereignty to regional or global loyalties; or down to ethnic or national identities? Is one form of identity displacing others or do we hold all these identities in a world of overlapping authorities?

A fourth and related question focuses on the source and nature of power in contemporary global society? Does it reside in geopolitical, geo-economic or knowledge domains? Is power bound up in global structures – whether military, economic or ideological – or in the unpredictable agency of countless entities? Is there a fixed hierarchy of power?

Finally, is the world undergoing a process of fragmentation or integration, and what meaning should we attach to these processes?

Image: The Concept

In developing the 'contending images' approach to understanding the main debate about world politics our first step is to clarify what we mean by 'image' and how we distinguish it from other concepts. By 'image' we simply mean a word picture. Like a photographic image, it foregrounds a particular aspect of the world and excludes others. An 'image' is not a reasoned proposition; rather it is impressionistic or suggestive of what is important, leaving a great deal of interpretation to the reader. It is a picture that draws us to what is thought to be an important feature. It seeks to simplify, and to influence, and to depict a complex reality.

As we employ it in this approach, 'image' is to be distinguished from 'theory' or 'theoretical perspective'. We see an image as being produced by a theoretical lens.[2] While the image represents a theory, then, it is not one itself. By 'theory' we mean a set of linked assumptions that claim to provide an understanding or explanation. It may seek to explain and predict in a strictly social science sense or aim to enhance 'understanding' through an explication of the ethical and normative parameters involved.

We also distinguish an 'image' from a 'model' (sometimes used interchangeably in International Relations texts).[3] We take a model to be a deductive system abstracted from the world that seeks to generate, via a theorem, something that can be taken back to the world as an assumption. It is, therefore, that part of the theory that involves deductive reasoning from first premises. It generates further assumptions.

The final distinction we need to clarify is that between 'image' and 'metaphor'. Strictly speaking, a metaphor is a figure of speech in which a familiar thing is used to describe the unfamiliar as in 'balance of power', 'power vacuum' or 'strategic chessboard'. However, in popular parlance, the terms may be used interchangeably. Walt Rostow, for example, refers to 'the coming age of regionalism' as a 'metaphor for our times' even though he is not strictly using the familiar to describe the unfamiliar. For those following a Nietzschean line, it is not only all images, but all language that is metaphorical. Roland Bleiker, for example, develops this view in Chapter 16.

The contributors to this volume, and the image-makers they review, employ 'metaphor' in each of these senses. The 'balance of power' employs metaphor in the first sense, that of using the familiar to convey the essence of the unfamiliar. But not all images are metaphorical. The 'end of history', for example, is not using a known thing to depict the unknown. This distinction between metaphorical and non-metaphorical images allows us to highlight the particular type of power inherent in the deployment of the familiar to depict the unfamiliar. The security and accessibility of the familiar can be very influential in creating a particular understanding of the unfamiliar. In fact, a major claim of this approach is that there has been little attention to the power of the metaphor in international relations thought and practice.[4]

'Contending Images' and Political Practice

In adopting a 'contending images' approach to the contemporary debate on the questions outlined above concerning the shape and possibilities of world politics, we proceed on the assumption that images are not only a useful way into thinking about the prominent perspectives on these questions, but that they are also powerful in their own right. Many of these images have been deployed in the policy debate. This is demonstrably the case for images of world politics such as 'the clash of civilizations', 'the end of history', the 'end of sovereignty', 'the borderless world', the 'coming anarchy', and the 'unipolar moment', which have all had enormous influence in framing an academic and policy debate about the contemporary international system. They have also begun to frame the debate in universities and defence colleges.

This political influence is partly due to the origin of the images. Despite their global reach and their implicit claim to a universal truth, they predominantly emanate from the United States. They are essentially part of an American debate about foreign and domestic policy, and in many cases the supporting analysis concludes with an explicit reference to the implications for American policy. It is unlikely that the images would have the same impact and influence if they were projected by authors in Nigeria, Colombia or Australia. Their impact is also due to their deployment in key world policy journals which inform both the academic and the policy communities: *International Affairs*, *National Interest*, *Foreign Affairs*, *International Security* and *Atlantic Quarterly*, or in popular books like Barber's *Jihad vs. McWorld* (1996), Friedman's *The Lexus and the Olive Tree* (1999), or Pfaff's *The Wrath of Nations* (1993a).

The timing has also been crucial in enhancing the impact of these images. Many of them began to emerge in the aftermath of the Cold War, a period in which the long-held assumptions about the structure of international order dissipated with the collapse of bipolarity. Simultaneously, the powerful impact of transnational and global forces discussed above was becoming increasingly evident. These events and processes demanded of theorists and commentators an explanation, but also freed intellectual space for more wide-ranging conceptualizations of the actors, forces and processes involved in world politics. In this complex and fluid environment, those that have a policy role, and particularly those in the United States, have been very receptive to new frameworks to guide them through the uncertain terrain of the contemporary order.

There is also something in the nature of an image which contributes to its potential influence. An image is, by definition, accessible. It is recognizable as an idea about how the world is or should be. An image is pithy, evocative, and simplifies a complex reality. It is often dramatic, or familiar, in the case of a metaphorical image. And, unlike a detailed theoretical perspective, it can be visualized. 'The end of history', 'the clash of civilizations' or 'the coming anarchy', for example, are nothing if not dramatic, even melodramatic. They present an interpretation of a complex reality that is easy to grasp. They are also put forward with certainty. They claim to capture the primary thing about world politics; they are not put forward as tentative explanations but as confident descriptions of reality. This has an appeal at a time of uncertainty.

Some images gain further influence and authority through repeated deployment. They can thus become unquestioned concepts or categories within the social sciences, in policy discourse or media descriptions. Such images contain such power that they no longer need justifying. They are categories or concepts which become 'naturalized'. We simply forget they are images. 'Globalization', for example, is a heavily contested characterization of the international system but its deployment by journalists and politicians would suggest that this has been forgotten. It is often accepted, not as one representation of our current reality, but as reality itself. The widespread use of the image of 'the international community' as an assumed entity provides a further example of this type of power. We forget that 'the international community' is an image which competes in a long-standing debate about the nature of international relations between those who see a 'society of states', those who see international life as a 'jungle' without society, and those who see it as going beyond a minimal society of states to a community with values and authority. The 'balance of power' probably provides the longest testimony to the establishment of this kind of authority.

'Contending Images' and the Theory of World Politics

The scholarly inquiry into world politics is conventionally approached through the theoretical perspectives offered by various strands of realism and liberalism, and sometimes of Marxism and feminism (Brown, 1997; Baylis and Smith, 1997). For many practitioners and others seeking to make up their minds about world problems and to determine their own actions in regard to them, this can appear to be a process removed from the world and geared more to theory-building than to providing understanding of contemporary problems. The 'contending images' approach developed in this volume is, by contrast, one that begins with the grand characterizations of world politics that have figured in the public policy and academic debate, and in media commentary, and works back into the theoretical perspectives that produce them. In particular, we are concerned with locating the ideas underlying these images in broader theoretical traditions so that the assumptions on which they are premised may be better understood and critically reviewed. In this way we hope both to demonstrate the relevance of International Relations theory in helping us to make political and moral judgements about prominent ideas put before us, and to provide an accessible entry point to International Relations thought.

The approach, however, should not just be seen as an heuristic or pedagogic device to make the world of theory more accessible and to appear relevant (although this is an important contribution in our view). For theorists, the approach also uncovers a broader range of theoretical perspectives from various disciplines and shows their interplay in producing characterizations of world politics that have a political impact. It delivers different insights than if we had simply projected a realist, liberal or Marxist image of world politics from the intellectual lens provided by these perspectives.

For a start, the prominent images that have political impact on practice do not necessarily equate with just one of the established theoretical perspectives in International Relations thought. While there is such correspondence between, say, the 'back to the future' image and the neorealist theoretical perspective, in other cases there may be several different perspectives that produce the same image. In relation to those seeing regions as the key organizing feature of the future, for example, as captured in such images as Peter Katzenstein's 'world of regions' (in Kohli *et al.*, 1995) or Rostow's 'coming age of regionalism' (1990), the same image is produced by antithetical theoretical perspectives: mercantilists (allied to realists), on the one hand, and free traders (allied to liberal economics), on the other. Other images – the 'world of tribes', for example – are difficult to locate in relation to International Relations perspectives at all. In some cases, an image may only draw on particular aspects of a general International Relations theoretical perspective while rejecting others. The 'end of history', for example, is a product of a very particular form of liberal thought combined with other non-liberal influences, and the 'clash of civilizations', despite departing from state-centrism, has a close correspondence to other aspects of realism. Finally, an image may be produced by perspectives not usually considered as part of the International Relations theory debate at all such as those from ecology, or social and political theory.

This approach, then, not only allows a novel exploration of a combination of International Relations theoretical perspectives; it also exposes the academic study of international relations to a broader range of ideas. It opens international relations to the influence of other disciplines and to influential theoretical frameworks created outside the academy. Just as International Relations as an academic field is broadening its focus beyond the relations among states in its understanding of the exercise of power in the world, so political scientists, political theorists, and sociologists, are lifting their gaze from their examination of self-contained states to broader powerful global forces in order to understand the challenges presented to the location of rights, responsibilities and citizenship. In fact, those creating the influential frameworks about world politics are now as likely to be political scientists (Samuel Huntington, Benjamin Barber), political theorists (David Held), international lawyers, journalist commentators (Robert Kaplan, Thomas Friedman, William Pfaff), business people (George Soros, Rupert Murdoch,

Kenichi Ohmae), civil servants (Francis Fukuyama), international agency officials (the World Bank), non-government organizations (Greenpeace), politicians (Patrick Moynihan, Tony Blair), economists (Walt Rostow), or sociologists (Anthony Giddens), as scholars within the formal discipline of International Relations.

Arguably, the most important contribution of this approach to the study of world politics is, however, the foregrounding of images as potentially powerful in influencing political outcomes.[5] Here, our central contention is that images or metaphors that are deployed to understand world politics should also be seen as contributing to the constitution of world politics. In this we build on the efforts of others who have sought to bring the power of language and knowledge-making into what is studied as part of world politics. In the 1990s, mainstream scholars have been much more receptive to the notion that ideas are a form of 'soft power' (Goldstein and Keohane, 1993), and that social norms matter in influencing international behaviour (Wendt, 1999; Klotz, 1995). Also increasingly influential is the more radical idea that theories of international relations play a constitutive role in international affairs (George, 1994). Drawing on poststructuralist ideas, this perspective sees such theoretical frameworks as 'realism' as powerful discourses that shape, as much as depict, international politics. It sees knowledge, and the language employed in knowledge-making, as framing the possibilities of political practice.

Our particular focus on prominent images deployed where academic knowledge meets policy making and media commentary is particularly influenced by Edward Said (1978b) whose concern was the power of images contained in authoritative knowledge which depicted the Orient, and particularly the Arab, in ways that were not only belittling or dehumanizing but, because of the link between the image-makers and colonial power, became part of the power of Europe over the Orient. With adaptation, Said's thesis can be generalized to an insight about the power of images in international relations when deployed authoritatively in policy-related commentary.[6] We contend that such images can be more powerful than the theoretical perspectives of the academy in creating the presuppositions of policy makers and framing the possible in the 'public mind'.

Power, Order and Inter-State Politics

We are now in a position to introduce the images selected for review in this volume. The first part of the book examines images that are primarily concerned with aspects of inter-state politics: the prospects for perpetual peace, the possibilities of society among states and its moral basis, the nature of inter-state order, and the nature of power at the centre of inter-state relations.

James Richardson opens the section with a review of 'the end of history' (Fukuyama, 1989, 1992), which was, as we have seen, the most dramatic early picture of the tectonic shifts taking place at the end of what Eric Hobsbawm (1995) has called 'the short twentieth century' (1914-1991). Fukuyama's main thesis was that the end of Soviet–US rivalry meant not only that liberalism had won a battle with Soviet communism, but also that it had won the long war between the universalist Enlightenment ideologies. It is then a reference to 'the end of history' in the Hegelian sense of the end of the conflict between the big ideas about how society should be organized, with liberalism emerging triumphant. For international relations, the implications are startling: nothing less than the end of inter-state war in the longer term. In the meantime, the world is divided into a post-historical world of liberal democratic states in which there is perpetual peace and a continuing historical world in which war and conflict continues between states. Fukuyama was joined by other neoliberal scholars throughout the 1990s who saw an 'end of history' in the possibility of a 'democratic peace'. It is this broad band of ideas largely drawing on nineteenth-century liberal ideas about the conditions of peace, and not just Fukuyama's Hegelian-derived formula, that forms the focus of Richardson's review of this important image of world politics.

The 'back to the future' image, reviewed by Jim George, is the antithesis of 'the end of history'. Generated by John Mearsheimer (1990a), an international relations theorist of the neorealist school, this characterization represents the quintessential statement about the unchangeability of international life. While focused on the future of Europe as seen in 1990, the image represents a broader view of future world politics as familiar travelling; it is just the names of the places that are changing along the way. States remain powerful, the balancing of power continues, and war between states remains a real possibility. In this view, globalization, regional integration, and the spread of liberalism, capitalism and democracy do not change the facts of international life. It is this broader meaning of this important image, propounded by realist theorists and inherent in the practice of states, rather than Mearsheimer's specific claims about Europe, that George explores in his chapter.

Richard Little surveys an image which forms a central part of the 'back to the future' characterization, and has probably been the most powerful image of inter-state politics for the last 500 years, that of the 'balance of power'. It is deployed in many ways and with various meanings by strategic studies scholars and permeates defence department policies. In the contemporary policy-related academic literature it appears in several competing guises: as 'the unipolar moment' (Krauthammer, 1990/91), as a 'concert of power' (Rosecrance, 1991), as an emergent multipolar balance (Dibb,

1995; Waltz, 1993; Mearsheimer, 1990a) and as civilizational balances (Huntington, 1993a). And yet the metaphor of 'the balance' is deployed unquestioningly in each case. Little demonstrates how the 'the balance of power' has acted as metaphor and myth historically and how it continues to be deployed in both senses in the contemporary debate about world order.

Finally, Paul Keal surveys a long-standing picture deployed most prominently in the English School of International Relations, that of 'international society'. The picture of the international system as a society of states with norms and rules, and perhaps a sense of moral progress, has become increasingly prominent in the post-Cold War environment in relation to issues where the collective action of the 'international community' has been sought, such as intervention and assistance in complex human emergencies. Keal investigates a number of different interpretations of the image of international society. The image suggests the existence of an international community, comprising states, constituted on common practices and rules, and embedded in the institutions of international law. Keal probes the extent to which 'international society' is seen to represent a genuinely universal and inclusive community or one which is hierarchical and prescriptive, effectively representing the interests of its founders and most powerful members from the West. He also considers the potential ethical tension posed to international society by the pursuit of international order, a primary goal of international society, on the one hand, and the broader moral and normative goals of world order, on the other.

Globalization and the Transformation of Community

The second section reviews images that emphasize changing notions of sovereignty, community and identity. It considers pictures of global politics that suggest the state is a declining force, that authority and identity are increasingly fluid and overlapping, and that globalization is a dominant process. Ian Clark explores the claims of globalization focusing on the image made famous by Ohmae (1990) of a 'borderless world'. Ohmae's thesis was premised on the idea that the forces of economic globalization are making territorial borders less relevant by shifting the organization of production and exchange from the state to the global level, progressively liberating economic activity from local political constraints. The image has, of course, been deployed, in these or other words, by any number of commentators, practitioners and theorists. We could have as easily selected 'globalization' itself as the most prominent image of the decade. For some, such as Thomas Friedman (1999), globalization has replaced the Cold War as the primary driving force in the international system. Clark's brief is to focus on the

claims underlying the economic side of the globalization image. He elucidates the arguments that territorial borders are becoming more porous,
obscured or transcended by economic and technological forces and agents.
In considering both the advocates and the debunkers of the image that suggests the state is in the process of fading away, Clark observes a continued
preoccupation with the role of the state. This prompts him to ask us to consider the potential synergy between the processes of globalization and of
state transformation and the extent to which the state itself may act as an
agent of globalization.

Jo-Anne Pemberton then follows with a review of the closely related characterization of the 'end of sovereignty'. She focuses on 'globalization' in its
more political, cultural and even metaphysical guises, thus complementing
the Clark chapter. Pemberton critically examines a number of discourses of
globalization, depicting it as encompassing forces that generate fluidity and
heterogeneity that are juxtaposed to the fixity and homogeneity underlying
conceptions of the sovereign state system. Pemberton provides an interesting parallel between contemporary discourses of globalization and those of
'rationalization' that were prominent earlier in the twentieth century. She
questions if globalization actually describes a set of incontestable facts
about forces currently assailing the state, or if, by contrast, it is a rhetorical
device, a set of arguments aimed at persuading us to view the world as a
more fluid environment. She also critically examines the 'conceptual inflation' of sovereignty suggesting, like Clark, that it may be useful to examine
the constitutional evolution of state sovereignty rather than to assume its
demise.

Richard Falk examines the 'new medievalism' image that has featured
prominently in academic analyses of the transformation of community in
world order, particularly in normative works seeking to devise future social
practices and institutions for global society. Originally coined by Hedley
Bull in his 1977 classic *The Anarchical Society*, it depicts a system of overlapping jurisdictions and authorities modelled on medieval Europe. In the
1990s this image was embraced as a picture of what the next phase could be
after the Westphalian states system. Evidence of change and the model of
this neomedieval future are often seen in the European Union. Falk examines how accurately the medieval analogy describes the actors, forces and
structure of world politics. He also considers to what extent it facilitates prediction and provides useful normative prescriptions for contemporary
world politics. In doing so, Falk highlights features of today's complex
world politics that this image might obscure through, for instance, its
Eurocentric focus.

Greg Fry then considers another image which claims to capture a process
of changing identity and authority in world politics, that of Rostow's 'coming age of regionalism'. He demonstrates that this image of a world in
which regions are becoming increasingly significant as loci of identity and

authority has a wide and diverse range of advocates, many of whom attach very different meanings to the rise of regions. Some focus on the rise of regions in the context of trade; others on the field of security; others again examine the growth of regional solidarity based on cultural identity or on activism in the realm of governance. Fry explores these varying interpretations, some of which view regions as emerging actors in their own right, others that view them as agents for broader forces of integration. This debate can be related to the broader debate with regard to how the international system is being shaped by forces of fragmentation and globalization. Fry demonstrates that these varying interpretations of regionalism are underpinned by very different normative and theoretical assumptions and often have very different ethical implications.

Fragmentation and Cultural Identity

The third section of the volume focuses on characterizations that emphasize the importance of cultural identities in world politics and which suggest fragmentation rather than integration in future world politics. It opens with Jacinta O'Hagan's examination of another very prominent image in the public domain, Samuel Huntington's 'clash of civilizations' (1993a). This more than most of the images reviewed here is generated by one person. Huntington is an influential political scientist, prominent in both academic and political circles in the United States. The image he proposes suggests that culture is becoming the central organizing principle of world order, replacing political and ideological boundaries as the flashpoint of conflict. It is one of the most controversial and deeply contested images of contemporary world politics. O'Hagan examines the context of international and domestic unrest in which the image emerged. She suggests that the image seeks to explain the apparent emergence of new forces and actors related to cultural, ethnic and religious identities in world politics, but is also deeply concerned with defining the interests and role of the West in the post-Cold War world. She argues that while it highlights significant issues relating to culture and identity often neglected in the study of world politics, it does so in a way that could exacerbate suspicion and antipathy rather than foster cooperation and understanding amongst peoples from different cultural and civilizational backgrounds.

Gavin Mount continues to examine the theme of cultural identity as a source of fragmentation in world politics in his discussion of the image of 'a world of tribes' evoked by texts and commentaries such as Robert Kaplan's influential essay 'The Coming Anarchy' (1994) and Daniel Moynihan's book

Pandemonium (1993). The image is drawn from a range of works that suggest world politics are becoming progressively engulfed in ethnic insecurity, violence and genocide. He argues that although there are some positive references to tribal and ethnic identity, they are most often associated with something ancient and primordial, and with tribal forms of community that carry with them connotations of political regression, rather than more positive, civic aspects. Mount reflects on how this image draws from the past a perception of a threat posed by the 'barbarian' to the peace and equanimity of the 'civilized' world. In examining how this image is constructed and deployed, he notes how it has been employed by local elites to mask their agency and to legitimate policies of violence, but has also been perpetuated by leaders and commentators in the international community. He further considers why, in certain contexts in world politics, the use of violence is depicted as something necessary and even progressive, while in images such as those associated with the 'world of tribes' the perpetrators of violence are depicted as irrational and primordial.

In examining the image of 'Islam and the West', Amin Saikal explores a powerful contemporary image of a world in which Islam and the West appear as coherent communities that face each other with suspicion and hostility. This image draws strength from the selective reading of relations between Islamic and Christian societies in the past, including the legacies of the Crusades, of colonialism and of the Cold War. This image blends religious with political identities, but it is also interwoven with the politics of development. Saikal points out that both Western and Islamic sources have generated this image. He examines the way in which it has been reinforced by political developments in key states, such as Iran, Afghanistan, Pakistan and Israel. But he also explores the way in which Western readings of these developments and engagement with these states has further enhanced the image. Western, and particularly American, engagement, he suggests, has often lacked sensitivity to the complexity of the particular political environments and to the implications of its actions that have at times strengthened radical Islamic groups. The consequence has been the exacerbation of suspicion and hostility in Western and Islamic societies and the enhancement of this image of antagonism.

Knowledge, Power and Inclusion

The final section introduces more radical departures from conventional images of global politics. These chapters address images which are as much about providing new pictures of how we create knowledge about world politics, and new perspectives on the forces and structure which shape world order, as providing conventional metaphors that sum up political processes. Johanna Sutherland discusses various interpretations and implications of the image of 'an endangered planet'. This image, drawn from the title of Richard Falk's 1971 book, *The Endangered Planet*, evokes a sense of crisis and insecurity generated by fears about global warming, rising sea levels, increased pollution and environmental degradation from industry, technology run rampant and poor agricultural practices, and a growing shortage of water, food and resources for an ever-expanding human population. All of these could threaten the health of the planet and the survival of those that inhabit it. Going back to their origin in the 1960s, Sutherland reviews the complex range of images which today surround debates about the environment, but have also permeated discourses on security, development, human rights and governance. These include the pessimistic images of potentially cataclysmic threats to human and planetary security, but also the increasingly prevalent optimistic images surrounding debates about sustainable development that suggest the emergence of pluralistic cooperative governance. Sutherland examines not only the contending images of global environmental politics, but also the knowledge/power networks that produce these images. She demonstrates that different discourses convey different understandings of the nature of the threats and of the best means to meet these.

The image of 'a gendered global hierarchy' is drawn originally from a title of an earlier work of Spike Peterson (1997a). It brings to the fore a perception of the inequality and disempowerment generated by the construction and deployment of gender differences in both domestic and international politics. These inequalities were brought to the political fore by the burgeoning of feminist activism and scholarship from the 1960s onward. Peterson uses the image of a 'gendered global hierarchy' to explore the ways in which feminist approaches provide the opportunity for a radical rereading of the theory and practice of world politics. Peterson argues that this perspective forces us to reflect on not only what issues we choose to consider when we study world politics, but how we obtain our knowledge. She suggests this perspective reveals first, the frequent omission of women and their experiences from examination of world politics, but it further reveals the way in which politics frequently privileges the masculine and denigrates the feminine, disempowering and silencing women. This forces us to seek to reconstruct theory to more accurately reflect the range of experiences and to dismantle the implicit hierarchies of power, based on gender and on other forms of discrimination or oppression. However, Peterson does not seek to articulate a single feminist voice or standpoint; rather, she recognizes the multiplicity of feminist positions ranged along a continuum.

Sanjay Seth continues this theme of problematizing and challenging conventional images of world politics as too partial and exclusionary. Seth uses the image of a 'post-colonial world' as a starting point from which to examine how a postcolonial perspective unsettles traditional images of the assumed universal structures and processes of world politics. The image is not one drawn from any particular author or work but rather from the growing body of work in history, literature, politics and a range of other disciplines, represented by texts such as Edward Said's *Orientalism* (1978b), that explore the experiences of colonization from the perspectives of the colonized. This body of work, notes Seth, is interested in the way colonization shaped the sense of self of both colonizer and colonized and in the ways in which knowledge of, and the capacity to represent, the colonized non-West provided a significant form of power to the colonizing West. This perspective questions the extent of the changes wrought to world order by decolonization. Seth's discussion explores how universal and inclusive the postcolonial international system is from the non-Western perspective, and the extent to which it can be seen as continuing to be based on the projection of Western structural power. Similarly he questions the extent to which the discipline of International Relations can accommodate and acknowledge the legitimacy of alternative models of political community that do not conform to the Western nation state model.

The final image discussed is 'the end of modernity'. Again, this is not drawn from any one author, but used here to investigate the proposition that we are entering into a new era in which central tenets of Enlightenment thought are no longer dominant. Roland Bleiker employs the image of 'the end of modernity' to examine some of the premises of postmodern thought and to explore one of the central conceptual themes of the book: the importance of representation in constituting the political world. Bleiker, although wary of employing categorical definitions and declaring 'the end' to things, suggests that the universalizing modes of thought are profoundly challenged by postmodern perspectives. The authority of the 'all-encompassing gaze' that represented reality as capable of being observed and represented in 'Grand Narrative' is undermined by those who seek to include a broader range of previously marginalized voices and perspectives in their understanding of reality. Bleiker shows how postmodern perspectives view the world not as one of facts, but of representations. Certain of these become naturalized, masking their constitutive nature and the interests and power that lie behind them. In his discussion of terrorism, Bleiker explores the implications of employing the postmodern perspective by examining how representations can legitimate or delegitimate certain actors or actions. This perspective, he argues, is driven by an ethic of inclusion and of embracing, rather than containing or excluding, difference.

In the concluding chapter, we offer an exploration of the interaction of these images in relation to fundamental questions concerning the shape and possibilities of future world politics. We believe that there is something to be gained in moving beyond the reviews of individual images to consider them in juxtaposition in a comparative frame. They represent, after all, different understandings of the world and of the central questions concerning its future political organization. We conclude with an exploration of the significance of the fact that the prominent images of world politics originate in the West and in the United States in particular.

PART I

POWER, ORDER AND INTER-STATE POLITICS

CHAPTER 2

The 'End of History'?

James L. Richardson[1]

Francis Fukuyama's 'end of history' image (1989) epitomized the triumphalist mood in the United States as the opening of the Berlin Wall led to the rush of events which culminated in the breakup of the Soviet Union.[2] In a crude sense the 'end of history' was taken to signify the end of the great twentieth-century conflicts: the triumph of liberal democracy over communism held out the prospect of a peaceful 'new world order' in line with the liberal vision of Woodrow Wilson.

This sanguine image could not survive the upsurge of ethnic conflict in the early years of the post-Cold War decade. Yet, this chapter will argue, there is far more to Fukuyama's thesis than this over-simple image would suggest. It articulates certain assumptions which underpin the liberal discourse which has become the *lingua franca* of contemporary international relations, and in doing so it incidentally draws attention to some disturbing features of contemporary political culture in Western societies.

The 'end of history' image is multifaceted. This chapter will distinguish four different ways in which it may be understood, but makes no claim that these are exhaustive. First, and not especially associated with Fukuyama, is the perception that the end of the Cold War signifies the end of the two centuries of ideological conflict unleashed by the American and French Revolutions. Second is Fukuyama's Hegelian interpretation of mankind's political evolution, culminating in the liberal–democratic state which alone fulfils human needs and aspirations. Third, the 'end of history' is closely associated with certain characteristic liberal doctrines, in particular the democratic peace, which signify the onset of a fundamental transformation in international relations – the end of major war as the ultimate arbiter of international conflict. Finally, the chapter will draw attention to a latent function of the image, its association with the systematic downgrading of 'history' – historical experience, knowledge and reflectiveness – in contemporary (Western) political culture.

The question addressed here is not the ultimate validity of the 'end of history' image. In view of its many aspects, this would be a pointless exercise. The chapter seeks, rather, to reflect on the ways in which the image is associated with some of the most prominent themes in contemporary international discourse. It is appropriate that these themes be examined critically, since the liberal discourse in which the 'end of history' image is embedded may reasonably be regarded as hegemonic at the present time – the language of those elites best placed to shape the 'international order' at the start of the millennium.

The End of Ideological Conflict?

The first of the four meanings of the image may be noted quite briefly, since it does not capture Fukuyama's thought. The success of liberal democracy in the Cold War, following the defeat of fascism in the Second World War, has suggested to many the passing of a certain phase of world history – the two centuries during which politics in Europe and much of the rest of the world was characterized by intense ideological conflict. The liberal, and later the socialist, challenge to the traditional monarchical-aristocratic order was followed by the twentieth-century struggle between fascism, communism and democracy, and finally the Cold War between the two adversaries. The strengths of liberal democracy finally asserted themselves over all ideological rivals. The United States, its original home, initially held out no more than a model for emulation, but by the time of the Second World War and the Cold War it had become the leader of the armed conflict against the successive totalitarian challenges. The worldwide influence of liberal democracy at the present time is inextricably bound up with the expansion of American power.

How complete and lasting this ideological supremacy will prove remains, in terms of this initial perception, an open question. For the time being no other ideology appears capable of mounting a general, worldwide challenge, even though political Islam may well enhance its influence in certain societies. However, to those not viewing the future through Fukuyama's Hegelian lenses, the longer term holds major uncertainties. Can liberal democracy maintain its ascendancy in the face of ecological challenges, mounting inequalities, the erosion of the autonomy of the state under the pressures of globalization, the 'democratic deficit' first noted in relation to the European Union but even more pronounced in other international institutions[3] – and so forth? The images of the future discussed in this volume foreshadow a range of alternatives to the inexorable triumph of liberal democracy. How, then, does Fukuyama substantiate his prognosis?

The Hegelian Conception

Fukuyama's reading of Hegel provides him with a distinctive version of a longstanding Western conception of the development of political organization, a 'grand narrative' of mankind's progress from tribal societies through monarchies, city-states and empires to the modern 'nation-state', first in its absolutist form, culminating in today's liberal democracies. Often dubbed the Whig interpretation of history, it lost credibility during the first half of the twentieth century, above all in Europe, but remained deeply embedded in American political culture.

For Fukuyama the end of the Cold War signifies much more than just the end of a particular phase of history. It is 'the end point of mankind's ideological evolution and the universalization of Western liberal democracy as the final form of human government' (Fukuyama, 1989, p. 4). History, thus understood, is not just the welter of events but the clash of great ideas which shapes the larger contours of human development. There will still be countless events to fill the columns and screens of the media, but these will no longer have world-historical significance. Moreover, while liberalism has won the battle of ideas, its final success in the material world may still be some time off. Indeed, Hegel had already discerned the end of history in 1806: Napoleon's defeat of the Prussian monarchy at Jena marked the victory of the ideals of the French Revolution – 'the imminent universalisation of the state incorporating the principles of liberty and equality'. Much remained to be done, but 'the basic *principles* of the liberal-democratic state could not be improved upon' (Fukuyama, 1989, p. 5).

On what does Fukuyama base his confidence that political evolution has reached its final form – that the present is not just another phase in the development of political communities? The argument, as developed more fully in his subsequent book (Fukuyama, 1992), is surprisingly thin. Liberal democracy alone – though always integrally associated with the market economy – can satisfy both mankind's material needs and what he terms *thymos*, the need for respect and recognition, an idea which formerly evoked images of glory and valour associated with the quest for empire, but is now associated with human dignity and human rights (Fukuyama, 1992, pp. 162–91). However, in the concluding passage of his article, in which he laments the passing of history, he had already cast serious doubt on this thesis. The 'common marketisation' of the world, it appears, will not lead to the universal realization of *thymos*, but rather to its suppression:

> The end of history will be a very sad time. The struggle for recognition, the willingness to risk one's life for a purely abstract goal, the worldwide ideological struggle that called forth daring, courage, imagination, and idealism, will be replaced by economic calculation, the endless solving of technical problems,

environmental concerns, and the satisfaction of sophisticated consumer demands. In the post-historical period there will be neither art nor philosophy, just the perpetual caretaking of the museum of human history. I can feel in myself, and see in others around me, a powerful nostalgia for the time when history existed. (Fukuyama, 1989, p. 18)[4]

Not far beneath the surface there would seem to be a second sense in which Fukuyama understands 'history': sacrifice, courage, imagination, art and philosophy are associated with all manner of human struggles, not merely ideological conflict. These are echoes of Napoleon's scorn for a nation of shopkeepers or the later nineteenth-century identification of peace with decadence, and vitality and progress with war.

Nonetheless, for those already perceiving world history through liberal lenses, Fukuyama offers supporting argument – indeed a novel form of support for a conception of history which, as we have seen, is embedded in Western, and especially American, culture. But he does not address the concerns of those who do not share this view of history: the social theorists critical of 'grand narratives' and the 'Enlightenment Project', or those concerned with the acute tensions generated by globalization and 'turbo-capitalism', the marginalizing of environmental issues, or the perception that political communities are becoming more fragmented and attenuated.

If Fukuyama's 'end of history' image lacks depth, however, it gains a different kind of support from its association with a number of other images which are also widely accepted in Western/American political discourse, and which constitute much of the contemporary liberal views of international relations. Fukuyama endorses most of these liberal doctrines in the more extended discussion in his 1992 book.

Associated Liberal Images

The most prominent of these is the idea of the democratic peace – the claim that since liberal democracies do not go to war against one another, a liberal-democratic world would be a peaceful one. This has become an axiom of American foreign policy thinking, and with it the assumption that the best way to achieve a peaceful world order is to support the process of democratization that has been so striking a feature of recent world politics. The idea of the democratic peace, first voiced in the eighteenth century and later powerfully invoked by Woodrow Wilson, appeared for most of the twentieth century to be no more than one of those 'utopian' liberal ideas that were irrelevant in the real world in which the democracies were constantly threatened by or at war with non-democratic powers, and there were relatively few democracies outside the West. The picture changed radically with the demise of the Soviet Union and the acceptance of democratic institutions in Russia and the other former Soviet Republics. Whatever the obstacles to the consolidation of democracy in these societies, there are no rival claims to political legitimacy; and at the same time, non-democratic regimes elsewhere experience difficulty in maintaining their claim to rule.[5]

The image of the democratic peace has captured the imagination of American international relations scholars: no longer merely a liberal aspiration, it is now supported by a substantial body of social science research (see Russett, 1993). There are no convincing examples of full-scale war between liberal democracies, as these terms are now understood. If these findings have strengthened the confidence with which policy makers endorse the image, however, its appeal owes little to such studies. Its appeal in the United States and elsewhere rests partly on its promise to realize one of the last and most ambitious liberal aspirations – world peace. But it also rests, even more, on the way in which it highlights those aspects of the present international milieu which promote the self-esteem of Western, and especially American, political and economic elites, as well as their material interests.

That is to say, it presents the currently prevailing international order as Washington would like to have it appear – as essentially benign, so long as the American model continues to win greater acceptance. Here the image of the democratic peace merges with that of the end of history. Those who do not conform with the prevailing norms are presented as culturally and historically retarded, their norms and values outmoded and not worthy of preservation. These images, in turn, evoke a related liberal image, that of the bifurcated world – divided between a liberal core, the zone of the democratic peace, regulated by liberal norms and regimes, and a violent, Hobbesian periphery where war remains deplorably frequent. Thus the 'end of history' image can retain its credibility in the face of the brutality of ethnic conflict in the 1990s. As Fukuyama (1989, p. 15) expresses it, large parts of the world remain 'mired in history'.

In this bifurcated world, intervention by the liberal democracies is justified partly in terms of maintaining order but more in terms of correcting flagrant violations of human rights. In practice, as in the past, intervention remains selective: the liberal West ignores mass killing in central Africa but perceives an imperative to intervene against 'ethnic cleansing' in Bosnia or Kosovo. In a bifurcated world Western governments, contemplating the evils of the backward, can permit themselves the luxury of choosing when and where to intervene. The sporadic nature of public interest in foreign policy ensures that while there may be occasional 'great debates' over particular cases of intervention, the larger pattern of opportunism or arbitrariness which underlies these choices passes unnoticed.

If intervention remains a divisive issue among liberals, and the image of a bifurcated world is not necessarily reassuring, the democratic peace is a unifying image. It evokes long-standing liberal themes, and it does not appear to require painful choices. There is a widespread perception that the risk of war among long-established liberal democracies is indeed negligible, and that the risk of war among the major states has receded dramatically since the collapse of the Soviet Union. But is there good reason to assume that, as circumstances change, the further spread of democracy will ensure peace, in the long run? The attempts by liberal theorists to explain why this should be so remain surprisingly meagre (Russett, 1993, pp. 24–42).

The two principal explanations may be termed the institutional and the normative. According to the former, it is the dependence of democratic governments on popular election which ensures that they will not go to war against one another: even if they wanted to, such governments could not persuade the people to accept the costs of war against others with similar institutions, whereas electorates can be persuaded of the need for war against threats posed by brutal dictatorships. This first explanation appears to presuppose the second, the normative: that democracies are committed to the norm of resolving their mutual disputes by non-violent means – to observe the same norms as in internal politics, having recourse to discussion and persuasion, ruling out the use of force.

However, it is evident that there is something missing in this second line of argument. Internally, democracies do not rely solely on discussion and persuasion, but also on the popular election of governments. The idea of the recourse to violence to resolve major issues does not arise so long as elections are accepted as the final arbiter.[6] But in the international system there is no such final arbiter, short of war. The explanations of the democratic peace, then, rest on the assumption that there are no issues which electorates in countries deeply at odds with one another – over territory, resources, or ideology/religion – would regard as justifying war. This assumption is obviously questionable, as contemplation of such cases as Israel and a prospective Palestinian state, India and Pakistan, or Russia and some of its neighbours would suggest. This line of thinking also allows for the possibility of civil war within a democratically governed society (such as the nineteenth-century United States) – a major anomaly which theorists of the democratic peace fail to address because they limit their theory to the discussion of 'external' war – war between states, not within states.

There is merit, then, in one of the familiar objections to the democratic peace hypothesis – namely, that the absence of war between democratic states this century may be due to other reasons as much as, or more than, their common democratic institutions. Put differently, there have been no differences among the Western democracies, or so far among those more recently established, which have been serious enough to persuade electorates to go to war, or even to give it serious consideration, against a background of extensive shared interests. It is surprising that liberal theorists have been so ready to argue from a correlation to a general law and a policy prescription, when the explanations which are offered for the presumed law are so unpersuasive.

The neglect of the economic dimension of contemporary international relations is a striking feature of this strand of liberal theory – the neglect, that is to say, of the magnitude of today's dense network of transnational economic and financial linkages and the expansion of transnational elite networks – developments which, under the rubric of globalization, are often seen as fundamentally transforming the character of the international system. A world dominated by independent sovereign states is seen as giving way to a more complex transnational system in which political structures lag behind economic and social developments, even though the concept of 'regime' may serve, up to a point, to bridge this kind of gap.

Regimes and norms, of course, represent a different aspect of contemporary liberal thinking, not least that of Fukuyama. They are invoked, as we have seen, in the image of the bifurcated world, even though any examination of current international institutions and regimes, with their diversity and overlap of membership, would raise major problems for the image of two worlds. What is perhaps most striking about these interrelated liberal images – the democratic peace, the end of history, the world of norms and regimes, and the bifurcated world – is how superficial are the observations and reasoning which underpin them. Notably absent is the role of American thinking and American power in projecting these images, yet to those outside the United States the contemporary liberal syndrome is unmistakably American, and its widespread acceptance is an indication of the pervasiveness of American power in the broadest sense.

It is reasonable, then, to ascribe the current popularity of this liberal syndrome to its appeal to the American political culture, on the one hand, and to the transnational elites which prosper in the present international milieu, aptly termed a global business civilization (Strange, 1990). In short, the liberalism espoused by Western governments may be regarded as the ideology of a privileged minority in a world characterized by massive and increasing inequalities. The experience of the less privileged is reflected in powerful counter-images – for example, in place of the liberal/Hobbesian bifurcated world, the image of global *apartheid* (Falk, 1995a), and in place of the democratic peace, that of insecurity, a world in which few societies outside the privileged West are free from the threat or the reality of violent conflict. If the liberal images are, essentially, the world as the privileged would like it to appear, it is not surprising that they are so widely rejected.

The 'end of history' has not been so long-standing an aspect of the liberal vision as the democratic peace or the world of norms and regimes, nor is it so politically charged as the bifurcated world. Yet, arguably, it articulates a latent assumption which underpins all of these like the closely related image of progress, which remains an article of faith with respect to the natural sciences and technology. It provides reassurance that the liberal societies are indeed more *advanced* than the rest, whose claims thus need not be taken altogether seriously. The liberal democracies are entitled to prevail – no longer in the crude sense of colonial rule but through institutions such as the International Monetary Fund (IMF) and the World Bank, and in the last resort through sanctions and intervention. In effect, the norms of sovereignty and equality apply only among those at an equal level of development.

The 'end of history' is at odds with the traditional image of progress insofar as it implies an end to progress in the social and political realm. If the idea of progress applied universally, we should be prepared to anticipate the next phase in mankind's political development: liberal-democratic institutions would be as transient as their predecessors. The 'end of history' provides reassurance that this is not the case. The same, presumably, holds for the market economy and the individualistic society resting on norms of universal human rights. History can improve on none of these. In this sense, the 'end of history' is revealed as a profoundly conservative image, one which seeks to buttress the political, economic and social order that prevails in the Western world at the present time. Yet this is a conservatism of a particular kind, greatly at odds with most traditional forms of conservatism, precisely over their respective views of history. An exploration of this tension serves to bring to the surface a number of less familiar but highly consequential features of the 'end of history' image at the present time.

The Downgrading of History

The invoking of history – the historical experience of the political community, its conflicts, its traditions, the development of its institutions – has always been prominent in conservative political thought. While this could lead to serious distortion and was seldom free from ethnocentric bias, conservatism kept alive a strong sense of the community and its values, and at its best could prompt a reflective, critical view of that history, not simply an affirmation of tradition. The conservatism associated with the 'end of history' image is of quite a different kind. If 'history', with all its violence and ideological turmoil, has reached its natural end, if the present order is manifestly superior to what preceded it, then it is easily assumed that historical experience is of little value or relevance. The image thus endorses a disregard for and forgetting of historical experience which serves to eliminate awareness of alternatives to the present order of things. Instead of being recognized as the product of a particular history, and particular choices, present institutions and practices are perceived as universally valid: history has completed its task of eliminating wrong-headed alternatives.

The downgrading of history is a paradoxical consequence of the grand narrative of human progress, the quintessentially historical Hegelian view of human society, yet in the contemporary political culture this is its principal consequence. A thorough reading of Hegel might prompt a genuine interest in history, but this is not the point: read in the context of an ahistorical culture such as the American or of the pressures working against historical reflectiveness elsewhere, the 'end of history' image merely reaffirms prevailing ahistorical prejudices. Moreover, if contemporary popular culture is ahistorical – this year's fashions, images and sound replace last year's, everywhere in the same way, with less and less attention to local, historical differences – contemporary elite culture may be seen to be anti-historical, subordinating historical values to current preoccupations of all kinds.

One telling indication of this disdain for history, in the broadest sense, is the attitude of the powers-that-be to libraries, whose holdings provide the essential repository not just for the study of the historical discipline but of human development, experience and culture in all their dimensions. Evident in many quarters – the local public library as well as major university and state libraries – is a readiness to invest heavily in electronic resources, with all their emphasis on the contemporary, at the expense of adequate holdings of books and journals – the prerequisite for fundamental scholarly research. In varying degree, most libraries seek to maintain a balance, but there are startling instances where this is abandoned. Two instances known to this author must suffice: readers may be aware of further examples.[7]

The first is a case of a policy decision by a major public library, the National Library of Australia. Until the mid-1990s it had maintained impressive holdings of broad scope and historical depth in the humanities and social sciences. In a radical change in policy, it then resolved to maintain comprehensive holdings only in relation to the Asia-Pacific region. Coverage of the rest of the world, and especially non-English-language sources, was left to under-resourced university libraries. In short, Australia would no longer have a major research library in the humanities and social sciences. Despite the implications for broader cultural as well as historical scholarship, the decision provoked remarkably little public debate.

The second instance relates to the policy of a funding authority, that is, the city/state of Berlin in the later 1990s, when the library of the Free University of Berlin was reduced to the point where journals were discontinued wholesale and the ordering of newly published books sank to negligible levels.[8] Again, a valuable research collection will rapidly cease to be usable as such. As in the former example, the absence of public outrage or political debate is testimony to the contemporary indifference to the downgrading of a major historical/cultural asset.

A further indication of the devaluing of history may be found in current attitudes to institutions, especially in the public domain. Institutions embody particular histories, and 'institutional memory' depends on a certain continuity of structures and personnel. This enables institutions to enjoy a degree of autonomy which is conducive to their performing their designated functions. The current 'managerial' fashion embraced by public authorities is wholly destructive of institutional autonomy. Institutional continuity is viewed with suspicion, 'restructuring' – the forced amalgamation or dissolution of existing institutions – is in vogue. Not only the upper echelons of managers are appointed on limited contracts: the trend is to limit all appointments. Along with continuity, institutional memory and indeed identity are sacrificed. That this may degrade the capacity of institutions to carry out their essential tasks in no way distends the managers and those who appoint them. The focus is on short-term, measurable indicators of 'performance'; the erosion of those intangible normative commitments on which the good working of institutions depends passes unnoticed. Universities provide especially attractive opportunities for the introduction of such fashions, but the same trends may be observed much more widely.

The devaluing of history in the public consciousness which is associated with developments such as these meets with little effective resistance, above all from those institutions which might be expected to serve as custodians of the values embodied in the humanities – the universities. History, in the broad sense, is central to the preservation and reinvigoration of those values: without a lively awareness of the history of philosophy, language and literature, for example, the subjects themselves must atrophy. Yet the universities offer little resistance to the prevailing anti-historical mindset.

This can be attributed to the way in which the universities are incorporated into society. As large institutions, they seek to expand their resources at a time of shrinking public funding. The growth areas, where the demand for specialist skills are high, are mainly in the 'information sciences' and in business and economics-related subjects. It is not surprising that university managers should divert resources into these areas at the expense of the humanities – and for that matter the traditional natural sciences. Far from resisting the prevailing cultural fashions, the universities tend to reinforce them. Scholars in the humanities are thrown on to the defensive, either forced to 'compete' through 'selling' their offerings in ways which run counter to the values to which they are committed, or else are increasingly marginalized.

As if this were not enough, the wider role of history as a taken-for-granted underpinning of a broad range of subjects, especially in the social sciences, has been under attack for some time by those who seek to extend the 'economic approach' far beyond the subject matter of economics, as traditionally understood (Becker, 1976). Whereas the historical mode of analysis involves not just a knowledge of the past, but a broader awareness of the complexity and particularity of human and social life, the economic mode favours 'parsimony', abstraction and extreme generality. In the form of game theory and rational choice theory, economic modes of analysis have become especially prominent in political science, but the ambitions of proponents of the economic approach extend to the social sciences as a whole. While this might appear to be a rather arcane issue, remote from the 'real world', it may on the contrary point to a mindset which can have the most serious practical consequences.

Two examples must suffice. During the past two decades Western official thinking and policy on development assistance has been dominated by approaches derived solely from neoclassical economics, by policies of universal application without regard for historical and institutional particularities. Except in East Asia, where many countries no longer require such assistance and where the reasons for their exceptional economic growth remain a matter of debate, the development experience during these two decades has been far less encouraging than previously, yet the neoliberal orthodoxies are barely questioned in official circles. An even more striking example is the economic and political situation in Russia. Those Westerners (essentially American) who advised the Russian government on the introduction of a market economy were exponents of orthodox economics. The possibility that this might not be sufficient, nor even appropriate – that so profound a transformation would raise a whole host of social, political and cultural issues, requiring a knowledge of Russia and its institutions available to few outsiders – does not appear to have occurred to the advisers, nor to the American government which provided them. At best, they were aware of these factors as obstacles to the success of their model, but never as indications of the need to develop a model more appropriate to the particular conditions of the society.

The ascendancy of economics in Western political culture would appear to be integrally linked to the 'end of history' – the 'other side of the coin'. The examples suggest, however, that this mindset cannot be enduring, however congenial it may be to the 'international business civilisation'. It would be ironic if 'history' – a return of violent geopolitical conflict as well as new ideological struggles – were to be revived thanks to the blindness of the 'end of history' mindset.

Conclusion

The 'end of history' image, then, may be seen not as a momentary aberration of post-Cold War euphoria but as a pointer to the distinctive character of international liberalism at the beginning of the new millenium. It underpins an optimistic view of the world as one regulated by liberal norms in which the aspiration to achieve world peace through the spread of liberal democracy is close to achievement. The pessimistic counterpart to this, however, is the claim that while there may be further technological progress, no further general improvement in human economic and political institutions is possible. An even darker side of contemporary liberalism is the social and cultural impoverishment which results from the degrading of historical memory in the practical realm, and its devaluation in the realm of ideas. The current version of liberalism is best viewed as an ideology which promotes a certain kind of international political/economic order and the interests of those who prosper within it. It has the strength that derives from powerful support, but in the long run the 'end of history' image is likely to prove one of its crucial weaknesses.

CHAPTER 3

'Back to the Future'?

Jim George

The Struggle for Memory

As one of the most enduring and most powerful metaphors in the International Relations (IR) lexicon the 'back to the future' theme, recently resurrected by John Mearsheimer and others, represents current and future world orders as little more than historical *déjà vu*. Or, in Martin Wight's terms, it represents a pessimistic image of global life beset by the 'recurrence and repetition' of an inter-state arena in which effectively unbridled egoism and structurally induced violence are fundamental and intrinsic characteristics (Wight, 1966a, p. 26).

In the era beyond the Cold War this pessimistic perspective has re-emerged, often within a neorealist literature inspired by the conservative structuralism of figures such as Kenneth Waltz. This is not at all surprising. Nor is it entirely inappropriate. Much of the celebratory (neoliberal) litera-ture of recent years is little more than rehashed utopianism, reflecting a kind of wishful thinking that has often accompanied proclamations of new world orders after major wars or periods of sustained political anxiety (Fukuyama, 1992).

There is, moreover, good reason to be concerned about much that is hap-pening in the space beyond the Cold War. Events in the Balkans, in partic-ular, have only heightened an awareness that for all the obvious potentials and opportunities of the current era it is also characterized by the great dangers associated with the rapid and often dramatic realignment of geopolitical and conceptual orthodoxy intrinsic to it. Little wonder then that in regard to conflicts such as those in Bosnia and Kosovo, one sees a reassertion of pessimism in much of the analysis which seeks to explain the chillingly familiar images of violence and suffering which emanated from the European heartland at the end of the twentieth century. From this pessimistic perspective, consequently, the many examples of political and cultural persecution, genocidal violence and fearful flight of innocents in the post-Cold War era, adds up to one unassailable fact about the world in which we live – nothing fundamental has changed.

Indeed, this is precisely the claim Mearsheimer has made in establishing his 'back to the future' premise (Mearsheimer, 1991). He makes four broad assertions. The first, that it is the distribution and character of military power among states which is the root cause of wars. The second, that a particular kind of systemic distribution of power – multipolarity – is the primary catalyst for war, while bipolar structures (for example, as in the Cold War) are a catalyst, if not for peace then for order. The third, that in any age states are driven by the Westphalian security dilemma rather than by other secondary motivations – such as economic prosperity. The fourth, that the Cold War security dilemma was solved by nuclear deterrence, thus Europe needs more nuclear weapons in order to make it more secure (Mearsheimer, 1991, pp. 90–195; see also Mearsheimer, 1994, p. 478).[1]

Similar themes characterized Mearsheimer's contention, first propounded in 1990, that we will soon miss the Cold War (Mearsheimer, 1994). To contemporary ears more attuned to the progressivist incantations of neoliberals this is undoubtedly a rather strange-sounding proposition, unless one takes into account that for figures such as Mearsheimer the Cold War stand-off between the nuclear superpowers, its balance-of-power logic and its hierarchical fixity were perceived as the only rational and realistic solution to the systemic anarchy which threatened the global community after the Second World War.

In this context the post-Cold War era becomes an ever more unstable and dangerous one as the structural and conceptual status quo of the bipolar world order is unravelled (in particular) by those intent on enhancing global economic, cultural and political liberalization and interdependence. Samuel Huntington's concern about a coming 'clash of civilizations' is infused with the same sense that beyond the traditional order scenario lurks anarchical potential and intent (Huntington, 1996). It infuses the commentaries of others, such as Robert Kaplan, who interpret the perceived breakdown of the post-Westphalian world order as the catalyst for a future global chaos analogous to that experienced in desperate West African contexts (Kaplan, 1994; see also Maynes, 1995).

These are insights on the contemporary global scene, I suggest, that need to be taken seriously, not just because they are important conservative contributions to a debate increasingly overtaken by a rather shallow market radicalism, nor necessarily because they have had a significant impact upon policy communities, particularly in the United States (Maynes, 1995).[2] Their value lies elsewhere, in the demands they make upon scholarship and contemporary political analysis in general. More precisely the importance of these variations on the 'back to the future' metaphor lies in the location of this metaphor at the core of a (power politics) tradition of IR thinking which for all its silences and omissions is still integral to any evaluation of new world orders in the twenty-first century (see Krasner, 1995; Booth, 1998; Smith, 1997;Vasquez, 1998; George, 1994).

This is a theme acknowledged in interesting fashion by Ken Booth in his recent analysis of the debate over the end of the Cold War and its implications for the global future (Booth (ed.), 1998). Here, the so-called 'new pessimism' of the current era is located more accurately as part of a much older tradition of theory and practice which continues to live on in very potent form. The power of 'power politics' in this context is contained in what Booth describes as the 'cold war of the mind' which, he argues, is actually a 'culture of global conflict' which became evident in the thirteenth century and which, by the 1970s and 1980s, 'had reached its apogee and cosmically destructive potential in the 50,000 nuclear-warhead confrontation between the United States and the Soviet Union' (Booth, 1998, p. 31) This mindset, he suggests, is far from dead in the 1990s, but is at the heart of the current struggle over the real history of the Cold War. Or, more precisely, the struggle over how the real story of the Cold War is to be told and who is to tell it.

The point at issue here is simple enough but it is one too often ignored by an IR community rarely concerned in any serious way with the relationship between history and reality, theory and practice. It is that there is no history that is independent of the way we give meaning to it, in the present. Or, more generally, our knowledge of past, present and future can never be totally independent of the way we interpret it – and because our interpretations of real things (events/facts) are always socially and politically grounded they are often contested, sometimes violently so. Thus, as Booth suggests, 'rethinking the past is a highly political activity' (1998, p. 3) This is particularly the case at the end of the Cold War, at a moment when so many of our traditional reference points for coherent meaning and policy practice have been rendered problematic. In this conceptual and structural vacuum the telling of the real story becomes a great political prize for those seeking to impose new (present and future) realities upon complex hazy historical pasts. The prize?: *the right to shape the future in line with the reality of the past.*

This was always the prize in regard to the Cold War, as anyone pondering the impact of George Kennan's famous 'X' telegram in 1945 could attest. Here, at another moment of confusion and indeterminacy within the Western IR community, Kennan' s representation of Russian history – as brutal and expansionary – and of the Russian character – as '[i]mpervious to the logic of reason' and 'seemingly inaccessible to considerations of reality' – became a central factor in subsequent Western interpretations of Soviet behaviour in the past, present and future (see Nathanson, 1988, p. 456). As such it became an integral component of Cold War practice, via the strategy of containment which, in one form or another, became the basis of 50 years of Cold War conflict on the part of the Western alliance.

This struggle for memory remains a crucial politico-strategic issue right up to the present. The nationalist extremists in the Balkans – the Milosevics and the Tudjmans – are certainly well aware of the prize associated with it, in a context where control over cultural and ethnic memory becomes the rationale for genocidal practice, a practice given its meaning in the theory of ethnic purity and a history of perpetual, naturalized hatred. Here, moreover, the struggle to tell the real historical story of the Balkans becomes the struggle to silence other stories of reality – the reality of centuries of cross-cultural integration, intermarriage and cooperative, intimate human engagement.

Francis Fukuyama is another who understands the implications of this struggle. Hence his promulgation about the end of the Cold War marking the 'end of history' (Fukuyama, 1992). This, of course, was not meant literally. Rather, what is at stake in Fukuyama's proposition is not human history *per se* but the post-Enlightenment struggle between the great modern 'isms' (liberalism and socialism) to claim history in the name of modern rational man. Fukuyama's proclamation of victory on behalf of liberal rational man – as global exemplar – is thus a victory which consigns socialism and not its liberal counterpart to the rubbish bin of history. But, as indicated above, there is an even more profound dimension to this claim for victory which renders it not just a statement of truth about the ideological past but which, just as importantly, gives it the right to explain, direct and shape the future in line with the reality of the 'past'.

This is the context in which Huntington's 'clash of civilizations' (1996) is also usefully understood if one sees it as an appeal to Western 'civilization' to heed the lessons of the past in confronting a perilous future. Huntington's 'past' is similar in many respects to that of Fukuyama, but whereas Fukuyama perceives the truth of modern history to lie in the power and logic of liberalism and market forces, for Huntington it resides in the underlying social and strategic order which allows market liberalism to flourish in the modern era. This should come as no surprise to anyone reflecting upon Huntington's earlier intervention in the debate about liberalism and order in the 1960s, when his preference for the latter (via support for ruling political and military elites in the Third World) infused US modernization theory and practice with a harder edged order-based dimension (Huntington, 1968).

Thirty years on Huntington's fears about 'too much liberalism' are apparent again in his warnings about the West's engagement with other 'civilizations' in the twenty-first century. His main fear in this regard is that Western peoples, rendered sanguine by their victory in the Cold War, will fail to understand that to maintain their power, wealth and global status, they must be prepared to protect it. More precisely, Huntington's fear for the future centres on the proliferation of the liberal and democratic faith in the age of globalization which, he warns, will raise expectations and ambitions among other 'civilizations' around the world that ultimately cannot be fulfilled. This will lead to major conflicts with some civilizations in particular (for example, Islam) and with those more generally who seek to take advantage of a rising sense of injustice directed at the West. For Huntington then it is imperative that the post-Cold War future be a continuum of the past – but that the past be understood as the triumph of a particular kind of global liberal order, rather than of liberalism *per se*.

This, in many ways, is also the keystone of Mearsheimer's 'back to the future' theme, in which the Cold War becomes a contemporary exemplar of historico-political continuity centred on systemic struggle between the major powers. From this perspective the meaning accorded the end of the Cold War is simple enough – as the victory of traditional geopolitical premises (balance of power, deterrence) and the triumph of post-Westphalian politico-cultural norms *per se*. From this perspective, accordingly, it is entirely rational and indeed entirely desirable that future responses to global order and prosperity remain centred on this geopolitical and cultural equation.

I will return to this issue in more detail shortly. For now a broader, related point needs to be made on the discussion thus far concerning the way in which the 'back to the future' metaphor has influenced the contemporary struggle for memory in the 1990s. It is, simply put, that there are other ways of giving meanings to the Cold War and to modern global history *per se* – meanings either ignored or marginalized by various 'back to the future' perspectives.

There is, for example, the story of the Cold War recently told by Lebow and Stein in *We All Lost the Cold War* (1994) which chronicles (from both Soviet and US viewpoints) the dangers and inadequacies of the 'back to the future' theme. Here, one encounters not the triumph of power politics strategy, but of spiralling arms races out of control, 40 million dead in the proxy wars of the central-balance superpowers, frightened, incoherent policy communities lurching from one crisis to another, fortunate (rather than rationally calculated) survival and a legacy not of future security but of future generations left to their insecure fate as global nuclear hostages.

On the question of the Balkans, too, there are other ways of according meaning to the contemporary tragedy in that region, meanings which offer no simple solutions, but which suggest that there were always other policy options than those accepted by the West in its dealings with the nationalist extremists in Bosnia. Such options, however, meant listening to other than the simple histories of 'tribalism' and ethnic hatred and giving meaningful resources and support (including perhaps military support) to those struggling for multicultural and pluralist outcomes among communities long used to such interactions (Campbell, 1998a). Had this historical reality been given the credibility it deserved, the peoples of the region might have been spared some of the horrors of the Bosnian conflict, and in 1999 NATO might not have become engaged in a brutal confrontation with the Milosevic regime in the quest to force upon it a multicultural and pluralist Yugoslavia.

To reiterate the point, while there are no simple solutions to any of the problems of past, present and future touched on above, it is important that this simplicity be challenged in some of the orthodox approaches to these problems in the post-Cold War era. This is not because they are valueless. The perspectives of the 'new pessimists' are often intelligent, insightful accounts of global reality from the perspective of those at its political, institutional and economic apex. Their simplicity, and the danger of it, lies elsewhere, in that which is excluded from their images of the real past, desirable present and possible future. And in the case of the 'back to the future' metaphor, I suggest, what is excluded is almost everything that does not fit within the orthodox Westphalian model of global modernity (see Krasner, 1995).

In the discussion to follow I will say something more substantial about the implications of this Westphalian model and in particular what it excludes from its story of past, present and future. In this regard it is worth keeping in mind Booth's proposal that while Westphalia might, on most accounts, represent simply the historical moment when modern sensibilities (for example, religious tolerance) and state structures began to emerge, it can also 'be read *as who the ruler? whom the exterminated?*' (Booth, 1998, p. 32, author's italics).

This is worth keeping in mind because if nothing else it indicates in very powerful fashion what many critical and post-colonial analysts have argued over many years – that the new world order after Westphalia was primarily about the rule of white, Western, christian, capitalist, males increasingly committed to systemic global dominance via a modern state system centred on structural hierarchy and the developing principles of power politics.

This, I suggest, is an increasingly dangerous situation at the beginning of a new millennium, with the experiences, perspectives and capacities of so many of the global community effectively excluded from serious concern and calculation in the struggle to shape the future world order. Hence, my contribution to the issue of the 'back to the future' metaphor here – which understands it as part of a much larger struggle for modern memory and which, in the first instance, critically engages the 'new pessimist' perspective in the most influential context in which it has claimed the past on behalf of the future – via the Westphalian model of global modernity.[3]

The Westphalian Model

The end of the Thirty Years War in 1648 and the treaty signed at Westphalia in that year is commonly represented as a historical point of origin for the modern state system. It represents, in this sense, the moment when *Res*

Publica Christiana, the world of the Holy Roman Empire, of Papal decree and the moral and legal unity of the Medieval age, gives way to a recognizably modern age of state sovereignty, moral and legal independence and religious tolerance and diversity. It sees the universalist conception of political and moral community established under Church and Emperor, displaced by a new world order centred on the rule of sovereign princes and established in territorial and secular-legal terms. More precisely, the shift from ancient to modern associated with the Treaty of Westphalia sees the political, religious and cultural architecture of the Medieval era superseded by a new framework of principles, ideas and structural norms representative of an emerging world of states.

In this form the dominant story of the modern world of states has intersected with the larger traditions of Western political history and modern philosophy (Walker, 1993). And in this Westphalian context a model of interstate relations has become embedded at the core of modern IR history, a model centred on the intrinsic conflict of a modern world order of autonomous power-seeking actors pursuing their egotistical systemic interests. Embedded too within this moment of original systemic creation is a paradox inherent to the system and an attitude necessarily drawn from that paradox. The paradox is that most famously associated with Rousseau which laments the tragedy of a system set up to allow for greater autonomy and freedom *within* the modern state becoming simultaneously the basis of systemic anarchy in relations *between* states. The attitude is that which inserts pessimism, an emphasis on structural constraint and a sense of tragic necessity as the only realistic responses to this paradoxical new world order (see Berki, 1981).

The point, however, is that this model of Westphalia is hardly an accurate historical representation of the emerging world of states in the seventeenth century, nor of the complex empirical realities of the state system in the centuries that followed (see Walker, 1993; Knutsen, 1992; Philpott, 1995; Watson, 1992). The point, more precisely, is that after 1648 there was never a single universally experienced reality within European borders capable of providing a 'modelled' understanding of the modern world of states. In particular, the post-Westphalian reality for the peoples in the east of the Continent was distinctly different from that of those in the west and along its Atlantic seaboard. In the east, the post-1648 experience was essentially that of the pre-Westphalian period, where feudal power relations and traditional structures of monarchical hierarchy remained intact and where medieval religion continued to dominate the everyday experience of the modern age of international relations.

In Western Europe, however, the freedoms of Westphalia served a crucial modern purpose, primarily for those states now energized by bourgeois ambition, growing industrial workforces and a new source of power, centred on naval expansion and the principles of mercantilism. In this context, and without for a moment underestimating the old world tendencies in some of its territories (for example, France), the modern world of anarchical states was, from its beginnings, invested with the kind of dynamic economic dimensions now associated with the process of (neoliberal) globalization. From its beginnings thus International Relations (represented in terms of post-Westphalian statist principles) was, for many, always International Political Economy. Moreover, from the beginning of the anarchical state system there was always a rudimentary but significant interdependence centred on complex political and economic norms and rules of behaviour – not just power politics anarchy. Or, as Ian Clark has recently emphasized, there was always unity and fragmentation at the core of the modern new world order (Clark, 1997).

There is, of course, nothing terribly original about any of this. Historians and medieval scholars (and some IR scholars) are well aware of the themes outlined above and, as such, of the problematic nature of any single model of the post-Westphalian world which does not take into account its complexities, paradoxes and ambiguities. The IR community in general has, nevertheless, traditionally invoked just such a model as the basis of its claim for real knowledge of the modern global past – a model which effectively divorces the 'political' from the 'economic', the 'internal' experience of states from their 'external' interaction and, most ironically, which effectively ignores the many instances of difference integral to a modern world of states (ostensibly the defining feature of a post-Westphalian world order) in favour of a universalized systemic sameness (ostensibly the defining feature of a pre-Westphalian order).

At the end of the twentieth century this Westphalian model has retained its status and power within the IR mainstream. Indeed, Stephen Krasner has recently re-emphasized its significance in the current era, as the 'basic concept for all the major approaches to IR in the 1990s ... including neo-realism and neo-liberal internationalism and the international society [English School] approach for which it is an "empirical regularity" ' (Krasner, 1995, pp. 119–20). Consequently, two fundamental assumptions remain embedded at the core of this Westphalian model at the beginning of the twenty-first century. The first, echoing security dilemma perspectives from Hobbes to Morgenthau to Waltz, is that global life is all about an anarchical world of sovereign states seeking to maximize their interest and power. The second, echoing market place logic from Adam Smith to Charles Kindleberger, is that the fundamental determinant of global behaviour is, and always was, egoistic self-interest (Waltz, 1979; Gilpin, 1987; Krasner (ed.), 1983; Keohane (ed.), 1986; Stein, 1983).

The result: an orthodox model of the contemporary global arena (and of its past) which sometimes appears to acknowledge the complexity, ambiguity, contingency and contestability of all human thought and behaviour but which then, logically and rationally, reduces that thought and behaviour to a particular representation of it. A model of global reality which, in short, reduces the world to a representation of it to be found in some of the great early modern texts touched on above (for example, Thucydides, Machiavelli, Hobbes) and to the great contemporary rearticulations of their eternal wisdom (E. H. Carr, Morgenthau and Waltz).

In this regard the Westphalian Model is the location of a crucial site of *preference* in modern Western theory and practice. Intellectually, it represents a preference for Hobbes' pessimism about the human condition over, say, Cruce's sense that the modern individual is capable of and inclined towards a fuller exposition of the human capacity. More significantly it represents a preference for the whole philosophy of the egoistic and anarchical imperative over, say, the Kantian perspective on the ethical imperative and its associated inclinations towards a democratic world order.

It represents, moreover, a preference for asking certain questions, in certain ways and referring other options to a very powerful language and logic of exclusion (for example, as utopian, idealist, ideological, irrational, normative). Put simply, the *Westphalian model represents a preference for a particular kind of world order and a particular kind of individual and global identity.* This preferred order and identity serves, in turn, a particular kind of interest, the interest it has in effect served since the seventeenth century; that, primarily, of the most powerful states and those sectors within them most advantaged by capitalist modes of production and exchange.

This is not to suggest that the Westphalian model is entirely bereft of insight or value. As intimated earlier, it has important insights to offer about how the world is viewed from the perspective of the most powerful and most privileged. Its problem, magnified in the contemporary period, is that it does not speak to the many realities outside that of the global elite. This renders it not only inadequate analytically but dangerous politically in terms of its inability to comprehend the implications of its global theory as practice.

This is clear enough with regard to the recent debate over the Cold War which saw Mearsheimer's 'back to the future' support for (bipolar) Cold War structures and deterrence theory articulated as a future programme of nuclear proliferation in Europe and a systemic status quo dominated by the major Western powers (that is, the USA and Britain). It is clearer still, perhaps, in the more general insistence that states must seek security in the traditional fashion, at a moment when attitudes towards security in a globalizing world have, like many other facets of the global agenda, taken on a decidedly unpredictable and non-traditional character. It is in this context that I conclude this chapter in outlining a case for, at least minimalist optimism in the struggle for memory with the Westphalian politics of preference and its 'back to the future' perspective.

The Case for Minimal Optimism

Perhaps the starkest illustration of 'back to the future' inadequacy in this context concerns the most obvious anomaly in its lexicon of (power politics) meaning – the willingness and capacity of the Soviet Union to confront its own dominant story of the past and seek to go beyond it, peacefully. Hence, the acknowledgment in word and deed of the wrongness of Soviet-style socialism and of the narrative of single truth, rationality and reality espoused with such tragic consequences by the CPSU. Hence, the acknowledgment of a new generation of Soviet citizens willing and able to engage their own struggle for (Soviet) memory with a sense that fundamental change was possible, absolutely necessary and realistically achievable (Booth (ed.) 1998, pp. 350–4).

Whatever else these changed perspectives indicate they suggest that, even in a closed and repressive society such as the Soviet Union, there was a sense by the 1980s that the old world game was over, that its traditional rules were destructive, and anachronistic, and that its lexicon of meaning was increasingly irrelevant. It suggests, more precisely, a shift in thinking about what it means to be secure in an age beyond deterrence theory, an age when security must include the development of more inclusive modes of political governance and effective economic and social integration within the international community.

There is, of course, still plenty of room for concern about the old Soviet Union, where anger and disillusionment at the unfulfilled promise of the Western way of life has already led to a rekindling of simple nationalist narratives and a sense of nostalgia for simple power politics as answers to complex questions. But this, I suggest, does not add up to a post-Soviet version of the 'we will soon miss the Cold War' scenario, nor Huntington's 'clash of civilizations' thesis. It adds up to a situation replete with both danger and opportunity, which requires neither posturing nor triumphalism but sensitive, nuanced and generous responses on the part of the Western powers, in particular, in order that pessimistic self-fulfilling prophecies be thwarted.[4]

In this regard also it is important to confront such pessimism with the cautious reminder that even at a moment of dreadful conflict in the Balkans, ex-Warsaw Pact countries are already part of NATO, and others are eagerly lining up for entrance; that for all its understandable anger at the NATO bombing of its Belgrade embassy, the Chinese are clearly less interested in conflict with the West than in becoming a major global trading power via entrée to the World Trade Organisation; that for all the desperate problems on the African continent, the apartheid system, for so long seemingly invulnerable to global opprobrium has, in fact, been defeated in South Africa and a tenuous but significant first step taken towards a multiracial, democratic future;

and that in Southeast Asia, previously unassailable dictators and autocrats have been challenged, and toppled, and important first steps taken towards more pluralistic forms of political governance.

Above all, perhaps it is worth remembering that in the anarchical heartland of the Westphalian model a quite remarkable experiment in cooperative/integrative behaviour is going on among European peoples who for centuries were engaged in 'tribal' warfare but who, since 1945, have quite consciously intervened in their own historical story in order to fundamentally change it. In this regard Richard Falk is correct, I think, to perceive the post-Second World War European attempts to create a different, safer and more secure human environment for (often) former mortal enemies, as the 'most significant political innovation' since the Treaty of Westphalia (Falk, 1994, p. 136).

It is, once again, easy enough to be cynical about such a claim. The EU undoubtedly has elitist dimensions and the concerns of its major actors are sometimes clearly prompted by narrow self-interested agendas. There is also deeply embedded racism in some quarters of its population and lingering suspicions and tensions are still evident enough in the everyday encounters of many of its citizens. And yet the new Europe, only a 50-year intervention in a thousand-year-old history, works efficiently and peacefully at all kinds of levels and is becoming a new and naturalized reality for this and future generations. As it does, it infuses great numbers of its citizens with the sense that a multi-ethnic, multicultural future is possible; that difference need not necessarily be feared and that it is also possible and, indeed, rewarding to live with the mild schizophrenia which accompanies multi-identity.

There is, to be sure, something of a 'democratic deficit' in all of this and it is the question of democratic possibility under globalization that is conventionally regarded as the criterion by which any meaningful future optimism, even of the minimalist variety, might be judged. In this context I can only touch on one element of the contemporary democracy debate in IR to indicate why such optimism might be warranted.

It concerns, in the first instance, the highly sceptical perspective of some commentators on this issue who represent the post-Cold War enthusiasm for liberal or 'low intensity' democracy as a strategy designed to facilitate the global economic ambitions of the major Western states, particularly the USA (Gills and Rocamora, 1992; see also Barber, 1996; Hirst and Thompson, 1996). There is, it seems to me, a good deal of validity to this claim. On the other hand, there is more to liberal-democratic internationalism than the egoism under anarchy thematic of many neoliberals. Just as important is a rekindled concern for global community and an ethic of democratic inclusiveness to be found under this broad rubric, aimed fairly and squarely at the global elite and its policy-making sectors. In this context the Report by the CGG (1995) is a significant statement about issues of

future global security which confront the Westphalian politics of preference with a sense of global community and global responsibility.

The Report is under no illusions as to its task, acknowledging widespread
violence, spiralling poverty and major ecological threats to the life-support
systems of the planet as crucial factors in any evaluation of the global scene
on the eve of the millennium. Nor does it shy away from the downside of
globalization in confronting the possibility of future worst-case scenarios,
which see a world divided between 'a prosperous and secure part' including most of Western and Central Europe, East Asia and North America and
'a larger part' characterized by impoverishment, violent conflict and unstable government, made up from most of Africa, the Middle East, South Asia
and parts of Central and South America (Commission on Global
Governance, 1995, p. 17).

It is in this rather daunting context that a critical liberal internationalism
emerges from the Report, one that acknowledges that states 'remain primary public institutions for constructive responses to issues affecting...the
global community' (p. 4) but which advocates significant structural and ethical changes to the ways in which states and all other actors operate within
the global system. Above all, it argues, the answer to the problems we face
do not lie in resort to traditional geopolitical or more recent neoliberal solutions. Rather, if the worst case scenarios are to be avoided, the Report suggests, there is 'no alternative' to the principles of equity and democracy, as
a global political practice designed to 'foster global citizenship and work to
include poorer, marginalized and alienated segments of national and international society' (p. 5).

It is on the issue of security, in particular, that this politico-ethical agenda
is most strikingly different from its more orthodox counterparts along the IR
spectrum. This is because, on this issue, the Report emphasizes the necessity
of inclusiveness as the keystone of a security format designed to anticipate
and prevent conflict occurring rather than desperately (and violently) seeking to suppress it. Thus, at the core of the Report's concerns regarding future
global security one finds a serious concern with issues of poverty, religion,
gender, class, mass migration, ethnicity, and environmental devastation,
and for the everyday realities of non-Western, non-christian, non-elite, non-
capitalist peoples of the world.

The necessity for this inclusiveness is bound up in the logic brought to the
question of what is most likely to make us insecure in the future. The answer
is that future security risks are unlikely to follow traditional patterns of
(inter-state) conflict but much more likely to be triggered by the processes of
Westernization and globalization integral to the contemporary globalization
project. Accordingly, the keystone of security theory and practice in the
future lies in more nuanced and sensitive understanding of empirical realities on the ground and preventative strategies which 'remove or alleviate

the factors that cause peoples, groups and governments to resort to violence' (CGG, 1995, p. 97).

This, I suggest, is a conclusion with direct empirical resonance, particularly in regard to complex areas of conflict such as Southeast Asia where a concern for questions of poverty, religion, gender, migration and uneven capitalist development allows for more useful insight and problem-solving potential on issues of future security in the region than does the conventional focus on global trade-flows and/or traditional geopolitical logics (see George and McGibbon, 1998).

The Report has its faults, of course, as one might expect from an enterprise of this magnitude and complex ambition. It is, for example, sometimes vague, even vacuous in its promotion of notions of 'global community'. Nor does it explain precisely how peoples and institutions embedded within a corporate capitalist frame of global reference might be persuaded to engage in radical processes of democratic change. These, however, are precisely the criticisms currently levelled (albeit unfairly) at the most sophisticated of recent critical philosophical works which seek explicitly to explain the transformation of patterns of global exclusion into cosmopolitan inclusion (see Geras, 1999, pp. 157–63, on Linklater, 1998). Consequently, and if one acknowledges its limitations, the Report represents a valuable perspective on the post-Cold War era which recognizes that a cautious, pragmatic approach toward global democratic change is an essential first step if worst case scenarios are to be overcome.

There is, nevertheless, a dimension missing from the critical liberalism of the Report which is, for me, an important component in my guarded optimism about the future – a dimension evident in much of the literature which addresses the democracy and globalization theme as part of a larger concern to resist modern processes of hegemonic control (Mittleman (ed.), 1996; Barber, 1996; Hirst and Thompson, 1996; Cox and Sjolander, 1997). Here, amid scepticism concerning 'low intensity' democracy, one finds the more positive recognition that globalization, for all its more obvious inclinations towards the (cultural, political and economic) hegemony of a Westphalian-based IPE, is perceived as 'in true dialectical fashion, impregnated with its opposite' (Cox and Sjolander, 1997, p. 151; see also Inoguchi, 1995), an opposite articulated in the wide-ranging attempts of peoples around the world to resist the power of global corporatism and great power intrusion upon their lives.

I have some reservations about change prescribed in dialectical terms, and there is good reason in the context of a chapter such as this to treat cautiously any appeal to teleological progress or (grand theorized) global consciousness. My own preference is for an explanation of contemporary change in terms of the always evident contingency of global political life and of the *radical indeterminacy* which, I suggest, is a central characteristic both of globalization and of any valid meaning of democracy associated with it.[5]

Two recent examples of radical indeterminacy in practice might indicate why, at least in minimalist terms, there is room for optimism on the global future. The first concerns the conflict between the Mexican Government and the (predominantly) Indian population of the Chiapas region where, for years, there had been a desperate hand-to-mouth existence and increasing anger at the unwillingness of the Government to provide help. This sparked off a concerted guerrilla campaign against the Mexican Government in January 1994 and a predictable and ruthless response from the Mexican military.

The difference between this conflict and many others of its kind, however, concerns the responses it triggered around the world via internet support networks. The point being that rather than leave the Chiapas Indians to their fate in the face of overwhelming military power, a whole range of human-rights activists, indigenous peoples representatives and supporters of democratic political movements rushed to the Chiapas region after being alerted to the conflict via a global communication network set up for decidedly 'opposite' purposes. The result was that these groups, in concert with the Zapatista leaders, were able to exert decisive (global) pressure on the Salinas government to end the immediate conflict and engage in meaningful negotiations with people previously treated with contempt (see Ronfeldt et al., 1998).

Another and different example of radical indeterminacy at work comes from the Southern Indian state of Kerala where, against great odds, the people of the region have embarked on 'the largest democratization project in the world today' (Shalom, 1999, p. 3). The significance of this project is that it has been undertaken as a conscious effort to resist the impact of IMF strictures and neoliberal globalization on India per se. Thus, while India as a whole has a per capita income 50 per cent higher than Kerala, on all other 'development' indicators Kerala stands as a promising indicator of what democracy from below might mean. Its infant mortality rate is lower than that among black Americans (and of other Indians) and many other richer countries; its female life expectancy rate (age 72) is significantly higher than the rest of India, and many other richer countries; its female literacy rate (87 per cent) is more than double that of India generally and many other richer countries; and in terms of wages, working conditions, nutrition, anti-caste discrimination, social security and gender equality it leads the low-income world (Shalom, 1999, p. 2). And it has achieved all this by prioritizing precisely those themes (land reform, universal education, social welfare, workers' rights, democratic elections and a free press) invoked by the Commission for Global Governance as essential to future global security and the amelioration of local, regional and international conflict (Shalom, 1999, p. 2).

The problems of the Indian peoples of Central and South America will not be magically overcome by the action in Chiapas, of course, nor, regrettably, will this be the last occasion when the remnants of indigenous peoples seek to rescind their poverty by force. And, extraordinary as events in Kerala appear to be, there are still enormous difficulties to be confronted before meaningful democratic change can become a reality for the mass of peoples on the subcontinent. But for all this, the events in Chiapas and in Kerala and elsewhere around a changing complex world indicate, at the very least, that power relations under globalization might be a little more indeterminate than either 'new pessimists' or orthodox liberal internationalists might imagine.

This, I suggest, will be the broad tendency in the foreseeable future, a future in which the basic conceptual and structural premises of the Westphalian state system will remain integral to human life. Under globalization, however, there will be change, and increasing space for the radical indeterminacy which is also integral to human life. Whatever else this means for the global future it surely cannot be comprehended by recourse to images of historical *déjà vu*.

CHAPTER 4

A 'Balance of Power'?

Richard Little

During the initial euphoria that accompanied the end of Cold War, serious thought was given to the idea that international relations no longer needed to be governed by a balance of power. For the previous 40 years, such a notion was widely regarded as heretical. It was often taken as axiomatic that it was neither possible nor desirable to move away from the nuclear balance that structured the international system. But the speed with which the nuclear balance collapsed, along with the failure to anticipate either the end of the Cold War or the demise of the Soviet Union, encouraged the belief that the balance of power and the associated realist approach provided an inaccurate or, at best, incomplete guide to world politics. Indeed, Fukuyama (1992, pp. 245–53) insisted that although it had been sensible to think in balance of power terms during the Cold War, such an approach was completely inappropriate in the emerging 'post-historical' world.

The importance of transcending the balance of power is not, of course, a new idea. In the eighteenth century, Kant argued that the possibility of creating world peace on the basis of a balance of power is a 'chimera' and he went on to suggest that the balance of power 'is like a house which was built by an architect so perfectly in accordance with all the laws of equilibrium, that when a sparrow alighted upon it, it immediately fell' (Clark, 1989, p. 55). But Kant is only one of many critics who has argued that the balance of power, far from being a source of stability, is perhaps the major cause of war. Certainly this negative assessment of the balance of power has prevailed in the United States for much of its history (Craig, 1976; Vagts, 1941). At the end of both world wars there was a desire in the United States to abandon balance of power thinking. At the end of the First World War, President Wilson insisted that balance of power politics were now redundant. And Cordell Hull, the US Secretary of State during the Second World War made a similar claim (Vagts, 1948, p. 82). But with the onset of the Cold War, balance of power thinking was soon being extensively deployed and enthusiastically endorsed in the United States. And interest in the balance of power persists in the aftermath of the Cold War.

The aim of this chapter is to explain why, despite the renewed desire in the post-Cold War world to dispense with balance of power thinking, it continues to be such a widely used image to characterize world politics. One of the most crucial policy debates now centres on whether the United States should endeavour to preserve a unipolar international system or encourage a move to a multipolar world. The persistence of the balance of power as a characterization of world politics, however, can only be adequately accounted for when attention is drawn to its metaphorical and mythical origins. Before examining the debate that revolves around unipolarity and multipolarity, therefore, attention will be focused first on the metaphorical and mythical role played by the balance of power in the analysis of social reality.

The Metaphorical Status of the Balance of Power

Metaphors are frequently dismissed as figures of speech that add nothing to our understanding of the world. From this perspective, saying that someone has told a pack of lies does no more than provide a graphic image that can quite easily be replaced, without any loss of meaning, by a literal statement. Metaphors are seen, therefore, to get in the way of clear and accurate descriptions of reality. In the case of the balance of power this argument has been pushed even further because the metaphor is inherently ambiguous and it can generate multiple meanings (Claude, 1962; Haas, 1953; Wight, 1966b). So although the metaphor often denotes an equal distribution of power, it can also carry the connotation of an unequal or even an unspecified distribution of power, with analysts identifying a shift in the balance of power without indicating what this entails. Indeed, Claude (1962, p. 24) notes how historians and international theorists can slide, without any acknowledgement, from one meaning to another leaving it to the reader to infer the meaning from the context in which the term is used. It is often concluded that such a protean concept should be avoided or replaced with terms whose meanings are literal and unambiguous. Waltz (1979, p. 120) makes a slight concession to this stern injunction; he refers to the balance of power because the employment of a metaphor can 'make one's prose more pleasing'.

These lines of argument, however, run directly counter to what has been depicted as the major strength of metaphors. The aim of metaphors is not to provide pleasing prose, nor should metaphors be eschewed on the grounds that they fail to provide a precise or literal meaning for a particular term. Instead, metaphors are used to transform the established meaning of a term, or in the case of a root metaphor (Pepper, 1942) to encourage us to look at reality in a new or distinctive way. As Nisbet (1969, p. 4) notes, metaphors involve a cognitive process whereby 'the identifying qualities of one thing are transferred in an instantaneous, almost unconscious flash of insight to some other thing that is, by remoteness or complexity, unknown to us'. In the case of the balance of power, both of these effects were achieved by the metaphor when it was initially devised. In the first place, it helped to transform the established conception of power, but in doing so, it also helped to consolidate a new and distinctive view of the international system.

The use of the metaphor has been traced back to Guicciardini's account, written around 1536, of the invasion of the Italian city-states at the end of the fifteenth century (Nelson, 1943).[1] Guicciardini (1966) starts his account in the years before the invasion and argues that the independence and peaceful relations of the city-states in these years can be attributed to the existence of a balance of power. The effect of the metaphor is to reveal that the city-states were all interconnected and formed a complex whole. But this new and distinctive view of the Italian city-states was premised on a transformed conception of power. By thinking of power in terms of a balance it became possible to reconfigure the established hierarchical conception of power.

Throughout the medieval period, the world was conceived in hierarchical terms. Power was exercised from above. The root metaphor that operated during the medieval period has been identified as 'the great chain of being' with God exerting power from the top of the chain (Lovejoy, 1936). A 'descending thesis of government' (Ullmann, 1975, p. 31) prevailed and even the dispute between the Pope and the Emperor resisted resolution by being depicted in 'equipoising' terms (Vagts, 1948, p. 89). The idea of a balance of power made it possible to reconceptualize power in non-hierarchical terms.

The Italian city-states represented a moment of transition between the medieval and the modern world. Metaphors helped to make sense of what was going on. But the metaphors deployed did not all point in the same direction. Machiavelli, Guicciardini's contemporary, failed to depict the Italian city-states in terms of a balance of power. On the contrary, he developed metaphors and images that were designed to make sense of a world that he saw as 'endangered and essentially unstable' (Condren, 1980, p. 99). Clegg (1989, p. 22) suggests that Machiavelli adhered, arguably, to what now looks like a postmodern view of the world where power can only be identified in the context of 'strategic manoeuvres made in contingent circumstances'. By contrast, Guicciardini's idea of a balance of power depicted a world where the city-states represented stable sites of power which could be drawn upon to counterbalance one city against another.

The Mythical Status of the Balance of Power

Guicciardini, however, did not simply transform the hierarchical conception of power by thinking of power as a system of weights pulling against each other on a horizontal plane. He also provided an account of how the system operated, demonstrating that city-states were able to maintain peaceful and stable relations amongst themselves. Since, in practice, the city-states certainly did not always maintain peaceful and stable relations, it can be suggested that Guicciardini drew on his balance metaphor to develop a political myth. In this context, myths are not fanciful or imaginary tales. On the contrary, a myth performs an important political function. From an anthropological perspective, myths 'provide values and meaning and ideas and plans and stratagems and alternative forms of political organization. Only through a myth does one see the "real" world. A myth is a form of pretence, an oversimplified representation of a more complex reality' (Bailey, 1977, p. 7). The aim of the myth perpetrated by Guicciardini was to demonstrate that peace is the natural condition of a system of independent states. There is a built-in tendency for peace to be maintained because war necessarily threatens the existing balance of power. If states go to war, then they confront the possibility of being denuded of some of their power.

Guicciardini identifies two mechanisms whereby peace was preserved amongst the five city-states (Venice, Naples, Milan, Florence and the Papal States) that constituted the system. In the first place, he identifies an automatic tendency within the system which derives from the adversarial relations amongst the city-states. This automatic and adversarial view of the balance of power was reinforced by a second mechanism which involved a deliberate attempt to manipulate the system in an effort to preserve peace (Little, 1989).

The mythical status of the balance of power has been drawn upon very regularly over the last 500 years. There has been a persistent assumption that, on the one hand, the balance of power is a self-regulating system that preserves the independence of states from the threat of hegemony, and, on the other, that the stability of the system can be reinforced by 'balancer' states which recognize that there is a common interest in maintaining peace and, in the process, ensuring that the balance of power is not upset.[2] It was on this basis that reference was made to a 'just equilibrium' in the peace settlements established at Utrecht in 1713 and at Vienna in 1815.

Across the centuries a whole series of metaphors have evolved to reinforce this aspect of the myth. In the eighteenth century, Fenelon (in Wright, 1975, pp. 41–2) thought of the balance of power in terms of both a body and an arch. Clausewitz (in Wright, 1975, p. xx) depicted the balance of power as a net. In the twentieth century, the balance of power has been depicted as a chandelier (Pollard, 1923) and a mobile. When these images are used, attention is not just being paid to the power of states, but also to their mutual interest in maintaining the balance of power. This use is very evident in Fenelon's discussion of the balance of power as an arch, where:

> All neighbouring states are so connected together by their mutual interests, that the least progress of any one is sufficient to alter the general balance, which makes the security of the whole; as when one stone is taken out of an arch, the whole falls to the ground, because all the stones sustain each other in pushing against each other. (in Wright, 1975, p. 42)

The Balance of Power as Metaphor and Myth

Metaphors can serve to reinforce the long-established myth that peace and the balance of power are mutually reinforcing features of a system of independent states. But metaphors can operate independently of the myth as the familiar image of the balance of power as a set of scales demonstrates. The idea that a balancer is prepared to move from one side of the scales to the other in order to preserve an equilibrium is an idea that obviously bolsters the myth. But metaphors can also be used to generate new insights into how the system operates. From this perspective, for example, the metaphor has been shown to reveal that power is very difficult to specify because it is only possible to determine the weight of any state in terms of the weight/power of the other states in the scales/system and this can only be done when the scales come to rest. As Bolingbroke (in Wright, 1975, p. 57) pointed out in the eighteenth century, those 'most concerned to watch the variations of this balance' will nevertheless 'misjudge' how the scales are moving because of their 'habitual prejudices'. According to Bolingbroke, they 'continue to dread a power no longer able to hurt them' and 'continue to have no apprehensions of a power that grows daily more formidable'.

The metaphor suggests that because the scales are almost always in motion any attempt to ascribe an exact measure to the power of a particular state is going to be an inherently flawed procedure. Analysts who are sensitive to the metaphorical status of the balance of power recognize this fact. Wight (1978, p. 173), for example, argues that the multiple meanings associated with the balance of power should be regarded as an advantage rather than a flaw. He suggests that part of the fascination of the balance of power lies with the difficulty of pinning down its meaning. We resort to balance of power terminology, he argues, because it is 'flexible and elastic enough to cover all the complexities and contradictions' encountered in the international system. Detailed historical research, according to Wohlforth (1993,

p. 306), 'reveals the multitudinous ambiguities surrounding power in world politics'.

What is perhaps most surprising about the balance of power, however, is its resilience and endurance, although this does not necessarily mean that either the myth or the metaphor is playing a useful role. Steiner (1975, p. 21) has noted how 'words go dead under the weight of sanctified use' and he suggests that, as a consequence, it becomes possible for a civilization to become 'imprisoned in a linguistic contour which no longer matches, or matches only at certain ritual, arbitrary points, the changing landscape of fact'. To the extent that the balance of power myth is used to impose meaning on a constantly shifting world, a gap between the facts and the myth is only to be expected. But there are other factors that have prevented the balance of power from becoming a dead metaphor or an irrelevant myth. One is the persistence of a counter-myth associating balance of power with perennial war rather than perpetual peace. A second factor is the ongoing divergence and tension that exists between the two balance of power mechanisms identified by Guicciardini. Finally, there is the protean nature of the metaphor which allows the balance of power to be constantly redescribed and reinvigorated by fresh images.

From Bipolarity to the 'Unipolar Moment'

A familiar description of the balance of power during the Cold War provides an example of how useful metaphors can be in redescribing a familiar phenomenon to take account of changing circumstances. The emergence of nuclear weapons in the United States and the Soviet Union appeared to have eliminated all the grounds for the high degree of ambiguity that has so frequently been associated with the balance of power. For many, during the Cold War, the power generated by nuclear weapons appeared to be anything but 'elusive' (Wohlforth, 1993). As a consequence, the metaphorical shifting scales were replaced by the image of two unambiguous and immovable poles of power, although situated East–West, rather than North–South. The United States and the Soviet Union also represented polar opposites and the tension between them was seen to reinforce the stability of the balance of power. Deterrence, which lay at the heart of the system, drew heavily on the myth that the desire for peace was reinforced by a perfect and unambiguous balance. It was only after the collapse of the Soviet Empire, swiftly followed by the demise of the Soviet Union itself, that it became apparent just how elusive the balance of power had been, in reality. And, unsurprisingly, the metaphor itself came under serious challenge as it was asked 'What was bipolarity?' (Wagner, 1993). Retrospectively, bipolarity appeared to have been an illusion. As the Cold War progressed, however, the balance of power myth was challenged at various junctures, when attention was drawn to concepts like interdependence and transnationalism (Oliver, 1982; Reynolds, 1975). But although these concepts resonated in the West, they failed to ring any bells in the East and the endless analyses of these concepts failed to undermine the image of the Eastern and Western blocs as polar opposites.

With the end of the Cold War the metaphorical and mythical utility of bipolarity collapsed. Despite the continuing existence of nuclear weapons, no one even attempted to suggest that the metaphor could begin to help to illuminate the essential characteristics of the emerging post-Cold War world. As always, in times of political turmoil, there was an instant and inevitable search for new metaphors in an attempt to impose meaning and make sense of the emerging post-Cold War world. President Bush conjured up the image of a New World Order. At the heart of this image lay notions of global multilateralism and collective security. The worldwide response to Iraq's invasion of Kuwait gave some substance to this image. But, as this book illustrates, a host of alternative images were thrown up in the wake of the post-Cold War world. Unsurprisingly, moreover, the imagery associated with the New World Order failed to resonate in a world where reference could also be made to the 'coming anarchy' (Kaplan, 1994). By contrast, Fukuyama (1992, pp. 276–7) presented an image of a bifurcated globe that quickly found favour. He paints the picture of a post-historical world where the rules of power politics have been abandoned, and a historical world that has survived the 'end of history' and where power politics persist. From this perspective, then, the balance of power has been transcended in the North while it continues to swing relentlessly in the South.

The image of a bifurcated world has garnered a good deal of support (Goldgeier and McFaul, 1992; Singer and Wildavsky, 1993). But it has also been challenged by an alternative, although related metaphor devised originally by Krauthammer (1990/91) who suggests that the end of the Cold War needs to be discussed in terms of a 'unipolar moment'. Krauthammer also bifurcates the world, into North and South, but in doing so he presents an image of the North which is very different from Fukuyama's post-historical world. During the twentieth century, Krauthammer suggests, the North has been torn apart by three great civil wars – the First and Second World Wars and the Cold War. But this era has come to an end and we have now entered a phase when 'an ideologically pacified North seeks security and order by aligning its foreign policy behind that of the United States' (Krauthammer, 1990/91, p. 25). This is the unipolar moment. There is, Krauthammer insists, only one pole of power which consists of the United States at the apex of the advanced industrial world. The idea that the North contains several poles of power and that these poles are collaborating on a multilateral basis is, for Krauthammer, an illusion. So the Gulf War, for example, is depicted as a case of 'pseudo-multilateralism'. The United States essentially acted alone, with the multilateral alliance being put in place to give 'unilateral actions a multilateral sheen' (Krauthammer, 1990/91, p. 25).

The Gulf War also helped to demonstrate that it is a 'materialist illusion' to imagine that economic power can be translated into 'geopolitical influence' (Krauthammer, 1990/91, p. 24). Potential poles of power such as Japan and Germany lack both the will and the military capability to create a genuinely multilateral force. Only the United States has 'the military, diplomatic, political and economic assets to be a decisive player in any conflict in whatever part of the world it chooses to involve itself'; and so the Gulf War revealed, at a very early stage, 'the true geopolitical structure of the post-Cold War world' (Krauthammer, 1990/91, p. 24). Although unipolarity is underpinned by a wide range of assets, in the final analysis, the structure is sustained by US military might. The US defence budget now accounts for around 35 per cent of the world's total annual military expenditures. As Gholz *et al.* (1997, p. 8) demonstrate, the United States 'towers over other nations in terms of its current and potential military power'; it not only 'leads the pack but out-distances its closest rival by more than a factor of three'. Krauthammer, however, is well aware of Kennedy's (1989) argument that endeavouring to sustain a hegemonic position in the international system can lead to 'imperial overstretch'. But he dismisses the argument that the United States cannot sustain its current unipolar position. He argues that the US is currently only spending around 5 per cent of its GNP on defence, around half the level sustained in the early 1960s.

Krauthammer is in no doubt, moreover, that the United States benefits from its ability to intervene wherever and whenever it wants to around the globe. Because the United States is a commercial, maritime, trading nation, it has worldwide interests which need to be defended. He is certain that there will be times in the future when these interests will be threatened and require protection. But because US interests are worldwide, Krauthammer insists that threats arise whenever any state anywhere in the international system attempts to destabilize the existing system. Destabilization occurs whenever a state endeavours to alter by force the way that the international system is currently structured. International stability, he insists, has to be carefully nurtured and he draws a comparison with the nineteenth century when international stability, from which the United States benefited, was achieved 'in large part, as the product of Britain's unrelenting exertions on behalf of the balance of power' (Krauthammer, 1990/91, p. 29).

There may appear to be a disjunction here between the analysis of unipolarity and the reference to the balance of power. But the disjunction disappears if it is acknowledged that in a unipolar system, the hegemonic state can choose either to establish an imperial system or adopt the role of a balancer and ensure that a system of independent states is maintained.

Krauthammer is arguing that in the nineteenth century Britain played this role and that in the post-Cold War world, it is appropriate for the United States to act as a 'balancer' in the global balance of power. From this perspective, the enormous power of the United States exists within a global balance of power which needs to be defended. From this perspective, Iraq's attack on Kuwait, for example, destabilized the system and, in doing so, disturbed the global balance of power. The balance of power metaphor is being used to stress the global significance of minor events. The suggestion is that the United States has a vested interest in rectifying even the most minor disturbance to the established balance of power. The argument contains a powerful normative element.[3] By preserving the global balance of power, the United States is providing a very important collective good. There are other metaphors and myths that can and have been drawn upon. Krauthammer could have used imperial imagery, referring to the Roman Empire and *pax americana*. But balance of power imagery is seen to be more effective because it is so closely associated with the idea of a system of independent states.

The normative dimension of the argument becomes even more apparent when Krauthammer examines the willingness of the United States to maintain its unipolar status. He argues that there is an incipient pull to isolationism within the United States which could pose a challenge to unipolarity. The most 'sophisticated and serious' expression of this sentiment is seen to come from the realist foreign policy school because not only does this school insist that US foreign policy should be driven by US interests but that these interests are generally defined 'in a narrow and national manner' (Krauthammer, 1990/91, p. 28). From Krauthammer's perspective, the United States has no real alternative but to preserve the world balance of power, by which he means defending the existing territorial arrangements across the globe. The major threat he sees coming from states that seek to acquire weapons of mass destruction, 'rogue states' as they have subsequently come to be called, and he acknowledges that it could be necessary for the United States to disarm such states. He also argues that only the United States, backed by as many allies as are willing to help, can carry out this task. More ominously, he suggests that the only alternative to unipolarity is chaos.

The Unipolar Illusion and the Rise of Multipolarity

Much of the euphoria that accompanied the ending of the Cold War has dissipated in subsequent years. The danger posed by 'rogue states' has not diminished and it has been joined by the threat of 'failed states' and civil wars resulting from the exploitation of ethnic divisions by leaders wishing to consolidate their domestic power bases. It is widely accepted, however, that the grand strategy outlined by Krauthammer for the United States and which, in essence, requires the United States to maintain the position that it adopted during the Cold War, has in fact been followed. As Mastanduno (1997, p. 51) has argued, the clear objective of both the Bush and Clinton administrations has been 'the preservation of the United States' pre-eminent position'. Nevertheless, the idea of unipolarity has come under attack on theoretical, empirical and strategic grounds. And competing images of the balance of power play a crucial role in the resulting debate.

On theoretical grounds, realists have argued that unipolarity is a highly unstable structure and that the United States will soon be challenged by other states with sufficient resources to create a multipolar system. From this perspective, it is an illusion to imagine that unipolarity will persist (Layne, 1993, 1997). Mastanduno (1997) acknowledges, however, that, so far, in the strategic arena, this prediction has failed to materialize. Moreover, he and Waltz (1993) suggest that, by judicious diplomacy, the United States could succeed in allaying the fears of potential rivals and if successful in this endeavour, these rivals might voluntarily restrain themselves from engaging in the military build-up that would result in the emergence of a multipolar world. The US would thereby prolong its position of pre-eminence. But as Mastanduno (1997, pp. 87–8) points out, it could be difficult to maintain the level of domestic support that would be necessary to operate as the 'stabilizer of last resort' in regional crises and he notes that over a two-week period in 1996, US officials found themselves managing the insertion of 20 000 US troops into Bosnia, prepositioning equipment for a possible renewed Iraqi attack against Kuwait, mediating a crisis on the brink of war between Greece and Turkey, and responding to China's military intimidation of Taiwan.

On empirical grounds, however, Dibb argues that the evidence is already available to discard the unipolar image. The argument is most easily made by focusing on Asia. Dibb (1995, p. 5) takes it for granted that we can talk about an evolving Asian balance of power where, for the first time in centuries, 'the future security of Asia will be shaped more by the large Asian powers than by external powers or foreign domination'. China already identifies itself as the second most powerful state in the world. Although it is not intending to challenge the United States on the global arena, it is seen by its neighbours to have every intention of becoming the dominant state in its own region. McLennan (1997) points out that although the Chinese are reducing the size of their armed forces, mobility and striking power are being enhanced. At the same time, they are transforming their coastal defence forces into an ocean-going navy. Despite these transformations, there is no certainty about the future power status of China (Gladstone, 1995; Huang, 1995). And there is the same lack of certainty about its intentions. Nevertheless, Dibb insists that East Asia is already operating as a distinct balance of power system and these uncertainties have to be regarded as a feature of the system. The automatic mechanisms identified by Guicciardini are already in play. It now remains to be seen whether the mechanisms linked to a more associative balance of power emerge.

From an Asian perspective, the unipolar metaphor lacks resonance. In the Cold War period three poles of power were identified: the Soviet Union, China, and the United States. With the collapse of the Soviet Union, China and the United States are now seen to be the 'defining poles of power' (McLennan, 1997, p. 59). There is no doubt that states in the region believe that but for the US presence, the Chinese would be pursuing a much more assertive policy. Although Japan has considerable naval power and is developing its naval air defences, it still relies, in the final analysis, on the United States to preserve its own security and the security in the region. Like Krauthammer, McLennan looks back to the nineteenth century when it is claimed that Britain acted as an 'offshore balancer' willing and able to act decisively whenever the established balance of power is jeopardized, and he presupposes, moreover, that the United States has taken over this role because it believes that its own security depends upon maintaining a global balance of power just as Britain did in the past. This presupposition, however, relies on the mythic status of the balance of power. In other words, McLennan's analysis accepts that peace and stability in the international system has been enhanced in the past by the willingness of a 'balancer' state to constantly adjust its policy to counteract the attempts of other states to alter the established balance of power. But McLennan is not suggesting that the United States or Britain ever took responsibility for every aspect of the global balance of power. He insists that 'it is nowadays only China that may need to be balanced against' (1997, p. 59). Although much more limited, McLennan is in no doubt about how crucial the US role could be, arguing that 'unless a stable balance is attained, there is no prospect of China and the United States working co-operatively and successfully to assure Asia's peaceful future' (1997, p. 63). McLennan's conception of the balancer, therefore, is much more limited than the one adopted by Krauthammer; nevertheless, both are relying on the mythic status of the balance of power to sustain their positions.

Even the limited balancing role accorded to the United States by McLennan is considered excessive and unnecessary by Layne (1997), although his main focus of attack is on policy analysts, like Krauthammer, who are arguing in favour of a grand strategy for the United States that will sustain its position of preponderance in the international system. Layne argues strenuously that such a strategy is simply not sustainable in the long haul. As we move through the twenty-first century, other Great Powers must emerge and the US commitment to maintain stability across the globe will become increasingly less credible. The best alternative strategy, Layne argues, is one of 'offshore balancing' but this position is very different from the one advocated by McLennan. Whereas McLennan accepts that the United States has crucial interests in East Asia , Layne (1997) advocates the definition of US interests in the narrowest possible terms. The definition would not extend beyond defending US territorial integrity and preventing the (highly unlikely) rise of a Eurasian hegemon.

Lane's strategy of 'offshore balancing' presupposes that the United States will be more secure in a multipolar world than in the current unipolar world. In a multipolar world, he argues, disengagement becomes possible. He accepts that the United States cannot cut loose without prior warning from its current commitments. Nevertheless, once disengaged, then the United States can be confident that its former allies will pursue strategies to ensure their own survival. For example, if Japan was cut adrift from its alliance with the United States, then it would without doubt become a major strategic player in the region. But this development would precipitate further consequences, as Dibb's assessment of the Asian balance of power already presupposes. The US alliance with Japan was always to give reassurance to Japan's neighbours as much as to offer protection to Japan. Once removed, other states would be pushed to pursue balancing strategies against Japan.

By contrast, as an insular power, the United States is in a good position to engage in 'bystanding' and 'buck-passing' behaviour, 'forcing others to assume the risks and costs of antihegemonic balancing' (Layne, 1997, pp. 117–18). The United States would only be required to engage in balancing behaviour when its own immediate and vital interests were seen to be affected. Since it is unlikely that any state would pose a direct threat to US territorial integrity and other states would very likely be able to cope with potential hegemonic threats, balancing activity would be minimal. By minimizing its overseas interests, the United States would be able to afford a much more expansive domestic programme. As a consequence, Layne (1997, p. 124) insists that the strategy can be seen to be 'ethically driven' and it presupposes that the primary interest of the United States is at home and not abroad. This grand strategy has the effect of forcing other states to defend the global balance of power and it is possible only because of the relative isolation and an apparently low level of integration into the world economy. These conditions are effectively outside the terms of reference of the balance of power; nevertheless, in postulating the assumption that the withdrawal of the United States from its global commitments will generate a multipolar balance of power, Layne too is forced to draw on the mythical status of the balance of power.

Conclusion

Although it has been argued that the balance of power 'is the best known, and perhaps the best, theory in international politics' (Jervis, 1997, p. 131), there has been little attempt in this chapter to explore or evaluate how the balance of power has been developed as a theory in the discipline of International Relations, although it has been noted inferentially that some of the contemporary theoretical discussion about the balance of power has long been anticipated in metaphorical analyses of the balance of power. Attention has been focused in this chapter on the metaphorical and mythical implications of the concept. Language is inherently metaphorical and it impossible to use language without drawing on metaphors. The metaphors that we use, however, encourage us to see the world in a particular way. And in doing so, they also discourage us from seeing the world in a different way. Too little attention has been paid in the analysis of International Relations to the metaphorical dimension of the subject. Other disciplines have been less reticent in this regard and the attention has paid substantial dividends (Morgan, 1997). What is most interesting about the balance of power metaphor is that from its origins it has been Janus-faced, looking in one direction at the competing interests between states and in the other at their common interests. Both faces of the balance of power, however, have underpinned its mythical status which links the phenomenon with peace and stability amongst a set of independent states. In examining the contemporary policy debate that revolves around whether world order will be built upon multipolarity or unipolarity what we find is that the competing arguments are all heavily conditioned by the mythical status of the balance of power. The myth is inextricably linked to the idea of a system of sovereign states and so long as there are advocates of sovereign states, the imagery associated with the balance of power will persist.

CHAPTER 5

An 'International Society'?

Paul Keal[1]

The idea of 'international society' forms a powerful image of world politics. Its power derives from the wide and now largely unexamined acceptance that a society of states or international society does actually exist. Indeed, the assumption that there is such a thing is implicit in much of the everyday discussion of world affairs. It underpins the idea of an 'international community', with 'society' and 'community' often being used interchangeably (Wight, 1966c, p. 93) and it is integral to international law. Thus for Martin Wight, international society 'is *prima facie*, a political and social fact, attested by the diplomatic system, diplomatic society, the acceptance of international law and writings of international lawyers, and also by a certain instinct of sociability' (Wight, 1991, p. 30). Nevertheless, whether it is a political and social fact should be questioned; for international society is essentially an image that may not be an accurate reflection of world politics.

The image of international society is one in which states articulate and agree upon rules, based upon their mutual recognition as sovereign states, concerning acceptable behaviour. It depicts states as acting in concert to achieve international order and as laying down criteria for the determination of which states are to be accepted as legitimate members of international society. Those that are so regarded are then entitled to be treated according to the norms and rules of the society. It is a view of political relations between states in which states are capable of creating and maintaining order in their relations (international order) without an overriding authority standing above them. It is depicted as a self regulating society without government; and this sets it apart from classical realism in which the lack of an overarching authority results in recurring struggle and disorder between states. Lastly, it is fundamental to the so-called English School of international relations theory. The image of international society has had its fullest discussion in the work of people located in this school, among whom Martin Wight, Hedley Bull and John Vincent have arguably been the most prominent. An account of the English School, its members and the centrality of international society in their work is contained in Tim Dunne (1998).

The following discussion first sketches facets of the image necessary to understanding the scope of its vision of world politics. These include the European origins of the society of states (or international society), the role of rules, the necessity of mutual recognition, the concept of legitimacy and the distinction between international and world order. Each of these crops up in subsequent sections. The discussion proceeds by next considering the way individuals and not just states figured in the intellectual roots of the image, which has important implications for both what the image suggests about future world politics and the moral purpose of an international society. Its purpose, the chapter argues, should be to promote the values of a world order in which individuals and not states have the primary place. Consequently the third section explains and rejects the suggestion that international society lacks the moral foundation to be anything more than a myth invented by academics. Following that, the focus of the fourth section shifts to the nature of the rules and common interests that supposedly bring states together in an international society. It begins by noting the centrality of rules in both international society and regime theory. It notices the similarities between the two approaches but argues that they are fundamentally different with regime theory lacking the breadth of comprehension of world politics contained in the image of international society. Discussion then proceeds to different conceptions of community encompassed by the image and the interests that underpin them. This leads into the fifth section which draws on the work of Fred Halliday and considers international society conceived of as an expression of the interests of states with similar domestic arrangements, economic systems or political ideologies and therefore as something that is inevitably confined to a particular group of states. The chapter concludes with comments about how the image has been deployed and a statement of five reasons for being discontented with it.

Facets of the Image

The *prima facie* evidence, mentioned by Wight, for accepting that international society is a political and social fact depends on a set of established practices known by inference from the way states and other actors behave. We conclude that there is an international society because states behave as if there were one. International society is, according to Wight, 'the habitual intercourse of independent communities, beginning in the Christendom of

Western Europe and gradually extending throughout the world' (Wight, 1966c, p. 97). And it was perhaps because of it being known by inference from the practice of states that Wight called international society 'a shadowy and insubstantial entity' (Wight, 1991, p. 30).

For Hedley Bull also, international society is implicit in and revealed by the practice of states; but in particular by the way they identify and articulate rules to guide their relations with one another.

> A *society of states* (or international society) exists when a group of states, conscious of certain common interests and common values, form a society in the sense that they conceive themselves to be bound by a common set of rules in their relations with one another, and share in the working of common institutions. (Bull, 1977, p. 13)

The primary function of these common institutions is to provide a foundation for order among states (international order). According to Wight, '[i]f there is an international society... then there is an order of some kind to be maintained, or even developed' (Wight, 1966c, p. 103). International society necessarily supports a normative order that accepts the legitimacy of states and the society constituted by them. The rules meant to maintain or develop order between states are, for the most part, determined by the great powers of the time, but their aims are not necessarily those of all states. If international society exists it is in theory for the benefit of all of the states that belong to it. An enduring question, however, is whether it does benefit all states or is, instead, never more than an expression of the interests of great or dominant powers.

Fundamental to the rules underpinning international order is mutual recognition, which Wight identifies as one of the distinguishing characteristics of historical states systems. For there to be a system of states, without which there cannot be either international society or order, states must mutually recognize each others' right to sovereign independence. An international society is for this reason a community of mutual recognition. Unless states do recognize each other as legitimate and sovereign actors there can be no basis for agreement over the practices that are to guide their mutual relations. 'It would be impossible to have a society of sovereign states unless each state, while claiming sovereignty for itself, recognized that every other state had the right to claim and enjoy its own sovereignty as well' (Wight, 1977, p. 135).

Coupled with mutual recognition is legitimacy, which for Wight meant 'the collective judgement of international society about rightful membership of the family of nations; how sovereignty may be transferred; and how state secession is to regulated, when large states break up into smaller, or several states combine into one' (Wight, 1977, p. 153). Further, in contemporary world politics the domestic arrangements of states are increasingly important in determining which states are regarded as legitimate. The status and moral authority of states depends, perhaps more than ever before, on factors such as their human rights record, their treatment of indigenous populations, whether they are governed by democratic institutions, and the degree of social justice that obtains in them. In earlier phases of world politics legitimacy was also an important question in relations between Christendom and what lay beyond it, especially whether non-Christian rulers could be accepted as legitimate (Wight, 1977, p. 156).

The legitimacy or otherwise of including non-Christian or non-European peoples is a vital but often neglected part of the story of international society. Bull and Watson (1984, p. 1) tell this as a success story of states in which a society of initially European states expanded 'across the rest of the globe' to eventually become 'the global international society of today'. A global international society was not possible before the 'numerous and extremely diverse political entities' of the world 'had come to resemble one another at least to the extent that they were all, in some comparable sense, states' (Bull, 1984a, p. 121). The expansion of Europe resulted in both the state becoming a universal form of political organization and the evolution of the body of rules and institutions, based on mutual recognition, that constitute international society. Until Europe unified the globe there was no common legal and moral basis for 'relations between states and rulers that were members of the different regional international systems'. The rules and institutions that eventually provided that basis were a response to the development of both inter-state relations within Europe and Europe's expanding relations with the rest of the world. But hidden under this success story of the expansion of international society is another story of moral failure with respect to the indigenous peoples of the world, many of whom had to struggle to be accepted as legitimate members of international society and even of the human race.

The state, as a universal form of political organization, was not, however, regarded by Bull as the end of the story. States, he pointed out, 'are simply groupings of men, and men may be grouped in such a way that they do not form states at all'. Consequently there are questions of deeper and 'more enduring importance' than those connected with international order; questions 'about order in the great society of all mankind'. In this way he introduces the idea of world order based not on an international society of states but a world society of individual human beings, with world order defined in terms of a concern with 'social life among mankind as whole' (Bull, 1977, p. 20). It is 'something more fundamental and primordial than [international society]' and is morally prior. '[I]t is order among all mankind which we must treat as being of primary value, not order within the society of states. If international order does have value, this can only be because it is instrumental to the goal of order in human society as a whole' (Bull, 1977, p. 22). Bull appears to have regarded international society buttressed by international order as a way station on the long journey to a normatively preferable world society and world order, giving international society the moral purpose of promoting world order. The difficulty with this is that the requirements and rules of international and world order may clash as, for instance, in cases where promoting the values of world order would require armed intervention in the affairs of a sovereign state. Of which an example is arguably the 1999 NATO bombing of Serbia in defence of the Kosovar Albanians.

Individuals

Hugo Grotius is accepted as a key early exponent of the idea of international society. His conception of it was not confined to states; it included individuals and non-state groups, it built on natural as well as positive law, regarded international society as being universal, and it included not just European rulers and peoples but non-Europeans as well. Concerning individuals, Cutler (1991, p. 45) argues that Grotius' writings reflect 'the absence at the time of a clearly perceived distinction between individual and state personality'. For him international society was 'not just the society of states, it is the great society of mankind' (Bull, 1992, p. 83). Natural law was fundamental to this reasoning because natural law theories concern the 'rights and duties attaching to individual human beings, rather than those attaching to states or other groups' (Bull, 1979, p. 171), and these rights and duties are both universal and held by 'individuals, alongside states ... under international law' (Cutler, 1991, p. 45). Cutler (1991, p. 46) contends that natural law contained the 'element of universalization' Grotius needed to conceive of a universal moral order. but that in contrast Bull's rejection of natural law meant that his conception of international order is one that has no basis for a universal moral order (Cutler, 1991, pp. 53–8).

The universal scope of natural law that allowed the inclusion of both individuals and non-Europeans meant the latter had, in theory, the rights that Europeans granted to one another. Consequently, Grotius has been represented in the history of international law as holding the opinion that non-Europeans possessed sovereign rights (Lindley, 1926; Anaya, 1996; Keal, 1995). In both international law and political theory the history of European relations with others can be represented as one in which there was a retreat, over four centuries of contact, from at first recognizing the sovereign rights of non-Europeans to finally denying them. There is, however, an alternate view which suggests that from its inception the international law on which international society was based discriminated against certain categories of people. From the beginning, international law codified difference, which meant that discriminatory practices were built into international society (Darian-Smith and Fitzpatrick (eds), 1999).

Grotius, and Francisco de Vitoria before him, both defended the sovereign rights of non-Europeans over the lands they occupied at the time Europeans arrived. But both allowed that there were circumstances under which those rights could be legitimately violated. These included actions taken in the defence of Christian teaching, and the use of force against people engaging in practices contrary to Christian belief. Grotius' view of international law was thus one that allowed an inner and an outer circle of membership with the latter having an unequal sets of rights against the former. At the same time as his conception of international society included individuals, he relegated certain categories of individuals to a status that denied them the full rights of membership and did not allow equal rights.

With the passage of time natural law with its focus on individuals everywhere gave way to the positive law of relations between states. The membership of international society was progressively limited to states and the element of universal moral order Cutler discerns in Grotius was displaced by the morality of states and their purposes.

A Myth Invented by Academics?

The possibility or otherwise of universal moral order is also at the root of one line of inquiry into whether international society is a myth. In his elucidating study of the English School, in which international society is the key concept, Timothy Dunne cites E. H. Carr writing to Stanley Hoffmann about the origins of the academic study of international relations: 'I suspect that *we tried to conjure into existence an international society* and a science of international relations. We failed. No international society exists, but an open club without substantive rules' (Dunne, 1998, p. 35). Dunne's interpretation of this is that Carr thought the society of states was a myth because of 'the structural inequality built into the system. Any society which accepts as "normal or permissible" discrimination between individuals, "on grounds of race, colour or natural allegiance", lacks the basic foundation for a moral order' (Dunne, 1998, p. 35). By implication there is no such foundation and so there can be no actual international society. Charles Manning voiced a similar concern by citing *The Times* of 19 April 1960 as having stated that 'international society is a metaphorical expression'. Manning interpreted this as the suggestion that moral judgement in international affairs is not well grounded and 'the idiom of international obligation ... [is one] of make believe and nothing more'. Moral order underpins the coexistence of men and women but not the coexistence of states (Manning, 1962, pp. 42–3).

Was Carr right about there being no basic foundation for moral order? If there is a moral basis for international society, what is it? As already mentioned, Bull rejected natural law in favour of positive international law and for Cutler this meant that his conception of international order is one that cannot accommodate a universal moral order and is necessarily confined to a morality of states (Cutler, 1991, pp. 53–8). Contrary to this, Dunne argues that Bull's conception of international society is underpinned by moral universalism. In support of this he cites Bull's contention, also noted above, that the 'society of states' is 'an instrument for delivering the moral value of world order', and goes on to say that 'the underlying moral universalism in Bull's thinking concerns his insistence that individuals are the ultimate moral referent. International order is only to be valued to the extent which it delivers "world order", which Bull makes the litmus test for the ethical claims of the society of states' (Dunne, 1998, pp. 145–6). The meaning of this is clear: international society has a universal moral basis so long as it fosters the well being of individuals everywhere.

For international society to do that, the practices of its member states would have to include those intended to either induce or enforce right conduct by member states towards the citizens within their borders. Clearly there are states that murder, torture, commit genocide, impoverish and in other ways deny the individual and collective rights of their citizens. In some cases the only way of ending such practices may be by armed intervention, which would violate the fundamental norms of inter-state relations. In that case the requirements of international order conflict with those of world order and international society may not at all be a viable route to the values of a world society.

Rules, Regimes and Common Interests

It was noted earlier that for Hedley Bull the existence of international society is revealed by the way states agree upon the rules and norms that govern their mutual behaviour. These norms and rules may, but need not have, the status of law, and they may include the kinds of rules that govern regimes. Indeed, the emphasis on rules in much of the discussion of international society has led more than one writer to suggest that regime theory is the American version of the English School (Evans and Wilson, 1992; Buzan, 1993; Slaughter-Burley, 1993; Keohane, 1989). Both emphasize the rules, norms and institutions that govern the behaviour of states and mutual relations between them; both are concerned with what might loosely be termed 'management structures' (Evans and Wilson, 1992).

Alongside the similarities are some crucial divergences. First among them is that regime theory is no substitute for the tradition of thought in which the idea of international society is set. International society is the centrepiece of a tradition that is much more holistic and far reaching than the study of regimes. The bulk of writing about regimes has been concerned with particular issue areas: security regimes, environmental regimes, communication regimes, economic regimes and so on. Regimes are a part of, and contribute to, the working of international society but international society cannot be reduced to regime theory. International society, Buzan observes, 'might be seen as a regime of regimes, adding a useful element of holism to the excessively atomized world of regime theory. But it is also the legal and political foundation on which the whole idea of regimes rests'. He goes on to say that international law, which is a fundamental constituent of international society, 'is not merely a regime but something much more basic: the political foundation that is necessary before regimes can come into play' (Buzan, 1993, p. 350).

The study of international society has been constructed on an historical depth that is absent from regime theory. Equally, it has included speculation about the future and poses a set of normative questions that are not congenial to regime theory. As it has been developed by writers located in the English School, discourse about international society includes consideration and prescription about what is good for the society of states as a whole. At its best the discussion of international society includes an element of critical theory and reflexivity, whereas regime theory is more closely wedded to explanation and problem solving. The essential intellectual temper of each is different.

The two diverge also over global governance to which regimes and regime theory are directly relevant. Regimes amount, in important cases, to the global governance of particular issues and areas. The more such regimes there are the more there can be said to be global governance, and for many that is both good and necessary as a means to dealing with problems that cannot be dealt with by states acting alone. Global governance is, however, not something that has loomed large in thought about international society. It involves both a variety of non-state actors and a lessening of the authority of states. Were global governance to be greatly extended it would ultimately mean the transformation of the states system. It would not necessarily entail the end of states but would certainly mean that states had a different role. The tradition to which the metaphor of international society belongs is too deeply wedded to states and the states system for it to countenance this and, indeed, the preference has been to conclude that for the foreseeable future the state as a form of political organization is here to stay.

In the lexicon of international society it is by articulating and observing rules and norms that states advance their common interests; but what exactly is the nature of these common interests? One answer to this can be located in the distinction Terry Nardin borrows from Michael Oakeshott between *purposive* and *practical* associations (Nardin, 1983; Brown, 1995, p. 187).[2] A purposive association is one in which the constituents are associated in a cooperative enterprise to promote shared values, beliefs, or interests [and] are united by their convergent desires for the realization of a certain outcome that constitutes the good they have come together to obtain'. In contrast, the

> values of practical association ... are those appropriate to the relations among persons who are not necessarily engaged in any common pursuit but who nevertheless have to get along with one another. They are the very essence of a way of life based on mutual restraint and toleration of diversity. (Nardin, 1983, pp. 9 and 12)

International society can be characterized as a practical association. The common interest of states has more often been simply to coexist without conflict than to achieve common values. During the Cold War, for instance, the United States and the former Soviet Union both articulated and agreed upon rules meant to guide their mutual relations, but they were implacable rivals without much common purpose other than the important one of avoiding nuclear war. Consequently, they found rules that would allow them to coexist without direct armed conflict (Keal, 1983). Rules of practical association impose restraints that allow states to coexist and they may be expressed in custom, in positive international law; or in unspoken rules. The goal of coexistence is achieved primarily through respecting the so-called basic norms of inter-state behaviour: sovereign equality, independence and the rule of non-intervention.

Yet international society can also be interpreted as a purposive association. For example, at the end of the nineteenth century the great powers of Europe proclaimed 'the standard of civilization' as the criteria for membership of international society. To be counted as members of international society and so subjects of international law, political entities had first to attain this standard which stipulated a level of political and social organization recognized by Europeans. The Standard of Civilization was thus a crucial instrument for drawing the boundaries between the 'civilized' and 'uncivilized worlds', and for determining who did or did not belong to international society. In this way the international society of that time was purposive. At the present time its place has been taken, as Gerrit Gong rightly suggested in the early 1980s, by the human rights record of states (Gong, 1984). It is now this, above all else, that confers the degree of legitimacy on states necessary for them to be regarded as rightful members of international society. In its constabulary role of determining legitimacy international society is a purposive association.

It is nevertheless more often presented as a practical association that 'both reflects and promotes the pluralism characteristic of the modern world'. Viewed from this angle it represents 'an attainable form of international order which is desirable in its own terms, and in no sense a "second-best" option'. And this is, in Chris Brown's opinion, 'the central position of the international society approach to international relations theory' (Brown, 1995, p. 188). He points out that those who do see it as a second-best option envisage an international order that is based on a broader sense of community than can be found in inter-state relations and that would require a purposive association to achieve it.

Later in the same article Brown makes the telling argument that there are 'real difficulties in finding *any* sense of international society with universal applicability' and that 'the only functioning international society today is that which exists between and among the advanced industrial countries' (Brown, 1995, p. 194). At the same time as there has been 'a deepening sense of community in the advanced industrial world' it is not matched by any deepened sense in relations between either that 'community and the rest of the world or – and in relations amongst and between the states that make up the rest of the world' (Brown, 1995, p. 196). The sense of community among the advanced industrial countries is fostered by the growth of the global economy and by commitment to a doctrine of human rights that is, Brown points out, 'essentially ... *intolerant* ... [and] stands against the pluralism that characterizes international society understood as a practical association' (Brown, 1995, p. 193). States that do not conform to the standards adopted by the advanced industrial states are excluded from whatever community is developing.

Brown's discussion of international society resonates with John Charvet's earlier consideration of international ethical order in which he divides states between an inner, middle and outer circle. States in the inner circle share a conception of the good and may be thought of as 'a federation of republican states' of the kind suggested by Kant. The second or middle circle contains the society of states and the third or outer, states that are self-interested and form a system but not a society. States belonging to the inner circle of republican states can belong to the circle comprising the society of states but for the latter there is no dual membership. At the same time both interact in the system of states. Membership of the inner circle is based on 'cooperative practices which are restricted to members and extended to others who may wish to join only on the basis of their internal constitution' (Charvet, 1992, p. 65). Charvet's division of states and the search for a moral international order in this way reinforces the suggestion that the idea of international society inescapably involves a hierarchy of levels or circles of moral community and criteria for inclusion or exclusion. Crucial to this is legitimacy understood as the collective judgement of the members of international society.

A Homogeneous International Society?

Legitimacy is a central element of the conception of international society discussed by Fred Halliday which renders 'society' as inter-societal and inter-state homogeneity. This sense of international society incorporates the links between the internal structures of societies and the international pressures that shape them. It refers, in essence, to the idea that as a result of international pressures states are compelled, increasingly, to conform to each other in their internal arrangements. An international society is then one in which states in the same vicinity have similar governments and uphold similar, or at least compatible, ideals. Halliday elucidates this by referring to three seemingly very different thinkers: Edmund Burke, Karl Marx and Francis Fukuyama (Halliday 1994).

Halliday observes that Revolutionary France was perceived by Burke, and others, including European heads of state, to be a threat to the peace of Europe. From their point of view, peace and order could be assured only by France having the same sort of internal constitution as the other states of Europe. In Burke's own words: 'It is with nations as with individuals. Nothing is so strong a tie of amity between nation and nation as correspondence of laws, customs, manners, and habits of life...' (cited by Wight, 1966c, p. 97). Thus Halliday explains that in Burke's mind 'revolutionary France was a mortal danger, merely by dint of its being. The stability of other societies in Europe required that France too be like them. Without homogeneity, there could be neither internal nor international peace' (Halliday, 1994, p. 110). Halliday interprets Burke as having argued

> that relations between states rest above all not on the conduct of foreign policy in the narrow sense, but on convergence and similitude in domestic arrangements, in other words on the prevalence of a homogeneous international society ... for any international order to maintain peace it needs not only to evolve norms of inter-state behaviour, but to produce a community of states with broadly similar internal constitutions. (Halliday, 1994, p. 112)

Conceived in this way international society is necessarily limited to states with similar domestic arrangements based on a shared political culture. It is in effect the inner circle of republican states distinguished by Charvet and closely resembles the prescriptions of Kant's First Definitive Article in *Perpetual Peace* (Kant, 1970, p. 99). In this conception states without similitude in political and social organization are excluded, if not entirely, then at least from full membership of the society. They are accordingly not regarded as subject to the same rules of conduct as those governing the conduct of like minded states. This is not a pluralist international society in which, so long as there are rules to guide mutual relations, the internal arrangements of states should not matter.

Another implication of this conception of international society is that it requires casting the world in the image of the dominant power or group of powers of the time, just as the United States sought to do after the Second World War and again after the Cold War. At both times the United States has been impelled by its vision of a liberal world order to attempt remaking the world in its own likeness. On a global scale, broadly similar internal constitutions would most likely have to be imposed and not represent the interests of all states but mainly those of the state or group of states able to impose them. This alone would probably be enough to ensure that the membership of a society of this type would remain limited.

Halliday emphasizes the immense divergences between Burke and Marx but identifies important points of convergence between them. He notices resemblances between Marx's conception of international society and that found in transnationalism, but concludes that 'the focus of Marx's analysis is not only the growing links between societies ... but also the degree to which, across the globe, societies increasingly come to conform to each other'. And for Marx 'the workings of the economy, and the ownership patterns associated with it, perform those functions which manners and customs do for Burke' (Halliday, 1994, p. 115). In the case of Fukuyama, the convergence of states is driven by a combination of the dynamics of modern science and the push toward liberal democracy. Modern science influences both military competition and economic development in ways that force states into conformity with one another 'to produce that resemblance, that similitude, that Burke identified'. Liberal democracies, it is argued, don't go to war with each other and so the spread of them spells the end of inter-state conflict and in the long term, 'the end of international relations as we have known it' (Halliday, 1994, p. 119).

Halliday's richly suggestive discussion has at least two important implications. First, it reinforces, once again, the point that the membership of international society is always proscribed. The criteria for membership at any given time means that certain entities do not belong to the inner circle of states in which there is a similitude of domestic arrangements. International society is only ever the conception of a particular society abstracted from a broader context. Second, Burke's sense of international society rests on a common culture, essentially the culture of the Concert of Europe and the states that comprised it. This begs the important question of whether there ever can, in a culturally plural world, be an international society that includes more than a particular group of dominant states.

Conclusion

This chapter began with the claim that the image of international society is a powerful one because it is assumed that there is actually such a thing. Part of the power of the image is derived from the way state leaders and their critics deploy it in arguing for actions both taken and not taken. Great powers typically justify actions that violate the rule of non-intervention as being in the interests of international order. Their critics then make the counter-claim that the actions taken were self-serving and do not at all serve the interests of international society as a whole. Underpinning such disputes is the argument that there are rules for the conduct of inter-state behaviour and that they should be observed for the sake of preserving what is ultimately a fragile international order.

To be sure the rules are contested. Increasingly, the rule of non-intervention is challenged by events, the most obvious being genocide, that seem to call for action by 'international society'. Wight observes that '[o]ne of the most notable means of coercion for upholding standards and maintaining order in international society is intervention' (Wight, 1966c, p. 111). He argued that in international life intervention is sometimes necessary but that it is an unfortunate necessity that should be the exception rather than the rule, and that 'in a moral scale, to maintain the balance of power is a better reason for intervening than to uphold civilized standards, but to uphold civilized standards is a better reason than to maintain existing governments' (Wight, 1966c, p. 116). It is now slightly more than 30 years since Wight wrote this, during which time the demand to uphold human rights standards as a contemporary version of civilized standards has undoubtedly altered the balance of his moral scale.

Regardless of whether international society is invoked to support or oppose intervention, it is essential to the legitimacy of whatever action or inaction occurs. Coupled with this is the belief that international society is sufficiently well formed to have agency and so take action to either prevent particular wrongs from occurring or to redress them after the event. In effect, this refers to the actions or inactions of the great or dominant powers of the time; and the emphasis on them is one of the reasons for being dissatisfied with the image of international society as a means to understanding world politics.

The story of international society has been a story of states and, in particular, great powers and in this respect it coincides with realist understandings.

But in contrast to the self-interested states of realism the idea of international society posits the good of the society of states as a whole. By implication this requires individual states to sometimes act against their own interests for the common good of international society. The problem is, who decides the common good? If it is the great powers, can they set aside their own self-interests for the sake of it? If international society is as Brown, Charvet and Halliday all suggest, essentially one in which the rules of interaction, terms of membership and questions of legitimacy are decided by an inner core of like-minded powerful states, it is something that inevitably rests on the structural power of the few. If they act as 'great responsibles' rather than as 'great irresponsibles'[3] this need not necessarily be a bad thing, but even so it is bound to ignite and perpetuate resentment from those who do not share that structural power.

A second reason for discontent relates to the emphasis in discussions of international society on the value of order between states, which has been given priority over questions of justice. There are, of course, good reasons for defending order, an important one being that without it the conditions for achieving justice might not exist. Equally, without more justice it might be impossible to sustain order. International order supports the continued existence of international society, but what, for instance, is the point of an international society that allows millions of children to die because the states they belong to are in debt? The image of international society has been one that pays insufficient attention to justice and has no well-developed theory of it.[4] A fruitful way of giving it more prominence would be to emphasize the moral purpose of international society as being that of working wherever possible toward the normative goals of world order. This would involve both a concession to cosmopolitanism and, to use Bull's words, states acting as local agents of the global good. In some cases it would mean being prepared to violate sovereignty and override norms of inter-state behaviour as NATO did in defence of Kosovar Albanians.

Third, it was noted earlier that in the early phases of its development the idea of international society included individuals and non-state groups. It has not since those times done this in any consistent or sustained manner but the inclusion of individuals is an element immanent in it. The norms of international society developed in a way that has denied international personality to individuals and sub-state groups. At this conjuncture many individuals and sub-state groups need international legal personality as a defence against the states in which they are encased. This is especially true for many groups of the estimated 250–300 million indigenous peoples scattered around the globe. To the benefit of these peoples states are increasingly bound by human rights instruments that make it difficult for them to hide from international scrutiny by claiming that the treatment of their indigenous populations is a domestic matter.

Fourth, unlike most other approaches to international politics, the study of international society has included the story of its expansion from a society of European states to one that is supposedly global or all inclusive (Bull, 1984a). The story of encounters between European states and non-European entities it tells has, however, been an incomplete one. It has excluded the story of peoples destroyed and dispossessed in the process of expansion. The story of these peoples needs to be recognized and recovered as a central part of the story of expansion.

Finally, clarification and critical analysis of the moral basis and assumptions of international society has been neglected and needs to be more fully articulated. As part of this one consideration is whether states that lack moral legitimacy, because of the way they treat the individual and collective rights of their citizens, undermine the legitimacy of international society. A major purpose of international society has been to maintain the autonomy of the state as a form of political organization. If that means maintaining states that have contested and unresolved questions about their moral legitimacy then the legitimacy of international society itself may be questioned.

PART II

GLOBALIZATION AND THE TRANSFORMATION OF COMMUNITY

CHAPTER 6

A 'Borderless World'?

Ian Clark

It is largely, if not exclusively, at the hands of the high priests of economic globalization that the imagery of 'a borderless world' has been crafted (Ohmae, 1990). Their central argument is that the organization of production and exchange, in the contemporary world, pays little attention to borders of states since both have now 'shifted' to global forms (Dicken, 1992). Corporations base various elements of production at a number of sites around the world and compete in a global market. Capital is highly mobile and financial markets transfer prodigious volumes around the globe on a daily basis. In this context, it becomes increasingly irrelevant to think in terms of distinct national economies. If borders no longer cage anything in, they become analytically superfluous.

While predominantly associated with the global economy, the image also has resonance elsewhere. Since its intent is either to establish that borders no longer work, or to argue that it is undesirable in some cases for them to do so, it occurs in discussions of the environment (Holden (ed.), 1996), migration (Collinson, 1993), drugs trafficking (Stares, 1996), and a range of normative debates related to human rights (Dunne and Wheeler (eds), 1999). As to the last of these, there is, of course, a venerable tradition of cosmopolitan moral theory which tends to eschew the salience of borders in its judgements. Such ideas are now strongly to the fore in the new literature on political community, itself derived from the currently perceived destabilization of existing borders and communities (see, for example, Linklater, 1998; Archibugi *et al.* (eds), 1998). The bottom line of all such usages is that peoples' lives are no longer predominantly shaped by what is decided within sets of national borders. This may be positively welcomed as heralding an incipient global society. At the same time, it is lamented by others who regard it as the loss of an important form of social protection in the face of rampant global capitalism or Western cultural penetration.

These views bundle together a range of disparate senses in which the world might be thought to be losing its borders. In some versions, the point is simply that the aggregate level of activity across borders is so dense that the borders themselves become obscured: they may still exist but have little visibility and hence do not tell us much about the nature of these transactions. Others concentrate more on the implications of these flows for the powers of states to manage them: the decreased salience of national borders indicates a political shift away from the jurisdiction of state managers. In yet other accounts, it is the very sameness of the way states react to new economic circumstances that justifies our relative neglect of them. If borders do not individuate the political and social processes that occur within them, why bother with them at all as part of the analysis? The image thus covers a spectrum of challenges: at one end borders are thought to virtually disappear; at the other, their persistence is accepted but their relative significance in shaping the contours of social interaction is denied. The predominant implication is of a decline in the role of the state with the result that the state is deemed to be everywhere in retreat (for example, in Ohmae, 1995; Strange, 1996; Reich, 1991).

The debate engendered by the image is not confined to the empirical evidence alone. To the extent that these changes are actually taking place, there is additionally disagreement about whether they are desirable or not. The optimists, like Ohmae, see them as beneficial since they allow economic rationality to prevail over 'unnatural' political interference. In this analysis, the disappearance of borders symbolises the final liberation of economic activity from the tyranny of politics, and the hopeful projection is that this will further unlock the great productive potential of the world economy. As against this, the pessimists deplore what they regard as the subjection of political self-determination to the dictates of hegemonic economic forces. It is not the 'abstract' states which are losing out to the global economy, but the political preferences of the individual citizen. What some then see as economic liberation, others are disposed to interpret as political disempowerment. The mixed verdict is returned because, while they may negatively impede, borders can also positively protect.

So what specifically might be happening to borders? Scholte (1997) has developed three distinct conceptions of the infringement of borders: the first refers to cross-border relations; the second, to open-border relations; and the third, to transborder relations. According to the first, borders remain steadfast, but there is simply a great deal of traffic that passes across them. As regards the second, borders are extremely porous, either because they are ineffectual or because they have been opened as a matter of policy (as in the case of abandonment of passport controls between certain European Union member states). In terms of the last, 'borders are not so much crossed or opened as transcended' (Scholte, 1997, pp. 430–1). Scholte certainly believes that it is this third development which 'is the newest and offers the most distinctive and helpful insight into contemporary world affairs' (p. 430). If the contemporary world is becoming borderless, it is of developments in this third sense that we must take special note.

Clearly, any requirement that International Relations as an academic discipline think in terms that transcend borders presents a formidable challenge to standard conceptions of the field. Even when not largely state-centric – and there is no convincing reason why it should be – International Relations has been reluctant to edge much beyond cautious notions of pluralism (a variety of actors) and transnationalism (relations across borders not controlled by governments) and, in either guise, remains firmly rooted in (partitioned) territory. When theorists have attempted to take the analysis 'beyond' borders (as in discussions of moral responsibility), this has been presented in language which manifestly recognizes the *existence* of borders, but merely questions the ethical *significance* attaching to them (Hoffmann, 1981). Equally, since standard definitions of transnationalism describe it as activity *across borders*, undertaken by non-governmental agents (Keohane and Nye, 1977), it is evident that IR's language of transnationalism falls very far short of Scholte's notion of the transcendence of borders. IR has regularly flirted with the notion of borders that are porous, but it baulks – understandably enough – at contemplating a world in which they are deemed scarcely to exist.

However, it can be questioned whether the image of 'the borderless world' is itself fully convincing or, even if valid in some respects, whether this feature can be regarded as sufficiently widespread to constitute anything but minor exceptions to the general rule. Apart from a few isolated, and oft-repeated examples – such as the Internet and financial networks – most other human activities and relations appear to be steadfastly grounded, even if not wholly territorially enclosed. There is then the danger that 'a borderless world' focuses attention on a limited, and atypical, range of relationships: it might not be 'wrong', but can nonetheless distort by being unrepresentative.

In any case, there is a more deep-seated issue that needs to be addressed. Surely there is something profoundly paradoxical about an image that invites us to discard borders as part of our mental map but which, at the same time, analyses the consequences of so doing primarily in terms of implications for borders? While denying the relevance of borders, the proponents of this position remain surprisingly preoccupied with the residual capacity of states, and make claims about the extent to which the state has been rendered uniform (in its impotence) by global forces. Simultaneously, we are enjoined to abandon borders conceptually, but to confine our appraisal resolutely to the impact upon them.

The Image: Meaning and Significance

How is the image of 'a borderless world' normally sustained? To provide some overview, it can be summarized in two overlapping versions, drawn from opposite ends of the disciplinary spectrum but showing remarkable consensus nonetheless about what is happening to the state. The first points to the obsolescence of the state as manager of its own functional activities, especially in the economic realm, a view succinctly presented in the assertion by an orthodox economist that there 'will no longer be national economies' (Reich, 1991, p. 3). Hoogvelt, although writing from a critical developmental perspective, adopts much the same position in her claim that 'the integrity of the national territorial state as a more or less coherent political economy is eroded' (Hoogvelt, 1997, p. 67). This is associated with the widespread notion that the state has been impoverished by its loss of controls to the impersonal structure of the market itself. In this vein, Susan Strange has drawn attention to the generic shift in the balance of power 'from states to markets' (Strange, 1996, p. 29). 'Where states were once the masters of markets', she insisted, 'now it is the markets which, on many crucial issues, are the masters over the governments of states' (p. 4).

A second, and more modest, version is that the state's powers are diminished, in the sense that it is now simply one actor jostling with many others in the management of the world economy. In this variation, the argument is not particularly novel and has basically been around since the 1960s, especially in the form that presents the state's powers as being usurped by the multinational corporations (Vernon, 1971). Strange, typically, has written of the TNCs as encroaching on the state's jurisdiction, and 'exercising a parallel authority' alongside it (Strange, 1996, p. 65). This argument extends beyond the economic domain alone. Other writers accept the diminution in the stature of the state brought about by the emergence of other actors, since they compete with the state in diverse areas of functional responsibility. Thus Richard Falk attributes the subversion of the state's generic capacity 'to control and protect the internal life of society' to the roles played by now multitudinous non-state actors, such as INGOs and elements of an emergent transnational civil society (Falk, 1997, pp. 124–5).

Whatever the specific version of this diminution in state capacity, it is thought to manifest itself in a number of distinct ways: the seeming depoliticization of economic processes, and their subjection to forms of 'technical rationality'. Such a development itself takes multiple forms, but typically is illustrated by the ceding of overt political control over the setting of domestic interest rates, via central banks or other similar devices (Teeple, 1995, p. 70). Macroeconomic policy is thereby taken out of the hands of reportedly scheming politicians, thought to have only short-term interests on their minds, and passed over to the expert managers who will take decisions on 'objective' economic grounds. Alternatively, control of economic policy, where it has not devolved 'downward' in such fashion, has devolved 'outwards', and now takes the form of international 'coordination efforts' with respect to monetary and fiscal policy (Webb, 1991, pp. 310–11). Obviously, such coordination has taken a much more advanced and institutionalized form within parts of the European Union (on currency and interest rates), but it can be seen as an element of multilateralism within the world economy more generally. Again, the effect of such efforts is to reduce the scope for unilateral governmental action.

By what specific mechanisms is economic globalization deemed to sap the policy autonomy of states? There are three recurrent accounts of the forces at work. In terms of the first, the range of policy options is narrowed by the need to remain internationally competitive. This reveals itself in the pressures to reduce levels of governmental borrowing, as well as in constraints on public expenditure. The need to do as much as possible to balance budgets is itself an element within the new competitiveness, unlike the halcyon days when the United States could dominate the international economy while persistently running enormous budgetary deficits. Phil Cerny, for example, maintains that the quest for competitiveness is not only the driving force of contemporary state policy but that, additionally, 'states are transforming – marketizing – *themselves* in the search for competitiveness' (Cerny, 1996a, pp. 124–5). Implicit in this notion of 'marketizing' is the unwillingness or inability of states to put up any policy resistance to the economic environment in which they find themselves. To do so would invite economic harm by rendering key economic sectors less able to compete. The depressing result, in the eyes of the critics, is a 'race to the bottom: lower wages, lower taxes, less accountability' (Greider, 1997, p. 101). States subject themselves to this competition because they see no choice: the fear is that production and investment can move elsewhere, insofar as 'a borderless world' is predicated on assumptions of the complete 'substitutability of locations' (Storper, 1997, pp. 31–4).

The second imperative is that states must inspire confidence externally. A state that is unsuccessful in this international competition risks being burdened by higher levels of social expenditure, most obviously with regard to the costs of higher levels of unemployment and welfare payments. At the same time, high social costs diminish the ability to compete. To break out of this cycle, governments must be seen to pursue policies that are considered sound by the international markets. 'Governments increasingly measure their performance according to criteria acceptable to the financial markets', and accordingly, 'they must be seen as "strong" or "sound" if they are to retain the confidence of the international financial community' (Cerny, 1996b, p. 87).

The resulting necessity to be mindful of the scale of deficits is, in its turn, driven by the third factor. When capital markets were largely national in character and operation, governments were less vulnerable to them.

However, in conditions of high mobility, such as have characterized the period since the 1980s, budgetary excesses are now prone to be punished by the markets. Thus commentators speak of 'the disciplining power of global capital movements' which has resulted in governments 'curbing public expenditure, giving priority to the control of inflation and enhancing the strength of private power' (Wilkin, 1997, p. 24). Typically, Milner and Keohane (1996, p. 17) locate their discussion of the reduced efficacy of national fiscal policy in this context of capital mobility. Otherwise expressed, the contention put forward is that 'national governments neither can nor should control the flow of capital across borders, and hence cannot regulate interest rates, fix currency values, or pursue macroeconomic policies' that do not conform to market preferences (Schor, 1992, p. 1). If they attempt to do so, they will simply invite a flight of capital and place pressures on exchange and interest rates.

In each of these areas, it is implicit that borders no longer work to keep out powerful transnational economic forces. At the same time, however, the costs of an inability to respond to these pressures are experienced within individual states. Borders seem too porous to prevent the incursion of these outside forces. They remain nonetheless sufficiently impermeable to retain the damaging consequences that result from them. They are powerless to keep the causes out, but powerful enough to keep the effects in. The core of the globalization thesis is itself tinged with the paradox that, faced with universal forces, the nonconformist state will suffer particular penalties: borders do not determine the distribution of benefits but they appear still to influence the distribution of costs.

The related claim is that economic globalization not merely reduces the policy autonomy of states, but that the evidence for this resides in the increasing uniformity of state behaviour. The theme of similarity in state behaviour is striking in this context. '[A]ll of the governments', Webb avers, 'responded in a similar, though not identical, fashion to change in international capital mobility' (1991, pp. 312–13). Uniformity thereby becomes the clearest expression of state impotence. The most striking formulation of this analysis has been provided by Falk, who laments the passing of the humane and compassionate state in the face of the new economic orthodoxy. Such is the pressure for uniformity and conformity that 'Sweden can no longer be Sweden!' (Falk, 1997, p. 130; compare Weiss, 1998, p. 113).

It is at this point, however, that a possible tension within the 'borderless world' case begins to reveal itself. If the above suggestions are taken to be equally plausible, we are led to believe that states are no longer the unit of account in understanding the workings of the world economy. At the same time, we are told that states are now, as economic actors, behaving in largely similar ways. Does the force of the one argument not call into question the plausibility of the other? If national economies have disappeared, how can we tell that they are responding uniformly?

The Counter-arguments

Much of the debate about 'a borderless world' is about the 'facts' of the matter – whether or not the empirical evidence substantiates the claim to a world without significant borders. On the economic dimensions of this issue, the matter is pursued vigorously in works such as Hirst and Thompson (1996), who give voice to a general scepticism about many claims made about the unprecedented degree of 'openness' in today's world economy. Likewise, detailed case studies demonstrating the tenacity of the state as an economic institution have been powerfully set out by Linda Weiss (1998). In this section, the analysis will eschew this kind of evidential approach and concentrate instead upon wider theoretical issues that have been raised by way of questioning the appropriateness of this image of world politics.

It will explore some of the reasons why there remains an ambivalence about the relevance of borders, at once partly dismissive, and yet at the same time obsessively preoccupied with them. In brief, the ambivalence may be attributed to the ways in which the seeming erosion of state power can itself be explained in statist terms. The point of these arguments is not straightforwardly to deny the evidence about the declining salience of state borders but instead to suggest that, in however shadowy a fashion, there is a lurking state presence behind many of the transformations that are currently taking place. In order to understand these trends more fully, we need to look beneath their surface manifestations to the dynamics that are driving them.

The primacy of the political

For many, the view of the state/globalization relationship as zero-sum is basically misconceived, as it fails to take into account the degree to which the state itself is the architect of globalization. To the extent that it is so, the global economy falls within the state's own structural power, and it is contradictory to imagine the state losing power to its own creation.

This particular dimension of the debate goes to the heart of traditional concerns of IR theory. It asks whether globalization is some kind of independent force – driven by technology, economic organization, communications or cultural patterns – or whether it is politically shaped by distributions of international power (Clark, 1997). Liberal versions tend to adhere to the former point of view insofar as 'states and governments are bystanders to globalization: the real driving forces are markets' (Hurrell and Woods, 1995, p. 448). If the driving force is not markets, then in other accounts it lies in uncontrollable technological developments. This is the heart of James

Rosenau's argument: 'For globalization is not so much a product or extension of the interstate system as it is a wholly new set of processes, a separate
form of world politics, initiated by technologies that have fostered new
human needs and wants' (Rosenau, 1997, p. 221).

The alternative standpoint denies that globalization has 'its own inexorable logic' (Waters, 1995, p. 46) and thereby allows that it may well be dis-
continuous and reversible. For example, further globalism within the world
economy has been described as being 'as much a dependent as a driving
force' and one of the things on which it depends is the strength of 'democratic forces' (Albrow, 1996, pp. 92–3). Armstrong, while aware of the powerful pressures of globalization, reminds us also that these come up against
the equally potent force of international society. Its norms and institutions
function as a bulwark for orderly states: borders are its touchstone.
International society, as a 'club' of states with membership rules of sovereignty and nonintervention, leaps to the defence of the state when it is confronted by marauding 'borderless' forces (Armstrong, 1998, pp. 461–2,
468–9).

Relatedly, there is the view that the persistence of globalization is contingent upon political dynamics and frameworks. Thus Hirst insists upon the
necessary role of 'appropriate public institutions' in sustaining a liberal
trading order (Hirst, 1997, pp. 414–15). Accordingly, as against the 'erosion-
ists', there are those who continue to insist upon undiminished state capacity: some even go so far as to suggest that states are more potent now than
ever. 'So-called "globalization" is not likely to displace state power' is one
such confident judgement. 'If anything, it will make it more salient' (Weiss,
1998, p. 13).

This position derives, in its most general sense, from realist views of international political economy (Gilpin, 1987). The case rests on continuing state
efficacy, and on the assumption that 'markets and companies cannot exist
without a public power to protect them' (Hirst and Thompson, 1996, p. 188).
If that is true of markets in general, it has been contended that it is true of
so-called 'free' markets in particular: 'free markets are creatures of state
power' (Gray, 1998, p. 17). From this initial assumption, the argument can
readily be developed that globalization itself has been fostered by cumulative state choices and actions.

One of its most vocal champions attributes the dynamic of globalization
to various policy decisions taken since the late 1950s, amongst which the
most important were: liberalization initiatives which favoured the market;
abstention from controls on capital movements; and the prevention of major
financial crises (Helleiner, 1994, p. 8). By these various decisions and non-
decisions, states created an economic climate conducive to the intensification of international financial integration.

The general drift of these passages is that we must subject the global economy to close scrutiny. It is not something that has evolved by accident, or

without some degree of authorship. Certain groups of states, pursuing their own interests and exercising their national power, have helped bring it into being. This does not entail that any one of them remains fully in control of its creation. But it suggests that state power, collectively, remains a presence. No image should discard this too lightly if it is to be taken seriously.

New state forms

A second theme is to approach the issue as one of redefinition of the state's functions rather than as about state retreat (Moran, 1994, p. 176). This points to a second form of refutation of the idea of a 'borderless world'. To appeal to this image is to mistake the evidence of state transformation as evidence for state disappearance.

The depiction of globalization as locationless may be quite misleading if it fails to capture that dimension of globalization best described as 'state transformation' (Clark, 1999). This alternative perspective recognizes that globalization is itself in some measure a reflection of the changing character of states, and not straightforwardly the cause of that change. Rather than view the global economy as an objective set of material conditions, which then constrains what states might do, it is important also to see the reciprocal sense in which the global economy has been built on profound social, political and cultural transformations within states. The citizens of states now have different expectations from state policies, and domestic bargains are in train of being renegotiated (Ruggie, 1998). Over the past two decades, and in contrast to the 'embedded liberalism' of the post-1945 generation within which the welfare of citizens was nurtured, social compacts between state and citizen are being reformulated. What has emerged in the shape of the present global economy is partly a consequence of these developments: it should not be thought of solely as their cause.

This is fundamental to any understanding of globalization but such a perspective is endangered by superficial appeals to the 'end of geography'. Such mantras reinforce the stereotype that globalization is something going on 'out there', above and beyond the terrestrial activities of states. To describe the key attribute of globalization as the transcendence of borders risks losing sight of this 'statist' dimension. Accordingly, the more mystical accounts of globalization need to be grounded in appropriate theories of the state, and not presented simply as descriptions of spatial transcendence.

The construction of any dichotomy between globalization and state power is bound to deceive. In other words, the important conclusion to draw from these debates is not that state powers persist under the constraints of the global economy but rather that globalization and the redefinition of the state are fundamentally interrelated processes. To speak of globalization is, by the very act, to address the evidence for the reconstitution of the state.

This is an issue on which analysts remain deeply divided. For instance, there is Palan's judgement. 'The study of the relationship between the state and the global economy', he insists, ' must not be founded, therefore, on the premise of an inherent contradiction between them' (Palan, 1994, p. 47). Yet elsewhere, others seem to take the opposite very much for granted. They highlight precisely the contradiction between the differing organizational bases of state and global economy – territorial and non-territorial – which inevitably pull in antagonistic directions. But this is exactly where the ambivalence of the 'borderless world' image becomes most conspicuous. How is the requisite politico-institutional support for the global economy to be sustained when it is itself seen to be undermining the state's principal claims to legitimacy? Globalization needs the legitimacy of the state but is simultaneously the greatest threat to it. The global economy throws into question the legitimacy of a territorially demarcated political structure while, at the same time, being fully dependent upon it for its own sustainability.

A clash of capitalisms

Even those who accept some elements of the globalization thesis vehemently deny that it renders borders meaningless. One respect in which they do so is a vision of a world of many and competing capitalisms. It is implicit in much of the 'victory of capitalism' and 'single market' literature that the world is thereby destined to experience a fundamental convergence of economic system: globalization is taken to mean, at the very least, such homogenization. It is this assumption which has been widely challenged and nowhere more so than by an insistence on many roads, rather than a single track, to capitalism. 'Globalization is often equated with a trend towards homogeneity. That, again, is just what globalization is *not*' (Gray, 1998, p. 57).

In this style of argument, the point is insistently made that there remain profound differences between current forms of capitalism – American, 'Asian', Japanese, Chinese, Russian, German and so on. They differ on a wide range of fundamental matters concerning the role of the state, state-society relations, and the nature of society itself. Gray holds that in 'Asian cultures market institutions are viewed instrumentally, as means to wealth-creation and social cohesion, not theologically, as ends in themselves' (1998, p. 192). This reflects the culture in which the economic system is embedded. All systems are affected by global pressures, but not uniformly. Differences remain, and may be accentuated, because of 'long-term historical divergences in cultures' which continue to manifest themselves 'in the different public policies of nation-states' (Gray, 1998, p. 74).

Does the survival of many forms of capitalism have significance for understanding the role of borders? The thesis is, of course, challenged altogether by those analysts who detect greater convergence amongst these separate systems. Even if the case is partially conceded, the inference we can permissibly draw from it remains indirect at best, since the varieties of capitalism should not be identified exclusively with national economic systems. In the same way that 'the clash of civilizations' is not a straightforward transcription of classical inter-state geopolitical conflict – but nonetheless has implications for it – so a clash of capitalisms does not fully restore the state as economic actor but enjoins us not to dismiss it either. The clash of capitalisms is more diffuse than the economic rivalry of nation-states. The strength of the connection depends upon the extent to which rival capitalisms are nationally constituted and reflect the political and social characteristics of their host states. This is presumably a variable condition, and one changeable over time.

Conclusion

The image of a borderless world is a powerful one. However substantiated, it posits a degree of 'one worldism' within which global interconnection assumes a significance far in excess of any residual elements of national separateness. If once extended from its empirical base in the global economy, it has powerful potential to reshape political programmes and normative agendas. A doctrine of human rights, for instance, is but one transcription of it as a normative condition in which all human beings enjoy certain fundamental rights, regardless of the specific community to which they belong and the particular borders within which they are contained.

However, the above discussion enjoins a degree of caution before rushing to reach such 'one world' conclusions. If it is true that there is the lurking presence of states (and of some states in particular) in the contemporary structure of the world economy, it may equally be the case that states 'lurk' in other quarters as well. The sharp encounters between cosmopolitan claims to rights and the defensive 'cultural' resistance to them – on grounds that what is being universalized is not some abstracted set of human rights but a view of rights located, say, in Western liberal traditions – pose questions about the extent to which universal rights is simply an agenda of Westernization. In the same way, its critics regard the wider processes of globalization as a similarly motivated economic and political project, grounded in sectional interests. A clear appreciation of the relationship between 'borderless' economic activities, and the state activities which may give rise to them, is critical not only for its own sake. It is equally important as a means of retaining a sensible discussion of the entire range of issues to which the image has also been extended, and often dubiously applied.

To say anything positive about borders is to court charges of conservatism, both in the disciplinary IR sense, but more importantly in the political symbolism of the act. To cast doubt on a 'borderless world' might be thought myopic at best: it is to seek refuge in a Westphalian temple from the confusions of a transforming world. At worst, it is to undercut the basis of all humanitarian action and to sell out whole populations to vicious governments. Borders serve not just to keep the barbarians outside the walls, but can equally give licence to the activities of the barbarian within.

But scepticism need not be the servant of such conservatism. Confusion about the role of borders is as likely to undermine the cause of humanitarianism as it is to advance it. Borders can, and do, help preserve human rights, just as states can help sustain wider projects, such as global economies. The trick lies in getting the balance right: this requires recognition of the legitimate achievements of borders coupled with acceptance that they are neither permanent in general, nor immutable in parts. To appeal to 'a borderless world' is perhaps to wish away those very nuances necessary for striking that balance.

CHAPTER 7

The 'End of Sovereignty'?

Jo-Anne Claire Pemberton

To think globally might be to picture a planet submerged in a swirling flood of people, ideas and things. It is a scene of intense mobility as well as rupture and breakdown. Wayward flows of transport, finance and information dissolve traditional boundaries and habits of thought. The world becomes a brilliantly lit riot of noise, colour and movement.

Global visions may also be conceived along more formalistic lines. To think globally could be to indulge in the science fiction fantasy of a glittering technopolis in which trained experts busy themselves with designing blueprints for world order. Countering the chaotic effects of globalization might require social planning on a grand scale. It could also be believed that electronic communications are fostering a growing sense of social solidarity among peoples and that this in turn forms the basis of a cosmo-political state. The notion of a clean, rationally governed and harmonious universe is the regulatory ideal in this case.

Science and technology can thus be seen as sponsoring thrilling and emancipatory global anarchy or a more secure and communal way of living on this earth. Nature has been interpreted in ways that support both of these perspectives. Those favouring a more fluid world tend to emphasize the explosive and indeterminate side of its operations. However, those advocating greater organization and coordination at the global level depict nature as an infinitely complex, organic unity with each of its sub-systems functioning in the interests of the whole.

Variations of these images and analogies feature prominently in contemporary narratives of global transformation. Such narratives are treated in this essay as rhetorical constructions: patterns of utterances designed to give credence and add lustre to preferred understandings of world society. I examine strategies and images common to arguments that suggest that

91

sovereignty is eroding in the face of a profusion and intensification of activity across state borders.

A crucial question is whether globalization is less a distinguishable feature of experience than a discursive effect. An array of items and processes, not all intimately or clearly related, have been grouped under this heading. Rich in subjects, the term has been reified and converted into a force that is active in the world. It is as if weapons capable of rapidly traversing continents, transborder environmental problems and international criminal networks, all of which have been cited as instances of globalization, arise from a single impulsion, one which propels them to shatter traditional lines of authority, and established political categories.

The attractiveness of representations of reality spun around the theme of globalization is achieved through the interplay of seductive metaphors, moral suasion and emotional and aesthetic appeals. These aspects of the rhetoric are therefore central to the following discussion. This essay illustrates that the line between metaphors and metaphysics is blurred and in this regard it attempts to bring into focus the metaphysics or cosmology presupposed by, or implicitly underlying, recent theories. The contrast between the richness and vitality of a pluralistic cosmology, evoked in international theories centred on the ideas of speed and temporality, and the strained metaphysics associated with the principle of sovereignty is revealed. This chapter also examines the breach between those critics of the state who favour the notion of a world of profuse and varied social formations and those who see experience in a universal light and lean towards the ideal of one world.

Beyond this, I argue that it is conceptually promiscuous to invest globalization with an epochal significance and represent it as an agent of the demise of the sovereign state. As the concept of globalization has been inflated so the term has been cut loose from its empirical anchors. This may not matter, in that global images can prove compelling even though possessing only a vague air of verisimilitude. Indeed, in most contexts their prime function is to persuade rather than to describe. Global images are dangled before audiences in order to win their acceptance and move them to action. Thus, we find the particular interests of corporate empires being swathed in light, shiny cosmopolitan cloth. Meanwhile, those pressing on us the absolute need for, and possibility of, global governance offer arresting descriptions of the dangers as well as opportunities that might stem from globalization. This chapter is sympathetic to those who, from a pluralist perspective, are doubtful about the project that is global governance while also seeking to address the concerns that lie behind its advocacy. It concludes by arguing that investigation and elaboration of traditions of thinking about sovereignty, and its normative bases, might suggest useful ways of thinking about international society in the new millennium.

Rhetoric of Globalization

The rhetoric of globalization is not univocal. In popular forums merchant princes and their publicists have projected efforts to expand commercial empires as leading to a new age of peace and enlightenment. The international lawyer and theorist, Richard Falk, also appeals to global images but he has drawn a sharp line between corporate globalism and the 'New World Order' designs of great powers, which he has called 'globalization from above reflecting the collaboration between leading states and the main agents of capital formation', and 'globalization from below'. The latter, he wrote,

> ... consists of an array of transnational social forces animated by environmental concerns, human rights, hostility to patriarchy, and a vision of human community based on the unity of diverse cultures seeking an end to poverty, oppression, humiliation, and collective violence. (Falk, 1993, p. 39; see also Falk, 1995a, p. 205)

For Falk, this transnational movement continues the 'evolving normative project' which began with the Hague Peace Conferences of 1899 and 1907. Interestingly, he describes this project as a 'global constitutional process culminating in a progressive form of geogovernance'. (Falk, 1995a, p. 87) Importantly also, he stresses that geogovernance, as he understands it, is not a static thing but should be seen as fluid; he writes of it as a 'continuous unfolding', leading to 'humane governance'. The precise legal and political contours of this form of governance remain somewhat obscure. It seems certain, however, that humane governance in practice would be inhospitable to the principle of sovereignty as it is commonly articulated in the political arena. Nonetheless, and because of Falk's scepticism as regards the global images projected by powerful interests, he concedes the sovereign state a role for some time to come. He recognizes that for vulnerable communities in the South, sovereignty can serve as a protective shell in the face of the predatory behaviour of global economic and political elites. Yet what is of utmost significance is that while Falk treats particular rhetorics of globalization with suspicion, his own proposals for change also draw on global imagery. He argues that threatening forms of globalization need to be answered by globalization of a constructive and inclusive kind (Falk, 1995a, pp. 81, 86, 90).

The 1995 report of the UN Commission on Global Governance entitled *Our Global Neighbourhood* employed some similar lines of argument, although in a less sophisticated and nuanced manner – not surprisingly, given its wider audience and overt polemical purpose. It argues that as 'territorial sovereignty' is under increasing pressure as a result of globalization in the form of transnational pollution, the drug trade, terrorism and financial liberalization, there is a pressing need for more extensive global cooperation. This argument was supplemented by the more positive claim that the erosion of physical, cultural and intellectual boundaries facilitated greater sociability among the world's peoples (CGG, 1995, pp. 10–11, 45, 68–71, 78, 82, 356).

The Commission stacked the deck in favour of its own recommendations, tending to represent the state as a weak and often oppressive institution while presenting global governance as necessary for global security and for the sake of humanity. The strategies employed in the report are replicated in numerous other polemics. Yet the main point I want to make in highlighting particular aspects of the arguments posed by the Commission, as well as those of Falk – taking these to be influential representatives of certain tendencies of thought within the public and intellectual arenas respectively – is that while it might be recognized that global models and metaphors are not always used innocently, their utility or appropriateness, when it comes to either empirical narration or political prescription, has not been widely contested.

Speed and Space

This last point brings us to a deep theoretical fissure. Falk's scepticism in relation to much globalist propaganda hits the mark. Yet his alternative version of globalization, however beneficent, might run into problems with those who tend to valorize notions like difference and plurality. His conception of humane governance might be seen as favouring unduly the idea of an essential oneness to which ultimately we can all be reconciled. Expressions such as 'benevolent global civil society' and appeals to the notion of 'diversity in unity' underline this. Falk employs at points a postmodern idiom and acknowledges social plurality. Yet from the perspective of the radical pluralist his ideal order may seem too rounded and complete (Falk, 1995a, pp. 81, 88). Humane governance is evocative of the idea of 'manyness' in onenesss and, to translate that into political terms, this seems to imply a world in which differences bloom and flourish, albeit in the midst of a larger, holistic framework. This picture can, however, be contrasted with the more anarchic and fragmented depictions of social affairs that feature in postmodern international theory.

In the sphere of international theory, R. B. J. Walker has been conspicuous for grounding a critique of sovereignty in a metaphysics of process and multiplicity. He emphasizes the plural, changing and uncertain side of existence. This is perhaps why he is intellectually uncomfortable with those designs for a better and more gracious way of living on this planet which tend to favour the collective over the distributive aspects of experience. Yet Walker's greater concern lies with oneness represented by the sovereign state and the implications of the multiplication of this form. The process metaphysics which informs his work is largely deployed against the sovereign state. Walker does not avow any adherence to process metaphysics but its presence is implied by references to the early-twentieth-century philosopher of change, Henri Bergson, and the adoption of key terms in that philosopher's vocabulary. The clash between a cosmological view resembling Bergson's descriptions of reality as 'undivided flux', 'becoming' and 'duration' and a more static picture which has a manifold experience carved into discrete units, is enacted vividly in his discussion (Walker, 1993, pp. 2, 10, 101, 119–20, 183).[1]

Walker also evokes the galactic scenes portrayed by Gilles Deleuze and Félix Guattari in their earlier account of the state and its struggle to regiment experience, *A Thousand Plateaus* (1980). These authors counterpose the defined and organized space of the state model to Bergson's conception of 'true positivity' as an 'unseizable multiplicity', an idea which Bergson thought was supported by the study of evolutionary biology and which he contrasted with a scientific outlook which typically spatially disperses and freezes the indeterminate rush of life.[2]

A Thousand Plateaus is thick with metaphysics, so much so that it is almost as if the political actors and institutions which the authors manoeuvre into battle are but individual articulations of larger conceptual systems and cosmologies. The forces gnawing at the state are presented as expressions of an underlying vital current while the state itself is projected as the deduction from a posited geometrical order. This reflects Bergson's influence as he viewed particulars as congealed expressions of an energy flow and rigid social systems as the by-product of mechanistic thought (see Bergson, 1984, pp. 196, 209–11, 239; Bergson, 1915; Deleuze and Guattari, 1988, pp. 361–7, 373–5, 407).

Walker is like Deleuze and Guattari to the extent that he sees the sovereignty principle as reflecting that 'fixing of temporality within spatial categories that has been so crucial in the construction of the most influential traditions of Western philosophy and socio-political thought'. Thus, the theory of sovereignty is projected into the political realm as an extension of the 'spatial metaphysics' of geometricians and scientists, of whom Newton is presented as an archetypal representative. For Walker, this helps explain why, in many accounts of international relations, the real is divided into structurally identical units called states which are placed under the sway of 'unchanging rules' such as the balance of power. In such a world nothing new can occur; all that can happen are periodic redistributions of power, just as in the universe of the classical physicist change is confined to redistributions of particles in space. Walker wonders, however, how long this 'spatial order' can be maintained in a 'world of profound temporal accelerations', a description he prefers to that of globalization, 'and spatial dislocations'; in fact, he thinks that already this frame is cracking (Virilio, 1986, pp. 133–51; Deleuze and Guattari, 1988, pp. 363, 386–7; Walker, 1993, pp. 4–7, 22, 95–8, 102, 128–9, 133, 155, 161–6, 176–8, 180; Walker, 1995a, p. 28; Walker, 1995b, pp. 314–15).[3]

Where the sovereign state system is treated as a microcosm of the cosmology of Newton, destabilizing the former involves challenging the scientific authority of the latter. Concepts thought to spring from the fields of astrophysics, chaos and quantum theory are called into play in order to underscore the image of a world characterized by indeterminacy and speed. Social theorists continue to uncritically embrace the idea that according to twentieth-century science the truth about reality is 'becoming' and that this renders dubious the continued division of the world into 'inviolable sharply delimited space[s]' (Deleuze and Guattari, 1988, pp. 371–3; see also Walker, 1993, pp. 5, 96, 129, 178; Walker, 1995b, p. 314; Kuehls, 1996, pp. 11–15, 37–40, 130).

It is beyond the scope of this essay to provide a sustained critique of the asserted relation between Newtonian physics and the theory of sovereignty as well as the belief that modern physics underwrites a metaphysics of becoming. Suffice it to say that the importance of ancient magic in Newton's thought undermines representations of him as a supreme rationalist and chief designer of that dubious construct, the Enlightenment Project. Conversely, to see in modern physics support for process metaphysics and a perspectivist account of knowledge is to invest in it a mystical significance that would not be apparent to the empirically austere.[4]

These points may not matter much if the relations posited between Newtonian cosmology, the sovereignty principle and certain contemporary scientific ideas, on the one hand, and a more complex, mobile and less bounded conception of political space, on the other, are analogical rather than conceptual (Deleuze and Guattari, 1988, pp. 365, 367; on the metaphorical dimension, see Walker, 1993, p. 98). However, where the injunction to rethink sovereignty is accompanied by proposals concerning 'rearticulations of political space/time', there is a strong suggestion that the relation is conceived to be of the latter kind. It seems fair to say of Walker that he considers the sovereign state system to be in part a deduction from the cosmological order sponsored by Newton. He certainly implies a relation between the conceptions of space associated with relativity theory and contemporary physics and those ideas and phenomena, such as temporal acceleration, indeterminacy and flux, which he associates with both modern and postmodern experience (Walker, 1993, pp. 127–9, 176–83).

Ecological Analogies

The conceptual motifs, imagery and vocabulary used by Deleuze and Guattari infuse and colour numerous writings on the state and theories of global transformation. In their account, the state institution is ascribed a weighty and imposing presence. By contrast, forces which escape or 'stand against States', be they vast, piratical, commercial complexes or 'local mechanisms of bands, margins, minorities' are endowed with all the fluency and sheen of quicksilver; they are treated as terminal expressions of a 'diffuse and polymorphous' energy which both challenges and is appropriated by the state. This imagery has been drawn on explicitly by Edward Said in contrasting the settled, established and administered existence inside the state with the 'unhoused, decentered, and exilic energies' of the migrant whose 'consciousness' he compares, although with qualifications, to 'the intellectual and artist in exile' (see Deleuze and Guattari, 1988, pp. 360, 386; Said, 1994, pp. 42–3). And Thom Kuehls, draws on their notion that global flows, whether in the form of people, technology or commerce, are generating expanding zones of 'smooth space'. He too puts these flows in dynamic interaction with the 'striated space' of the state (Kuehls, 1996, pp. 37–42).

Kuehls is interesting because of the marriage he effects between Deleuze and Guattari's conception of space and the ecological paradigm. The principle of sovereignty has been portrayed as a threat to human survival in so far as it allows states to refuse to cooperate on environmental issues. The depiction of the state as an ecological hazard is powerfully complemented by the suggestion that state borders are contrary to nature. These points are evident in writings urging the adoption of a planetary politics. In an especially lurid example of this genre Patricia Mische argued that we needed to 'reconceptualize sovereignty' because:

> The Earth does not recognize sovereignty as we now know it. Existing concepts and systems of state sovereignty are incongruent, even antithetical, to the prerequisites for global ecological security ... the sovereignty of the Earth is indivisible.

This line of argument displays more than a hint of anthropomorphism. Particular conceptions of the biosphere are reified and endowed with human capacities of wanting, knowing and feeling. It is also evident that the naturalistic fallacy (which in this case involves drawing inferences to do with political organization from certain ideas regarding the contours of the natural world) is alive and well in contemporary political discussion (Mische, 1989, p. 396).[5]

The all-absorbing nature of these analogies presents problems for those authors who are wary of global visions that look too much like projections of the sovereign state onto a larger canvas. While a world state based on more humane and ecological principles might be preferable to the present system it might go too far in privileging unity over complexity. Jean Chesneaux cautions against an 'eco-globalist levelling of the New Age variety' which might submerge older forms of solidarity (Chesneaux, 1994, pp. 92–3). These points explain why the organic analogy is modified in some writings, Chesneaux's included, so that it would appear to accommodate difference while allowing for an underlying interconnectedness.

Yet the question remains: can a universe in which differences merge into each other at some deep level be described as authentically pluralist? Must there not be, from the radical pluralist point of view, the possibility of differences which, go 'all the way down'?[6] Kuehls goes some way to overcoming this problem in respect to the ecological paradigm. He renders the natural world in kaleidoscopic terms, emphasizing its dynamic, 'complex, contingent, chaotic' side. While this more open-ended picture is intended to undermine the bounded space of the sovereign state it is also intended as a rejection of all-encompassing global institutions. Kuehl's model does not include a plane on which all differences melt into unity (Kuehls, 1996, pp. 15, 92–3, 130).[7]

Metaphors and Metaphysics

If the metaphysical complement to the state system can be described as homogeneous discontinuity – that is, a world comprising discrete entities which are each of them structured along similar lines – the pattern traced by those working in the Bergsonian tradition is one of heterogeneous continuity. Heterogeneous continuity allows us to think of reality as a moving and endless stream comprising diverse elements and relations which are of varying degrees of intimacy and proximity. Unities can be built out of this stream but, in so far as the novel and alien keep appearing, nothing can absorb everything.[8]

To translate this into political terms, a universe thought of in terms of diversity in unity can be seen as recommending a federal republican model of governance. Such a model is not ruled out by an understanding of experience in terms of heterogeneous continuity. However, such an understanding would dictate, at the minimum, that a fringe of anarchy must surround any organizational structures we establish (Laski, 1925, p. 250).

I am not presenting this last metaphysical conception as the truth about reality. In counterposing a metaphysics of heterogeneous continuity to one of homogeneous discontinuity I am contrasting one metaphorical description of the world with another. This suggests, further to a remark made at the outset, that the distinction between metaphor and metaphysics is not only not always sharply defined but is also prone to collapse. This is starkly apparent in cases where metaphysical conceptions are invoked for strategic reasons rather than as objects of investigation in themselves. International Relations scholars who have adopted the vocabulary and motifs that appear in the work of Deleuze and Guattari are not primarily engaged in theorizing about the structure and texture of reality. Rather, the main game is one of destabilizing certain political and legal constructs and categories. If audiences can be persuaded to think of experience in terms of flux and fluidity then the hold on the imagination of the ideas of territorial borders and state sovereignty may be weakened. Acceptance might also be won for more supple and loose-ended organizational forms. At the same time, to the extent that the distinction between metaphorical redescriptions and metaphysical claims remains vague the former are imbued with the air of authenticity which surrounds the latter.

From Rationalization to Globalization

To invoke process metaphysics against the idea of the state is not a novel move. In the interwar period the notions of flux, fluidity and temporal acceleration were conjured with in order to suggest that state borders were breaking down. Electric machine power, in the form of the radio, aeroplane and telegraph, was believed to have unleashed a torrent of transborder activity; money, industry and knowledge were described as flowing across borders as never before (Young, 1933, pp. 6–7, 9–10, 12–13, 16–19, 23, 34, 52). These developments were treated as aspects of a cosmopolitan movement called rationalization; this was depicted as a force that was annihilating the 'age-old physical barriers of time and space' (Brady, 1933, pp. 401, 411).

As in the present, in the interwar period the sovereign state was decried as a backward-looking institution that was fading in influence. It was also depicted as artificial, as a denial of that reality of process which physical scientists were uncovering. It was claimed that since matter had dissolved into electricity, thus rendering reality a 'seething state of material flux', so too must states dissolve into the 'social and economic flux' of modernity (Young, 1933, pp. 18, 28, 33–4, 36–7; Greaves, 1931, pp. viii, 60).

There were two distinct responses to these ideas. Aesthetic pleasure could be taken in contemplating a world of hustle and excitement, in imagining living amidst a constant maelstrom of events. More typically, however, it was argued that with science and commerce breaking down barriers and generating powerful forces it was both possible and necessary to institute rational coordination of industrial and social policies through the League of Nations' technical organizations. Rationalization thus additionally meant a scientifically planned order at the international or world level (van Kleeck, 1931, pp. 34–6, 39; Young, 1933, pp. 176–81).

Here it should be noted that proposals for a rationalized world order in the interwar period, with their strong emphasis on the streamlining of social life, were seen by critics as recipes for social absolutism and a toneless mass culture. In order to counter these charges the liberating potential of rationalization was emphasized. Proponents of rational organization of social and industrial life argued that far from eliminating cultural 'diversity' and producing 'one dead level' once 'minimum levels of comfort' had been achieved, positive differences and creativity would flourish. It was similarly pointed out that rationalization in the commercial sphere had led to a world, not of grey uniformity and lacking in spontaneity, but of 'speed, kaleidoscopic change, size, color, variation' (Brady, 1993, pp. 408–13).

One of the most notorious advocates of cultural diversity in the interwar period was the conservative author Oswald Spengler. In *Decline of the West* (1922) and *Man and Technics* (1932), Spengler pointed to the devitalizing impact of modernity, warning that the mechanization and organization of the world would extinguish national and regional distinctiveness. He told of a coming struggle between tribal energies and a sterile, secular internationalism. Spengler was condemned for his dark, operatic tale of the collapse of Western civilization and for revelling in the politics of blood and soil. As one would expect, enlightened opinion, as expressed at the League of Nations and by its many sympathizers in the intellectual arena, tended to view national and cultural divisions as reactionary and dangerous. Further, a progressive air and scientific glamour surrounded the idea of conscious control of social forces in the interests of solidarity (Spengler, 1926, I, II, pp. xiii, viv, 100–2; see also Spengler, 1932, pp. 93–8, 102–3).[9]

In the contemporary intellectual context, science cannot be used convincingly to authorize monistic social theories. Further, philosophical and political pluralism has been theorized in an increasingly sophisticated manner over the last quarter of a century. There is a greater emphasis in contemporary writings on the hyphenated nature of our loyalties.[10]

That aside, it should be clear that the term rationalization was invested with many of the significations that are also borne by the term globalization. In their respective historical contexts, these two words have been used to connote transnational flows and the notion of a borderless world and to point, because of the turbulence they generate, to the need for more systematic world governance. These historical parallels suggest that contemporary claims about sovereignty may say less about the shape of things to come than about early twentieth century dreams of modernity.

They also provide support for the argument that the term globalization denotes a set of persuasive strategies rather than a stark and incontestable fact of life. It is telling that in many accounts of globalization we meet the same repertoire of arguments and images which were assembled in the early decades of the century and invoked against state monism and particularism. Further, if globalization – where this word is used to refer to a set of social and economic forces assailing the State – is a rhetorical construct, as was international rationalization before it, its grasp on our thinking is rendered far more tenuous. To a great extent, its existence becomes contingent upon a will to believe.[11]

Thinking about Sovereignty

The same holds for the principle of state sovereignty, as well as any alternative legal and political order that might be proposed. Whether or not flux is the final word about reality no one would dispute that the sovereign state is a work of contrivance. Where past theorists have accounted for this form by appeal to physical or cosmological conceptions, they were doing no more than those contemporary theorists who link their political ideals to chaos theory, ecological paradigms and process metaphysics: attempting to locate legal or political prescription in a dimension of the real. Those who look to geometrical conceptions for the origins of sovereignty are thus treating metaphorical relations as evidence of profound conceptual continuities.

If we concede with Bergson that we must draw lines through and spatially organize nature if we are to act, then much of the contemporary controversy surrounding sovereignty can be reduced to the pragmatic question as to which lines and spatial arrangements best serve as instruments of happiness (Bergson, 1984, pp. 44–5). As we have seen, for some the answer to this question is strengthened world institutions. Others prefer a less formalistic, more open-ended approach to governance – something along the lines of the neomedieval scenario which itself can be interpreted in a more or less anarchical fashion (Kobrin, 1998).

The concept of state sovereignty has been dismissed by its critics as unnatural, factually dubious and morally objectionable. To some extent the success of such an onslaught depends on an act of conceptual inflation. As Robert Jackson finely expresses it, the term has been 'detached from its legal mooring' and invested with an assortment of philosophical, sociological and economic meanings (Jackson, 1990, p. 33). Such a move has been justified on the grounds that sovereignty denotes more than a legal concept; it drags along with it a whole discourse. The construction of the sovereignty discourse clearly expands the terrain on which the intellectual battle can be fought. It offers a means of identifying sovereignty with political absolutism, social monism, isolationism and physical self-sufficiency. As we have seen, this discourse is inscribed with cosmological meanings to the extent that a geometrical conception of space and a spatial understanding of time are seen as immanent in the sovereignty principle. As there seem to be no limits to this sovereignty discourse, its analytical utility can be questioned. The concept of sovereignty has become so heavily burdened with meaning that it appears as though one is encountering less a coherent conceptual and historical presence than a license to build straw men.

That said, there is at least one good reason for approaching sovereignty as a discourse. The sovereignty card is central to the rhetoric of justification employed by rulers. It has been invoked as if it amounts to a right to do whatever one wishes. However, even John Austin, who has long been demonized as one of the chief proponents of the monistic state, emphasized that sovereignty was developed in opposition to the 'false and absurd' doctrine of 'might makes right' (Coker, 1921, p. 194; Austin in Brown, 1906, pp. 186–7). Nonetheless, if sovereignty means, drawing on Alan James's useful definition, 'constitutional independence' and this condition applies in practice then governments are well positioned to do what they can (James, 1986, p. 24).

Jackson believes that the world in one hundred years will still be organized along the lines of the sovereign state system – even though some states may disappear and statuses other than sovereign statehood may be reintroduced (Jackson, 1997, p. 46). State practice suggests that membership of the United Nations and participation in international regimes is not seen as heralding the formation of a wider constitutional arrangement. For good and ill, states vigorously defend what they regard as their rights and these are not seen as insignificant. Taking these points into consideration, but also taking seriously the humanitarian issues raised by critics such as Falk, what scope is there left for thinking constructively about sovereignty?

To answer this question I want to revisit the notion of the sovereignty discourse that I will define as that discursive realm in which intense controversies and negotiations take place over definitions of the rights and obligations of states. This is a realm in which semantic anarchy is possible and ambiguity is necessitated in the course of navigating among myriad understandings and nuances.[12] Wilful silence may also be encountered. In some respects, then, sovereignty might be said to inhibit and distort communication. Yet it also facilitates it. To imagine international relations as a sovereign state system is to designate, in the midst of a potential confusion of tongues, a set of authoritative, legal voices. It is also to lay down a set of protocols governing discussion, and while distortion may be an effect of their observance, they are necessary if it is to proceed. Alfred Zimmern offered a somewhat similar view in 1934, noting that international 'etiquette' dictated that while sovereignty is 'compatible' with various means 'for minimising friction and settling disputes these means can only be efficacious if the limits within which they are employed are clearly understood' (Zimmern, 1934). Zimmern's notion of international etiquette necessarily addresses the obligations and not just the entitlements of states. I would suggest that there have been greater expectations in regard to the former than critics of the sovereignty discourse have allowed. These expectations are manifest in efforts, more or less vigorous, to redefine the duties of states in respect to their citizens. These have taken the form of legal and moral argument, diplomatic remonstrance and expressions of outrage. It might be thought that the accumulation of these, along with post-Cold War interventions, have pushed outwards and diluted the limits of international etiquette which Zimmern found so rigid in 1934.[13]

Such a development might approximate the evolving global constitutional process that Falk discusses. Others, however, would insist that while this century has seen a significant expansion of state responsibilities, the cumulative impact of declarations, conventions, and the hardening of certain norms of conduct, this has not laid the basis of a wider constitutional framework. Although I have indicated that state practice favours the latter interpretation, the scholar's choice of outlook is likely to hinge on normative preferences. It might make better strategic sense in certain contexts, however, for proponents of global governance to argue in terms that do not greatly offend established categories. It is perhaps in recognition of the fact that sovereignty remains entrenched in our thinking that we are being urged to rethink the notion rather than, as Harold Laski suggested, surrender it altogether (1925, p. 45). In 1992, Boutros Boutros-Ghali claimed that sovereignty had acquired a 'new meaning':

> Added to its dimension of rights is the dimension of responsibility, both internal and external. Violation of state sovereignty is and will remain an offense against the global order, but its misuse may also undermine human rights and jeopardize a peaceful global order. (Boutros-Ghali cited in Scheffer, 1992, p. 283n)

Here, he was making an effort to connect with the values of an international audience while at the same time attempting to shift opinion.

Yet it is worth developing the point that as sovereignty was in part a deduction from natural law principles the idea that it entails obligations to keep the peace domestically as well as internationally is hardly new. Many past theorists, jurists and diplomatists, Vattel and Westlake for example, have acknowledged that certain actions fall outside the 'limits of that authority within which the sovereign is presumed to act with reason and justice' (see Stowell, 1921, p. 53; see also Bentwich, 1934, p. 76).[14] A reinvestigation and elaboration of traditions of thinking about sovereignty might provide moral and legal ballast for efforts to challenge jurisdictional claims of the more abusive states. Such an exercise could also yield compelling arguments for enlarging the normative basis of statehood in general. One should consider here the way in which the customary principle of state responsibility has provided grounds for urging on states more extensive obligations in respect to the environment. The government of China expresses a common view in claiming that 'traditional' understandings of sovereignty support the conclusion that the 'global environment, democracy and human rights' remain 'essentially within the domestic jurisdiction' of a sovereign state (Qian, 1995, p. 136). Yet tradition might prove subversive of this line of argument where it is used as an alibi for malpractice. I realize my suggestion in regard to strategies of persuasion is a modest and incomplete response to the problem which is the abuse of sovereign power. My assumption has been that the type of punitive cosmopolitanism critiqued by Danilo Zolo is widely regarded as intolerable, although my analysis does not entirely rule it out (see Zolo, 1997).

Conclusion

Global imagery is a part of the rhetorical stock-in-trade of contemporary actors seeking to change political and intellectual priorities. Shimmering visions of a world criss-crossed and interlinked by streams of electronic energy or depictions of the planet as an integrated whole, crop up frequently in writings urging on us a global destiny. By contrast, the sovereign state is often depicted as an outdated, provincial and even freakish institution. In the more sophisticated theoretical works, critiques of the sovereign state and representations of globalization are informed by larger metaphysical themes. This is not surprising as some theorists see the sovereign state system as an effect of certain cosmological presuppositions and thus think destabilizing this system involves winning acceptance for alternative understandings of reality. Typically, we find the philosophical idea of reality as unpredictable and uncontrollable flux being contrasted favourably with static, deterministic conceptions of the universe. This metaphysical opposition may be seen as simply another case of contesting images or metaphors. Most importantly, it seems the principle of sovereignty retains a sufficient grip on the thinking of enough political actors to withstand the assaults of the army of images and metaphors deployed against it.

In regard to the intellectual divide between those critics of the State who see experience as fluid, manifold and untidy and those who see it in more holistic terms, I want to make a number of related points. To start with, those who mobilize the metaphysics of flux and becoming against the state system would concede the need to construct unities and draw lines around spaces within which we all can act and live. Yet if we consider the universe to be really open-ended we must deny the possibility of finality or any assurance of success in relation to whatever unities or bounded spaces that we will into being. There is a moral reason for declining to see history as an evolution towards a harmony of interests – that is, if we want the struggle against evil to be a genuine struggle rather than one in which the ultimate outcome is preordained.[15] Further, those who tend towards social holism do in fact accept that irreducible differences exist and will continue to erupt; talk of a global civil society is often accompanied by the demand that institutions of global governance be given teeth. To argue this is to concede that a harmony of interests may need, in some measure, to be deliberately produced and policed.

The spatial arrangement which is the sovereign state system also presumes the possibility of differences which go a long way down. Coexistence is seen as preferable, for prudential and ethical reasons, to campaigns to convert by the sword. The effect is a thinly based international society that is often indifferent to suffering behind state lines. Voices that demand a hearing are excluded or ignored. It is concern about these matters which often lies behind pictures of borders melting into air. Descriptive argument veils an attempt to impress on us the morally contingent nature of sovereignty. Yet, historically, sovereignty has been considered provisional for human purposes. Revivifying past patterns of thought would not only amplify this point but might provide compelling arguments for sharpening, deepening and expanding upon the responsibilities that must accompany this status.

CHAPTER 8

A 'New Medievalism'?

Richard Falk

The Quest

Putting forward a metaphor that offers to help us grasp the totality of international political life increasingly engenders debate. For decades the essential quality of world order seemed to rest upon a structure of anarchy that
had been formalized in the Treaty of Westphalia in 1648 at the conclusion of
the Thirty Years' War, which had such a draining, and apparently trauma-
tizing, effect on the European powers of the day. Continuing to rely upon
'Westphalia' or 'the state system' seems less and less satisfactory. It over-
stresses the Western heritage of the territorial sovereign state and the modern era of demarcated borders. At the same time it neglects the welter of
transnational, supranational and intranational actors and their interdependent activities, as well as the resulting diffusion of authority and the relevance of non-Western international experience. Yet finding a substitute for
Westphalia is no simple matter. Contemporary patterns of adherence to
divergent world pictures complicate the quest, perhaps making it futile to
seek a consensus metaphor at this stage.

This difficulty of establishing a new metaphor that captures the global
essence of the postmodern reality is undoubtedly, in part, a confirmation that
this is a time of transition. The Westphalian framework of thought is far from
dead, or obsolete (see, for example, Lyons and Mastanduno (eds), 1995). It
continues to frame the most influential foreign policy discourses which are
anchored, consciously or not, in various modes of realist thought. At most, the
more liberal brands of realism share the view that the proper posture to take
with respect to action in the world is what Hedley Bull has so influentially
called 'the anarchical society' (Bull, 1977; Buzan et al., 1993). Arch realists, in
the vein of John Mearsheimer, dissent sharply from Bull's coupling of 'anar-
chism' with 'society', and feel more comfortable relying upon a social science
terminology, such as 'the structure of anarchy' (Mearsheimer, 1990a; Waltz,

1979). Such a realist underpinning for international relations continues to rely on Hobbes and Rousseau as providing the most illuminating insight into the conflictual nature of the relationship among territorial sovereigns, typically reinforced by a selective reading of Thucydides.[1]

Realism as the continuing 'official' ideology of the ruling elites is coming increasingly under siege, not primarily because of a renewal of idealistic sentiment, but because of the frustrations associated with turning military superiority into political outcomes.[2] Realism is also implicitly being deeply challenged in the contemporary world by 'the discipline of global capital' as enacted through the prism of neoliberal thought and practice. The significance of this challenge directed at traditional realist accounts of world order is mainly responsible for the currency of various post-Westphalian images of 'globalization'.[3] Even within the four corners of realism, then, there is a concealed and subversive tension, as 'the new geopolitics' of the world economy, and its accompanying economistic ideology, deterritorializes the role of the state and the world picture of its leadership. Still, when it comes to the 'national security' of leading countries, the world seems as 'statist' as ever, although incorporating within statism a comprehension of inequality among states, the transforming effects of weaponry of mass destruction on international risk-taking, and recurrent tendencies toward hegemonic projects. Torbjorn Knutsen (1999) is an excellent recent example of scholarship that is substantially informed by this realist genre. As a major element of his 'rewriting' of International Relations, Knutsen does seek to enlarge and enrich the realist tradition. He argues that normative performance (relating to reputation with respect to morality and law) is the third component of state power, that needs to be added to the other two – military prowess and economic capabilities. In effect, then, the very search for post-Westphalian metaphors is bound to be beset by resistance from those who are not yet prepared to loosen their familiar Westphalian moorings, or regard such loosening as an unwelcome move by those who operate from a variety of 'utopian' standpoints.

Another inevitable aspect of this 'war of totalizing metaphors' is the degree to which language, and more specifically 'names', embody views about civilizational predominance and its global policy implications. As Knutsen (1999, p. 291) points out, what is 'globalization' for the dominant sectors of the world is often being experienced, and analysed, as 'Americanisation' and 'Westernisation' elsewhere, with very different policy inferences being drawn. As will be discussed, there is a closely related problem associated with 'the new medievalism' as a candidate metaphor due to its historical referent and relevance being so exclusively Western. Such a civilizational blinkering also pertains to the use of Westphalian metaphors, which draw exclusively on the historical experience of Western Europe, and then purport to generalize this imagery to encompass the world. As might be expected, a reliance on this Westphalian imagery in debate and discussion is pretty much confined to an internal Western dialogue. Yet, as Edward Said points out, there is no way to deprive non-Western partici-pants in global culture from appropriating such images, and re-endowing them with a quite different, no less valid resonance (Said, 1994).

Despite these difficulties those who are impressed by the discontinuities in international life are bound these days to posit a language that they find more descriptive (capturing the empirical reality better), predictive (reflect-ing sensitivity to emergent macro-trends), and prescriptive (affirming the more desirable potentialities for the future) than that being used in the tra-ditional realist/Westphalian discourse. For more than two decades one of the candidates to fulfil this post-Westphalian mission of renaming 'interna-tional society' is 'the new medievalism', or simply, neomedievalism. At least for international relations, it is interesting that it was Hedley Bull, a prime expositor of the realist approach to international relations, who first explored this possibility with any depth. Bull did so by associating an emer-gent 'new medievalism' primarily with the evolution of Europe in the decades after the Second World War, and not by reference to the entire world (Bull, 1977, especially pp. 264–76).[4]

In this chapter my main effort is to consider the strengths and weaknesses of this metaphor of neomedievalism from the threefold perspective of description, prediction and prescription. As an initial matter, it is necessary to clarify the various meanings being attached to the neomedieval metaphor, and their degree of compatibility.

Three Neomedieval Discourses

In my judgement there are three rather parallel invocations of the new medievalism that are not generally separated for purposes of analysis. Each proceeds from the view that something fundamental is changing in interna-tional life in a manner that recalls the essential experience of Medieval Europe. As with the reliance on a 'post-' terminology, as in post-Westphalian or post-Cold War, there is an acknowledgement of tentativeness whenever the prefix 'neo', or the idea of a 'new' version of a former age, is used to identify a change in macro-historical circumstances. In effect, the task of naming what follows from the ruptured past is deferred to the future, until the new situation yields a name that corresponds to its non-recurrent char-acter.[5] An underlying question, then, is whether 'the new medievalism' is helpful in this transitional period, and whether its use covertly serves some political project, such as weakening the hold of statism on the political imag-ination or perpetuating a Eurocentric imagery.

The first discourse: taking account of complexification

The most obvious appeal of the medieval analogy relates to the range of political actors that constituted world order, with an accompanying dispersion of authority that produced a variety of hierarchies and overlapping claims to control. The contrast of this medieval world is with the modern world that emerged from it, gradually assuming its defining character through the rise of the territorial sovereign state with its strong sense of boundaries. In this modern framework international relations is essentially shaped by the interactions among these states, and the core of this interaction consists of war, including the preparations for and consequences of war. Virtually everything else is left out of account. As such, it represents a deliberate exaggeration for the purpose of illuminating the essence of modern history. Expert commentators understood that there were always, even during the height of this modern era of statism, important non-state influences exerted by a range of actors (see Latour, 1993).

What the new medievalists claim is that this core modern reality is undergoing a process of change that is of such decisive significance that it warrants a new imagery. Instead of calling attention to the state and cycles of warfare, it is now more helpful to interpret world order as the outcome of several intersecting sets of economic, social and cultural forces. These forces can be reduced to three: the state, transnational market actors, and agents of global civil society. In addition, there are all sorts of hybrids, ranging from different types of international institutions and a spectrum of non-governmental organizations and citizens' associations, including those representing labour and religion, as well as such recent issue areas as human rights, environment, and nuclear disarmament.

The net effect on this new medievalist viewpoint is to diminish greatly the role of the state as the predominant source of identity, and to challenge its monopoly over the deployment of legitimate force. Noting 'the take' on reality provided by new medievalism, Anne-Marie Slaughter regards its outlook as '[t]he leading alternative to liberal internationalism', as an interpretative focus for change on a global scale. She goes on to suggest, perhaps hyperbolically, that '[w]here liberal internationalists see a need for international rules and institutions to solve states' problems, the new medievalists proclaim the end of the nation-state' (1997, p. 183). In the article, Slaughter argues impressively that what is really at work is the disaggregation of the state into its main functional domains, and their transnational coordination by a variety of formal and informal means. The state is not being superseded as the main organizing unit, but it is adapting to the challenge of complexity, changing its modes of action and its global role, yet still managing to retain predominant control over world politics.

Hedley Bull's influential formulation of a possible emergent new medievalism was hedged with qualifications, and restricted in its geographic scope to Western Europe. It was, in Bull's words, an empirical inquiry into whether there existed 'any evidence' that certain trends associated with what he calls 'a secular reincarnation of the system of overlapping or segmented authority that characterized medieval Christianity' are transforming world order (Bull, 1977, p. 264). It is a matter only of considering the evidence that might support such an inference. Nothing more. At the end of the inquiry, which included other alternatives to statism, Bull concludes sceptically that 'there is no clear evidence that in the next few decades the states system is likely to give place to any of the alternatives to it that have been nominated' (p. 275).[6]

Writing more recently, Andrew Linklater, while drawing inspiration from Bull, suggests that intervening trends regionally and globally in the last two decades give the neomedieval alternative greater plausibility than it had in 1977 (Linklater, 1998, pp. 179–212). Focusing primarily on changing ideas of citizenship and community, Linklater takes note of various ways in which loyalties and identities are shifting, involving overall a weakening of statist control over the political and moral imagination of 'the citizen', but not yet an attachment to a global ethos of human solidarity. In this sense, the significance of the new medievalist actuality is a complexification of the modern experience of world politics, but not yet in any sense the launch of a new era where the interests of *the whole* transcends the interests of *the parts* (whether these be states, regions, movements, or market actors). In Linklater's words, '[t]he post-Westphalian era will begin when societies act as cosmopolitan citizens who aspire to make progress together towards the ethical ideal of a universal community' (p. 211; compare Nussbaum, 1996; also Nussbaum, 1997).

In keeping with Bull's conception, the relevance of this first discourse on the new medievalism seems most useful as an interpretative focus for European integrative trends where the growth of institutions with supranational authority has proceeded rather far, and inroads on the supremacy of the state are of growing consequence. Europe, too, has been experimenting since the Maastricht Treaty of 1992 with a supplemental notion of 'Europeanness', which is intended to encourage a loyalty additional to that owed the state, but it is not offered as a substitute.[7] Furthermore, the initiation of the euro in 1999 and the prospect of a European Central Bank, does involve a major transfer of sovereignty from the level of the state to that of the region, but it is too soon to tell whether this innovation will be sustained. Also relevant is the idea that ethnic communities will be able to weaken their sense of subordination to the territorial sovereign by establishing a variety of linkages to the regional sovereign.[8] These moves all give the imagery of the new medievalism a degree of credibility, but they are not yet characteristic of the global setting. In effect, the cumulative development of the European Union is of systemic proportions, but nothing comparable can be observed in other regions or on a global scale.

Bull is careful also to emphasize the 'secular' character of this possible return of medievalism. Historically, medieval Europe was what it was largely because of the relevance of Christianity, particularly as the legitimizing foundation of political authority. A 'secular medievalism' in this regard is virtually an oxymoron. The empirical case for associating this 'postmodern' international relations with a new medievalism most persuasively derives from the various facets of complexification, especially the emergence of a range of non-state actors, the intensification of many forms of interrelatedness, and the many effects of a deepening of cybernetic unification.[9] But the essence of the medieval memory is connected with its religious aura, not with its authority structure.

The second discourse: the onset of the information age

There is another way of conceiving of the resemblance between salient features of the emergent world and that of the remembered medieval world. It focuses on identifying the essential analogical feature of both systems as consisting of organizational structures that cannot be reduced to bounded territoriality. In this regard, the transforming element in the present setting is associated with information technology (IT) that substitutes deterritorialized networks for territorially situated hierarchies.[10] Of course, the medieval reality was very much premised upon hierarchical relations, but not premised on degrees of territorial control or claims of sovereignty that could be calibrated in relation to distinct political spaces.

As expressed by Stephen Kobrin, '[c]yberspace is not physical, geometric or geographic. The construction of markets as electronic networks renders space once again relational and symbolic, or metaphysical. External reality seen through the World Wide Web may be closer to medieval Christian representations than to a modern atlas' (Kobrin, 1998, p. 365). In Kobrin's view,

> [t]he scale and complexity of technology and the emergence of electronically integrated global networks render the geographic borders and, more fundamentally the basic construct of territorial sovereignty problematic. A critical issue raised by globalization is the lack of meaning of geographically rooted jurisdiction when markets are constructed in electronic space. (p. 362)

Recourse to the medieval analogy is particularly tempting for those who see the future of international relations from the perspective of an integrating world economy emerging under the primary guidance of neoliberal convictions in the primacy of the market. As readers of *WIRED* magazine are well aware there is a spontaneous bonding taking place between market enthusiasts and 'netizens', the name given to those IT libertarians who have transferred their primary loyalties from geographic space to cyberspace. These overlapping constituencies share a belief in the workings of self-organizing systems based on rational criteria such as the maximization of profits or the unregulated flow of information. Neither respects government, nor sees much need for it. In an obvious sense, the medieval metaphor does not work at all. The medieval world was not at all self-organizing, but rested on the most elaborate metaphysical conceits that linked the humblest peasant to God in heaven by way of 'the great chain of being'. In this regard, the second discourse invokes the medieval analogy almost exclusively to express 'the basic disconnect between geographic space and cyberspace' that is posited as the definitive marker separating a terminal modernism from an ascendant postmodernism (Kobrin, 1998, p. 362).

A case can also be made for the analogy as a way of emphasizing the obsolescence of a diplomacy based on state-to-state relations mediated by governmental representatives. Governments are losing control over the flow of information; efforts at censoring Internet access and use being a futile rearguard action. At best, governments can make use of information either to gain control via military applications, which is the essence of what Joseph Nye has influentially dubbed 'soft power', or to tell its story quickly and effectively by shaping and dominating the global media (see Wriston, 1997, especially pp. 174–6). Here again any invocation of the medieval analogy seems quite far-fetched, as the essence of medievalism was such tight control over information that the time became known as 'the dark ages', almost the polar opposite of the sort of openness that IT facilitates, and may even necessitate.

In conclusion, then, except for admittedly crucial assertions about deterritorialization of authority and the virtues of self-organizing systems, the analogy to the medieval experience as a precursor of territorialized modernity, seems more misleading than illuminating. It is not a metaphor that can be carried very far in the reinterpretation of transformed international relations, except possibly by economistic ideologues. They perceive a mainly tacit alliance between market forces and IT as the foundation for a post-Westphalian utopia that brings peace, prosperity, and technological excitement to the peoples of the world.

The third discourse: the recovery of the sacred

Perhaps the most fundamental attempt to rely on the medieval metaphor relates to the postmodern experience of religious revival. This attempt emphasizes the modern scientific age as resting upon a deliberate separation of secular and spiritual domains, with public knowledge of a rational character belonging exclusively to the secular. As progress was based on the application of this knowledge to the human condition by way of technology, religion was at best a mode of consolation. For Marxists, of course, religion was an obstruction to the clear perception of class domination, which was the foundation of an emancipatory revolutionary project. In essence, modernity either marginalized or suppressed religious consciousness, endowing the political community with an essentially materialistic view of human fulfilment.

The new medievalists who invoke this third discourse are convinced that the most basic expression of an emergent postmodernism is the return of religion. The medium of scientific inquiry has itself become more prominently receptive to the limits of empirical knowledge and more awed than ever by the deep and pervasive symmetries and designs of nature (see Spretnak, 1997; and Griffin (ed.), 1990). A spiritual sensitivity has also followed from the encounter of modern society with its limit condition, a sense of involvement with cosmic destiny that follows, and an ecological metaphysics that provides various transcendent alternatives to the reductive materialism of the modern experience.

Various renewals of religious relevance to the public sector have attracted attention in this early postmodern era, including the proposals of Hans Kung for a global ethic resting upon the pluralistic base of the world's 'great religions' (Kung, 1998; for assessment see Falk, 1999b). Kung argues that a secular orientation can neither mobilize the peoples of the world for cooperative responses to the challenges and dangers of globalization, nor can inter-civilizational dialogue proceed very far without an acceptance of the central role of religion in establishing an ethical foundation for acting in the world. In an important respect, such religious thinking is anti-medieval insofar as it acknowledges the validity of religious pluralism as constitutive of world order, and repudiates any project for universalizing religion on the premise of a single true revelation. The medieval world picture rested on the ultimate truth of Christianity, which lent itself to the projection of Western power in the pre-Westphalian period of crusades, overseas expansion, and early colonialism. The Christian cross was a dedicated accomplice of the Iberian sword!

This historical memory of medievalism as deeply implicated in some of the worst forms of Westernization, discourages any serious reliance on neomedievalism as a metaphor disclosing the special character of postmodern history. At the same time, closing the book on Enlightenment dogmatics and secular fundamentalism signals a new openness to the spiritual dimensions of reality. Such openness is arguably a Pandora's Box as it releases various toxic forms of exclusionary religious tendencies that can breed intolerance and engender repressive political regimes. The positive neomedieval case rests on the possibility of activating inclusionary religious orientations that enable the respiritualization of political life (a rescue from the destructive narrowness of the consumerist ethos) in a normative climate that is dedicated to democratization and human rights. Whether this re-emergence of religion is sufficiently reminiscent of medievalism to warrant the label of 'neomedievalism' is far from assured, and even then the insight into the present seems one that is primarily suited to the possible evolution of Western civilization as primarily a regional phenomenon.

Evaluating 'the New Medievalism'

The case for and against reliance on a particular metaphor relates to the symbolic and substantive messages that it conveys. As suggested earlier, there seems to be three important evaluative standpoints: description, prediction and prescription. A short assessment will be made from each of these standpoints. The task of evaluation is further complicated, however, by the claim that the new medievalism should itself be conceived as consisting of three distinct, yet overlapping discourses. And it is even complicated beyond this, by acknowledging that a metaphor may be illuminating within a particular civilizational setting, but repellent if introduced into other such settings.

Descriptively, the neomedieval analogy seems most persuasive and important when invoked in the first discourse as an aid in the imagining of a world order that exhibits overlapping authority structures that are not specified by reference to territorial space. Similarly, in the second discourse, the organizational decentring associated with the Internet and IT seems to suggest ways in which social and political interaction occurred in the medieval world. Diplomats and monarchs were often chosen on the basis of transnational dynastic implications rather on the basis of a nationalist affiliation to a particular geographical space. By contrast, the third discourse reverses the focus recommended by Bull to secularize the medieval metaphor. This discourse maintains that its descriptive relevance is precisely an effect of an emergent reunion between religion and politics in the form of a recovery of the sacred, with the intention of globally overcoming the shortcomings of postmodern secularism. The metaphor of new medievalism calls attention to a multi-faceted, unexpected, worldwide religious revival that challenges the modernist view that science would supplant religion over time.

There are descriptive shortcomings that pertain to each discourse. In the first and second discourse the suppression of the religious ethos of medievalism seems like a fatal descriptive flaw. This flaw is rendered more serious in the second discourse by the degree to which IT works against hierarchical structures of authority as compared to the medieval preoccupation with a rigidly conceived hierarchy that is centred upon an unquestionable religious affirmation of God as the highest authority. Hierarchy is also misleading in relation to the first discourse, but less so. The organizational complexity of a globalizing world has blurred the lines of authority structure, except perhaps with regard to economic governance. Arguably a hierarchy topped by the World Trade Organization, and complemented by the International Monetary Fund and World Bank, is taking shape before our eyes. And for the third discourse, the pluralist nature of the religious revival, and the geographic dispersion of religious adherents, makes misleading any recall of the homogeneous unity of exclusionary religious belief that was characteristic of the medieval world.

As far as trends are concerned, to the extent that its descriptive deficiencies are ignored the medieval metaphor seems to have a certain predictive power. It seems likely that the first discourse's emphasis on complexification, the second discourse's focus on networking and the transforming role of IT, and the third discourse's contention of religious relevance will be sustained for the foreseeable future. But it can be doubted that a metaphor with such serious descriptive problems should be retained merely because it yields partial insights.

It may be that a metaphor should be promoted because it encourages a more desirable human future even if it suffers from descriptive shortcomings and predictive limitations. In this instance, the first two discourses, for the sake of clarity, presuppose a completely secular future for world society, which would seem to confirm the most regressive readings of the impact of globalization. In both discourses there is no counter to consumerism, materialism, and a neglect of human suffering. In the third discourse, a challenge to secularism is precisely what is being asserted by invoking the medieval analogy, but it seems so embedded in the Western experience – with its dubious memories and continuing deformations – as to be unusable on a global communicative stage.

Given the challenges and opportunities within the transforming setting of world politics, it seems critical to conceive of normative potential by reference to some conception of global humane governance.[11] At this stage, promoting normative potential is being most hopefully associated with some of the initiatives arising from global civil society, and from the turn toward the advocacy of 'cosmopolitan democracy' or some equivalent as the basis of an emancipatory ideology that extends the reach of democracy beyond state-society relations to embrace the entire social order.[12] The functional pressures to save the global ecosystem from deterioration, and possible collapse, suggests an institutional imperative to coordinate and implement standards of behaviour on a global basis. The medieval metaphor has a mixed relationship to such world order priorities. It seems consistent at a first level with the importance of further centralization of authority, but it is quite incompatible with the emphasis on the democratic spirit that needs to inform the dynamics of global reform.

Conclusion

On balance, then, it would not seem very helpful to rely upon the medieval metaphor as a way of understanding the passing of the modern. It fails to come sufficiently to terms with the various contradictory features of this transitional interval in which a transformed world order is taking shape. Arguably, it may be constructive to use the medieval metaphor for a consideration of the evolution of Europe, as a source of regional insight and assessment. Such a regional notion avoids many of the problems connected with seeking to globalize an essentially Western precursor to modernity that had and has so many unpleasant connotations for non-Western civilizations.

But even within Europe, the metaphor must be used with caution. After all, with large Muslim minorities in several important European countries, it is difficult to think of Europe as 'a Christian Europe'. Relevantly, Hans Kung discerns and decries just such a project as the objective of the Papacy in Rome (see Kung, 1998, pp. 138–9).[13] Despite this problematic side of the metaphor, the European comparison of 'before' and 'after' the Westphalian period of statism lends itself to illuminating inquiry if done in a sufficiently critical spirit.

CHAPTER 9

A 'Coming Age of Regionalism'?

Greg Fry[1]

When W. W. Rostow was asked in 1990 by the journal *Encounter* to suggest a 'metaphor for our time' he offered 'the coming age of regionalism' (Rostow 1990).[2] He argued that it was the single image of the future that had the virtue of relating significantly to 'the other major dynamic forces' shaping global society. The outcome of such forces would, in the worst case, be 'fragmentation, violence and stagnation'. To manage these forces in an age when the capacity of the state is declining, he contended, we require a primary role for regionalism in a 'federal pattern of regional and global cooperation' (1990, p. 7).[3] While claiming that his vision should not be seen as utopian, he was clearly suggesting the 'coming age of regionalism' as a desired and necessary path. This places him in a familiar tradition of regionalist doctrines and schemes put forward since the Second World War by those who have sought a greater role for regional organization in global governance to promote various normative projects such as free trade, trade protection, collective self-reliance, security, order, or welfare (Fawcett, 1995; Taylor, 1990).

In the following decade a less grand, but ultimately more significant, claim was made on behalf of a region-centric characterization of world politics. Academics, policy makers and commentators began to speak not only of a 'new regionalism' to capture a new institutional and policy emphasis on regionalism in the 1990s but of a new status for regions within the emergent world order (see, for example, Palmer, 1991, particularly chapter 1; Fawcett and Hurrell (eds), 1995; Hettne and Inotai, 1994; Gamble and Payne (eds), 1996; Lake and Morgan (eds), 1997; Grugel and Hout (eds), 1999; and Robson, 1993). Peter Katzenstein (in Kohli *et al.*, 1995, pp. 14–15), for example, offers the image of 'a world of regions' to capture what he sees as the move towards a new arena for world politics, while prominent security theorists such as Barry Buzan (1991, 1999), Mutthiah Alagappa (1995), and

Mohammed Ayoob (1999), suggest that global security must now be seen largely as the sum of its regional parts rather than as a product of global logic. Some leading economists ascribe a new prominence to regionalism (Arndt, 1993), or refer to the emergence of a 'second regionalism' (Bhagwati, 1994), or the advent of a 'new regionalism' (Ethier, 1998), whether or not they support such a development. For other scholars, the region offers a possible new site of promotion of world order values of democracy, and human rights and a possible site of resistance to globalization (Falk, 1995b). While these scholars may not go as far as Rostow in seeing regionalism as providing the single metaphor for 'the coming age', in other respects their image of a 'world of regions' represents a more dramatic claim, for it asserts that regions are in fact becoming an important locus of world politics rather than simply suggesting that they should do so.

The central claim underlying this cluster of images, prominent in the policy and academic domains, is that regions – geographically contiguous states and peoples – are, or are becoming, key actors, identities or arenas in world politics. Although the proponents of region-centric thinking do not necessarily dismiss the agency or identity of other entities – such as ethnic groups, states, civilizations, international agencies, or transnational corporations – or dismiss the importance of other political arenas, they necessarily see regions as significant in their own right, and not merely derivative of state or global power. While they recognize that there has been a 50-year history of regional schemes and doctrines of various kinds, they see these previous efforts either as having been ineffective, or as having been idealistic non-starters, or as derivative of hegemonic power. This, they argue, is the first time that developments in regionalism are occurring in a form that really matters in world politics. This therefore amounts to a claim to fundamental transformation of the global order.

This chapter is principally concerned with the question 'what kind of transformation?' It is one thing to accept the claim that regions are now an important locus of power in world politics, but this tells us little about the significance of such a transformation in terms of structures, processes, values and interests. In exploring what the assumed transformation means we consider four specific questions. The first concerns the changing political role of regions. What kind of political entity or site is 'the region' becoming? Is it to be seen increasingly as a locus of authority, identity, community or agency in world politics? The second question takes this a little further by exploring the relative power of regions as against other centres of power, notably global institutions and states. Third, we explore the contending normative projects underlying the 'new regionalism' and the normative implications of the various regionalist doctrines that cluster around these projects. The fourth question links these values to contending political interests and asks how we might characterize the interplay among them. It asks 'which interests prevail?'

In exploring these questions, the focus is on the intellectual and normative lenses that produce this region-centric image of world politics. As will already be apparent, the 'world of regions' image is produced by some very different, and often conflicting, theoretical perspectives and normative orientations. As with a 'world of states', different interpretations of a 'world of regions' can offer very different possibilities for peace and war, or conflict and cooperation, depending on the interpreter's ethical and theoretical commitments.

Before exploring the way in which various contemporary regionalist positions interpret the above questions concerning the kind of transformation a region-centric world polity represents, we examine their shared starting point in the rationale for the claim that *regions* matter in world politics in a way they did not before, that *regionalism* is now a major trend in world politics, and that this in turn suggests a transformation of world order.

The Rationale

The proponents of a region-centric picture of world politics argue that the regionalism of today differs in a substantial way from the regionalism of the last 50 years (see Taylor, 1990; Fawcett, 1995). They observe that from the late 1980s the world has seen a substantial strengthening of existing regional institutions and the creation of a significant number of new regional associations among states (Fawcett, 1995; Hurrell, 1995). The so-called 'new regionalism' is usually taken to have its roots in the Single European Act of 1986 and the move by the Reagan administration to negotiate 'regional' preferential trade agreements with Canada and Israel. The subsequent profound deepening and widening of European integration in the 1990s culminating in the Maastricht Treaty, together with the creation of the North American Free Trade Agreement (NAFTA) in 1992, are cited as the most impressive institutional developments. However, more tentative developments in the economic arena in East Asia around APEC and ASEAN, and the dramatic increase in the number of new regional preferential trade agreements elsewhere in the world have also been very important in encouraging a region-centric orientation among commentators. The developments in Europe, Asia and North America, in particular, had by the mid-1990s suggested for many that the fundamentals of future world politics were to be found in the interaction of these three powerful economic blocs (see Wyatt-Walter, 1995).

In the security realm, they point to the re-invention of the North Atlantic Treaty Alliance as a broader European regional security organization and the expansion of regional security cooperation in Asia in the ASEAN Regional Forum. Supporters of the notion of a 'new regionalism' also point to the creation of new regional institutions and the reinvigoration of established ones in Latin America, the Middle East and Africa (see Fawcett and Hurrell (eds), 1995; Gamble and Payne (eds), 1996; Axline (ed.), 1994; and Grugel and Hout (eds), 1999).

A second part of the rationale draws attention to the fundamental change in the role expected of all regional institutions by the United Nations and the United States after the end of the Cold War (Alagappa, 1995, pp. 359–60). In 1992, the then UN Secretary-General, Boutros Boutros-Ghali, proposed that regional organizations take a greater share of security management – in such areas as peacekeeping, peace making, and preventive diplomacy – but in partnership with the UN and consistent with the principles of the Charter (Boutros-Ghali, 1992, section VII). Although hardly successful in outcome, developments in West Africa, with the operation of the ECOWAS peacekeeping force in Liberia, and in Europe in relation to Bosnia, were also seen as suggesting a trend in that direction.

The supporters of a region-centric characterization of world politics assert that a similar shift towards regionalism is evident in United States policy. In the security field, the US government expects regional institutions to carry more of the burden, particularly in areas of the world in which it has no vital interest. This expectation has increased over the decade as direct US involvement has become less politically tenable and UN Security Council backing has become harder to obtain. In economic policy there has also been a discernible shift from a global multilateral approach to a regionally focused approach to trade liberalization. This was most evident in the creation of the North American Free Trade Area but has also been expressed in plans for a broader hemispheric regional economic grouping (Payne, 1996, pp. 102–29).

Third, the region-centric position points to the fundamental transformation of the global structures and processes within which regionalist doctrines operate. It argues that an old idea like regionalism now assumes greater importance because of the changing material and ideational context. The prime development is the geopolitical change associated with the end of the Cold War and the role of the United States within the world polity. This particularly affects the security realm. Here, the argument runs, regionalism becomes more important because of the limitations on US reach and political will in a 'unipolar' world (Alagappa, 1995, p. 359). Developments in global economic arrangements in the early 1990s constituted a further important stimulus. These include the dynamism of the Asia-Pacific economies, the stalling of progress at the global level in free trade, the spread of economic liberalization policies in the 1990s, and the effect of the end of the Cold War on the world economy (Wyatt-Walter, 1995). Another claimed change is the perception of a declining locus of power at state level as a result of globalization. In such circumstances, it is argued, regions become more important actors and arenas (Grugel and Hout, 1999, pp. 3–4).

Political Community, Identity, Agency

We are now in a position to consider the persuasiveness of this rationale. But in doing so we need to press beyond the claim to a new and qualitatively different regionalism to the claim to a changed role for the region as a polit- ical locus in world politics. We will do so by exploring whether the 'new regionalism' suggests a changing political role for regions as political com- munity, political agent, political identity, or knowledge/policy category. In exploring in what sense 'the new regionalism' represents a shift both in thought about political *community* as well as its practice, a useful starting point is the European experience because it is here that the case is most per- suasively made. The European Union has all the hallmarks of a community: free movement of people within its borders, common laws and sanctions enforced by regional rather than national institutions, citizens with common rights and responsibilities, a move towards a single market and a common currency, and even, from 2000, the beginnings of a European defence force (outside NATO). There are also, increasingly, shared norms about social organization, and shared understandings about the basis of exclusion from, or inclusion in, the community. There has been a political transformation in terms of loyalties, transactions, power, authority, values and norms. The result is not, however, a new 'super state'. The resultant community has no police force and has a layering of rights and responsibilities, with various entities having overlapping jurisdiction and authority.

Beyond Europe, however, we do not find the same kind of transformation taking place. In the regional schemes of Asia, Africa, South America, the South Pacific, and the Middle East, we find a much 'thinner' kind of com- munity and one in which generally only states, or state elites, participate. Unlike Europe, where some pooling of sovereignty has occurred, non- Western regionalism aims to strengthen rather than weaken the power of national governments. However, within this group of 'thinner' communi- ties there is further variation. Some regional groupings clearly have almost no claim to community. The classic case is South Asia, and its regional grouping, the South Asian Association for Regional Cooperation. Other regions resemble more what Mohammed Ayoob (1999, pp. 3–7) usefully described as a 'regional society', a region in which, in security terms at least, the states consciously pursue shared norms and rules in their interaction. Southeast Asia and its regional association, ASEAN, is arguably such a 'regional society'.

But the concept of 'regional society', or even the 'thicker' concept of 'regional community' as employed by Ayoob (1999, pp. 3–7), refers only to levels of community among states and it assumes that one of the shared norms of that community is the non-intervention principle. These concepts therefore obfuscate other forms of transformation of community which are being promoted both by state and non-state actors. There are, for example, moves within ASEAN by some democratic states (the Philippines, Thailand) to move beyond the non-intervention principle. There are also developments at a non-government level which suggest moves beyond these state-centric regional societies to a 'thicker' form of regional community in areas such as the environment and human rights. The burgeoning of free trade areas also has the potential to create more economic integration that can further enhance political community or, conversely, lead to a break up of community if badly handled, as in the economic integration attempts of the 1960s.

There is also a strong case for arguing that the 'new regionalism' represents a transformation in political *identity* in increasingly providing a rallying point for 'identity diplomacy'.[4] The appeal to regional identity in cultural and civilizational terms as helping to constitute boundaries of inclusion and exclusion, and as part of battles over the nature of the social, political and economic organization which will prevail within states, is not new.[5] The 'new regionalism' of the 1990s, however, has gone a step further in the deployment of cultural and civilizational identities although these are often contested. The increased salience of cultural, and even civilizational, identities at the regional level has appeared partly as a reaction to the more blatant promotion of Western values as part of a post-Cold War global governance agenda and their attachment as conditions to economic assistance.

The increased deployment of a regional cultural identity in the 1990s has been prominent in European and Asian regionalism. The Asian financial crisis, which clearly set back the agenda and confidence of the two principal 'regional' institutions, APEC and ASEAN, nonetheless produced an upsurge in identity regionalism and identity diplomacy. It is evident that there was more determination to promote an Asian challenge to the domination of Western institutions and experts, and to pursue this regionally. This position seemed to enjoy wider support in Asia than the Malaysia/Singapore-sponsored 'Asian values' variant of identity regionalism of previous years. Proposals to establish an exclusive East Asian economic area gained unprecedented support at the end of the 1990s. In Europe we see the other side of the coin. The post-Cold War period has seen an upsurge in the cultural identity aspects of defining European regionalism. This was seen, for example, in the conditions of membership attached to East European entry and in the military intervention in Yugoslavia in the name of a 'standards of [European] civilization'.

Turning to the region's role as a political *agent* in world politics the evidence is more mixed. Again Europe provides the most developed common foreign policy but even in that case the limitations are many (Gamble and Payne, 1996, pp. 255–7). The promotion of joint positions by other regional associations are less common. But two developments do suggest that this will develop further. One is the increasing tendency of international agencies to expect *regional* positions and reactions to global issues such as the environment, biodiversity, population control, sustainable development, human rights, gender issues, 'good governance', and social issues, seen, for example, in the approach to the series of global summits that took place in the 1990s. This demand from above for regional agency is complemented by a demand from below, by member states, for regional institutions to take a more active role in representing their interests in global economic fora. In particular, it has been argued that the development of the 'new regionalism' in the 1990s in marginalized areas such as Africa has been stimulated by a perception that a collective voice is needed to protect state interests in relation to what are seen as the forces of 'globalization' (Grugel and Hout, 1999).

The region has also assumed a more powerful political role in world politics in relation to its use as a *category* in knowledge systems, whether by academics, policy makers or international agencies. The naturalization of the idea that the world is divided up into entities larger than states, called 'regions', has evolved over time in association with the expansion of European interests throughout the globe. This is a powerful idea because it has facilitated the tendency to generalize about conditions or peoples or customs within the regional boundaries. This in turn nourished the preconceptions underlying policy responses by colonial administrations attempting to manage developments in these regions. Made famous by Edward Said's *Orientalism* (1978b), this colonial relationship between knowledge, power and regional images continued into the post-colonial period. Those attempting to manage development and security in a post 1960s world of hundreds of states found the idea of region indispensable. Region-centric thinking has arguably increased after the end of the Cold War in the social sciences, in international agencies and in policy areas of major powers. Regionalism has become a subtle but powerful tool of analysis and policy in the management of world politics.

Finally, it does appear that whatever our view on the changing political role of regions in terms of political agency, community or identity, there can be little doubt concerning their increased role as an *arena* or *site* of politics. Sitting between states and global forces and agencies, the region and its institutions are increasingly a place where business gets done. The region now stands alongside state and global institutions as a site where contests occur over what values, practices and concepts should prevail within the societies of that region. The region often has the capacity to confer legitimacy on practices (such as intervention) and on important concepts (such as 'security' or 'development'). It distributes resources, legitimates procedural norms, and adjudicates on the legitimacy of states and governments by policing the right to membership. It is also increasingly a site of the generation of international law. In all these roles it is a site of contest between contending ideas and is particularly an arena in which the tension between the global and the local is mediated.

Overall, then, the region has multiple political roles. It is sometimes an independent political agent, it sometimes acts like a political community, and it is sometimes called up as a political identity. It is always an important arena, and a significant analytical and policy category. Each of these roles has arguably become more important since the end of the Cold War, suggesting that the 'new regionalism' does increasingly matter as a locus of world politics, and therefore that the rationale underlying the 'world of regions' is persuasive, albeit with the qualifications noted above.

Relational Power

The next step in our inquiry into the kind of transformation implied by region-centric imagery is to ask whether the increasing political significance of 'region' suggests the displacement of global or state power. It is here that those behind the banner of a 'world of regions' start to diverge from each other. While they can all agree on the increasing political significance of regions, they hold different views concerning whether this is at the expense of the power of global or state arenas.

We turn first to the relationship between regionalism and globalism, a prominent issue since the emergence of regionalist doctrines in the 1940s (Potter, 1943). In his famous text on international organization, *Swords into Ploughshares* (1956), Inis Claude asked: should we see regionalism as a stepping stone to universalism, an alternative to world order or a supplement to global organization? The first of Claude's approaches, regionalism as the stepping-stone or building block to an effective global order, was popular in early regionalist doctrines such as those of the free trade economists or the liberal idea of 'peace in parts', moving beyond state sovereignty through regional integration towards global peace (Nye, 1971). This view sees regionalism ultimately as subordinate to globalism and as withering away as global peace or global free trade is achieved. Claude's second category, that of creating an alternative order to global order, is a radical perspective suggesting no significant role for global organization. It is implied in the ideas of competitive trading regions or the neorealist idea of a set of competing 'regional states'. The third approach, the supplementary role, emulates the federal pattern of regional and global organization suggested by Rostow. It does not explicitly suggest either globalism or regionalism as superior but implies a more varied relationship in which regionalism is sometimes derivative from, and sometimes complementary to, universalist approaches. This suggests the need for a fourth category, that of a fully derivative relationship where regionalism is simply the agent of global organization.

What do contemporary doctrines envisage about this relationship between region and global order? The *stepping-stone* position is most influentially held by some economists. Whether committed to 'open regionalism' or 'discriminatory regionalism', they hold that the ultimate goal is global free trade. Regionalism simply provides the building blocks to a world of free trade.[6] The *'alternative world order'* position is most prominently held by neomercantilists who see ongoing competitive regions much as in the realist world of states (in the short term the 'discriminatory regionalism' of the free trader does not look very different to this neomercantilist alternative order). This is a world of fragmentation between competing blocs. It is not a stepping stone to a new global order; it *is* the order, one that may undermine the core of a global liberal trade system. The idea of separate existence, as providing an alternative order, not in partnership with global order, is most closely approached in the assertion of a counter-hegemonic position like that of the East Asian Economic Caucus proposal.

The *supplementary* role in which regional and global institutions coexist in a kind of federal arrangement is envisaged in the state-centric security management doctrines. In this view, regions are not seen as stepping-stones to a global order or as providing an alternative order, but as continuing in partnership with global institutions. The idea of regions as simply *agents* of global organization appears not to have any support in contemporary world politics. Although increasingly seen as conduits for a global governance agenda, they are not simply agents. This would suggest some independence for the region as a political locus.

In practice, the relationship with global institutions and globalism varies significantly according to region and to issue. But they all fall within Claude's third category, the supplementary role, in which there is a federal relationship between the regional and the global. Even in the most extreme cases of regional dependency, as in some Third World regional institutions, they are not simply agents of global governance. And at the other extreme, where regionalism has formed a sophisticated political community as in Europe, there is still some agency for global institutions. The EU, for example, is subject to global regulations in the economic sphere. An alternative order of a solely regions-based world does not seem plausible given the global reach of economic and political forces.

How, then, does the region-centric view see the changing political power of the regional arena in relation to state power? For some observers, the changing political role of regions is a product of the decreasing power of states under the impact of globalization. The region is seen as the new alternative to the state after the fall of state sovereignty. As we have seen, this was the basic premise on which Rostow was working. Thus the region is seen as a new site of community and of society, and as replacing the state's role in protecting local societies against the deleterious effects of globalization (Falk, 1995b). Others see an increased role for regional arenas as consistent with the maintenance of state power. Here the region is just another layer or arena in an increasingly complex and overlapping system of global governance.

There are also those who see regionalism as enhancing state power and maintaining state sovereignty and the non-intervention principle in the face of global encroachments (Grugel and Hout, 1999). Some who hold this view see this situation as legitimate. They argue, for example, that this is a counter-hegemonic strategy. Others who hold the same view of the relationship between regional and state power see this enhancement of state power as legitimating inexcusable behaviour by governments. This is seen, for example, in the objections of some human rights activists to the creation of *regional* human rights commissions. They see them as obstructing a more probing *global* human rights approach (Sidney Jones quoted in Rae and Reus-Smit (eds), 1996, p. 42). This tendency is also referred to by Muthiah Alagappa in relation to security issues:

> ... instead of containing and terminating domestic conflict, regionalism can prolong and intensify it. By strengthening the hand of the government, as for example in Burma, regional support increases the persecution and insecurity of groups seeking political change (1995, p. 385).

The relationship between state and regional power clearly differs significantly from region to region. Thus we could identify real aspects of a new form of political community in the EC that implies diminishing state sovereignty. For example, we could note the fact that the European Court of Justice is seen as a powerful weapon for local communities against national governments. But as we have seen this differs sharply from the experience in South Asia where state sovereignty is fully intact and the understandings between regional players are very undeveloped. In Southeast Asia, we might argue, in Ayoob's terms, that a 'regional society' made up of states has emerged, but it is one in which non-intervention and state sovereignty are the paramount norms. The South Pacific is a little further along the continuum towards Europe, and the East Asian region is closer to the South Asian experience. Even in Europe, however, we would have to question whether popular loyalties have been transferred to the regional level. There is very little evidence in Europe that Brussels has supplanted national capitals as a location for identity or loyalty.

According to those propounding a 'world of regions' image, such a characterization of world politics does not imply a world in which regionalism displaces globalizm. But, as we have seen, for some adherents it does mean a displacement of the power of states. In practice, neither state nor global arena appears to be displaced by the 'new regionalism'. Rather, the view (Gamble and Payne, 1996, pp. 263–4) that what we are seeing is an emergent system of overlapping authority and jurisdiction with the relative power of state, regional and global, arena varying from issue to issue, over time, and according to the region concerned, seems more persuasive.

Contending Values, Contending Interests

The claim to an increased political importance for 'the region' as a locus in world politics, whether as arena, political agent, community, identity or category of knowledge, begs the question 'what values and norms are served in this "world of regions"?' Regionalism provides a common vehicle for very different ideas about how the world should be organized socially, politically and economically. Behind the 'new regionalism' discourse we can detect several key clusters of normative concerns. Around each of these normative concerns we can distil contending regionalist doctrines promoting different approaches to their achievement. They in fact represent different values.

One cluster of normative concerns focuses on economic welfare, economic survival and economic justice. The most influential doctrinal approach is a form of neoliberal economic doctrine that sees regionalism as a stepping-stone to a global free trade order that would maximize growth and welfare. Within this general camp, however, there is an important distinction to be made between those supporting 'open regionalism', influential in the APEC model, and those supporting discriminatory regionalism, as in the European Community and NAFTA. The 'open regionalism' advocates argue that if regionalism is to be a stepping-stone to global free trade then it should not be discriminatory. For those advocating discriminatory regionalism, on the other hand, regional-level discrimination is seen as a necessary evil to pressure outsiders into making concessions on reducing barriers to trade. There are, however, pure market liberals who oppose regional approaches, whether discriminatory or open, arguing that they are not as effective as a global approach, that regional free trade areas are likely to be turned into trading blocs, and that regional arrangements are an unnecessary interference with the market mechanism.

Tracing its lineage to the ideas underlying the European Union in the 1950s and the free trade areas among developing countries of the 1960s, the pro-regionalist neoliberal position received new impetus from the end of the Cold War, and from the increased influence of neoliberal ideas in the foreign policies of great powers, and their ascendancy within states as governments grapple with the perception of an impinging globalization. It has also been driven by disillusionment with progress in multilateral talks at the global level. For Jagdish Bhagwati:

> The conversion of the United States [to supporting 'preferential trade liberalisa-tion'] is of major significance. As the key defender of multilateralism through the post-war years, its decision now to travel the regional route ... tilts the balance of forces at the margin away from multilateralism to regionalism. (1994, p. 150)

In direct contention with this neoliberal position is a regionalist doctrine built on neomercantilist premises. While these perspectives share a norma-tive concern with economic welfare, neomercantilism sees the role of regionalism in a very different light. It assumes that regional free trade areas are competitive trading blocs, or could become so. Here, advocacy of region-alism is motivated by the need to survive in the face of regional consolida-tion (Hurrell, 1995, pp. 340–1; Bhagwati, 1994; Payne and Gamble, 1996, pp. 1–2). In the contemporary context this is expressed in a perception of European developments as 'fortress Europe' (see Harris, 1999, pp. 4–5; see also James Kurth, cited in Harris, 1999, p. 6) that, when taken together with North American and Asian regional developments, constitute a world of competing trading blocs potentially engaged in trade wars. For an individ-ual state, prudence dictates joining a regional bloc for economic survival. It is argued that we cannot afford to assume that regional developments are moves towards a harmony of interests at the global level. Moreover, with the loss of global hegemonic stability, it is argued that regional hegemonic stability may be desirable. Such a doctrine is given impetus by the ambigu-ity of 'new regionalism' in its economic form. While lip-service is paid to building something that contributes to global free trade, the strategic trade doctrine that actually informs regional developments is a half-way house between protectionism and free trade. Thus even free traders may have an incentive to be reluctant neomercantilists in this context. In practice, then, we can detect both neomercantilist and neoliberal free trade doctrines in regional institutional developments such as APEC, NAFTA or the EU.

A second cluster of normative concerns focuses on peace, security, stabil-ity and order. Here a corresponding neoliberal and realist doctrine can be discerned. One expression of the neoliberal doctrine represents a contempo-rary manifestation of Joseph Nye's 'peace in parts' approach (Nye, 1971) and of the political aspects of economic integration theory. It sees regional economic interdependence as making war among participating states less likely, a regional expression of nineteenth-century liberal ideas particularly associated with writers like Richard Cobden. Another variation is expressed in seeing regions as vehicles for promoting liberal-democratic political val-ues (as demonstrated by the insistence on the acceptance of such values for membership of European institutions), thereby leading to peace. This echoes the long-standing democratic peace thesis of the liberal thinkers, most notably Immanuel Kant. Each of these liberal positions has in common the claim that regional integration on the basis of free trade and liberal-demo-cratic norms makes war unthinkable among the participating states.

For other neoliberal regionalists, the aim is more modest. It depends on a less structural determination of peace, emphasizing regional arrangements which feature collective security arrangements, peacekeeping forces, the building of regional norms of peaceful resolution, confidence-building measures, preventive diplomacy, and arms control. This doctrine views regionalism as a means of assisting the participating states to move beyond the security dilemma through cooperative security. This position can be seen in the rationale offered for the ASEAN Regional Forum, for example.

There is also a realist doctrine supporting regionalism on security/order grounds. This doctrine promotes inter-state security and regional order as part of global management. It sees regionalism as an informal alliance against other states, or as a hegemonic sphere of influence of a great power. This idea of 'regional security' emerged during the Cold War, particularly in the 1960s as decolonization made various areas of the world uncertain for great powers.

This cluster of regionalist ideas also includes a doctrine that questions realist and neoliberal definitions of 'security' and 'regional security'. It sees the dominant doctrines as being primarily concerned with the security of *states*, and particularly hegemonic states, rather than with societal or human security. It is also more expansive in its definition of what constitutes a secu-rity threat. It includes environmental and economic threats and threats from the state to its own citizens. It argues that 'regional security' as defined by the dominant doctrines not only leaves out human security; its promotion actually undermines it by legitimizing state-centred security. While such a doctrine has usually been the preserve of non-governmental organizations (NGOs), it has recently made inroads into mainstream state-sponsored regionalism. Following the Asian financial crisis, the Japanese government has promoted 'human security' as part of Asian regionalism. This initiative has gained a good deal of support from regional think-tanks and elites. Such ideas were already influential in European regionalism where social and human security has been enforced by regional courts and law-making bodies.

A third cluster of normative concerns focuses on questions of the moral/cultural kind such as how society is organized. On the one hand are those who view regionalism as a way of promoting values of 'good gover-nance', human rights, liberal democracy, and sustainable development. They have also been motivated by a desire to use regionalism as a way of legitimating and facilitating humanitarian intervention when states break down. This normative project, referred to as 'intrusive regionalism' by

Amitav Acharya (1999, pp. 18–22), is really a new development outside Europe. It has become an important stimulus to the regionalist impetus within the UN, international agencies and in the foreign policies of larger powers, particularly the EC, Japan and the US. This position has also been shared by NGOs and global humanist thinkers in academic international relations (Falk, 1995b).

However, regionalism has also been promoted as a way of countering or mediating intervention from what is seen as these hegemonic Western influences. Here regionalism is used to protect local cultural mores. Regionalism is seen as an anti-hegemonic strategy to control great power and particularly American or Western dominance. This is most prominently demonstrated in the promotion of Asian values.

Clearly, then, the nature of the transformation suggested by a 'world of regions' is highly contingent. As the regionalist project is promoted by doctrines that stand for quite different, and often antithetical, values, what it ultimately stands for depends on which doctrine prevails politically. These doctrines are not free-floating sets of ideas that will be evaluated according to rational criteria. They are connected to contending interests. For many observers, this contest comes down to hegemonic versus counter-hegemonic interests. While they each see hegemonic interests as predominating, they emphasise a range of candidates for the label of hegemon: globalization, capitalist interests, large global powers, important regional powers, and states. These are sometimes seen as consistent rather than conflicting propositions. For example, such a position might hold that the 'new regionalism' should be seen as a state-centred project in which the regional power takes the initiative to act as agent for creating a regional order based on the norms and values associated with Western values and capitalism through the promotion of a neoliberal conception of economic, political and social order. The 'neorealist' and the 'neo-Marxist' positions on the nature of political interests involved in the 'new regionalism' are not far from sharing such a view (Hout, 1999; and Hurrell, 1995).

Such a position even has some support in global humanist circles. Richard Falk, for example, while hoping that regionalism might adopt a counter-hegemonic role towards what he calls 'negative globalizm' (by which he means unfettered capitalism), is pessimistic based on the experience thus far (Falk, 1995b). He argues that post-Cold War regionalism has largely promoted the neoliberal economic doctrine, while failing to promote what he regards as the worthwhile 'positive globalizm' agenda of human rights, sustainable development and democracy, at least outside of Europe. His is a more nuanced position, however, in that he does admit to regional differences and to the possibility that regions were becoming sites of contest rather than simply the agents of these hegemonic interests (Falk, 1995b, p. 15).

The idea that regionalism is simply a hegemonic project of Western capitalist interests, an agent of 'globalization from above', is far too simplistic on a number of scores. Falk's latter suggestion that regions could be seen as sites of contest, born more out of hope than his emphirical observations, seems closer to the mark, and worthy of exploration. This would still allow the hegemonic thesis, in its various hues, primacy of place but draw attention to what is undoubtedly a more complex picture.

There are several reasons for regarding this as a productive line of inquiry. Firstly, the hegemonic thesis overestimates the homogeneity of hegemonic interests whether of the West, of globalization, of regional powers or of capitalist interests. These interests are often in competition seen, for example, in the differences between Asian and trans-Atlantic capitalism, or between the values and norms promoted by regional hegemons and global powers. This competition takes place in the regional arena. Second, the hegemonic thesis underestimates the power of counter-hegemonic interests to moderate, modify or even reject so-called global practices and ideas. Even in the most marginalized case of the South Pacific, a region of micro-states, it can be shown that island state opinion has prevailed in the face of an attempt to impose a hegemonic order throughout the Cold War (Fry, 1993). Third, the mix of interests and the possible outcomes vary enormously from region to region. Generalization is impossible. Finally, the emphasis on regionalism as a project of states underestimates the role of NGOs in affecting the outcomes in many regions. The increasing links between peoples within a region and the promotion of a cultural identity and community by states is creating further demands for wider participation in the regional contest over values and practices. It is no longer simply a project of states.

FRAGMENTATION AND CULTURAL IDENTITY

CHAPTER 10

A 'Clash of Civilizations'?

Jacinta O'Hagan[1]

The relatively peaceful conclusion of the Cold War encouraged many to hope for the commencement of a new era of international relations; one characterized by co-operation and growth. However, by the early 1990s, there was a growing sense of pessimism and insecurity. This was reflected in the emergence of a new metaphor for future world politics, that of the 'clash of civilizations'. Introduced by the well-known American political scientist, Samuel Huntington (1993a), the metaphor suggested that world politics were being reconfigured with the 'fault lines' between cultures replacing political and ideological boundaries as 'the flashpoints of crisis and blood shed'. It invoked an ominous image of the inevitability of conflict, the immutability of difference and a doomsday-like scenario of a third world war fought along the fault lines and fissures of culture.

Few of the current metaphors of world politics have been so closely associated with the work of one commentator. Huntington's *Foreign Affairs* article has become one of the most commented upon articles ever published in that journal. The article and subsequent book have been widely discussed, not only in academic circles, but also by the media and politicians. The imagery and language which it employs, of cultural clashes, fault lines and 'tectonic plates', have powerfully entered the vocabulary of contemporary political and academic commentary.

While widely contested, the thesis became something of a centrifugal point around which much debate regarding the role of culture and civilizations in world politics spun during the 1990s. It provides a powerful image of the emerging world order at a time in which culture has become an increasingly prominent dimension of world politics and international conflict. As we enter the twenty-first century, culture appears ever more prevalent as a force which shapes the interests and identities of political communities. However, adopting this particular image as a framework for interpreting and understanding the role of culture in world politics could have

135

startling and far-reaching implications for the type of policies pursued in the international arena. This makes it very important to look more carefully at this image in order to better understand its underlying assumptions and its broader implications.

The Metaphor

Huntington argued that the end of the Cold War signalled the collapse of ideological identification as a central feature of international relations. However, he also saw modernization and technology as forces that are weakening the role of the nation-state as a political community and enhancing the role of cultural and religious identity. These processes enhance the sense of identity between culturally similar groups and heighten the sense of difference from others. For Huntington, these developments are expressed in economic and political cohesion *within* civilizational groups and increased tension *between* civilizational groups. In essence, Huntington's thesis is premised on the belief that difference accentuated by proximity encourages conflict.

His concerns, however, go further than this to focus on the implication of this world order for the West and its role in world politics. In contrast to commentators who argued that the end of the Cold War meant the victory of the West as a model for human development towards which the rest of the world would converge, Huntington presents an image of an increasingly fragmented world. The West is seen as in decline and under threat both at home and abroad. Huntington's analysis suggests that, rather than acting as a universal model for development, the West should abandon its universalist pretensions which are false, immoral and dangerous. Instead it should focus on enhancing its cohesion and protecting its own interests while recognizing the realities of a multi-civilizational world, and restraining itself from undue interference in the affairs of other civilizations. In this context, it should be recognized that this metaphor not only describes an image of world politics, but also advocates particular approaches and policies.

Why has this particular metaphor of post-Cold War politics generated so much interest and debate? Its impact derives, in part, from the influence and respect which its author commands in both academic and political circles, particularly in the United States. Huntington is a prominent Harvard professor who has written widely on American and comparative politics, on strategic studies and on theories of modernization. His work has consistently reflected a concern with order and the institutions of governance. In addition to teaching and research, Huntington has been an adviser to government, serving as coordinator of security planning of the National

Security Council from 1977 to 1978. A less well-known author may not have received as much attention or evoked so much reaction.

The impact of this metaphor also derives from its radical and controversial reading of post-Cold War world politics. Huntington's thesis was an attempt to understand and explain this post-Cold War world, a world of tremendous change which challenged the explanatory powers of existing International Relations theory. On the surface, this metaphor demonstrates a desire of theorists to escape the rigid modes of thinking of the Cold War, a period characterized by state-centric and realist theory, in order to account for 'new' forces and actors in world politics, such as religious 'fundamentalism' and ethnic nationalism. However, this approach does not seek to escape grand theory itself. It posits an overarching theory aimed at reducing the rich and bewildering complexity of world politics to a clear and simple pattern. Its accessibility as a tool to understand a complex environment is one of the factors which have made this metaphor such an appealing lens through which to view world politics (Welch, 1997).

Huntington's pessimism reflects important currents in the contemporary intellectual and political environment. The early 1990s saw the emergence of a sense of disillusionment with the post-Cold War 'New World Order'. Conflicts had erupted throughout the former Soviet Union.[2] The collapse of Yugoslavia escalated into an increasingly cruel war in Bosnia from which the chilling term 'ethnic cleansing' emerged to rekindle memories of the worst forms of ethnic and racial intolerance. In India, the Ayodhya mosque was destroyed in December 1992. Western involvement in the Persian Gulf, which had epitomized the spirit of the New World Order during the Gulf War, had soured with the United States' bombing of Baghdad. At the 1993 Vienna Human Rights Conference, differences between Western and non-Western governments became more evident. Racial and ethnic identity were increasingly perceived as significant, with many of these disputes involving different ethnic communities. Racial tensions and violence became more prominent in Europe, particularly in Germany and France, and in the United States, which had been rocked by the 1992 Los Angeles riots.

A 'new pessimism' was becoming evident amongst certain intellectuals in the United States and Europe. In contrast to the confidence and triumphalism of Fukuyama's 'end of history' view of world politics, 'the clash' reflected a sense of insecurity stemming from the perception of new threats in a less stable multipolar world. These included instability in regional politics, the risks of proliferation and tensions arising from economic and social causes such as migration and resource depletion. Attention increasingly focused on the 'threat from the 'South' rather than the East (Mearsheimer, 1990b; Kaplan, 1994; Moynihan, 1993). There was also a sense of domestic instability. Within the United States, there was debate with regard to the impact of multiculturalism on the cohesion of American society and on the polarization of American values (Schlesinger, 1991; Hunter, 1991). The metaphor emerged from a context of domestic as much as international insecurity.

Key Assumptions

What, then, are the assumptions that underlie this metaphor? The first relates to the structure of world order. The metaphor, and the supporting argumentation, suggest that culture is becoming a central organizing principle of international relations, shifting the focus away from states as the foundation of international order. It does not suggest that states are no longer significant actors in world politics, but it does imply that they are becoming the agents of civilizational identity, with their interests increasingly defined along cultural lines.

The interest demonstrated in the role of civilizations in world politics by this perspective is not completely novel. It returns to the precedents provided by scholars such as Arnold Toynbee, Oswald Spengler and Quincy Wright, who all explored international affairs at the macrocosmic level. For both Spengler and Toynbee, civilizations were the most significant units in world history. In fact, differing assumptions about culture, and the nature of civilizations and their interaction, can be found deeply embedded in many works on world politics. These assumptions vary widely. For some, civilizations are multiple and diverse; for others, the concept of civilization is singular and universal, incorporating the whole of humanity in a project of progress and development. Some view civilizations as innately conflicting, others as converging. There are, then, a variety of ways in which the 'cultural world order', the nature and interaction of civilizations, can be perceived.

The perception of cultural world order conveyed by the 'clash of civilizations' is a pluralist one, comprising a number of coexisting civilizations.[3] These are seen as dynamic, in that they rise and fall and are subject to redefinition. This metaphor implies that whilst civilizations blend and overlap, the differences between civilizations are real, if not always sharply defined. Significantly, civilizations are seen as largely incommensurable; their capacity to understand each other is limited. It rejects any suggestion that humanity forms, or is converging towards, a single, universal civilization. Civilizations are perceived as having 'core states' which provide leadership, authority and discipline within their sphere of civilizational influence. They also 'mediate' in cross-civilizational disputes. This is reminiscent of the realist image of a world order based upon the management of great powers, structured around competition and the distribution of power.

The world order suggested by the 'clash of civilizations' is also profoundly shaped by the assumed nature of interaction between civilizations, that of conflict as the predominant form of relationship. Such disputes are seen as protracted, difficult to resolve and having a strong potential to escalate. Their protractedness appears to derive from the sense that these disputes are ancient and primordial. Their potential for escalation derives from the perception that states and peoples will increasingly rally to assist other 'kin countries', cultural brothers and sisters, when in distress. The image of 'torn countries', countries in which the elite seeks to manoeuvre the community into one civilization, but the popular culture remains entrenched in another, further promotes the sense of conflict in the context of civilizational heterogeneity. These images undoubtedly exercise a powerful appeal at a time when world politics is full of disputes which appear to reflect ancient cultural rivalries, such as that between India and Pakistan, with 'ethnic' cleansing in Europe and Asia, and debates which posit 'Asian' in contrast to 'Western' political values.

'The clash' metaphor implies that cooperation is more likely amongst peoples of a similar civilization. This has ramifications for political, military and economic policy. It suggests, for instance, that economic cooperation is most likely to succeed within rather than across civilizational communities. Consequently, the prospects for the European Union are considered better than those of the more culturally diverse ASEAN (Huntington, 1996, pp. 130–5). Therefore, regional integration is not perceived as representing a broader trend towards integration on a global basis. Rather than a building block of globalization, this image suggests regionalism is a reaction to globalizing trends, with societies resisting universalizing tendencies by strengthening their cultural identity within larger blocks.

This highlights a second body of interesting and contentious assumptions: that globalization and modernization do not necessarily lead to cultural homogenization or Westernization. The metaphor acknowledges the impact on world politics of the growth of contact between different societies, enhanced by developments in transport and communications. Peoples of the world are now more familiar with, and affected by, each other. However, this perspective contradicts the perception that increased interaction brings greater understanding and convergence of ideas across societies and cultures. Instead, it suggests that contact increases awareness of difference between civilizations and invigorates animosities.

Huntington argues that modern societies have no need to resemble one another any more than traditional societies have done. Although modern societies have commonalities, they remain culturally distinct. He goes further, suggesting that modernization can accentuate such differences through increasing contact; through the confidence generated by prosperity; and by creating the need for stronger local identities to respond to the social problems caused by modernization (Huntington, 1996, p. 78). This implies that, for Huntington, modernization does not necessarily mean Westernization. In fact, this suggests, to the contrary, that modernization enhances indigenization. Modernization contributes to dislocation and alienation from traditional community and structures. This leads to people seeking a renewed sense of identity in their own culture or religion, the basis for the revival of religions such as Islam and the Hindu faith as powerful social and political identities. In this context, the 'clash of civilizations' perspective suggests that modernization can stimulate a certain amount of resentment towards the West's power and dominance. Modernization also empowers non-Western cultures. Huntington argues that modernization may initially have encouraged non-Western people to adopt aspects of Western culture, but as societies have grown more powerful and wealthy, they have increasingly gained greater pride and confidence in their own culture. A similar argument has been put by key advocates in the Asian values debate, such as Kishore Mahbubani (1992, 1993) and Lee Kuan Yew (Zakaria, 1994). They argue that Asia's economic success in the late twentieth century was based on borrowing selectively from the West whilst retaining core social principles such as communitarian values, respect for authority and a strong work ethic.

Unlike more liberal commentators, Huntington firmly rejects the idea that the end of the Cold War will produce the universalization of liberal democracy. For him, this argument suffers from the 'single alternative fallacy' in failing to acknowledge the persistence of other secular and religious challenges to Western liberal democracy (Huntington 1993b, p. 191; 1996, p. 66). Similarly, he rejects the notion of an evolving international society. Instead, he treats the global level of interaction as involving an elite culture, the 'Davos Culture', rather than one which encompasses all humanity (Huntington 1996, pp. 67, 76). Therefore, the 'clash of civilizations' presents an image of world politics where the forces of modernization and globalization lead to fragmentation rather than integration.

A third set of key assumptions underlying the 'clash of civilizations' metaphor relates to the West. The metaphor portrays the West as a once-dominant civilization now under challenge. In proposing this metaphor, one of Huntington's central preoccupations is the position of the West in future world politics. For Huntington, 'the central axis of world politics in the future' is likely to be the conflict between 'the West and the Rest' (1993a, p. 41), the West being seen as comprising the United States and Western Europe. Although it is principally a Judaeo-Christian community, it excludes Orthodox Christian societies, including Greece, which is commonly viewed as the political and philosophical font of the modern West! The West suggested in this image is a powerful community which has dominated the institutions and regimes of modern international relations. However, for Huntington, the West's decline is illustrated by the retreat of colonialism and a faltering US hegemony in the post-Cold War world. Internally, economic and social decline are manifested in falling productivity, growing crime rates and social problems such as the growth in one-parent families and drug abuse (Huntington, 1996, pp. 82, 304).

As noted above, the 'clash of civilizations' metaphor reflects contemporary concerns with the instability of world politics in the 1990s. It focuses on specific challenges to Western security and stability, both external and internal. Externally, the focus falls upon the perceived challenges arising from resurgent Islamic and Confucian societies. The Islamic challenge is portrayed as essentially anti-modern. Its hostility to the West is conceived of as embedded in ancient cultural and religious antipathy aggravated by envy of Western success, the legacy of imperialism and the social dynamics of contemporary Islamic societies. Islam is also portrayed as an innately unstable society which lacks a core state, a type of civilizational 'loose cannon' (Huntington, 1996, pp. 174–8, 248–52). However, the second source of external challenge that the West is perceived as facing is the more substantial one: the growth and assertiveness of East Asia. In fact, critics such as Chandra Muzaffar (1994) argue that the 'clash of civilizations' derives from the West's efforts to contain this challenge. For Mahbubani (1993), the thesis is symptomatic of the West's failure to deal with the shift in the balance of power away from the West and towards the peoples of the developing world. Written prior to the 1997/98 East Asian financial crisis, Huntington's thesis suggested that Western dominance is challenged by East Asian economic dynamism and by the growing stature of China as a military and economic force. Huntington views this strength as enhancing the cultural assertiveness of these societies, manifested, for instance, in the criticisms of Western society emanating from Southeast Asia in the early 1990s (Huntington, 1996, pp. 103–9, 225). The East Asian challenge, therefore, is cultural, as well as economic and strategic. Furthermore, it is not anti-modern, but presents an alternative model of modernization. In both cases, the 'clash of civilizations' blends old with new rivalries, blending the ancient fear of 'holy war' and the 'yellow peril' into a modern 'Confucian Islamic conspiracy'.

'The clash' also suggests that challenges to civilizational cohesion can emerge internally. Concerns with regard to immigration relate perceptions of external challenge to internal challenges to the West. The fear is one of Western societies becoming swamped by peoples of other cultures. Huntington suggests this could lead to Western society becoming divided. His concern is not with immigration *per se*, a practice that was fundamental to the creation and building of the United States. It is rather with the cultural heterogeneity produced by the perceived non-assimilation of contemporary migrants into the norms and institutions of Western societies. In the US context in particular, the fear is that multiculturalism is undermining the homogeneity of Western society. Huntington fears the norms and values upon which Western society is built; norms such as individualism, equality and democracy, are under threat from new principles such as minority rights (Huntington, 1996, pp. 4–6). Similarly, James Kurth (1994) articulated concerns that intellectual movements, such as postmodernism, feminism, and multiculturalism are deconstructing Western civilization and the Enlightenment ideas on which it is based.

These concerns highlight the importance of norms and values to conceptualizations of civilizational identities. While territory, ethnicity or even religion are often seen as providing the objective features of civilizations, norms and institutions provide substance and meaning to these objective boundaries. This is also the case in the 'clash of civilizations' approach. For instance, for Huntington, it is norms and values which define but also distinguish the West, making it unique rather than universal. Consequently he argues that others do not value the norms such as individualism and the rule of law most valued by the West.

The significant twist which this approach introduces to the discussion of the importance of norms to civilizational identity is the argument that the projection of norms onto other societies provokes conflict rather than cultural convergence. This provides a distinctive reading of the impact of Western values. The spread of Western values and institutions such as democracy has been a superficial process, it is argued, predicated on the strength of the West as a military and economic power; not on the innate relevance of these values to all societies. The promotion of these norms as universal simply masks the underlying promotion of Western interests. Curiously, this is an argument not uncommon in postcolonial and some postmodern perspectives. Huntington's analysis led him to conclude in 1996 that the promotion of Western norms and values as universal was false, immoral and dangerous. It was false, because Western values are not universal. It was immoral since values could only be effectively spread through the projection of force, suggesting some form of imperialism. It was dangerous since it posed the risk of counter-reaction. In contrast, the 'clash of civilizations' thesis suggested civilizations should pursue policies of consolidation at home, and non-interference with other civilizations abroad. For the West, this implied the consolidation of the Atlantic alliance, united fundamentally by common ideas, values and histories, and respect for the 'sphere of influence' of other civilizations.[4]

Critique

The image of world politics which the 'clash of civilizations' metaphor presents can be criticized from a number of perspectives. The first is that it over-rates the influence of culture as a force shaping world politics. For many analysts, states remain the principal actors in world politics, and it is states that manipulate culture rather than themselves acting as culture's agent (see, for instance, Ajami, 1993; Walt, 1997; Welch, 1997). Such a conception continues to see relations and conflicts between states as the principal focus of world politics. The 'clash of civilizations' has also been criticised for overemphasizing the degree of cohesion within civilizational groups. This neglects the prevalence and violence of intra-civilizational conflict as demonstrated, for instance, by the Rwandan conflict of 1994. This also raises questions about the precise definition of civilizations. As Welch (1997) points out, in Huntington's work, the definition of what constitutes a civilization is somewhat ambiguous. It is unclear whether the criteria for civilizations are primarily linguistic, historical or religious. At times, this makes it difficult to judge whether conflicts should be seen as inter or intra-civilizational. For instance, should the ongoing conflict in Sudan be regarded as an instance of inter-civilizational conflict, or intra-civilizational conflict between peoples of different faiths?

A second common theme of critique is that the image of world politics presented in this metaphor is too determinist. In focusing on civilizational difference as the source of conflict or cooperation, it masks political, social and economic issues which may also be the source of tension (Rubinstein and Crocker, 1994; O'Hagan, 1995; Groves, 1998). For instance, the sectarian violence which erupted in the Indonesian province of Ambon in 1998–99 can be viewed as revealing the incompatibility of Christian and Muslim communities living in close proximity without the 'firm hand' of an authoritarian political structure to suppress innate civilizational animosity. However, this reading of the situation may mask the problems created by policies such as transmigration and the uneven distribution of wealth in the province. It may understate the significance of the broader political context which fuelled these tensions. Similarly, in 1998, the rivalry between India and Pakistan intensified with both states testing nuclear weapons. This could be viewed as an escalation of inter-civilizational tension, suggested, for instance, in the media's depiction of Pakistan's nuclear capacity as 'the Islamic bomb'. However, as Denise Groves points out, focusing on these events as primarily instances of civilizational conflict masks the role of other contributory factors. These include severe domestic socioeconomic pressures on both governments, perceptions of national security, and the quest for international status which joining the 'nuclear club' is perceived to bring. 'The real issue', argues Groves, 'are the Haves versus the Have nots': culture is merely a side-show (1998).

Similarly it could be argued that conflicts such as those which have riven Serbia, Bosnia and Yugoslavia in the 1990s have been perceived and depicted as perpetuating ancient tensions between neighbouring civilizations, but entail at their heart contemporary conflicts over resources and influence. In his 1993 article, Huntington used the conflict in the former Yugoslavia and the Gulf War as instances of inter-civilizational conflict in which 'kin–country rallying' was evident (Huntington, 1993a). Huntington noted the success of Saddam Hussein in appealing to Pan-Islamic solidarity, amongst Arab elites and publics, and Islamic fundamentalists during the Gulf War. He also noted the declining active support of the Arab governments for continuing pressure on Iraq in 1992 and 1993. With regard to the Yugoslavian conflict, which is described as falling along the ancient fault lines between Western, Orthodox and Islamic civilizations in Europe, Huntington argued that leading actors in Western civilizations rallied behind their co-religionists along kin–country lines.

Huntington's analysis of both conflicts was roundly criticized by commentators as largely swallowing the rhetoric of the conflicts which has cloaked the material and power interests of the main protagonists. The Iraqi regime was one of the most secular in the region; it had fought a ten-year war against the revolutionary Islamic Iranian state. One of the staunchest allies of the anti-Iraq coalition was one of the most orthodox Islamic regimes in the region, Saudi Arabia. Huntington's analysis of the position of Arab governments did not acknowledge factors such as the potential impact of the total defeat of Iraq on the regional balance of power (Ajami, 1993; Kirkpatrick, 1993; Salamé, 1993).

Huntington was similarly criticized for his interpretation of the breakup of Yugoslavia and the war in Bosnia as primarily instances of inter-civilizational conflict. For many, these disputes are based on modern rather than medieval sources of conflict (Banac, 1993–94; Job, 1993; Pfaff, 1993b). As Pfaff has argued, the differences between the peoples of the Balkans are largely historical rather than racial or primordial. The same might be said of the Kosovo crisis in the 1990s which entails both significant historical dimensions but was also spurred by competition for land, resources and status. However, the selective deployment of history in the context of escalating tension permits this conflict to be read as ancient, primordial and inter-civilizational.

There is a serious danger of misreading these conflicts if they are simply seen as a continuation of ancient conflicts. Focusing on culture as the essential source of conflict can inhibit dispute resolution and even exacerbate tensions further. If conflicts over economic or political issues are interpreted as collisions of civilizations based on primordial differences, they are transferred from the realm of the negotiable and the solvable into that of perpetual unsolvable conflict (Pfaff, 1993b). Furthermore, the focus on the irreconcilability of civilizations, rather than on their techniques for coexistence, can become a self-fulfilling prophecy. The rhetoric of the inability of peoples who see themselves as culturally distinct to peacefully coexist, can generate and legitimate policies, such as 'ethnic cleansing' which can decimate previously heterogeneous communities. One of the dangers of the 'clash of civilizations' as a metaphor is that it can be used to legitimate policies such as ethnic cleansing.

However, the appeals made to the rhetoric of civilizational identity by leaders such as Saddam Hussein or Slobodan Milosevic are very significant. Through these appeals, they seek to escalate conflict to a different level, to present cultural difference as the primary source of conflict in a bid to win broader support. This indicates the power and influence of civilizational identity.

Does Culture Matter?

Such criticisms of the weakness of cultural and civilizational approaches to understanding international relations are important and significant. However, they do not explain why the language of civilizational identity and cultural difference has emerged; and why it is so prominent in contemporary world politics. As Michael Mazarr (1996) has observed, instead of asking 'does culture matter?' perhaps we should be asking 'how does culture matter?' It must be acknowledged that the 'clash of civilizations' metaphor has brought to the fore the important if often neglected analysis of the role of culture and identity in world politics. Once we accept that civilizational and cultural identity does matter in world politics, we move to a new and deeper level of critique of *how* civilizational identity and interaction are represented through this metaphor.

The 'clash of civilizations' reintroduces the concept of civilizational interaction into considerations of world politics. However, its treatment of civilizations is reductionist, portraying them as rigid 'hermetically sealed' and largely incommensurable communities. It underrates the extent and significance of tension within cultures. For instance, Huntington's treatment of Islam has been widely criticized as underrating divisions and tension between Muslim societies, and exaggerating the influence of Islamisist elements in these societies (Camroux, 1996; Maswood, 1994; Muzaffar, 1994).

A second key problem with the treatment of civilizational interaction in this metaphor is its focus on conflict and its neglect of cooperation. This focus on conflict ignores the 'creative constructive interaction and engagement between civilizations' which, as Muzaffar observes, is a more constant feature than conflict. There are other agents of civilizational encounters in addition to warring soldiers. These include, for instance, businesspeople, scholars, tourists and journalists. There have even been constructive and cooperative dimensions to relations between the West and Islam. Islam provided the foundations for the growth of mathematics, the sciences, architecture and agriculture in medieval Europe (Bozeman, 1960; Puchala, 1997;

Muzaffar, 1994). The impact of the interaction of different cultures and civilizations through such agencies as trade or the exchange of ideas may be gradual and occur over a long period of time, but they are surely as significant as bloody conflict.

The focus which this metaphor places on conflict at the expense of cooperation parallels its focus on difference at the expense of commonality between civilizations. There is little space in this perspective for exploring points of commonality which link groups and societies across civilizational boundaries. Nor does it answer the question of why civilizational identity becomes the principal form of identity at certain points in time, superseding other sites of identity or interests, such as class, corporate identity or gender.

Finally there is a sense conveyed in this metaphor that culture is something which has only become relevant in recent years as non-Western societies have become sufficiently powerful to become actors in, rather than objects of, world politics (Huntington, 1993a). This implies that the politics of non-Western societies are only relevant to the extent that they impinge upon the West. It also neglects the degree to which the institutions and study of international relations are embedded in Western culture. Therefore, whilst this approach encourages the serious consideration of culture as a factor in international relations, it does so in a way that limits exploration of the complexity of culture as an influence.

Similarly, this metaphor of world politics acknowledges the significance of cultural identity as a factor in world politics. However, it links the politics of such identity primarily with the establishment of irreconcilable differences and with threat. In the 'clash of civilizations', the outsider is always a potential enemy threatening the strength and cohesion of the civilization. Of course, the sense of threat, in itself, provides a sense of cohesion within (Bigo, 1994). Huntington himself has remarked: 'How will we know who we are if we don't know who we are against?' (Huntington, 1993c, p. 37). Whilst the politics of differentiation are critical to the formation and maintenance of identity, this raises the question of whether 'the other' must always be seen as threatening. Such an approach, in and of itself, inspires a degree of hostility and precludes the possibility of cooperation.

Huntington's focus on conflict emanates from his conception of cultural world order. As noted above, this is one of a plurality of incommensurable civilizations. It is widely contested, particularly by liberal critics whose image of world order conveys a much stronger sense of the convergence of societies towards a universal, modern civilization. For instance, in his commentary on 'The Clash of Civilizations?' Robert Bartley is decidedly more optimistic than Huntington with regard to the impact of globalization and increased interaction. He sees communications, for instance, as a powerful force which reduces the power of oppressive governments and encourages world integration along a Western, liberal model. Bartley sees a profound linkage between the forces of economic development and the emergence of democracy and human rights (Bartley, 1993, p. 17). However, Bartley's analysis does not effectively explain the resurgence of 'civilizational' conflict in contemporary world politics. For some liberals, like Francis Fukuyama (1992) or Michael Mazarr, these conflicts are a passing phase in modernizing societies. Mazarr treats cultural clashes as symptoms of 'transitional instability' as societies move from the industrial to the information age. If properly managed, these instabilities will give way to an era in which 'the impact of unique cultures in world affairs subside' (Mazarr, 1996, p. 178). Others treat 'civilizational conflict' as symptomatic of discord caused by the worldwide diffusion of industrial technology. The current discord is the product of systematic differences between developed and developing societies (Sato, 1997). These explanations privilege the material, socioeconomic dynamics of societies over the cultural. However, they *also* implicitly entail significant assumptions about the nature of cultural world order, assumptions that are in marked contrast to those found in the 'clash of civilizations'. These assume a 'progressive' and convergent cultural world order in contrast to Huntington's fragmented one.

A central point of contention within the debate surrounding the 'clash of civilizations' metaphor is whether globalization or fragmentation is the dominant force in future world politics. Related to this is the question of the role of the West in any future world order. Is the West a model of universal civilization or simply one of many civilizations, one in decline in an increasingly fractious cultural world order? Robert Cox sees the forces of fragmentation and globalization as not mutually exclusive but involved in a dialectical relationship. For Cox, the alienation caused by globalization is expressed in the resurgence of identity politics, and particularly by the affirmation of national and class identities. For Cox, '[g]lobalization is countered by the affirmation of civilization in this dialectic of homogenization and diversification'. For Cox, this is not a temporary process. The management of relations between coexisting civilizations will become an increasingly significant dimension of world politics in the twenty-first century (Cox, 1998, p. 2).

How does Cox's perspective contrast to that of the 'clash of civilizations'? Cox defines civilizations as having two key dimensions: the material and the inter-subjective. As noted above, the 'clash of civilizations' also recognizes the importance of the intersubjective dimension of civilizations. As the material boundaries of civilizations become increasingly mingled in the contemporary world, Cox suggests that conceptualizing civilizations as analogous to territorial communities becomes less relevant. The concept of territorial 'fault lines', so prominent in the 'clash of civilizations' metaphor, becomes increasingly problematic. The 'clash of civilizations' perspective advocates the containment of these processes of intermingling through policies which encourage homogenization and enhanced cohesion. This suggests some level of segregation which Cox's analysis implies is becoming less and less feasible. In contrast, Cox's analysis accentuates the need for mutual comprehension and dialogue between civilizational identities as paramount for world order.[5]

Implications

What then are the implications of adopting the 'clash of civilizations' as a metaphor for world politics? One of the underlying aims of Huntington's original thesis was to challenge the optimism of post-Cold War Western liberalism, to undermine what he called its 'illusion of harmony', and to dispel its faith in Western universalism. Huntington appeared to want to shake the West, and the US in particular, out of the confident complacency that it had defeated its major threats. This had led to what Huntington and others saw as inappropriate policies such as arms control, a reduction in military preparedness and growing divisions between Europe and the US on foreign policy issues towards non-Western states such as China. Huntington warned Europe and the US that they must 'hang together or hang separately' (1996, p. 321). He advocated that current policy trends be reversed, suggesting instead universalism at home and multiculturalism abroad. Huntington's image of world politics appeared to seek to stimulate Western cohesion by conjuring up new monolithic and essentialized enemies to replace the old, the terror of the East with the threat from the South combined with the 'Yellow Peril'! (Bigo, 1994; O'Hagan, 1995).

The metaphor also has significant implications for domestic politics by legitimizing and even encouraging the politics of homogenization. Homogenization encourages the assimilation and promotion of clearly identified and authorized interpretations of cultures. Yet cultures are often diverse and contested. There is a danger that such policies could feed increasingly static and monolithic images of cultures, which could be both reductionist and exclusionary (Lawson, 1996). This metaphor also has major implications for our reading and understanding of world politics more broadly. It could further exacerbate existing tensions and stimulate a new security dilemma based on perceptions of likely civilizational interaction. Expectations of cross-cultural cooperation are not eliminated in this metaphor, but they are substantially weakened. It suggests a system in which order is maintained through an ethos of non-intervention which substantially undermines the concept of an evolving cosmopolitan framework, replacing this with an ethos of cultural relativism.

Huntington's discussion of this metaphor in relation to the West suggests that this civilization needs to consolidate its own identity and prepare to defend this in an anarchical world of inter-civilizational power politics, rather than seeing itself engaged in processes of progress or cultural convergence through globalization. This entails acknowledging the diminution of Western power in the face of the resurgence of non-Western civilizations. How the West continues to promote its own interests and project power, yet maintain a policy of non-intervention is unclear, but it does imply a policy of constructive interaction, particularly amongst the core states of particular civilizations. This prescription sounds strangely reminiscent of a 'civilizational concert' or balance of power. Indeed, although Huntington argues that his thesis offers a new paradigm for understanding world order, this metaphor has a familiar ring of a civilizational 'war of all against all'. In this 'new' paradigm, the significant units of the international system may be civilizations rather than states, but the structure of the international system continues to be defined primarily by conflict between self-regarding units. This world view is informed by the concept of power politics leading to a vision of the world dominated by conflict, and the assumption that power continues to be contested in an anarchical environment. In effect, this metaphor seeks to capture the concept of inter-civilizational relations for the realist paradigm. This could well deprive academic International Relations of the richer insights which the study of civilizational interaction and cultural world order could bring to the discipline.

CHAPTER 11

A 'World of Tribes'?

Gavin Mount[1]

Many of the most disturbing images of the last decade of the twentieth century depicted horrific episodes of 'ethnic cleansing' and protracted ethnic or communal conflicts. In fact, post-Cold War world politics seems to have been 'engulfed in convulsive fits of ethnic insecurity, violence and genocide' (Lake and Rothchild, 1996, p. 41). These events have generated extensive intellectual debate among policy makers, academics and other commentators. In particular these debates have revealed two sets of assumptions about the underlying causes of ethnic antagonisms. Some argue that these conflicts represent a revival of premodern or 'tribal' identities, whilst others argue that they are part of a late-modern 'fragmentary' reaction against homogenizing tendencies of globalization.

Some of the most disturbing images of the last decade of the twentieth century portray post-Cold War ethnic conflicts as a backward or regressive phenomenon. For example, Francis Fukuyama argued that ethnic and nationalist violence were caused by irrational '*impulses* incompletely played out, even in parts of the post-historical world' (1989, p. 18; my italics). Similarly, Samuel Huntington (1993) argued that contemporary ethnic conflicts were most likely to occur in 'torn countries' divided by old civilizational 'fault lines'.[2] A prevalent view in the early 1990s was that the end of the Cold War 'released' suppressed ancient ethnic hatreds that had been 'frozen for almost two generations in the ice of the Cold War' (Bernstein, 1993, p. 12).

In the ethnic studies literature, 'primordialist' understandings of ethnic identity – as fixed pre-given 'traits' – have been widely discredited (see Comaroff, 1996). More importantly, ethnic conflict specialists challenged the historical determinism of these 'raised lid' or 'gene out of the bottle' images and derided International Relations scholars for overdrawing the causal relationship between the end of the Cold War and the apparent 'resurgence of nationalism' as 'shallow and misleading' (see Smith, 1995, p. vii; Gurr,

1994).[3] At the same time, Diamond and Plattner seem justified when they observe that these struggles have 'unquestionably gained new *salience* with the decline and fall of European communism' (1994, p. 1; my italics).

An alternative view portrays ethnic conflicts as the product of modern or even postmodern anxiety. Alberto Melucci argues that these struggles are part of a late-modern response to 'new forms of exploitation' such as globalization. According to this view, ethnopolitical struggles are part of a wider attempt to negotiate 'personal and collective identity in highly complex societies' (1996, p. 368). Stjepan Mestrovic goes even further in suggesting that 'balkanization', and the reassertion of traditional cultures in modern societies, is a 'genuinely postmodern phenomenon, if one understands postmodernism to be a rebellion against the grand narratives of the Enlightenment' (1994, p. 176).

Perhaps the most common euphemism used to characterize the current widespread phenomenon of ethnic conflict is 'fragmentation'. Just as the idea of 'globalization' has emerged as one of the main ordering principles that best explains the 'transition of human society into the third millennium' (Waters, 1995, p. 1), the idea of 'fragmentation', broadly conceived as a worldwide pattern of disintegrative tendencies, has emerged as a profoundly unsettling 'metaphor of our time' (Ahmed, 1995). In fact, one of the more baffling paradoxes preoccupying International Relations scholars in the contemporary period is the tension created by an 'intense trend toward political fragmentation within the context of globalizing economy' (Holsti, 1993, p. 407; also Clark, 1997). More specifically, the core issues at stake in ethnic struggles concerned with preserving traditional ways of life, anxiety over an attachment to place and the erosion of cultural identity have a much wider resonance in contemporary debates about globalization, democracy and governance (see Held, 1995).

Terms such as 'tribalism' or 'barbarism' are rarely explicitly referred to as the dynamic force that underscores late-modern accounts of fragmentation. But the absence of a discernible *theory* of tribalism in contemporary International Relations thought belies the existence of a more general *discourse* of tribalism that continues to pervade International Relations theory and practice. For example, images of tribalism have always served as relational categories which orientate and reify civilizational imagery.

This chapter, arranged in four sections, will show how late-modern images of a 'fragmenting world' are informed by a much older and deeply embedded discourse of tribalism. The first section considers the prominent image of 'the coming anarchy' and shows how ethnic conflicts have become salient concerns in popular commentaries on international affairs. The second section shows how certain metaphorical devices are deployed in the rhetoric of political elites to embellish the image of a 'fragmenting world'. The third section traces the vacillating discourse of tribalism in International Relations thought as a way of situating the contemporary imagery of fragmentation. The fourth section considers the normative and policy issues associated with a 'multicultural world'. The chapter concludes with some reflections upon other manifestations of 'tribalism' at the beginning of the twenty-first century. Whilst most references to tribal peoples or tribal behaviour tend to be negative or pessimistic, there have always been more romantic and nostalgic images. Both negative and positive images of tribalism have a contemporary resonance.

A Coming Anarchy?

One of the most famous expositions on the significance of post-Cold War ethnic conflict was written by the journalist, Robert Kaplan, in his 1994 essay, 'The Coming Anarchy'. This essay has been widely influential, especially among policy makers. For example, it was considered important enough to be faxed to every US embassy in the world and was reputably so successful in 'rattling' United Nations officials that a confidential meeting was called to discuss its implications (see Richards, 1996, p. xiv).

Kaplan argued that the explosive combination of environmental degradation, poverty, crime, the collapse of the modern nation-state, and the transformation of war were creating the conditions for a coming upheaval which had the capacity for 'destroying the social fabric of our planet' (1994, p. 44). His survey begins with a description of the restless 'hordes' of young men that he encountered in six cities of West Africa. They behaved like 'loose molecules in a very unstable social fluid, a fluid that was clearly on the verge of igniting'. Kaplan argues that the collapse of order in West Africa serves as a preview, or even 'the symbol', of a worldwide anarchy 'that will soon confront our civilization' (1994, p. 46).

> Africa may be as relevant to the future character of world politics as the Balkans were a hundred years ago prior to the two Balkan wars and the First World War. Then the threat was the collapse of empires and the birth of nations based solely on tribe. Now the threat is more elemental: nature unchecked... Africa suggests what war, borders and ethnic politics will be like a few decades hence. (1994, p. 54)

Much of Kaplan's focus is on the link between societal collapse and environmental scarcity. This pressure is compounded by three other factors: cultural and racial clash, the transformation of war and geographic destiny. But for each of these *late-modern* concerns he recommends looking back to *pre-modern* epochs and drawing upon the insights of early modern philosophers. In particular, he draws upon the nineteenth-century writings of

Thomas Malthus to understand the significance of environmental pressures in the twenty-first century. Likewise, he agrees with Van Creveld (1991) who tells us to look back to a time immediately prior to the birth of modernism to understand the future of war. Van Creveld argued that future wars 'will have more in common with the struggles of primitive tribes than with large-scale conventional war' (cited in Kaplan, 1994, p. 73). Kaplan's arguments about 'geographic destiny' led him to conclude that world politics will become increasingly bifurcated. 'Part of the globe is inhabited by Hegel's and Fukuyama's Last Man, healthy, well fed, and pampered by technology. The other, larger, part is inhabited Hobbes' First Man, condemned to a life that is "poor, nasty, brutish, and short" ' (1994, p. 60).

As we shall see, Kaplan's technique of infusing his discussion on the late-modern characteristics of fragmentation with early-modern (or ancient) understandings of barbarism is indicative of a much more pervasive tendency in commentaries on the significance of ethnic conflict in contemporary world politics.

A Fragmenting World Order?

The term 'fragmentation' is used to describe a collapse of order at various levels: national, regional or global. Political and social life within 'fragmented', 'failed' or 'weak' states is seen to have deteriorated into a 'Hobbesian universe' (Brown (ed.), 1993). When legitimate bureaucratic institutions collapse, the population is thought to be caught up in a 'security dilemma' (Snyder, 1993). As a regional phenomenon, the image of fragmentation or 'balkanization' refers to a crisis that spreads from one country to another as violence and population flows 'spill over' into neighbouring countries. As a global force, fragmentation is seen to threaten international security because it contributes to the international flow of refugees, small arms proliferation, environmental devastation and terrorism (Brown, (ed.), 1993). At a normative level, it undermines legal doctrines of sovereignty and is a principal source of gross violation of universal human rights (Ryan, 1990).

Frequently, the spectre of fragmentation is described in highly alarmist or even apocalyptic language. For example, Premdas (1991, p. 10) warned of, 'ethnically ignited strifes becoming contagious and uncontrollable ... threatening world stability and mankind's future'. Several metaphorical devices are used to highlight the perception that these crises are inevitable, spreading and chaotic. In particular, ethnic conflicts are characterized as ancient, natural and savage.

Ancient animosities

The view that ethnic conflicts are the consequence of primordial or ancient hatreds reflects a core assumption in modernist thought that *'[p]rogress, science and rationality'* characterize the modern West; and *'tradition, tribe and religion* represent the outmoded and obsolete past' (Ahmed, 1995, p. 6 my italics). It also makes struggles over ethnic identity appear predetermined and intractable.

The most virulent exponents of this view are political elites within ethnic conflict situations who 'play the communal card' (Human Rights Watch 1995) to make conflict between ethnic groups appear destined, natural or inevitable. In the case of the Yugoslav crisis, for example, a highly selective and deterministic view of the past was used to rationalize the view that the conflict between ethnic groups was inevitable and that extreme measures were necessary. Noel Malcolm (1994, p. xix) noted that 'ethnic' leaders such as Milosevic and Tujdman propagated the myth that, 'what they and their gunmen were doing was done not by them but by impersonal and inevitable historical forces beyond anyone's control'.

But many Western leaders, journalists and academics have also resorted to historically deterministic views by assuming that contemporary struggles are the perpetuation of ancient animosities. For example, former British Prime Minister John Major represented the conflict in former Yugoslavia in terms of the reappearance of entrenched 'ancient hatreds' (cited in Malcolm, 1994, p. xx). Similarly, former US Secretary of State Warren Christopher commented:

> Yugoslavia raised the lid on the cauldron of ancient ethnic hatreds. This is the land where at least three religions and a half-dozen ethnic groups have vied across the centuries. It was the birthplace of World War I. It has long been a cradle of European conflict, and it remains so today. (Christopher, *New York Times* 7 February 1993, p. 81)

The characterization of ethnic conflict as a continuation of ancient animosities is a discourse of disempowerment that consigns two or more ethnic groups to a condition of perpetual struggle.

Natural disasters and epidemics

A second metaphorical device employed to make ethnic conflicts appear beyond human instrumentality is to either characterize the protagonists as sub-human or describe the conflicts more generally as being like natural disasters, epidemics or paranormal phenomena. Both rhetorical strategies dehumanize the participants and make the conflicts seem both more unpredictable and contagious.

The earliest references to *ethnos* in ancient Greek writings referred to a threatening mobile and undifferentiated mass, or swarm of animals (see Homer, 1951, Part 2, p. 87). But the most sustained and devastating example of this rhetorical strategy has been perfected over 500 years of European colonialism. For example, nineteenth century social Darwinists used the science of eugenics to legitimize evolutionary arguments by showing how cranial features of the 'black' races were comparable to 'apes' (see Todorov, 1993).

Once again the technique of dehumanization is a favoured image deployed by elites in ethnic conflict situations. It is especially common in xenophobic discourses that cultivate a sense of fear of being swamped or flooded by aliens. Leo Kuper (1981) argues that dehumanization is a universal characteristic that precedes all incidences of genocide. Invariably these analogies refer to animals that are scavengers, parasites or vermin.[4] The more that target minorities are portrayed as 'dirty' or 'parasitic', the easier it is to rationalise a hygienic policy of 'cleansing'.

In the post-Holocaust world international statespeople rarely describe the participants in ethnic conflicts as animal-like. However, they frequently depict the conflicts themselves as being like 'natural' phenomena. These comparisons have a similar effect of obscuring human agency and making the violence seem predetermined. A particularly common image in the post-Cold War period has been that of a 'cauldron of hot liquid which boils over when the lid is removed' (Roberts, 1995, p. 395). This image corresponds with the prevailing view that ethnic conflicts are a symptom of structural collapse or imperial breakup that unleash suppressed ethnic hatreds. Fire is another common naturalist image. As Christopher warned, 'If something isn't done to quell the fires of nationalism burning out of control ... we'll have 5,000 countries rather than the hundred plus we now have' (Christopher, *New York Times* 7 February 1993, p. 1).

Another prevailing metaphor of natural phenomena is that of the 'contagious' disease or epidemic. For example, in a speech before the French National Assembly in 1994, US President Clinton warned that ethnonationalism was a 'cancerous prejudice, eating away at states and leaving their people addicted to the political painkillers of violence and demagoguery' (cited in Kegley and Wittkopf, 1995, p. 458). Similarly, former UN Secretary-General Boutros-Boutros Ghali characterized the spread of ethnic conflicts as follows:

> Just as biological disease spreads through a body, and as an epidemic spreads geographically, so also a political disease can spread through the world. When one State is endangered by ethnic conflict, others will be endangered as well. (cited in Roberts, 1995, p. 394)

When ethnic conflicts are not being equated with natural disasters, they are sometimes portrayed as paranormal or supernatural phenomena. A contemporary example of this sort of analogy was made by former Soviet President Mikhail Gorbachev who alerted the world to how the 'demons of nationalism were coming alive and...putting the stability of the international system to the test' (cited in Kegley and Wittkopf, 1995, p. 445).

Savage war

A third set of metaphorical techniques that dehumanize ethnic conflicts is to describe them as distinctively irrational and savage. The discourse of tribalism has always incorporated a belief that barbarians or tribes are more prone to resolve disputes through violence and warfare. For example, Auguste Comte, the father of modern sociology, noted that savages were like large children who got bored easily and 'found escape from boredom in warfare' (cited in Laffey, 1993, p. 49).

Sometimes ethnic elites deploy the image of savage tribalism as a deliberate attempt to mask the culpability and rational agency of their governments. For example, a Human Rights Watch report argued that those authorities that orchestrated the genocide in Rwanda underlined the supposedly 'tribal' nature of the killings to make the violence appear the result of 'spontaneous, uncontrollable rage'. The report argued that this emphasis was explicitly designed to manipulate Western observers and to take advantage of the 'susceptibility of foreigners to explanations of "ancient tribal hatreds" among Africans' (Human Rights Watch, 1995, p. 6).

Again, Western political leaders in post-Cold War international politics have characterized contemporary ethnic conflicts as incidences of savagery and barbarism. Sometimes these references are subtle. For example, the moral purpose of former US President Bush's epochal vision of a 'New World Order' was to ensure that the conduct of nations would be governed by 'the rule of law', not 'the law of the jungle'. He envisaged a world where the international community would be united in sending belligerent tyrants back to the 'dark ages where they belong' (Bush, 1991). At other times the language is more overt. Clinton described Bosnia as 'a tribal feud no outsider could hope to settle' (cited in Hirsch, 1995, p. 9). More recently, a Portuguese diplomatic envoy recently declared: 'The situation in East Timor is barbaric, the fundamentals of human civilization are at stake' (Gomez, 1999).

In particular, ethnopolitical 'struggles' are distinguished from inter-state 'war' through the use of different language to describe these scenarios. For example, in the Falklands and Gulf Wars, or for that matter the NATO intervention in Kosovo, acts of killing were described as 'surgical' strikes, 'smart' bombs, 'collateral' damage and 'friendly' fire. This language creates the impression that the violence is somehow more 'sanitised' (Cohn, 1990; Scarry, 1985). In fact, the United States government has legislated against the use of the words 'killing' or 'murder' in official reports to describe human rights abuses in *allied* countries. Instead the phrase used is 'unlawful or arbitrary deprivation of life' (see *New York Times* 15 February 1984).

In contrast, ethnic conflicts are frequently characterized as passionate, mad and irrational. The language of violence also appears to be differentiated as more or less savage depending upon its spatial proximity. Whereas high-technology modern warfare is becoming increasingly detached and depersonalized (Cohen, 1996), ethnic wars pitch neighbours against each other in a condition of 'visceral hatred' (*Economist* 21 December 1991, p. 45 and Rapaport, 1996). The contemporary discourse of savagery tends to be attributed to incidences of face-to-face or proximal violence.

Finally, the policy of 'ethnic cleansing' has emerged as a synonym for contemporary forms of genocide. Ever since Lemkin (1944) coined the term, genocide has been seen as the ultimate act of barbarism. As Omer Bartov puts it: 'We see genocide as a throwback to another, premodern, barbarous past, a perversion, an error, an accident' (1996, p. 4). But the distinction between 'genocide' and other acts of killing, such as 'war', can be misleading. There is an obvious temptation to distance one from the other as war has traditionally been seen as a legitimate 'institution' of international society (Bull, 1977). War has also been associated with civilization inasmuch as it has historically been a precursor for state formation and served as the ultimate disincentive to tyranny and conquest. Today, as wars between democracies have supposedly become obsolete, 'humanitarian wars' are portrayed as civilizational imperatives. Clearly, acts of genocide are not understood to have the same civilizing qualities.

However, as any historical study of violence will attest, genocide has long been acknowledged not only as 'a structural and systematic destruction of innocent people by a state bureaucratic apparatus' (Horowitz, 1976), but as a distinctively 'modern' form of violence. The British invented the modern 'concentration camp' during the Boer War and the allies perfected the strategy of 'total war', involving pattern bombing of civilian populations in factories in German cities such as Hamburg and Dresden. Many argue that the acts of total annihilation in Hiroshima and Nagasaki should be thought of as incidences of genocide (see, for example, Kuper, 1981). Critics point out that this history of state-sponsored genocide is obscured or forgotten in contemporary accounts. Accusations of genocidal violence are exclusively reserved to describe and discredit the behaviour of 'murderous' tyrants in the past such as Hitler or Stalin, and Hussein or Milosevic in the present.

This survey of images and metaphors has sought to highlight three points. First, both the earlier discourse of tribalism and the contemporary image of fragmentation create the impression that tribal or ethnic peoples are caught up in a primordial, predetermined frenzy that is outside the realms of normal human instrumentality. Second, contemporary accounts of a fragmenting world are informed by an old and deeply embedded discourse of tribalism or barbarism. Third, the terminology is not just deployed by 'tyrants', but also by Western politicians, scholars and other commentators.

The deployment of discourses of tribalism and images of fragmentation by scholars and officials should be scrutinized because they inform policy. As Adam Roberts has observed, 'the words used to characterize a conflict matter deeply. They often imply the type of interpretation to be placed on it, and even the policy prescription to be followed' (1995, p. 390). The way in which the long-standing discourse of tribalism served to rationalize centuries of colonialism and genocide has been well documented (see Wolf, 1982; Kuper, 1981). Correspondingly, the contemporary discourse of fragmentation creates the impression that the appropriate policies should be to 'contain', 'exorcise' or 'quarantine' ethnic violence.

The Discourse of Tribalism in International Relations Thought

The terminology of 'tribes', 'savages' or 'barbarism' seems old fashioned and anachronistic for a contemporary text on International Relations. In the second half of the twentieth century, this language has been studiously avoided in political and social thought because of its Eurocentric, racialist or colonial overtones. Consequently, there have been very few explicit studies in contemporary International Relations literature that have seriously contemplated the significance of 'tribes' in world politics.

It is, then, perhaps not surprising that we should find the few essays that focus explicitly on the subject of 'tribes' or 'barbarians' amongst the so-called 'traditionalist' writers in International Relations literature (see Gong, 1984; Bell, forthcoming). The most famous of these is Wight's (1991) philosophically reflective essay which showed that the assumption that there was a deep chasm between civilizational order and barbaric anarchy has always been an important theme informing each of the three main traditions of International Relations thought. For example, barbarian activity could be rationalized within the realist ontology of anarchy. Beyond the anarchic arena that existed between states one could expect an even more savage anarchy. Similarly, the idea that civilizations have an historical imperative to expand,[5] as well as a moral obligation (or discretion) to assist barbarian peoples to develop, have been important motifs in the 'rationalist' as well as the 'revolutionist' traditions.

During the Cold War period, references to tribalism as a force in world politics almost completely disappeared from International Relations thought. This shift in attention was informed by two broad changes in social science and the norms of international society. First, political scientists assumed that tribalism and ethnicity would disappear as societies modernized (see Horowitz, 1985). Second, the normative changes accompanying the process of decolonization and the expansion of international society discredited the term. Furthermore, studies of ethnicity more generally tended to be regarded as matters of 'low' or 'domestic' politics and consequently were seen to be outside the purview of the International Relations discipline. Stephen Ryan identified three principal reasons why the study of ethnic conflict was neglected in International Relations during the Cold War period. In addition to the general assumption that ethnicity would disappear with modernization or increasing supra-state integration, the discipline was overwhelmingly focused on the ideological conflict between Western liberalism and Soviet-style Marxism, and preoccupied with interstate behaviour (1990, pp. xix–xxi; also see Schecterman and Slann (eds), 1993).

The end of the Cold War eventually redirected the focus of International Relations thought towards internal war. But, as much of the initial discussion was preoccupied with debates over the causes of the end of the Cold War, the theoretical importance of studying ethnic conflict continued to be underdeveloped. By 1993, Carment could justifiably argue, 'it is no longer possible to ignore the widespread tenacity of ethnic conflict and the way in which it is deeply influencing current interstate behaviour' (1993, p. 137). However, in the same year, Holsti was equally justified in his complaint that 'almost all *theoretical* work in the field has ignored ... ethnicity, religion, language, and other primordial attributes' (1993, p. 407; my italics).

Today, the study of internal wars have not only emerged as a more important site of inquiry, they are now widely acknowledged as *the* principal source of contemporary war in world politics (David, 1998; Brown (ed.), 1996). Even the terminology of 'tribalism' seems to have returned to the lexicon of International Relations scholars and practitioners (see Horsman and Marshall, 1994; Barber, 1996). What was seen as being unimportant now saturates the discipline.

Normative and Policy Issues of a Multicultural World

Perhaps the most glaring ethical issue that arises out of the deployment of such imagery is that it obscures and objectifies ethnic peoples themselves. On the one hand, contemporary world politics is replete with images of 'ethnic', 'communal' or 'tribal' peoples as victims or perpetrators of horrific wars. On the other hand, as 'sovereign-free' agents their voices are muffled in a world that continues to privilege the legitimate agency of sovereign states.

The status or legal personality of ethnic 'peoples' is highly ambiguous in international law. In particular, the principle of self-determination tends to be celebrated as an ideal, but discouraged in practice. This tension is evident in legal instruments throughout international law, including the 1945 Charter of the United Nations.[6] Secession is rarely a peaceful process for those people directly involved, but the concern of the international community to control the proliferation of states into unmanageable units has always been as much about preserving the integrity of the states system as preserving peace. As former UN Secretary General Boutros Ghali warned: 'The United Nations has not closed its door. Yet if every ethnic, religious or linguistic group claimed statehood, there would be no limit to fragmentation, and peace, security and economic well-being for all would be more difficult to achieve' (1992, para. 17).

Paradoxically, whilst the claims of ethnic peoples are often at the forefront of contemporary negotiations over sovereignty, territoriality and human rights, ethnic peoples themselves continue to be denied any real legitimacy or recognized agency in these processes. This visibility of minority groups in international society is unsettling because it reveals 'a gap between the practice of state sovereignty and the principle of legitimacy' (Preece, 1997, p. 92). A recent example of this rift was the UN-mediated agreement between Portugal and Indonesia to have a ballot on the issue of independence or autonomy for East Timor. These negotiations were celebrated as a normative achievement for the international community, but there were no East Timorese representatives (even as observers) present in these discussions.[7]

A more gradual shift has also increased the visibility of ethnic and linguistic minorities within states. Policies of multiculturalism and the normative argument that modern nation-states should be culturally heterogeneous have been ascendant over the last few decades of the twentieth century. In earlier phases of state formation this century, policies of assimilation, and the forced relocation of populations to ensure stable, culturally homogeneous nations, were not only tolerated but encouraged and condoned. However, in the contemporary era both of these strategies are no longer acceptable on normative and international legal grounds (Preece, 1997). The momentum of this normative discourse has led some scholars to proclaim that we live in an increasingly 'multicultural world' (Young (ed.), 1993).

Similarly, the problem of 'protecting the dispossessed' (Deng, 1993) has drawn increasing international attention to the struggles of ethnic minorities. Some of this concern is driven by a new humanitarian ethics. These debates have undoubtedly been informed by the dual influence of an increasingly 'globalized' media and the proliferation of non-governmental organizations. The so-called 'CNN factor' is seen to be especially important in mobilizing opinion to 'do something' about the plight of refugees and displaced peoples (see Rotberg and Weiss (eds), 1996; Rotberg (ed.), 1996; Korten, 1990).

But these normative shifts towards multiculturalism and a concern for refugees have also been accompanied by a rise in xenophobic nationalism expressed primarily by extreme right-wing parties. The rise in popularity of these parties appears to be a worldwide phenomenon, especially in the 'Western' world. Their outspoken leaders attract a disproportionate amount of national and international media coverage which has allowed them to influence mainstream politics. For example, Bruno Mégret from the French National Front declared: 'We have achieved a great strategic victory. We are no longer demonised' (Younge, 1998, p. 24). Perhaps Hobsbawm is correct in speculating that, 'xenophobia looks like becoming the mass ideology of the twentieth century *fin de siècle*' (1996, p. 265).

Savagery within

> When confronted by the concept of barbarianism, the smug Westerner who is protected by his or her superiority complex thinks automatically of murder, crime, genocide or some other act committed by one human agent against another – and usually in some fictitious, remote, fourth world. (Meötrovic, 1993, p. xvii)

The preceding discussion has focused on images that depict tribalism as a belligerent phenomenon that only occurs in remote or backward contexts. The following comments briefly consider several alternative, and more benign, images of tribalism that appear within Western civilization.

Tribalism has always featured deep within Western world history – the sort of historiography that celebrates stories of the rise and fall of great civilizations. For example, the twelve tribes of Israel, or the twenty tribes of Rome, have been reified as the originary or foundational source of Western civilization. Barbarism is sometimes discernible within civilizations. A common explanation for the decline of civilizations has been the motif of civilizational decay. Rome was eventually overwhelmed by the Visigoths, but only after the social conditions within the empire had deteriorated.

Not all images of tribalism and fragmentation conform with the pessimistic Hobbesian view on the state of nature. There have always been nostalgic or romantic views of tribes. For example, early modern political philosophers such as Locke and Rousseau celebrated the state of nature in romantic terms as 'free' and 'noble'. Nineteenth century sociologists such as

Tonnies, Durkheim and Marx each displayed a sense of nostalgia for the 'tribal horde'. They warned that the industrial revolution would erode the sense of community and the warmth of small, traditional face-to-face social relations. The writers of the previous *fin de siècle* coined the term to describe more than simply the 'end of the century', but as a critique on the barbaric, degenerate and decadent perversions of an emerging industrial society. Thorsten Veblen's critique of the American leisure class, Sigmund Freud's study of the 'discontented' in civilization and Emile Durkheim's study of suicide were all examples of this anxiety.

In the contemporary context, similar fears of urban decay and a decline of moral order persist in accounts of late-capitalist society. For example, Moynihan concluded that 'the social condition of American cities is hugely deteriorated' and the clearest symbol of this at the time he was writing was the 1992 Los Angeles riots (Moynihan, 1993, p. 23). Other commentators such as Kaplan (1994) and Enzsenberger (1994) reflect upon the zones of turmoil within urban ghettoes of the Western metropolis.

If there are latter-day barbarians at the gate in the current age of globalization, they are not just war-torn refugees. They are also corporate conglomerates and 'hedge funds' that roam the world to overwhelm weak financial markets. Friedman (1999) has described these investors as 'electronic herds' or 'cybertribes'.

The supposedly *integrative* force of globalization has come to be portrayed as a major force of dislocation of social life. The logic of 'free trade', labour and capital mobility, deregulation of the welfare state and the imposition of a global cultural economy (Appadurai, 1990) are all seen to be responsible for the erosion of 'community' in late-modern society. As Zygmunt Bauman (1995, p. 161) argues, much of today's violence is a consequence of 'the privatization, deregulation and de-centralization of identity problems'.

Conversely, tendencies towards 'fragmentation' are sometimes portrayed as a guarantee, rather than a pervasive threat, to peace and prosperity. In the European Union, for example, the sharing of loyalties, the opening of territorial borders and the movement of peoples are celebrated as the foundational principles for securing peace and prosperity. The tendency towards smaller forms of governance and overlapping authority is recast in the positive and progressive terminology of 'devolution' and 'subsidiarity'.

Romantic and nostalgic views of tribalism seem to be flourishing in the contemporary context. Melucci's (1996) 'nomads of the present' are new social movements born out of the 1960s' emancipatory struggles and have overlapping interests and identities. In particular, he claims that these communities all share the following values: a concern about the way that the human body is objectified; the view that humans are an integral part of, rather than masters over, the environment; and, a new ethics that cultivates forms of spiritualism challenging conventional religious doctrine and a new collectivism that undermines narrow materialism and individualism. Some 'new ageist' social movements have retaliated against hyper-consumerism by advocating more communal and self-sufficient, 'alternative' or neo-tribal lifestyles. New ecological sensibilities are often informed by, or at least in coalition with, indigenous struggles over their sacred lands.

Conclusion

Fukuyama (1999b) was recently asked to reconsider his 'end of history' thesis particularly in light of the trends towards ethnic conflict and nationalism over the last decade. In response, he argued that, disturbing as events in Kosovo and elsewhere may be, they will not result in any fundamental 'world-historical' institutional change.

But this view ignores the indirect influence that these sorts of crises are having on redefining cherished liberal institutions. International Relations thought and practice has been forced to reassess fundamental assumptions about territoriality, sovereignty and, in turn, democracy and human rights. One of the more astonishing reactions to globalization has not been narrow-minded parochialism, but transnational collectivism that occurs in non-governmental and international organizations such as the United Nations Working Group on Indigenous Peoples (see Esman and Telhami, 1995; Tennant, 1994). A number of more critical International Relations thinkers argue that the influence of 'sovereign-free' agents on the inter-state system is part of a wider transformation in world politics. They claim that these changes are historically profound to the extent that they may signify the emergence of a post-Westphalian or more cosmopolitan era (Linklater, 1998; Held, 1995). But, as Bull (1977) proposed over two decades ago, this 'new' normative architecture of world politics may appear similar to the pre-Westphalian or neomedieval world.

Philosophical and popular commentaries on world politics have always been underscored by fundamental assumptions about human nature and juxtaposed against images of a premodern or tribal condition. Likewise, the dialectic between forces of integration and disintegration can be found throughout human history. The contending images circumscribing these phenomena are unlikely to disappear in the coming century.

CHAPTER 12

'Islam and the West'?

Amin Saikal

Relations between the Muslim world and the Christian West, led by the United States, are complex and multidimensional. Yet two strong but contradictory views continue to raise serious concerns about the state of this relationship at the dawn of the twenty-first century, and each view comes with varying nuances (for a detailed discussion, see Esposito, 1992; Said, 1997, especially Chapter 1; Halliday, 1995, especially Chapter 3). One view is that Islamic 'fundamentalism', as propounded by those political forces of Islam which are contemptuous or distrustful of Western, and more specifically American, values and international behaviour, lies at the core of problems between the two sides. This view presents the phenomenon of fundamentalism as poisonous, and calls for the arrest and if possible the elimination of its influence in international relations. This view, which gained salience in the late twentieth century following the Iranian revolution of 1978/79, still resonates strongly in the thinking and policy behaviour of a number of influential elements in various Western capitals – most importantly, Washington. The emergence on the international scene of such radical Islamic forces as the Taliban militia in Afghanistan, Harakat ul-Ansar and its successor Harakat ul-Mujahideen in Pakistan, a cluster of Kashmiri groups associated with the last two, the Lebanese Hezbullah, the Palestinian Hamas, the Egyptian Islamic Jihad, and the Algerian Islamic League – an outgrowth of the Islamic Salvation Front – has helped to perpetuate this view.

Another view, which has become widespread among Muslims, more as a reaction to the first view than anything else, is that the West has been swept by 'Islamophobia'[1] for a variety of self-serving political reasons. It claims that the 'Islamic threat' thesis is more of a myth than reality, and is designed mainly to promote an enemy to replace the Soviet Union, on whose enmity the US had staked its superpower operations for some 50 years. This view maintains that as long as the United States fails to change its attitude and come to terms with the changing dynamics of the Muslim world, relations between the latter and the West may continue to be as problematic in the new century as they were in the one that has just ended.

The objective of this chapter is not to provide a comprehensive coverage of the various dimensions of relations between the Muslim world and the West, or to conceptualize their dynamics in such a way as to provide a grand vision or prescription for the future. Its main purpose is rather to tease out some of the major areas of tension between these two political spheres, and to determine the extent to which the above polarized views correspond to the reality of the situation. In doing this, the chapter also seeks to explore the motives for such views and to make a brief assessment of their implications for those who uphold them and for those who are subjected to them. Finally, it investigates what possible patterns of development the relations between the two sides may experience in the foreseeable future, and the possibility of moving beyond 'Islam and the West' as a major image of world politics.

Sources of the Image

That the relationship between the Muslim world and the Christian West has been far from smooth since the advent of Islam as a revealed monotheistic religion in the early seventh century is to state the obvious. Despite the Islamic ordinance that Muslims must respect all other revealed religions prior to Islam, most importantly Judaism and Christianity, and provide protection for Jewish and Christian minorities in their societies, and despite the fact that this led to a period of highly tolerant coexistence between Muslims, Jews and Christians during the first four centuries of Islam, relations have grown uneasy and at times confrontational since then. From the perspective of Arab Muslims, the Christian crusades to take over Jerusalem, which the Muslims respect as their third holiest city after Mecca and Medina, marked a turning point in the process (see Maalouf, 1984). European (especially British and French) colonialism, beginning in the wake of European expansionism from the sixteenth century, simply reinforced the painful legacy of the Crusades. It caused wider humiliation for Muslims as many of their communities in the Middle East, South Asia and Southeast Asia fell to European colonialist rule and cultural subjugation.

In the meantime, Tsarist Russia's encroachment from the early nineteenth century upon Muslim territories in Central Asia and its growing enmity toward the Ottomans caused Muslims to become increasingly apprehensive. Soviet Russia's 'Godless' communist ideology, formal annexation of the remaining emirates in Central Asia, and repression of its Muslim minorities, especially during the Stalinist period, strengthened this apprehension. The rise of the United States to a global power, the American-Soviet Cold War rivalry for global influence following the Second World War, and the negative consequences of this for the Muslim world, as well as America's success in achieving dominance in the Muslim Middle East, further pained many Muslim peoples. These events made them highly distrustful and in some cases resentful of both powers, even though some of their ruling or opposition elites found refuge or comfort in alliance with one or other of the rival powers.

European colonialism bifurcated the subjected Muslim societies into secularist elites, dedicated to the goal of modernization along Western lines, and Islamic clusters, devoted to reforming and reorganizing their societies according to Islamic teachings. The latter, in the late nineteenth and early twentieth centuries, launched numerous ideological and combative challenges to Western domination. They ranged from Sayyed Jamal ul-Din Al-Afghani's Pan-Islamic efforts to Hassan Al-Bana's Society of Muslim Brotherhood's endeavours to unite Muslims at both national and regional levels against internal decay and outside intervention and subjugation. They did not succeed in achieving their ultimate goals, but were important in germinating a new awakening among Muslims, which would gain deeper and wider salience in the more conducive conditions created in the wake of post-Second World War globalism.

In recent times, three main developments marked a watershed in the process. The first was the Iranian mass revolution of 1978/79. This historical event, of an unprecedented nature and magnitude, was significant for a variety of reasons. However, the most relevant concerns the fact that it resulted in the overthrow of one of America's key allies, Iran's absolute ruler, Mohammed Reza Shah. The Iranian monarch had acted as the bridgehead for US influence in Iran and the broader region from 1953 when the Central Intelligence Agency (CIA), assisted by British intelligence, engineered the overthrow of the elected nationalist-reformist government of Prime Minister Mohammed Mossadeq and reinstalled the Shah on his throne (see Saikal, 1980, pp. 44–5). The Iranian revolution enabled the radical Iranian Shi'ite clerics, led by Ayatullah Khomeini, to seize the leadership of the revolution and to establish a staunchly anti-American Islamic regime. Khomeini's Shi'ite Islamic regime was by no means widely emulated in the rest of the mainly Sunni-dominated Muslim countries. Nonetheless, in many ways it reflected the aspirations of all those Muslims in the region and beyond who had felt humiliated and frustrated by their bitter experiences with the West. It inspired and emboldened many political forces of Islam to challenge the influence of the West in the Middle East and elsewhere in the Muslim world (see Ramazani, 1986, 1988; Hunter, 1998). They included the radical Islamic elements among the Lebanese Shi'ites who, with the direct help of the Iranian Islamic regime and its Syrian counterpart, formed the Hezbullah (the Party of God), as well as a host of other Islamist groups from both sides of the Sunni–Shi'ite sectarian divide in the Muslim world (Shapira, 1988). These forces were inspired to seek either a peaceful or revolutionary political and social transformation of their societies along Islamic lines, but free of Western hegemonic influences.

These developments, together with the seizure of some 50 American diplomats as hostages by Khomeini's Islamic militant student followers in Tehran – a crisis which lasted for 20 months from November 1979, and brought much humiliation for the United States – proved instrumental in moulding Washington's understanding of, and opposition to, radical or Jihadi (exertive and combatant) political Islam. In the wake of its bitter experiences with Iranian and Iranian-inspired Islamism, Washington developed a particular mindset about radical political Islam, shaped more by its own perceptions, experiences and interests than the reality of what the phenomenon was all about. It labelled as 'fundamentalist' many of those political forces of Islam which either challenged or refused to recognize America's hegemonic interests and accord it status as a global power. Washington considered these forces as a menace in the international system, therefore warranting suppression and isolation by the international community. Hence its deployment of 'Islamic fundamentalism' as a pejorative term to disparage and discredit them as irrational, irresponsible and extremist forces, dedicated, actually or potentially, to the goal of international terrorism (Saikal, 1993, p. 198). This was a development that played into the hands of those who ever since have been keen for one reason or another to promote 'Islamophobia' in world politics.

The second but simultaneous development was the Soviet invasion of Afghanistan in late December 1979. Moscow's prime objective was to maintain a pro-Soviet communist government in Kabul and pre-empt its replacement by an Islamic government as part of a perceived wider Islamic threat to the Soviet Central Asian Muslim republics. The invasion essentially confirmed all the disdain that many Muslims had held for Marxist-Leninist communism and the perceived Soviet historical ambitions towards the region south of the USSR's borders in the direction of the Persian Gulf and the Indian Ocean. This was an event which the Soviet Union's arch rival, the United States, and other adversaries, including the People's Republic of China, immediately utilized to achieve their long-standing goal of defeating Soviet communism. Washington found it opportune to let *realpolitik*, rather than ideological preferences, determine its counter-interventionist strategy. Without any moral qualms, it welcomed the deployment of Islam as an ideology of resistance to Soviet occupation. It immediately embraced the Afghan Islamic resistance forces, the Mujahideen, which emerged as a mixture of radical and moderate groups, divided along the lines of personality, sectarian, tribal, ethnic and linguistic differences. In this, however, it confined its support to the main groups that represented the majority Sunni Muslim population of Afghanistan and were based in Pakistan; it thus carefully avoided any action which could possibly help the Iranian-based Shi'ite Mujahideen groups or the Iranian Islamic regime.[2]

Washington sprang into action to forge a regime of international assistance to the Pakistan-based Mujahideen, and helped Pakistan, the newly emerged frontline state against Soviet communism, to enable it to act as the main conduit for anti-Soviet operations in Afghanistan. The CIA was given the prime responsibility for the conduct of America's proxy war. In a close alliance with Pakistan's military intelligence (ISI), the CIA not only helped thousands of Afghans to take up arms under the banner of Islam, but hundreds of Muslims from Pakistan and the Arab world to join the Afghans in a Jihad ('holy war') against the Soviets and their surrogates (for details, see Yousaf and Adkin, 1992; Khan, 1991). It also developed contacts with and forged an international network of Islamic activists (some of them more radical and traditionalist than others), including some who were based in the United States, to support its Afghan counter-interventionism.

The third development, which in its conception predated the first two, concerned the establishment in 1948 of Israel as a confessional Jewish state out of what was predominantly Arab-populated Palestine, at the cost of creating an enduring Palestinian problem and Arab–Israeli conflict. Although the US role in support of this development was initially driven by moral and humanitarian considerations, given the horror of the Holocaust, it nonetheless within a few years of the foundation of Israel took on a serious political and strategic dimension in the context of American domestic politics and the Cold War. As the United States committed itself to guarantee Israel's security and survival, and to embrace a strategic partnership with the Jewish state, America's position could no longer remain neutral in the conflict. Washington's massive financial and military assistance[3] to enable Israel to maintain a strategic edge over its Arab neighbours, and its political protection of Israel at the United Nations and in other international forums, could only alienate the Arab masses in general, and the radical Islamic elements among them in particular.

The turning point came with Israel's victory in the 1967 war, enabling the Jewish state not only to occupy more land, but also to capture East Jerusalem. Israel's annexation of East Jerusalem[4] to form with West Jerusalem the 'united capital of Israel for ever' caused more anguish than ever before in the Muslim world's relations with the West. The annexation of East Jerusalem and Washington's tepid reaction amounted to a major catalyst in galvanizing Muslim activists to grow more hostile towards Israel, and distrustful and even resentful of the United States. Many of them viewed the whole development as a Jewish–Christian conspiracy, ensuring the continuation of the Palestinian problem and the Arab–Israeli conflict, and acting as the main obstacle to finding a resolution to them sooner rather than later. Although the Muslim Brotherhood had established its cells in the 1940s in Palestine, it now found its biggest opportunity to expand its popular influence. Israel initially backed the Palestinian radical Islamic group Hamas (which had its roots in the activities of the Muslim Brothers) in order to counter the secularist Palestinian Liberation Organization (PLO) under Yasser Arafat, which Israel at the time rejected as a 'terrorist' organization. However, by the late 1980s, Hamas was well positioned to draw not only on the PLO's failures and the Palestinians' increased suffering under Israeli occupation, but also on the Islamic grievances of the Palestinians in particular, and Muslims in general, to play a leading role in the Palestinian Uprising (intifadeh), which started in late 1987. The intifadeh and Hamas's role in it were as much against Israel as they were in opposition to those who supported the Jewish state, most importantly the United States. In the end, Israel felt threatened more by Hamas than by the PLO, and while backed by the United States, it chose the PLO as a 'partner' in the Oslo peace process, which the two sides initiated in September 1993. But Hamas and its sister organizations in Palestine and the region still remain deeply troubled by the process and by their rejection by the United States.

Turning the Image into Reality

Although these three developments emerged from different bases and produced different outcomes, ultimately Washington's handling of them goes a long way towards explaining the tense state of relations that has developed between the United States and the political forces of Islam. It is clear that Iranian Islamic radicalism, the Afghan Islamic resistance, and Palestinian Islamic assertiveness interacted to induce an unprecedented degree of radicalization among Muslims, who have remained divided politically but have projected a semblance of unity in religious terms. Washington bears much responsibility for the way this radicalization has, at least from time to time, spawned and given rise to an anti-American – and for that matter, to some extent, an anti-Western – upsurge in the Muslim world. The US approach to these developments from the start was contradictory, naïve and self-centred, and lacking deep consideration for their long-term consequences. It showed little concern about the manner in which US policy actions could negatively affect the lives of ordinary Muslims, and their perceptions of the West. Nor did it pay much attention to the way in which America's policy behaviour could play into the hands of those elements on both sides who for political and ideological reasons would want the state of relations to remain disrupted and confrontational.

The irony is that the United States has persistently overlooked the role that it itself has played – advertently or inadvertently – in the creation of the current radical Islamic resurgence since the Iranian revolution, the Soviet invasion of Afghanistan, and the Israeli occupation of East Jerusalem. It has done so either by contributing to the development of situations that bred such radicalism, or by providing direct and indirect assistance to elements which have advocated radical Islamic orientations. Of course, the United States was not from the start necessarily opposed to Islamic radicalism and traditionalism *per se*. Its opposition came to be directed against those forces of political Islam that it could neither control nor influence in pursuit of its interests. The US demonized the Islamic radicalism of Khomeini's Iran and Hamas, Islamic Jihad, and Hezbullah, which emerged to challenge America's interests.

It did so without taking into consideration the Iranian people's serious grievances about America's unwavering support of the Shah's dictatorial rule since 1953 when the CIA successfully re-installed the Shah on his throne to govern Iran at the behest of the United States. Even when by mid-1978 the revolution against the Shah had reached an irreversible point and Khomeini's leadership of the revolution had been assured, the US still failed to open dialogue with the Khomeini camp. President Jimmy Carter finally announced on 9 November that the Shah might not be able to hold on for too long, but this was not translated into any policy measures to court the Khomeini camp and to reassure the Iranians of Washington's readiness to change course and redress some of their fundamental grievances. It was not surprising that Khomeini's leadership grew firmer in its anti-Americanism, resulting in the hostage crisis and the rupturing of relations between the two countries. Of course, since the rise to power of President Mohammed Khatami and Washington's increased realization that Iran is politically, economically and strategically too important to remain 'out of the loop', the prospects for an Iranian–American rapprochement have improved. But the situation for both sides still remains too complex for one to be very optimistic in the short run. Even if a rapprochement is achieved, the scars of the past and the conflictual nature of their ideological stands are unlikely to allow them to have a meeting of minds on too many issues for the foreseeable future – unless Washington drops its apprehension about the Islamic forces that do not avowedly support its interests.

By contrast, Washington showed no difficulty in embracing the various Afghan Mujahideen groups, but on one condition – that they, like the Saudi regime, remained either directly or indirectly under American influence. The US aided whatever group came forward to fight the Soviet occupation and was endorsed by Pakistan's ISI. It displayed little understanding of the nature of Islam in Afghanistan, which had never been extreme, but was vulnerable to manipulation under the right circumstances. It acted in such a way that it became entangled with several forces whose use of Islam for extremist purposes was bound to have serious repercussions for the future of not only Afghanistan, but also many other countries, including some of the allies of the United States, in the region.[5]

One such group, which emerged as more extremist in both its ideological and policy disposition than many of its counterparts in the Muslim world, was the *Hezbi Islami Afghanistan* (the Islamic Party of Afghanistan), led by Gulbuddin Hekmatyar. A self-styled Islamist, and a highly political opportunist, with unbounded power ambitions, Gulbuddin Hekmatyar caused much conflict and bloodshed within the Afghan resistance and subsequently destroyed half of Kabul at the cost of thousands of lives when he could not seize power following the collapse of the communist regime in April 1992. He also practised the worst of what he could justify in the name of Islam, with a special antipathy toward the West. At times he publicly condemned the United States as an evil power, and refused to meet American political leaders for fear of compromising his orthodoxy. Yet for most of the 1980s he was courted by Washington, and received the lion's share of American military assistance to the Mujahideen. Washington was repeatedly warned about him, but to little avail. Because he was the favourite of the ISI, which wanted him to head a pro-Pakistani post-communist government in Kabul to cater for Pakistan's wider regional interests, he was also regarded as useful in Washington, as long as he was under the control of Pakistan and served America's interests (Saikal, 1998, pp. 116–18).

In the end, Hekmatyar proved to be useless even for Pakistan, as he failed to gain popularity in Afghanistan or to dominate the Mujahideen Islamic government under President Burhanuddin Rabbani and his highly nationalist military chief Commander Ahmed Shah Massoud. This led the ISI to create in 1994 a fresh Islamic Sunni militia, the Taliban, more orthodox than any of the Mujahideen groups. The new militia was to pursue three main objectives: to secure a receptive government in Kabul, a degree of strategic depth in Afghanistan against India, and strong leverage for wider regional influence, especially in the wake of the disintegration of the Soviet Union and the opening up of a new, but resource- and market-rich Muslim Central Asia. The Taliban was raised, trained and equipped from both the Afghan and Pakistani sides of the border, financed by Saudi Arabia and the United Arab Emirates, and quietly endorsed by the United States – an issue which will be detailed shortly.

In a similar vein, Washington allowed its counter-interventionist activities to favour a variety of Arab mercenaries who volunteered from various Arab countries, ranging from Saudi Arabia to Egypt to Algeria. One of these volunteers was Osama Bin Laden, a wealthy Saudi who came to Afghanistan in 1984. Bin Laden, who joined a Mujahideen training camp in the Afghan eastern province of Nangarhar, was closely supported by the ISI and indirectly by the CIA. He soon emerged not only as an Arab Jihadi hero but also, by the turn of the 1990s, as a major Islamic opponent of the United States. He came to resent deeply what he viewed as America's maintenance of the Saudi regime to subjugate Islam's holiest land, and its support of Israel in enabling the Jewish state to control East Jerusalem in particular, and suppress the Palestinians in general. Bin Laden became more vocal in his criticism of the Saudi regime and the United States in the wake of their military response to the August 1990 Iraqi invasion of Kuwait – a response which was launched from Saudi Arabia (see Cooley, 1999, Chapter 10). As the Saudi regime disowned him, after a short stay in Sudan, he returned to Afghanistan through Pakistan in the mid-1990s, this time not to resist the Soviets, but to support the ISI's new orchestration, the Taliban. Bin Laden's wealth (estimated at about $250 million) and influence with Arab volunteers proved important in this respect.

Washington was aware of Pakistan's orchestration of the Taliban and Bin Laden's involvement in support of the militia from the start, but maintained a conspicuous silence over it, for two possible reasons. One was Pakistan's argument that the Taliban was primarily an anti-Shi'ite and therefore anti-Iranian militia – a feature which also appealed to Saudi Arabia and the United Arab Emirates, given the former's regional rivalry with Iran and the latter's dispute with Iran over three islands in the Gulf. Another was the impression that the Taliban would bring stability to Afghanistan, opening a direct route from Pakistan to Central Asia, where Washington was concerned about a perceived upsurge in Iranian influence, and through which American companies could export oil and gas from Central Asia, especially Turkmenistan, to South Asia and beyond. These factors interacted with financial support from Bin Laden to enable the Taliban to take over Kabul by mid-1996 and most of a socially divided and militarily exhausted Afghanistan by 1998.[6]

This was instrumental in empowering the Taliban to impose a medieval, very brutal and highly discriminatory form of Islamic rule, with the harshest treatment meted out to women and Shi'ites (Maley, 1998); and in enabling Bin Laden to secure a very friendly and effective base of operations. Bin Laden was now officially promoted as the esteemed 'guest' of the Taliban and reportedly married a daughter of the Taliban leader, Mullah Omar. While revered by the Taliban and their architect, the ISI, he rapidly enhanced a wide network of followers and activists who could get in and out of Afghanistan only through Pakistan, given the hostilities of Afghanistan's other neighbours to the Taliban. It was against this backdrop that he allegedly masterminded the bombing of American embassies in Kenya and Tanzania in August 1998, killing and injuring hundreds. Thus was born what America called a leading 'Islamic terrorist', and America's 'most wanted man'. As Washington has sought to bring Bin Laden to justice, and has prompted the United Nations to impose limited sanctions on the Taliban from late 1999, it has become entangled in a bloody struggle with another wave of 'Islamic fundamentalism', in the creation of which its own role cannot be underestimated.

Yet Bin Laden was only one of the many Arab fighters that the CIA had supported and the US government had endorsed when it suited its anti-Soviet activities. America's virtually unqualified support of Pakistan to help

America's operations in this respect proved to be fraught with peril from the start. Regardless of Pakistan's chronic fragile domestic structures, disastrous economic and social conditions, continued entrenchment of the military in its politics, and mounting problems of national identity and direction, Washington paid little attention to what its policies might bring for Pakistan and the region. As things turned out they proved harmful in many ways. They significantly assisted the military regime of President General Zia ul-Haq to overcome the illegitimacy of its usurpation of power and the execution of the former Prime Minister Zulfiqar Ali Bhutto, whom he had deposed. They also aided the regime to ensure its longevity, based on a politics of public deception, divide and rule, and Islamization of Pakistan, and to camouflage its drive to acquire nuclear capability. This, together with General Zia ul-Haq's granting of almost unlimited powers to Pakistan's military intelligence to enforce his dictatorship, as well as to handle Pakistan's Afghanistan and Kashmir policies, left a terrible legacy. On the one hand, it entrenched further the culture of the military and secret service in Pakistani politics and, on the other, it encouraged the growth of Islamic militancy and sectarian violence. Islamic militants found a new political climate of legitimacy to exalt their moral virtue, participate in the Afghan Jihad and receive training in warfare and develop an international network, involving hundreds of like-minded Arabs.

The ISI tapped effectively into this network not only to have a major hand in the Afghan Islamic resistance, but also to drum up the cause of Kashmiri separatists against India whenever appropriate, and to link up to different Islamic movements and groups in the region and beyond. This was a development that subsequently severely impaired the ability of civilian leaders, who came to power after Zia ul-Haq's death in a mysterious air crash in August 1988, to put Pakistan on a stable course of democratization. This in turn helped the military to regain power under General Parvaz Musharaf in the coup of October 1999. It also played a key role in generating extreme Islamic forces in Pakistan, many of which are now inextricably linked to Bin Laden, the Taliban and various Kashmiri Islamic groups, including the Haraktul Mujahideen. It was allegedly members of the latter group who were responsible for the late December 1999 hijacking of an Indian Airlines passenger plane, with 160 hostages on board, to an Afghan airfield in Kandahar – the headquarters of the Taliban. The hijacking ended within a week, but only at a very high price for India. As well as killing one of their hostages, the hijackers forced India to release three Kashmiri Islamic militants from jail. As the hijackers, together with freed militants, walked away free under escort from the Taliban, serious questions were raised about the role of the Taliban and Pakistan in the whole drama. Given the Taliban's failure to arrest the hijackers after the ordeal and the fact that the Kashmiri militants and the Taliban have been closely guided by the ISI, Pakistan's reputation as a state ostensibly supporting 'terrorism' came under serious discussion.

By the same token, the US could not be totally absolved of any responsibility for contributing, at least indirectly, to Pakistan's transformation into a potential cradle for the growth of Islamic extremism. The former Pakistani Prime Minister, Nawaz Sharif, expressed openly his deep concerns about this shortly before he was deposed by General Musharaf. He condemned the links between the Taliban and Pakistan's Islamic militants and by implication between them and the Kashmiri separatists (see Rashid, 1999), over whom a few months earlier he had, though at Washington's urging, averted a war with India by forcing them to withdraw from the Indian side of the Line of Control in Kashmir. However, his call for action came too late, and some might claim that the coup against him might have been partly prompted by a desire to pre-empt any action by him.

Beyond Pakistan, other elements who benefited from American policies were those Arab Islamic fighters who participated in the Afghan resistance but upon returning to their countries of origin, took up arms in opposition to their secularist governments. Two prime examples have been the Islamic militants in Algeria and Egypt, many of whom have reportedly been veterans of the Afghan Islamic resistance. Of course, this is not to claim that their struggle in each case has had no real local causes. To the contrary, in the case of Algeria, where their operations (some in the most gruesome form imaginable) have resulted in some 80 000 deaths in the 1990s, the militants' grievances are rooted in the military's cancellation of the February 1992 elections, which the Islamic Salvation Front (FIS) was poised to win. Yet it is also undeniably true that many of the militant supporters of FIS who took up arms to redress the situation had fought in Afghanistan under the guidance and watchful eyes of the CIA and ISI and had become involved in the wider network of Islamic militants whose growth had been encouraged by American policies. The fact that Washington remained conspicuously silent over the military's cancellation of the elections only added salt to the wound as far as their growing antipathy towards the US was concerned.

The case of the Egyptian Islamic militants, some of whom are now reportedly linked to Bin Laden, tells a similar story. Although the Egyptian authorities have now succeeded in containing their bloody operations, some of which resulted in the death of hundreds of foreign tourists in the 1990s, this has not led to their total eradication or inability to be nourished again by their international linkages at an appropriate time. In the meantime, Washington's policy of isolation of the Islamic regime in Sudan has done little to dampen that regime's support for those Islamic militants who can serve its interests against either the United States or its allies, which include the Egyptian regime of Husni Mubarak.

As for the part played by the US in contributing to the development of conditions which gave rise to the Palestinian Hamas and Islamic Jihad, as well as the Lebanese Hezbullah, America's unqualified strategic alliance with Israel has provided these forces with a great deal to chew on. There is a dominant view among these forces that if it were not for this alliance, committing the US to guaranteeing the survival of the Jewish state, and to maintaining its strategic edge over its neighbours, Israel would have not been able either to annex East Jerusalem as part of its united capital or to continue its occupation of Palestinian and Arab lands, with painful consequences especially for the Palestinian people. Many among them have perceived America's support for Israel's choice of the secularist PLO as its partner in peace as a confirmation of Washington's consistent opposition to that political Islam which, from their perspective, is dedicated to rebuilding and renewing Arab societies according to Islamic values but free of any bondage to the West.[7] They believe that the Oslo peace process is designed to deflect the impact of one important anomaly in American Middle East policy: one standard for Israel and another for the Arabs. They are not necessarily persuaded that it is devised to enable the Palestinians to have a truly independent, sovereign state of their own, and to free themselves genuinely from the constraints imposed upon them by the traditional alliance that has underlined the existence of the state of Israel. They strongly contend that Washington remains determined to influence and moderate Palestinian and Arab nationalism in a direction that would make it amenable to a settlement of the Palestinian problem mainly on Israel's terms.

Of course, they have not been alone in such a belief, which has also been widely shared across the Arab world in particular, and the Muslim world in general. As such, they have been able to tap into the grievances and frustrations not just of their own peoples but of wider Muslim audiences, to promote Islamic radicalism to focus public discontent on both Israel and the United States, and to justify their armed actions against them. Indeed, the intensity of their opposition to Israel and the US has lately somewhat moderated. Two factors account for this: a realization on the part of the Clinton Administration that Palestinian Islamic radicalism and outside support for it can be contained if there is real progress in the peace process; and the election in Israel in May 1999 of Prime Minister Ehud Barak (in place of his hardline predecessor Benjamin Netanyahu), who has shown more commitment to the peace process. However, should the peace process falter and the two parties in the process fail to achieve a final settlement, as they have agreed, Islamic radical opposition to the peace process may not prove to be too far from the surface.

Beyond an Image of Conflict?

Three important issues emerge from a close study of relations between the world of Islam and the West, led by the United States, in the second half of the twentieth century. The first is that radical political Islam, resulting mainly from the Iranian revolution, the Soviet invasion of Afghanistan and the Israeli occupation of East Jerusalem and other Arab lands, with a fairly diverse anti-American character, crystallized in response to diverse situations and challenges. As such, the phenomenon was divided from within from the start, and did not provide for a cohesive force and united front, whereby one could claim that it posed a collective challenge to Western interests. Nor could it at the same time be contained within a particular geopolitical setting, although naturally the Muslim Middle East–Central Asia–North African area, stretching from Kashmir and Pakistan to Algeria experienced a concentration of it. It was widespread, manifesting itself in different modes and shades, and locked in as much to internal conflict as to confrontation with the outside world, especially the United States.

The second is that it was shaped as much by its own internal dynamism as by the United States' poor understanding of the phenomenon and its politically and ideologically motivated response to it. Once Washington was subjected to a set of bitter experiences in relation to Iranian Islamic radicalism under Ayatullah Khomeini, it adopted a sweeping and at times highly contradictory mindset in its approach to handling the phenomenon. It let its changing interests and perceptions override the principle of consistency in its foreign policy behaviour. While it opposed Iranian-type Islamic radicalism, it supported the various shades of Islamic radicalism associated with the Afghan Islamic resistance to the Soviet occupation, and paid little or no attention to the consequences of this for Afghanistan and for the region as a whole. It let its strategy drift in favour of all kinds of Afghan and non-Afghan Islamic groups and elements, without an overarching strategy as to how to manage effectively problems arising from post-Soviet-occupied Afghanistan[8] and the outside Islamic groups and individuals associated with it. It left the whole task to Pakistan – or, more specifically, the ISI, which was nourished by an alliance with the CIA, but had grown to be an independent actor and interlocutor in the very network of Islamic activists that it had forged with the CIA's active participation to substantiate Washington's counter-interventionist strategy. It failed to see that many of these groups and individuals, while sharing America's stand against the Soviet invasion of Afghanistan, had their own grievances against the United States.

The third is that the United States – in some cases advertently and in others inadvertently – made a substantial contribution to the generation of Islamic forces opposed to its interests. Its policies, whether towards Iran or Afghanistan or the Arab–Israeli conflict, were formulated and conducted in such a way as to activate the very Islamic forces that it wanted to contain. They were frequently driven by a degree of self-delusion, and were distant from the reality on the ground. They created a mode of thinking in the United States that certain confessionally and politically motivated publicists and opinion makers could use to promote a stereotypical image of Islam as incompatible and even hostile to Western values and civilization,[9] leading to an acute bout of Islamophobia. Outside the United States, this Islamophobia was nowhere more evident than in France, where the incident in 1989 of a Muslim school girl being barred from attending school because she was wearing an Islamic head scarf epitomized the whole development (Cody, 1989).

Despite some perceptive changes in America's policy behaviour before the end of the twentieth century, relations between the West and the world of Islam continue to suffer from bouts of misperception, misunderstanding and, at times, conflict of various kinds. However, two favourable developments appeared to have some impact. One was the effort made by the Iranian Islamic moderate (or *ijtihadi*) President Mohammed Khatami to rationalize Iranian foreign policy and promote the concept of 'dialogue' as opposed to a 'clash' of civilizations. Although confronted by serious domestic and international obstacles, he has evidently laid the foundations for change in Iranian politics and made some contributions to relaxing the regional environment in this direction. If Khatami succeeds in his politics, then his achievement could have serious implications for regional and wider relations. The second was the election of the moderate Islamic scholar, Aburrahman Wahid, to the presidency of the predominantly Muslim Indonesia in 1999. Wahid has not only endorsed the concept of a secular government as acceptable in a Muslim country, but also, like Khatami, has called for wider dialogue and serious measures to improve relations between the followers of various religions in the world, most importantly Muslims, Jews and Christians. However, to change the situation in the direction of wider peaceful coexistence between Muslims and the West, there is an urgent need for a meaningful attitude shift on the part of both sides, although the United States, as the world's only superpower, bears the major responsibility to avoid its past mistakes in the new millennium.

PART IV

KNOWLEDGE, POWER AND INCLUSION

CHAPTER 13

An 'Endangered Planet'?

Johanna Sutherland

Many of the post-1960s images representing the state of the Earth's environment cast a global pall. They politicize and popularize repeated scientific warnings that the life-sustaining processes of the planet are imperilled. As a consequence, images of environmental insecurity are often projected in the International Relations (IR) discipline. But more reassuring images of 'sustainable development' achieved through global governance, have become increasingly prevalent. Institutions, non-state actors, and social movements are recognized and analysed as key actors for sustainable development. These images contrast again with the ecocentric but marginal images projected by ecofeminists and 'deep' ecologists.

This chapter provides a selective overview of these contending images. It argues that while a sub-group of IR academics debate the merits of various security analyses of the endangered planet, images of sustainable development achieved through security-promoting cooperation predominate. These cooperative and managerial images are projected primarily by the liberal institutionalist IR literature and by the kindred sub-discipline of international environmental law. Dominant images of actors, interests and institutions are inherent in IR analyses of binding instruments (particularly treaties and customary international law) and soft law (codes of practice, guidelines, standards, declarations of principles, and non-binding resolutions). But several of the core norms and principles in international environmental law also presage the finite history of humanity, if fundamental changes are not made to predominantly industrial lifestyle patterns. 'Deep' ecologists and social ecologists who are critical of the anthropocentric nature of global governance and the environment are the most marginal in the IR discipline. The Gaia approach to whole-Earth ecological interdependencies challenges the technological 'development' and 'rationalist' management strategies inherent in mainstream sustainable development approaches (Braidotti *et al.*, 1994; Cavalieri and Singer (eds), 1994; Birnie and Boyle, 1992, pp. 422–4). Images of animal rights and welfare are also scarce in the IR literature, and will not be considered further in this chapter. Ecofeminist images are similarly marginal, although there is also a more mainstream feminist agenda for sustainable development which generates significant levels of institutional activity.

Does it matter that there is such a diversity of contending images? This chapter suggests that it does, drawing on Foucaultian and constructivist theory (Ashley, 1987; George, 1994; Price and Reus-Smit, 1998). The chapter recognizes that images, and the discourses that parent them, are produced in a social context. They embody negotiated and contested norms and values. Images are often as persuasive as the relative power and authority of their supporting discourse. Discourses are frameworks and matrices of thought, language and practice which enable 'reality' to be understood and explained although they are often interwoven, overlapping and contested (George, 1994, pp. 29–30). The images conjured by discourses are often powerful, and can produce policy preferences consistent with the rationalities or emotions inherent in that discourse.

Images are also important because they can be resources that actors project and/or draw upon to encourage things to happen that may not have happened otherwise. Images are produced by knowledge/power networks, and the strength and influence of an image can be indicative of those networks' power. Images are most influential when allocative resources (material power and capacity to assert control over the physical world), and authoritative resources (knowledge/power and the capacity to influence human behaviour), are abundant. Authoritative resources include the capacity to influence the social and temporal organization of politics and society, to store and transmit information, and to mobilize people or influence others' life-chances (Haugaard, 1997: 107, 110–11). Dominant networks of knowledge and power, as embodied in discourse and image, can effectively shape governance options.

This chapter is concerned primarily with contending images of global environmental politics and 'the endangered planet', but the knowledge/power networks and/or authors which project these images, are also noted. It will be argued that doomsday scenarios have precipitated significant institutional change within the United Nations since the 1970s, but that the underlying trends justifying the warnings have not yet been effectively curtailed.

Warnings, Grim Scenarios and Environmental Insecurity

Many global environmental images verge on being apocalyptic, and warn that current production and consumption trends threaten humanity's survival. Rachel Carson's *Silent Spring*(1962) condemned the over-use of pesticides and insecticides as a threat to human health and ecosystems. Her warnings have been echoed in follow-up studies (Graham, 1970; Marco *et al.* (eds), 1987; Hynes, 1989). Images depicting the disappearance of species have been particularly common, exemplified by *Survival or Extinction* (Synge and Townsend (eds), 1979), *The Sinking Ark* (Myers, 1979), and *Extinction* (Ehrlich and Ehrlich, 1981). Concerns about disrupted ecosystems, excessive population, depleted food supplies, rampant militarism, and the exhaustion of non-renewable resources produced *The Limits to Growth* (Meadows *et al.*, 1972), *This Endangered Planet* (Falk, 1971), *The Closing Circle* (Commoner, 1972), 'A Blueprint for Survival' (Goldsmith *et al.*, 1972), *The Global 2000 Report to the President* (Barney (ed.), 1980–81), and *North-South: a Programme for Survival* (ICIDI, 1980). These images of imploding life have not dissipated. Flannery (1995) has more recently criticized us as *The Future Eaters*.

The 1987 report of the World Commission on Environment and Development (WCED) linked environment and security, but more clearly projected the image of a global political community. It recognized that unsustainable development promotes insecurity, and that competition for resources and environmental stress can be an important causal factor in the eruption of conflict and large-scale migration and refugee movements. It suggested that four issues of global environmental importance – tropical forests, water, desertification and population – could be funded with less than one month's global military spending (WCED, 1987, p. 303). However, the central message of the report was that a comprehensive reorientation towards sustainable development and multilateral cooperation was imperative, with poverty, inequality and environmental degradation needing to be addressed simultaneously. It recognized population, food security, loss of species and genetic resources, energy, industry, and human settlements as priority and inter-linked issues.

Writers in several disciplines still employ confronting images to convey the urgency of these issues. They include *The Ends of the Earth* (Kaplan, 1996), *Environment, Scarcity, and Violence* (Homer-Dixon, 1999), *Ultimate Security* (Myers, 1996), *Fighting for Survival* (Renner, 1996), *Shattering* (Fowler and Mooney, 1990), and *The Last Harvest* (Raeburn, 1995). Kaplan chose the image 'the coming anarchy' (1994) to convey his argument that the environment would be the national security issue of the early twenty-first century. Homer-Dixon (1999) argues that the incidence of civil and inter-ethnic violence will most likely increase as cropland, freshwater, and forests, become scarcer in many parts of the world. Examining environment and security projects involving 100 experts from 15 countries, he concluded that environmental scarcity, interacting with political, economic and other contextual factors, would precipitate increasing violence. In *Beyond the Limits* (Meadows *et al.*, 1992) scientists warned again that some consumption, population and pollution patterns have surpassed sustainable rates and that without a significant reduction, an uncontrolled decline in food output, energy use and industrial production is inevitable. Significant improvements in energy efficiency were also essential. But the potential for choosing long-term sustainability was also emphasized.

Population and security concerns are often linked in this environmental security genre, leavening Thomas Malthus' eighteenth-century warnings that population growth would outstrip humanity's capacity to feed itself. Over-population motivated Paul Ehrlich's *The Population Bomb* (1970) and the Ehrlichs' later *The Population Explosion* (Ehrlich and Ehrlich, 1990). Food security remains a priority for neo-Malthusians (such as Ehrlich *et al.*, 1993; Brown, 1999). But historical studies of colonial frontier conflicts over scarce resources, and contemporary conflicts over resource exploitation and degradation, suggest that conflicts over local resource use have been longstanding and are not necessarily macro-population-dependent (Reynolds, 1987, 1982; Claxton, 1998; Gedicks, 1993). Critics of Malthusian approaches urge that the political economy of resource use and institutional factors be given more consideration than population alone (Hartmann, 1995; Bandarage, 1997). Another suggests that notions of the earth's finite carrying capacity are simplistic, and naturalize poverty and underdevelopment (Ross, 1998). Some suggest that the ecological footprints which stratified segments of societies leave behind are highly variable (Wackernagel and Rees, 1996), so population trends alone tell little about future security, even within states.

Today the biotechnology revolution is a flash point which provides an added dimension to older debates. It is producing diverse images about food security and sustainable development. Bio-traders, bio-ethicists and bio-regulators compete for followers (Reid *et al.*, 1993; Hindmarsh *et al.*, 1998; Baumann *et al.*, 1996; Rojas, 1999; Krimsky and Wrubel, 1996; Gottweis, 1998). Proponents of the rapid expansion of gene technology industries argue that these can offer sustainable development and food security for the world's billions by increasing yield and reducing agro-chemical use. Sceptics suggest that biological diversity and local food security are being jeopardized by lax approaches to bio-safety risks, early emphases on chemical-resistant crop plants, and because consolidation in the agrochemical and seed industries has led to a handful of multinational corporate groups claiming broad patents in those industries, inhibiting affordable access to technology for developing countries (Thomas *et al.*, 1999; Griffin, 1998–99; Shand, 1997). Access, ownership and intellectual property rights issues for private and public sector users of genetic resources are still unresolved internationally. Furthermore, the use of genetically modified material in food products is resisted by consumers in many parts of the world (Sánchez and Juma (eds), 1994; Hoagland and Rossman (eds), 1997; Mugabe *et al.* (eds), 1997).

Concerns about water further add to the image of environmental insecurity. Water quality is significantly affected by agricultural practices.

Inadequate water supplies are more likely to be an environmental cause of human insecurity, civil conflict and inter-state war today than food shortages and population growth. An over-abundance of water conversely threatens the security of low-lying states as sea levels rise due to global warming (Homer-Dixon, 1999, p. 179; Myers, 1996, p. 18; Thomas, 1992, pp. 124–9). Climate change is also likely to impact adversely on food security.

Two 1997 UN reports document numerous sustainable development challenges, reinforcing the image of an endangered environment. They suggest that the natural regeneration rate of many interdependent life forms have been exceeded. The consumption of renewable resources including land, forests, topsoil, water, fisheries and urban air remains unsustainable. Little progress has been made in curbing either unsustainable consumption or production. Chemicals still cause widespread major health damage, environmental contamination and disposal problems. Ecosystems are imperilled by poorly regulated urbanization. Global biogeochemical flows are causing acidification, climate change, ozone depletion, unsettled hydrological cycles, and eroded biodiversity, biomass and bioproductivity. Energy output, fossil fuel consumption and pollution rates are all currently unsustainable. Agriculture and human settlements displace biodiversity at an increasing rate. Water quality and quantity, particularly in many developing countries, require urgent remedial action (UNEP, 1997; UNGA, 1997).

In 1999, further research findings about the declining ability of the earth to maintain the quality of human life were presented to the XVI International Botanical Congress. Attended by more than 4000 scientists from one hundred countries, the Congress heard that excessive fertilizer use and the burning of fossil fuel had more than doubled the amount of available nitrogen in the environment. Nitrogen and phosphorus run-off into major river systems and the sea had caused the death of some fifty areas of coastal ocean. Furthermore, 1998 was the planet's hottest year on record, as human activities increased the atmospheric concentrations of carbon dioxide and other heat-trapping gases. Human-induced change to the earth's environment, caused particularly by habitat destruction and invasive species, has increased extinction rates between 100 and 1000 times what they would otherwise have been (IBC Press Office, 1999).

The *Global Environmental Outlook-2000* (UNEP, 1999) reaffirmed many aspects of such dismal global environmental assessments.

Implications of the Image for Global Governance

The linking of environment and security projected by this image of an endangered planet has immediate governance implications. When issues are described as being of 'security' concern this can elevate them and associated remedial actions to a special status of urgency (Waever, 1995, p. 55). But which remedial actions are advocated depends on which security discourses an advocate supports. In general, security tends to be understood as a condition of being safe, secure and not threatened, but numerous governance options flow from the various ways the object and the realization of security are envisaged (Barnett, 1998).

Conventional or traditional concepts of security involve states entering into alliances, balancing power, and acting in military cooperation to deter others from seriously breaching international law. Collective security arrangements can be authorized by the United Nations Security Council or by regional arrangements or agencies, in accordance with the UN Charter. The environmental and opportunity costs of this traditional approach have long been of concern to environmentalists, because strategic planners and combatants rarely give priority to the environment in strategic assessments, military spending and military campaigns. Nuclear weapons and their decommissioning remain an acute concern.

'Comprehensive security' broadens the concept of security beyond managing threats to include political security (military, economic, social and humanitarian), and sustainable development (addressing environmental degradation and sustainable use) (Buzan, 1991; Barnett, 1998, pp. 129–30; Westing, 1989; Westing (ed.), 1989; Käkönen, 1992; Mandel, 1994). Even the United Nations Security Council has recognized that non-military sources of instability, including ecologies, had become threats to peace and security (Sands, 1993, p. 50). However, this broadened approach to traditional security concerns can continue to evoke traditional responses. Mathews (1989), for example, while making some innovative recommendations, has called for a renewed commitment to multilateral diplomacy and regional cooperation (regional security). She has also recommended enhanced monitoring (or intelligence-gathering), enforcement and compensation; the development of indicators of environmental health (or verification strategies), and new participatory development projects involving non-state actors. She also welcomes suggestions for the replacement of the UN Trusteeship Council with a new body having trusteeship of the global commons (the oceans, atmosphere, and planetary climate).

The UN's Food and Agriculture Organization is one global institution using traditional security language to convey its commitment to food security. Its Global System for the Conservation and Sustainable Utilization of Plant Genetic Resources, for example, includes a 'World Information and Early Warning System'. It monitors the state of the world's genetic resources and responds to potential threats from crop pathogens. In 1999, a warning of a global threat to wheat crops was issued (Sutherland, 1999). Similarly, an 'early warning centre' for global biological diversity within an international non-government organization (NGO), Conservation International, has been funded by private donors (Reuters, 1998).

The concept of environmental insecurity invites a departure from the increasingly obsolete concept of security being attained by states safeguarding their sovereignty over defined territory and populations, and managing the threats posed by other states in the international system. Environmental threats lack the intentionality and often territorial elements of this view (Prins (ed.), 1993; Mische, 1989). Therefore, responding to environmental insecurity demands a broader range of security strategies than those envisaged by traditional security concepts. 'Common security' is an alternative concept, which relies less on potential sanction and more on promoting security through trust and cooperation amongst states, based on a recognition of interdependence and a commitment to joint survival (ICIDI, 1980; ICDSI, 1982; WCED, 1987). It recognizes differential state responsibilities and transboundary interdependence. In 1995, the Commission on Global Governance expanded the concept of common security, and called for a universal commitment to the security not just of states, but also of all people and the planet, with a central role for the United Nations. It emphasized the need to prevent the development of crises and threats to security, and the need to maintain the integrity of the environment and the planet's life support systems (CGG, 1995, Chapter 3, echoing Walker, 1988 in many respects).

Like common security, 'cooperative security' also promotes stability and well-being through international economic and social cooperation, and it can encompass both common and collective security. Cooperative security promotes dialogue, multilateralism within international regimes, and peace-building preventative measures, such as promoting compliance with international sustainable development and human rights strategies. It involves addressing the underlying causes of disputes, conflicts and crises, so as to prevent threats arising or recurring. It also involves maintaining, restoring and enforcing peace (Evans, 1993, pp. 14–16, 39, 51; Birnie and Boyle, 1992, pp. 137–9). Many commentators note, however, that promoting and ensuring compliance with international environmental law remains a major challenge (Sands, 1993, p. 51; Birnie and Boyle, 1992, pp. 138–9, 212). Cooperative security seems to be the most dominant of the environmental security images portrayed in the IR literature, although the image is rarely described using explicit 'security' language. Rather cooperation for better environmental governance amongst a range of stakeholders is analysed and the pluralist image this generates is generally a positive one.

The image of an endangered planet has also encouraged a much broader re-visioning of security. There is increased academic and international institutional interest in the concept of 'human security', for example. Human security tends to be seen as a 'critical security' image. It includes individual and non-state-centred environmental, food, health, and economic security as a component of its revisioned security (Barnett, 1998; FAO, 1996; UNDP, 1995; Thakur, 1997; Walker, 1988; Tickner, 1995). This literature has not yet been able to settle on workable boundaries for the referent of security for IR purposes and debate continues over the utility of the 'human security' concept.

Recent critical security studies overlap to some extent with common and cooperative security studies, although the literature is diverse. Dalby, for example, advocates cooperative planning amongst neighbouring states and an avoidance of commodifying, enclosing, controlling approaches to nature. He has called for a pulling-back from current rates of unsustainable production, and for a reconfiguring of the social relations of production within and amongst states so that more equitable distributions of wealth, power and pollution are effected (Dalby 1992a, 1992b and 1998). Extant international agreements cover some of these recommendations and often go beyond them, but again implementation and compliance rather than prescription is a larger problem.

On the other hand, some critical theorists suggest that the environment and security nexus needs to be rethought, partly because the bleak security scenarios are overdrawn. Deudney (1992) proffers a counter-image: 'the mirage of eco-war'. Dalby suggests that security imagery can evoke authoritarian rather than humanitarian and participatory development strategies or other responses more appropriate for the complex, geographically specific, yet often unclear environmental and security interactions. Bringing environmental issues into the security concept may muddy the issues and reduce the likelihood of appropriate responses being developed. Dalby has criticized Kaplan for reinforcing neo-Malthusian themes and for representing Africa as a place of tribal, hostile and violent 'Others' (Dalby, 1996, p. 473). Dalby suggests that the long-term evolution of political and economic constellations of power, and the impact of the global political economy and international financial institutions on development trajectories, need to be more critically assessed. More cynically, Waever suggests that much of 'redefining security' debate is about elites vying for entry to the corridors of high politics and associated power which hitherto had not been accessible to them (Waever, 1995, p. 57). This cynical view is belied by mounting evidence of potentially irreversible environmental degradation, however, which academics and activists cite as justification for their political activities.

Although there is some evidence of a shift toward cooperative security strategies in environmental governance, concerns about environmental insecurity have not yet inspired UN member states to ensure that sustainable development strategies can become universal. Governments have committed insufficient funds to implement a range of multilateral environmental instruments that have already been adopted. Many commitments about the transfer of environmentally sound technologies to developing countries to aid in the latter's transition to more sustainable development are still unrealized (UNGA, 1997). Commitments to provide new and additional financial resources for developing countries, to meet agreed targets of 0.07 per cent of gross national product (GNP) in official development assistance from developed countries for developing countries, and to provide 0.15 per cent GNP for the least developed countries, have not been met. Despite replenishment, financial mechanisms such as the innovative Global Environmental Facility still need to be better funded. The continuing debt problems of developing countries also militate against sustainable development, despite periodic offers of respite (UNGA, 1997; Reed, ed., 1996; Rich, 1994).

Pluralizing Governance and Reassuring Images of Cooperative Security

The most dominant image since the 1992 UN Conference on Environment and Development has been that of a pluralist global body politic with proliferating inter-governmental institutions and environmentally active non-state actors. Proponents of sustainable development direct attention to the role of UN agencies, the corporate sector, women, youth, indigenous communities, and other local communities. This focus on the involvement of 'major groups' or stakeholders was a feature of many of the 1992 UNCED instruments, a feature not so evident in the instruments agreed to at the 1972 United Nations Conference on the Human Environment.

The reactive process of post-1972 global institution-building in response to the professional and popular environmental movement and environmental degradation has inspired titles such as *Governing the Commons* (Ostrom, 1990), *The International Politics of the Environment: Actors, Interests and Institutions* (Hurrell and Kingsbury (eds), 1992), *Institutions for the Earth* (Haas *et al.* (eds), 1993) and *Institutions for Environmental Aid* (Keohane and Levy (eds), 1996). In cooperative and reformist mode, commentators portray and assess the 'greening' of politics (Dobson (ed.), 1991), law (Sands (eds), 1993; Esty, 1994; Anderson and Blackhurst (eds), 1992), and ethics (Sylvan and Bennett, 1994). Environmental governance is seen to be increasingly global, as exemplified by titles such as *Toward a Politics of the Planet Earth* (Sprout and Sprout 1971), *Global Governance* (Young (ed.), 1997), *Global Accord* (Choucri, 1993), *The Global Politics of the Environment* (Elliott, 1998) and *Beyond the Limits* (Meadows *et al.*, 1992).

The UN agencies most closely associated with sustainable development images today include the UN Environment Program (UNEP), the UN

Development Program (UNDP), the Global Environment Facility (GEF), and the Commission on Sustainable Development (CSD). Sustainable development is also an agreed principle for the World Trade Organization (WTO), and many post-1970s global, regional and bilateral environmental agreements. The WTO has been criticized for not making stronger progress in promoting sustainability, however (Charnovitz, 1994, 1995, 1997). Other multilateral development actors, such as the Asian and Inter-American Development Banks and the World Bank, are also incorporating sustainable development discourse within their policies and guidelines, although financial institutions' structural adjustment policies have been criticized as an impediment to the attainment of sustainable development (Reed (ed.0, 1996).

Non-state actors are particularly welcomed. Publications which celebrate their contribution include *Reclaiming Paradise* (McCormick, 1989), *Environmental NGOs in World Politics* (Princen et al., 1994), *Activists Beyond Borders* (Keck and Sikkink, 1998), *NGOs, the UN, and Global Governance* (Weiss and Gordenker (eds), 1996), *Global Civil Society and Global Environmental Governance* (Lipschutz with Mayer, 1996), *Expanding Partnerships in Conservation* (McNeely (ed.), 1995), *Our Global Neighbourhood* (CGG, 1995) and *Our People, Our Resources* (Barton et al., 1997).

These images will remain powerful because the largest environmental global NGOs are growing in political legitimacy and authority. Environmental NGOs continue to proliferate in most countries of the world, and project diverse images of their priorities. In 1948 only 41 NGOs held consultative status with the UN's Economic and Social Council. The number expanded to 377 in 1968, and is now more than 1350. Fifteen hundred and fifty NGOs are currently associated with the UN's Department of Public Information. International non-government organizations (INGO) budgets can exceed those of the smallest and poorest states in the international system, and they have become the source of the second largest net amount of development assistance (United Nations, 1998a). This relative growth in power of NGOs follows many states' willingness to delegate, enter into partnerships, or opt out of some service delivery and/or resource management functions (Stamp, 1997; Peet and Watts, 1993).

The Green Web (Holdgate, 1999) conjures a powerful image. It depicts one of the most effective and influential quasi-NGOs – the World Conservation Union (or International Union for the Conservation and Natural Resources). Established in 1948, the Union has played a key role in conceptualizing and advocating changing conservation philosophies. It has instigated and influenced the negotiation and implementation of many global and regional international environmental treaties and its categories of protected areas and endangered species are recognized around the world. This has been an extraordinary contribution. In 1998, its members included 74 states, 110 government agencies and 743 NGOs, spanning 138 countries.

The IUCN's six global commissions have a combined membership of more than 10,000 volunteer scientists and lawyers. These commissions work in project teams and action groups, and promote community participation in species and biodiversity conservation and the sustainable management of habitats and natural resources (Holdgate, 1999, pp. vii, 243–5).

The WWF, another global NGO, is committed to protecting endangered spaces and species, and responding to global threats to the environment. Formed in 1961, it has sponsored more than 2000 projects in 116 countries. Its annual budget of US$300 million has exceeded that of both the United Nations Environment Program and the World Conservation Union (Holdgate, 1999, p. 216). In 1996, WWF claimed 4.7 million supporters in a global network active in 96 countries (Russell, 1996). The image of the panda gives WWF instant recognition. Other major NGOs include Greenpeace, Friends of the Earth, and Conservation International.

These large environmental NGOs have a global presence and operate with extensive international networks, often largely funded by over-consumers in developed states. The Internet enables NGO campaigns and other activities to be projected globally. Their images invite donations, support in kind, and urge societal change. Campaigns have become globally coordinated and are rapidly evolving. Glossy INGO publications, and sophisticated websites carry images of sustainable development around the world. The rapid expansion of NGOs' influence has been facilitated by the growth of global communications networks, and particularly the Internet, which enables campaigns to be effected relatively quickly and easily. The significant transparency of many inter-governmental environmental processes at instrument-negotiation and implementation stage has also stimulated stakeholders interest. The International Institute for Sustainable Development is a leader in raising awareness about inter-state negotiations. Its *Earth Negotiations Bulletin* (http://www.iisd.ca/) carries details of negotiations to followers' work stations around the world.

But images of powerful NGOs are not only made in developed states. Much of the expanding strength of the global environmental movement since the 1970s has come from the South, partly stimulated by UN activities (Rootes, 1999; Bahuguna, 1988). Although accurate figures are unavailable, estimates suggest that most of the 6000 NGOs in Latin America and the Caribbean have been formed since the mid-1970s. In Indonesia, WALHI, the Indonesian Environmental Forum, expanded from 79 NGO members in 1980 to more than 500 in 1992 (Princen *et al.*, 1994, p. 2). Some campaigns have become better known internationally. For example, the Chipko movement came to international prominence in 1974 from the Reni village of the Garhwal Himalaya. Women of the Chipko movement hugged trees in their local forest and challenged tree-fellers to saw their bodies along with the trees, emulating other Gandhi-inspired *satyagrahas* (Shiva, 1986). Deforestation in the Brazilian Amazon became politicized in the 1970s, with large international environmental organizations and local communities, including indigenous peoples and rubber tappers, mobilizing against some development plans. The struggle of the Dayaks against deforestation in Sarawak became an international issue from about 1987 (Keck and Sikkink, 1998, p. 152).

Such positive images of NGO contributions to sustainable development have been constituted in part by the ascendancy of liberalism in the post-Cold War era, and the UN's adoption of liberal-democratic discourses and processes in its environmental work. Non-government organizations exercise political influence in inter-governmental fora, despite not having voting rights. Accredited representatives may make oral or written interventions at meetings, comment on drafts of texts, and can lobby government delegations. Several UN agencies have entered into Memoranda of Understanding with partner NGOs and work closely with them in treaty development and implementation.

But not all commentators celebrate NGOs contributions. Edwards and Hulme (1996), for example, call for more accountability from, and critical scrutiny of, the non-government sector. Rubin denounces environmental campaigners for being part of *The Green Crusade* (1994). Other sceptics suggest that NGOs have insufficient power to challenge either the oligarchic features of the global political economy or authoritarian and anti-democratic states (Pasha and Blaney, 1998).

Transnational corporate activities and their environmental impacts have been relatively underassessed in the governance literature, although state-corporate and corporate-NGO strategies and partnerships for sustainability are attracting increasing attention (Murphy and Bendell, 1997; Holdgate, 1999, pp. 221–2; Dauvergne, 1997; Choucri, 1993). Academics are now suggesting more often that optimum regulatory approaches to promote sustainability may involve a combination of state, corporate and NGO strategies and instruments. Direct, state-based 'command and control' regulation has declined in relative influence, and diverse combinations of alternatives are being recommended as *Smart Regulation* (Gunningham *et al.*, 1998). The International Chamber of Commerce and the Business Council on Sustainable Development suggest that they will play an essential role in any transition to a sustainable future (Schmidheiny and Zorraquin, 1996; Schmidheiny with BCSD, 1992), and some of the largest NGOs are developing partnerships to ensure it (Murphy and Bendell, 1997).

However, not all NGOs are comfortable with positive images about corporate stakeholders' contribution to sustainable development. Some are critical of the corporate sector because international business associations have successfully lobbied to have the finalization of many international environmental agreements delayed, and their content weakened. They have also lobbied to have international trade agreements strengthened to protect their commercial interests. Many NGOs are unconvinced by corporate commitments to the environment and social justice, and have reacted with hostility to the current UN Secretary-General's invitation to industry to become more closely involved, perhaps even via a formal compact, in the pursuit of some of the fundamental goals of the UN (United Nations, 1999). Some NGO critics have also described the UN Development Programme's plan to accept voluntary donations from the corporate sector to finance a Global Sustainable Development Facility (GSDF), as 'greenwash', and 'a perilous partnership' which threatens the UNDP's independence and capacity to criticize corporate donors which breach international environmental, labour and human rights standards (TRAC, 1999). Paradoxically, various influential NGOs in developing countries, including the Third World Network, have opposed the incorporation of such standards in international trade agreements on the grounds that they could be used as a protectionist device by developed countries. It is unlikely that these negative images will survive intensifying imperatives for a transition to sustainability although they are indicative of the extent of the challenge remaining.

Images of 'Sustainable Development'

Much of the contemporary IR literature on environmental issues celebrates humanity's potential and actual capacity to effect global change in sustainable directions. 'Sustainable development' has become a popular and legal catchword which encapsulates diverse goals. It includes the integration of economic growth and development agendas with environmental sustainability, and recognizes that development cannot continue indefinitely on past and present trends. Wholesome images of careful planning and a generally precautionary approach to decision making are projected by the term. Advocates suggest that where there are threats of serious or irreversible damage, lack of full scientific certainty should not be used as a reason for postponing cost-effective measures to prevent environmental degradation. Other 'good governance' targets include transparency and public participation, effective environmental legislation, responsibility for environmental harm beyond territorial jurisdiction, and policies based on a recognition that peace, development and environmental protection are indivisible.

Although McGoldrick (1996) suggests that 'sustainable development' rests on the three pillars of international environmental law, international economic law and international human rights law, images of rational actors making market-oriented decisions are being projected increasingly by diverse actors globally. The relatively new sub-discipline of environmental economics advocates mechanisms such as new property rights to render the market and resource management more efficient and sustainable (Young *et al.*, 1996; Vogel, 1994). Other mechanisms include improved valuation and pricing systems for biological resources, pollution taxes and tradable emission permits. Rational game theory analyses attach values to direct use (trade, tourism), indirect use (ecological functions) and non-use (existence value, bequest value, and option value) of environmental 'resources' (Barbier *et al.*, 1990; Pearce and Turner, 1990; Pearce and Moran, 1994). Full-cost pricing is advocated, suggesting that the social costs of resource depletion and degradation – hitherto often considered externalities and market failures – should be reflected in the price of resource use, partly so that much-needed revenue for conservation can be generated. Other mechanisms include incentives, national accounting systems to include environmental resources, assessment of ecosystem support services, resource quotas, performance securities, debt for nature swaps, transferable development rights, watershed protection payments, and managed harvesting rights.

These optimistic images of clean green business and better priced environmental goods are being projected by several large INGOs, such as the IUCN and WWF, the World Business Council for Sustainable Development, a few NGOs in developing countries (see, for example, Sánchez and Juma (eds), 1994), and many governments, academics and several international institutions (such as OECD, 1996a and 1996b). Influential images, metaphors and book titles which project this approach include: *Blueprint for a Green Economy* (Pearce *et al.*, 1989) and subsequent publications in that series; *World Without End* (Pearce and Warford, 1993), *Reimbursing the Future* (Pearce *et al.*, 1996), and *Economics and Biological Diversity* (McNeely, 1988). Other influential organizations projecting sustainable market images include the International Institute for Environment and Development, Beijer International Institute of Ecological Economics, International Institute for Sustainable Development, and the Australian Centre for Environmental Law.

The 'universal' human component is also increasingly pronounced in images of sustainable development that identify stakeholders and 'major actors' who have an interest in, or responsibility for, the implementation of programmatic recommendations. Future generations, for example, have become a major stakeholder. A potentially finite future for humanity is implicit in the well-established norm of intergenerational equity (IUCN, 1995, p. 37). Development has to meet the needs of the present without compromising the ability of future generations to meet their own needs. Images of benevolent wisdom and precautionary restraint are projected by this norm. Women are another major group, and images portraying their contributions to sustainable development are noted briefly below.

Indigenous people[s] and communities in both North and South have also gained remarkable recognition as environmental actors since the 1980s. Postmodern pluralities of knowledge have gained legitimacy as the so-called 'Enlightenment project' of modernization has been questioned, and norms of 'racial' equality have become more widely constitutive. Images of the indigenous peoples living in harmony with nature have become popular since the 1980s. 'Expertness', particularly within UN environmental bodies, is now less the exclusive preserve of those with professional credentials or the support of a state or well-funded NGO. These bodies are still undoubtedly influential (Litfin, 1994; Haas, 1990), but increasingly indigenous people[s] and local communities are recognized as social actors having relevant local and traditional knowledge for environmental governance purposes. Commentators welcome *Indigenous Knowledge Systems for Development* (Warren *et al.* (eds), 1995), denounce *Monocultures of the Mind* (Shiva, 1993a), and advocate *Decolonizing Knowledge* (Apffel-Marglin *et al.*, 1996).

Images of Ecological Imperialism?

There is a body of literature which suggests that global actors promoting better environmental governance are really facilitating ecological imperialism. Local practices, especially in the South, have to be transformed to meet the new environmental goals of the North (Lohman, 1993, p. 158). International environmental agreements are said to prioritize issues of concern to donor states, and to marginalize issues of concern to grassroots movements (Shiva, 1993b).

But do the texts of numerous international environmental instruments portray stark images of hegemonic domination by the North? In 1989, developing country governments insisted on linking conservation and development in the UN General Assembly Resolution which called for the convening of the 1992 Rio Earth Summit. Essentially bipolar North-South negotiations did characterize the negotiation of the instruments produced at the Earth Summit, with the Group of Seventy-Seven (representing about 128 countries) insisting that their development agendas were not to be sacrificed to the environmental agenda. The Rio Declaration describes sustainable development as making 'environmental protection...an integral part of the development process'. That Declaration also recognizes the eradication of poverty as an 'indispensable requirement for sustainable development', with special priority to be given to the needs of developing and particularly the least developed countries. Developed countries are said to carry particular responsibilities for the pursuit of sustainable development because of the pressures they place on the global environment, and the technologies and resources they command. States are asked to reduce and eliminate unsustainable patterns of production and consumption, and promote appropriate demographic policies. As noted above, however, donor states are being criticized for providing inadequate resources to enable sustainable development to be realized.

The breadth and complexity of many environmental issues defy simple North-South images. Fluid coalitions of states negotiate outside the UN's regional groups depending on the issues at hand. 'Southern' groups include AOSIS (Alliance of Small Island States), the Group of 77, and Mercosur. 'Northern' groups include A-CAP (developed Pacific countries), CANZ (Canada, Australia and New Zealand), the European Union, the Group of Eight (seven major 'Western' economies and Russia), JUSSCANNZ ('Western' states outside the EU), the OECD, the 'Umbrella Group' and the Western European and Others Group (WEOG). But a significant range of groups include both donor and recipient states (North and South), including ASEAN (Association of Southeast Asian Nations), the Valdavia Group (various countries in the southern hemisphere), the Cairns Group (agricultural trade reformers), COBSEA (Coordinating Body on the Seas of East Asia), the Commonwealth, ESCAP (UN Economic and Social Commission for Asia and the Pacific) and SPREP (the South Pacific Regional Environment Program). So the image of a global 'local' may risk oversimplifying fluid and sometimes transitory coalitions or common negotiating positions.

As another rejoinder to ecological-imperialism images, several developing country governments have had aspects of United States trade and environment law declared illegal under the General Agreement on Tariffs and Trade and WTO Agreements. Unilateral trade restrictions on environmental grounds are illegal in the absence of genuine and prior attempts to negotiate multilateral solutions.

Diversifying Images

In the 1980s and 1990s expert warnings about the state of the world have not abated, but the tropes and images by which they are popularized have diversified. Ecofeminist images are the final example of contending images of the environment in world politics which will be considered. Feminism has claimed its place as a mainstream inspiration for change. Since the 1980s, the ecofeminist movement has denounced the masculine control of 'Mother' nature – personified in Gaia, Eve or Isis – and gendered science, technology and states. *Reclaim the Earth* (Caldecott and Leland, 1983), *Earth Follies* (Seager, 1993), *Earthcare* (Merchant, 1995), *Ecofeminism* (Mies and Shiva, 1993), *Re-Weaving the World* (Diamond and Orenstein (eds), 1990), and

Fertile Ground (Diamond, 1994) are some of the many publications in this diverse genre.

Some ecofeminists champion nature's emancipation from masculine domination and advocate more ecocentric interconnectedness for all (Warren with Erkal (eds), 1997; Runyan, 1992). Some essentialize women, arguing they are closer to nature because of their productive, reproductive and nurturing roles. They suggest women's empathy also derives from their experience of domination within the public/private, production/reproduction dualisms of many societies. Ecofeminist writings that condemn science and technology for perpetuating the exploitation of nature tend also to reject the development paradigm which envisages a more egalitarian technological capacity between 'North' and 'South'. 'Catch-up' development, they suggest, is illusory since the 'good life' or over-development of the North has only been made possible through the exploitation of the South, which continues. Moreover, some ecofeminists argue, a global 'good life' of technological universality is an ecological impossibility. Mies and Shiva (1993) argue that the dominant development paradigm and capitalist patriarchy are partly to blame for the erosion of biological diversity, with women, 'foreign peoples' and nature being colonized within this paradigm. Other feminists have highlighted the impoverishment of women, who have lost subsistence resources to cash-crop production which is highly vulnerable to market forces, and whose double burden as productive and reproductive workers has intensified with 'development' (Fairbairn-Dunlop, 1994).

The emergence of ecofeminist images and discourses partly reflects the growth of a heterogeneous global social movement, in which women and gender issues are prominent, that has gained increasing UN attention since the 1970s. Northern liberal feminism has had to make room for all manner of feminist diversity: socialist, cultural and gay. Claims based on gender-based productivity, poverty, basic needs, efficiency and equity also now have a place in this diverse movement. Advocates of women in development, and gender and development discourse have demanded responses from international institutions (Razavi, 1997), and these have been delivered to varying degrees of satisfaction. Following the Vienna and Beijing world conferences on human rights and women, gender (and not just feminism) has been made a mainstream issue for the United Nations (United Nations, 1998b and 1998c).

Gender and Development (GAD) and 'Women in development' (WID) are particularly mainstream. One of their concerns has been the failure of economists, development planners and national account systems to recognize and value women's contributions to development, and to analyse gender-specific aspects of development. Consistent with earlier feminisms, rights to equality for men and women were recognized in the UN Charter and have been recognized in many UN instruments since. Rights based on gender equality are implicit in much of the literature on women in development, gender and development, and ecofeminism.

Conclusions

This chapter has sketched a very partial history of the present and identified various images projected by literatures concerned with sustainable development, security, and gender and the environment. It has explored how complex and variable contemporary global images about security, sustainable development, and human rights have made sustainable development a matter of governance, and a site for interventions, and the exercise of power, by diverse actors. It has indicated the imperatives of change toward greater sustainability, if security for the endangered planet is to be promoted. It also notes the interrelationship between dominant images and longer-standing global discourses, including international law. The chapter has argued that although cooperative security is the dominant approach to managing global environmental problems, the security aspect of multi-stakeholder cooperation is rarely explicitly acknowledged. Rather, liberal institutionalist literature emphasizes rationality and mutual interests in cooperation.

This discussion of images surrounding that of 'an endangered planet' has emphasized the role of non-state actors, social movements and the promotion of environmental security. This prompts us to recognize that the emergence of pluralizing cooperative governance has important theoretical and political implications. It confirms the diffuse and contested nature of economic and social power within increasingly liberal forms of global governance. It also demonstrates the important roles played by knowledge/power networks, social movements, corporations, and academic disciplines and sub-disciplines within networks of governance. State and non-state actors both produce discourses and can be constrained by them as subjectivities evolve and respond to changing norms. The dominance of anthropocentric discourses is apparent from the literature, with images of the instrinsic values of species being less dominant.

CHAPTER 14

A 'Gendered Global Hierarchy'?

V. Spike Peterson

As a metaphor for our time, 'a gendered global hierarchy' may be an unfamiliar and even disconcerting image to many. Unlike other metaphors in this book, a gendered global hierarchy is not associated with any particular author, text or origin. In fact, at present this metaphor has no single meaning and therefore has perhaps less currency in the literature of International Relations than some of these other metaphors. Rather, there is a rapidly growing body of research, writing, teaching and activism we might label 'feminist IR'. In some respects, all variants of feminist IR are critical of a gendered global hierarchy, but they differ significantly on what constitutes this hierarchy, how it is produced and sustained, and how we might move beyond it. While there is, then, no single or simple image, an examination of the various interpretations of a gendered global hierarchy brings us to an important site that other pictures of world politics miss, one which has important implications for the theory and practice of world politics.

In many ways, a snapshot of mainstream IR itself depicts a gendered global hierarchy. The discipline is largely dominated by Anglocentric and Eurocentric male practitioners and by masculinist[1] constructs, such as sovereignty, national security, *Realpolitik*, and military might. It is also focused on public sphere activities – power politics, foreign policy, militarism, war – that are defined as masculine and dominated by men. More recently, the male-dominated activities constituting big business and global financial power have become a focus of IR as well. Moreover, mainstream depictions of IR represent a world of hierarchical social relations among inherently competitive, power-seeking nation-states. In sum, the discipline and its mainstream image renders women, the activities associated with women, and/or constructs, identities, practices and institutions associated with femininity virtually invisible. What feminists argue is that this gendered (masculinist) image is not only 'inaccurate' and hence generates flawed analyses of world politics; it is also biased in ways that effectively produce and reproduce a variety of global hierarchies that are linked by their denigration of the feminine as weak, dependent, irrational and uncivilized.

This chapter argues that feminisms provide powerful conceptual lenses which systemically challenge the givens and parameters of conventional IR theory and practice. This claim has several components. First, feminists transgress disciplinary boundaries to generate more wide-ranging and inclusive analyses of social relations. Their study of world politics draws upon and links areas of inquiry, such as family relations, domestic violence, welfare economics, and ecological issues, that are neglected in mainstream accounts. Second, feminists also transgress 'levels of analysis' and the public–private divide to generate more systemic or holistic analyses. For example, they examine how individual internalization of gender stereotypes (for example, masculinity as competitive, unemotional and 'in control') interacts with sociocultural inputs (for example, patriarchal religious beliefs, pornography, violent entertainment) and with gendered divisions of labour (for example, politics and the military as 'men's work') to fuel international relations that are competitive and conflictual (for example, dominated by men seeking autonomy and control through direct and indirect violence). Third, feminists acknowledge that their work is informed by normative/political commitments. The specifics of that commitment vary tremendously: there is no single feminist vision or agenda. But the very existence and acknowledgment of a commitment to 'improving the conditions of women' links and strengthens feminists even as it also works against feminist projects by fuelling resistance from those not committed to gender equality.

In sum, the lens that feminisms provide poses challenges to conventional analyses by integrating insights and research on gendered identities (how we think of ourselves and behave as gendered social beings), on gendered communication systems (how naming, concepts, language and world views are gendered and how this affects all social relations), and on gendered institutions (how divisions of labour and authority structure unequal divisions of autonomy, privilege, security, resources, and power). Given this array of issues, we begin to see how feminist IR is not easily captured by any single metaphor, and how it constitutes not only a critique of specific IR claims but a transformative project on no less than a global scale.

What then does the image of 'a gendered global hierarchy' encompass? What do we mean by feminist IR? And why has feminist IR emerged only recently? I begin by setting the context for the emergence of feminist IR and then consider several ways to depict its meaning and significance. The first of these has to do with epistemological differences that shape how feminists, and others, variously deploy the dichotomies of male–female and masculine–feminine. The second considers three overlapping feminist projects that underpin and inform feminist IR and provides examples from feminist IR texts. I conclude by discussing the strengths and weaknesses of viewing IR through feminist lenses.

Context: Why Feminist IR *Now*?

All images and perspectives are dependent on historical context for their meaning and salience. Feminist IR could emerge because feminist activism had politicized gender oppression (for example, inequality of rights, opportunities, resources; sexual harassment and violence), and made women's issues visible and global. Of particular relevance to IR, the United Nations Decade for Women (1975–1985) and its related conferences not only provided global fora for women's issues, but also instituted data-gathering on the actual conditions of women worldwide. At the same time, feminist scholarship demonstrated that gender influences not only who we are and how we act but also how we think and, therefore, how we make knowledge claims. In various academic disciplines, debates in social theory were unsettling conventional claims about objectivity and science. Referred to as the 'third debate' in IR,[2] critiques of the discipline's 'givens' raised or re-opened many foundational questions. These disruptions made it more likely that alternative vantage points and critical challenges could emerge.

But given the masculinist image of IR depicted above, the discipline has been particularly reluctant to acknowledge, much less welcome, feminist interventions. In Ann Tickner's words, 'international politics is such a thoroughly masculinized sphere of activity that women's voices are considered inauthentic' (Tickner, 1992, p. 4). From this, we begin to see how and why the discipline constitutes difficult, even hostile terrain, for women and especially for feminists. However, by the late 1980s, even reluctant disciplines were vulnerable to feminist pressure.

In 1988, the London School of Economics formally initiated the study of 'gender and IR' through a seminar course and a special issue of its journal, *Millennium: Journal of International Studies*.[3] Conferences, panels, articles, and books followed. The Feminist Theory and Gender Studies section of the International Studies Association provided institutional visibility in 1990. I circulated a thin but rapidly growing 'gender and IR' bibliography until 1993, when the volume of relevant material exceeded my ability to track it comprehensively.[4] Given its relatively recent and heavily resisted interventions, feminist IR has gained a remarkable foothold in the discipline. A very extensive and wide-ranging literature exists. IR feminists have institutionalized their presence at conferences and in curricula, and have recently launched a journal devoted to feminist international politics. As a particular sign of healthy growth, a 'second generation' of IR feminists is already visible, pushing in new directions and further eroding disciplinary, territorial, and race/ethnic/class boundaries.

Epistemology: What Difference Does it Make?

Whereas all proponents of feminist IR seek to improve the conditions of women in some sense, the variance among them in what this means and implies is considerable. Like any lens on social relations, feminist perspectives can be distinguished by reference to what issues (bodies, politics, economics, violence?) are focused on and how knowledge/truth about those issues or topics is produced (empirically, analytically, comparatively or intuitively?). It is important to note that the two questions are not separate but interactive. Stated simply, the latter refers to epistemology – or the study of truth claims, as in 'How do we make claims to know?' 'How do we generate evidence and conclusions and attribute validity to them?' I can only treat these complex issues briefly here, but they are important for grasping how feminist IR spans a range of positions, which generate multiple interpretations of the image of a 'gendered global hierarchy'. Epistemological positions also affect responses to feminist IR. I return to this point in the conclusion. Of course, epistemology is also key to current social theory debates, which centre on how we understand the relationship between knowledge and power. In this sense, epistemological practices are quintessentially political.

At the risk of oversimplification, the epistemological distinction I wish to draw between positivist and postmodernist orientations centres on questions of language and power (for fuller discussion, see Peterson, 1992; see also George, 1994). Positivists make two interacting assumptions: that subjects (knowers) can be separated from objects (that which is known), and facts (generated through the application of scientific method, which separates subject from object) can be separated from values (the subjective taint of the knower's desires, opinions, interests). A further assumption follows: that reality exists independent of the subject's participation in it, so knowers (and the power relations within which they exist and act) can be separated from that which they study.

Postmodernists are sceptical of these claims, and especially the dichotomized, either–or separations that are assumed. They argue instead that reality is better understood not as rigid boundaries but *relationally*. Specifically, they argue that the world we study is a social construction in the sense that humans/subjects 'create' meaning and intelligibility through the mutual (inter-subjective) constitution of symbols, language, identities, practices and social structures. This is not to argue that the physical world does not exist independent of subjects but that it has no social *meaning* independent of that which is 'imposed' by human thought and action. Hence, knowers cannot stand 'outside' of the reality they observe because their participation in that reality is a necessary condition for the object observed to have any social meaning. That is, *both* subject and object gain their meaning and intelligibility by reference to their location in a system of meaning and social relations, including power that encompasses both. From this perspective, subjects and objects are not categorically separate but necessarily exist in a relationship shaped by inter-subjective meaning and social/power relations. As a consequence, 'absolute' objectivity is illusory, the relationship between knowledge and power becomes central to evaluating all claims, and language becomes central – and political – insofar as it constitutes the meaning system of intelligibility and order.

By denying the categorical separations that are fundamental to positivism, postmodernists reject 'either–or' thinking (dichotomies) as a distortion of social reality. They emphasize instead the relationships that link beliefs and actions to language and power. This becomes crucial in feminist debates – and in feminist IR – because the dichotomies of male–female and masculine–feminine play so central a role in feminist claims. As one consequence, 'a gendered global hierarchy' means different things to different feminists.

Diversity and Complexity: a Continuum of Feminisms and Images

While there is overlap among all feminist projects, the diversity among feminists renders many different images of a gendered global hierarchy. To impose structure on the imagery, I identify three overlapping feminist projects and locate particular feminist IR projects along a continuum that spans positivists and postmodernist orientations.

Typically, the initial feminist project is a deconstructive one: exposing the extent and effects of masculinist bias. This exposes the omission of actual women and their activities while also documenting how 'woman' is represented as deviant from or deficient in respect to male-as-norm criteria. For example, the model of universal human nature (as atomistic, greedy, and competitive) that underpins IR is in fact based upon interpretations of the experiences of a particular subset of humans (males) in a particular context (modern Europe). Hence, these cannot be accurate claims about all *humans* or even all males. Consider how a model based on females who mother would foreground not independence, selfishness or competition but mutual aid, 'altruism', and cooperation – that is, *relationships* – insofar as these are essential for sustaining group existence. It is not simply that mothers are doing something different than the men depicted, but that the very existence of adult males *depends* on mothering and other cooperative activities. To ignore this is to misrepresent *human* social relations. In short, androcentric (male-as-norm) assumptions have generated systemic bias in knowledge claims and cultural ideologies. One sense of a gendered global hierarchy, then, is how the picture it projects focuses on men (only) and privileges only what they do and how they think. In this picture, women, and also 'private sphere' activities upon which men's lives depend, are rendered invisible.

Attempts to rectify the systematic exclusion of women constitute a second project: correcting androcentric falsehoods by *adding women* and their experiences to existing frameworks. To focus on women's lives and private sphere activities involves new sources and topics (for example, diaries, domestic activities) and prompts a re-evaluation of old ones. But adding women to existing paradigms also reveals how deeply the conceptual structures themselves presuppose male experience and viewpoint. That is, 'adding women' reveals the extent to which excluding women/femininity is a fundamental structuring principle of conventional thought. Indeed, women cannot simply be 'added' to constructions that are literally defined by being masculine: the public sphere, the military, rationality, political identity, objectivity. Either women as feminine cannot be added (that is, women must become like men) or the constructions themselves are transformed (that is, adding women as feminine alters their masculine premise and changes their meaning).

Probably the most familiar feminist IR work corresponds to the second project and asks 'where are the women?' and/or 'adds women' to conventional IR topics. For instance, Rebecca Grant (1991) recasts the stag hunt analogy by asking where the women are and how each man's relationship to family needs affects his decision making. By ignoring these aspects, the stag hunt is a misleading analogy for the behaviour of states, which also depend on domestic arrangements. Other feminists recast security by asking how women are affected by war and whether the pursuit of guns over butter is in *their* interest. Cynthia Enloe's pioneering work (1990) examines the unconventional topics of tourism, foreign military bases and domestic servants to illuminate a gendered global hierarchy operating in everyday lives and global dynamics. And adding women to models of economic development exposed, for example, how assuming Western divisions of labour paralleled those in Africa resulted in failed projects. Programs that directed agricultural training and credit to men denied women's traditional role as farmers and actually decreased their well-being and that of their children (Elson (ed.), 1991).

More recent literature adds women and some exploration of gender to international political economy (IPE), where women's work significantly shapes national productivity and resources.[5] Women are key, as ever, to the reproduction of future citizens and workers. They determine consumption patterns. They 'take up the slack' when states cut back on public provision of welfare. As cheap and flexible sources of labour, women are preferred workers in today's global assembly line economy. In short, feminists insist that acknowledging the work that women do is essential to economic analyses. Other research that takes women's lives and experiences seriously includes: women's rights as a dimension of international human rights discourse (Cook (ed.), 1994; Peters and Wolper (eds), 1995; Peterson and Parisi, 1998); the history and contemporary relevance of women's peace and ecological activism (for example, Reardon, 1985; Runyan, 1988; Shiva, 1988; Mies and Shiva, 1993; Sharoni, 1995; Whitworth, forthcoming); women's state, non-state, trans-state and international political activities (Randall, 1987; Stienstra, 1994; Whitworth, 1994; Tetreault, 1994; D'Amico and Beckman (eds), 1995; Peterson and Runyan, 1999); and women in militaries, nationalist struggles, foreign policy, and security broadly construed (Enloe, 1983 and 1993; Stiehm (ed.), 1983; Elshtain, 1987; Cohn, 1987; Elshtain and Tobias, 1990; McGlen and Sarkees (eds), 1993; Lorentzin and Turpin 1998).

Making women empirically visible in world politics is a valuable project. It exposes the androcentric assumptions of conventional accounts, inserts actual (embodies) women in our picture of 'reality', and reveals women as agents and activists, as well as victims of violence and the poorest of the poor (Peterson and Runyan, 1999). But it also forces a rethinking of foundational categories. For example, it suggests that the androcentric definition of 'human' conceals how women systematically suffer 'human' rights abuses. And it is a masculinist construction of 'work' that conceals women's labour and its relevance to IPE. In short, adding women also reveals how categories and frameworks themselves are biased toward male bodies, experience, and knowledge claims. Rethinking foundational categories entails the third project that is prompted by feminist perspectives: reconstructing theory.

It is here that the distinction between sex and gender is crucial.[6] In contrast to positivist notions of sex as a biologically 'natural' dichotomy of male–female, gender is a systematic *social construction* that dichotomizes identities, behaviours, and expectations as masculine–feminine. As a social construct, gender is not 'given' but learned and therefore mutable. Most significantly, gender is not simply a trait of individuals but a historically institutionalized, structural feature of social life. On the one hand, gender is a socially imposed and internalized 'lens' through which individuals perceive themselves and the world. On the other hand, the pervasiveness of gendered meanings shapes concepts, practices, identities and institutions in patterned ways. In short, gender is not simply an empirical category referring to substantive men and women but an analytical one, such that 'all of social life is gendered' (Nelson, 1989, p. 4). In Sandra Harding's words

> Once we begin to theorize gender – to define gender as an analytic category
> within which humans think about and organize their social activity rather than a
> natural consequence of sex difference, or even merely as a social variable assigned
> to individual people in different ways from culture to culture – we can begin to
> appreciate the extent to which gender meanings have suffused our belief systems,
> institutions, and even such apparently gender-free phenomena as our architecture
> and urban planning. (Harding, 1986, p. 17)

As a *structural* feature of social life, gender pervades language, which
shapes how we think and communicate. It structures divisions of power and
authority, which determine whose voices and experiences dominate culturally and coercively. It also structures divisions of labour, which determine
who does what kind of work and how compensation for work is distributed.
In short, a gendered global hierarchy operates at a deep structural level.

In the third project, reconstructing theory, feminists join other critics of
positivism who challenge essentialist categories and dichotomies. Gender
as an analytic category enabled feminists to criticize not only the exclusion
and/or denigration of females (as a sex category), but also the masculinist
constructs that underpin philosophy (reason, abstraction), political theory
(atomistic individualism, sovereignty), economic models (waged labour,
rational choice), and science (objectivity, dichotomies). Indeed, feminists go
beyond other critics of positivism to argue that 'the fundamental
dichotomies ... between subject/object, rational/irrational, culture/nature,
and reason/emotion are all a product of the basic male/female hierarchy
that is central to patriarchal thought and society' (Hekman, 1987, p. 68). For
example, Ann Tickner (1992) genders the state by arguing that IR theorists
simply project the assumption of masculine characteristics onto states,
which they then define as unitary, rational, competitive, and the primary
actors in IR. Historically, individuals are linked to states through citizenship that is constituted by (male-only) military and property-owning qualifications, and states act as warriors in the anarchic realm of international
politics.

The third variant of feminist IR focuses less on sex as an empirical variable and more on exploring the interdependence of masculine–feminine, the
centrality of gendered identities, and the significance of gender in how we
think as well as how we act. Conventional categories and dichotomies are
not taken for granted but problematized. Here we find more references to
symbols and language, and more efforts to rethink foundational constructs,
such as power, sovereignty, security, identity, development, violence, peace.
Consistent with this, there is typically more evidence of theoretical discussion and debate, and more self-consciousness about analytical assumptions
and how they frame the questions we ask and the methods we adopt.

For instance, Spike Peterson and Anne Sisson Runyan emphasize the
interaction of empirical and analytical gender by reference to two mutually

constructed dimensions: 'women's position in world politics' (how women and men differently act within and are affected by international processes) and the 'power of gender' (how gendered lenses shape our concepts, expectations and knowledge claims). Their book illustrates how gendered dichotomies – such as public–private, soldier–protectee, production–reproduction and culture–nature – underpin IR thinking about politics, security, economics and ecology (Peterson and Runyan, 1999). Jan Jindy Pettman takes the imagery of gendered global hierarchies to new sites by exploring the gendered politics of identities not only within states but also in relation to colonization, racism, nationalism, migration and postcolonial issues (Pettman, 1996). These remain neglected areas in IR but are increasingly the focus of feminist interventions (for example, Yuval-Davis, 1997; Alexander and Mohanty (eds), 1997; Agathangelou and Ling, 1997; Han and Ling, 1998; Ranchod-Nilson and Tetreault (eds), 2000; Eisenstein, 1996). This is due in part to the significance of gender in relation to identity politics more generally, and also to feminist concern with a broader range of oppressive politics than typically animates IR inquiry.

As we move through feminist projects and along the continuum, gender refers less to taken-for-granted categories of male–female, which simply reproduce the terms as a dichotomy, and more to the dynamic, multidimensional relationship between masculine–feminine. Here, gender is not a synonym for woman (Carver, 1996). Rather, gender as analytical construct means that claims about femininity are necessarily also claims about masculinity. Because they are interdependent constructs, the study of men and masculine activities *requires* the study of women and the feminine. In this sense, feminist IR does not just tell us something about women but necessarily transforms our understanding of men. As a corollary, on this 'side' of the continuum we find in works such as Marysia Zalewski and Jane Parpart's edited volume *The 'Man' Question in International Relations* (1998) not only more attention to men, masculinities and heterosexism (Zalewski and Parpart (eds), 1998; Weber, 1999; Peterson and Parisi, 1998; Peterson, 1999) but a destabilization of 'identities' more generally.

Postmodernists question whether we can refer unproblematically to collective social identities – such as 'the working-class perspective'. If all social identities are constructed through complex and intersecting histories, experiences, and structures, then there is no such thing as a purely 'working-class' identity. Rather, people have socially constructed identities other than, and in addition to, class, such as gender, race, national, and familial identities, that can conflict with or mediate their class identities. Therefore, there is no way to identify a single working-class perspective that can speak for all working-class people. Rather, we must recognize that, while generalizations about groups are useful, they are also always suspect insofar as they hide the differences 'within' the group being described.

Even as postmodernism problematizes universalizing claims, its critical orientation can serve feminist projects. Jill Steans identifies feminist postmodernism as 'affirmative' and able to contribute to critical projects of emancipation. Any fixed or universalizing construction of 'women' is rejected, but the possibilities of feminist resistance are not. For Steans (1998, pp. 182–3), feminist IR is perhaps better seen not 'as an attempt to 'reconstruct' the discipline, but rather as opening up spaces for critical engagement and dialogue'. (1998:182–3) Christine Sylvester (1994) develops a different theoretical point in regard to feminism and postmodernism. The latter's emphasis on the constitutiveness of masculinist language inclines it toward the deconstruction of authority and destabilization of places from which to speak/act, and hence, away from political commitment and action. In contrast then to feminist postmodernism, Sylvester argues for postmodern feminism, which inclines toward a negotiation between standpoint feminism – with its 'real' women and practical/moral implications – and postmodernism's scepticisms. So understood, postmodern feminism permits us to have meaningful identities even as we relentlessly question their political implications. Sylvester's postmodern feminism asks us to recognize, but not categorically resolve, our need for boundaries and identities. Rather, to transform gendered global hierarchies requires a shift to more fluid and relational orientations.

There is, then, no single feminist IR perspective but a continuum of overlapping perspectives/projects and even epistemologies. Hence, there is no single interpretation of how 'a gendered global hierarchy' is constituted or might be reformed, but the continuum outlined above illuminates key forms of hierarchy that other perspectives on world politics neglect.

Strengths and Weaknesses of Feminist IR

Given its diversity and range, feminist IR makes a number of contributions to our understanding of world politics and multiple interpretations of a gendered global hierarchy. These can be examined by reference to empirical, analytical and critical/political contributions.

From the vantage point of empirical contributions, feminists improve our understanding of world politics by including more of the world. As approximately one-half of the population, 'adding women' is not a trivial consideration. For example, the work that women do is consistently neglected in conventional accounts. Yet the reproduction of all social groups and all public sphere activities *depends* on activities in the 'private sphere' that are delegated to women. Moreover, today's global economy, which is inextricable from today's world politics, involves consumer identities, worker expectations and skills, divisions of labour, and financial arrangements that are all profoundly gendered. Hence, we simply do not adequately understand the world of economics – and politics – unless we take seriously how those worlds are gendered. We begin to perceive a gendered global hierarchy when we ask, where are the women?

The diversity among the world's women – differences of class, ethnicity/race, nationality, sexuality, and so on – poses urgent problems for feminists who implicitly or explicitly make universalizing claims about 'women'. Among feminists, the significance of differences and, especially, hierarchies among women is a challenging and politically crucial dilemma. At issue is how to bring an awareness of and respect for differences among women into productive relation with commitments to and action in support of 'women's' political agency and efficacy, insofar as the latter presupposes commonalities of experience, interest and strategic objective. Although all social movements confront this tension, feminists have gone further than most to acknowledge and address their complicity in reproducing hierarchies. However one interprets their record on this score, it is certainly the case that women's movements are a worldwide phenomenon and inputs to feminist IR reflect a diversity that corresponds more accurately to the world than inputs typical of mainstream IR.

Of course, including women in world politics also informs and should transform policy making. This extends from basic welfare provision to health care and family law and on to trade policies, citizenship laws, war crimes and human rights. In short, women and men differently affect, and are differently affected by, the practices, processes and institutions of world politics. Adequate analysis requires recognizing and coming to terms with these differences.

From the vantage point of analytical contributions, feminists join other critics of positivism in rejecting either–or dichotomies and simplistic notions of objectivity, rationality, and the neutrality of methods. Postmodern feminists extend anti-foundational critiques by identifying objectivity, rationalism, and even science itself as specifically masculine ways of knowing as shaped by patriarchal social relations. Locating masculinism at the foundation of Western thought and early state-making, they argue that the *hierarchical* dichotomies that typify Western culture and structures are both produced by and are a product of the gender hierarchy 'that is central to patriarchal thought and society' (Hekman, 1987; also Peterson, 1997b). It is in this sense that gender hierarchy underpins other structural hierarchies (see below). That is, the taken-for-granted, ostensibly 'natural' dichotomy of male–female is generalized to naturalize, hence depoliticize, the dichotomy of masculine–feminine and its historical *privileging* of that which is associated with masculinity over that which is associated with femininity. This naturalized hierarchy provides powerful legitimacy to discriminatory languages, practices and institutions that are linked by their denigration of the feminine.

Thus, feminists make a distinctive contribution to current debates. First, to the extent that masculinity remains privileged and positivism is identified with masculinity, critics of positivism meet resistance not only to their argumentation *per se* but to the 'demasculinization' of science their argument entails. Second, to the extent that Western thought constitutes, and is constituted by, the colonizing dualism of masculine–feminine as these feminists claim, moving beyond positivism requires moving beyond taken-for-granted gender dichotomies as well (Peterson, 1992). In short, effective critiques of positivism must involve effective critiques of masculinism, and vice versa.

From the vantage point of critique and political practice, feminist contributions are uniquely transformative. Their key contribution in this case is historical-empirical in providing analytical evidence of gender hierarchy as fundamental to domination in its many guises. First, females suffer disproportionally under systems of domination insofar as females constitute at least one half of most subordinated groups and are systematically rendered more vulnerable to sexual and other violence, inadequate health care, political subordination, and economic impoverishment. Second, the naturalization of women's oppression – taking gender hierarchy as 'given' rather than historically, politically constructed – *serves as the model for depoliticizing exploitation more generally*, whether of groups or of nature.

That is, feminists argue that domination of women, nature, and all who are constructed as (feminized) 'other' is not a matter of 'essential', atemporal qualities but of socially constructed, historically contingent practices. Eliminating the justification of oppression (as natural) does not eliminate oppression, nor preclude other justifications of it. But the ideology that treats hierarchies as 'natural' serves powerfully to legitimate and reproduce domination: through the internalization of oppression, the silencing of protest, and the depoliticization of exploitative rule and global hierarchies. By exposing how the denigration of the feminine legitimizes *multiple* oppressions – not just that of women – feminist critiques offer rich resources for re-envisioning, resisting, and transforming hierarchical social relations.

This is emphatically not to posit a feminist 'conflict-free' utopia, nor to argue that feminist critiques necessarily take precedence over other emancipatory discourses, nor to claim that gender hierarchy is always the most salient dimension of oppressive dynamics. It is to argue that feminist voices offer alternative visions; that gender domination is not reducible to some other form and, therefore, that 'progressive' movements must also be feminist movements; and that, while not always the most salient, gender is always a dimension of oppressive relations and 'taking it seriously' improves our critical understanding and possibilities for change. In sum, insofar as denigration of the feminine serves to naturalize (depoliticize) all manner of oppressive relations, we cannot eliminate oppression until we eliminate the hierarchical gender dichotomy that sustains it.

The weaknesses of feminist IR are clearest when we consider the context of its development: a discipline dominated by masculinist and positivist commitments. This shapes both what feminists themselves have produced and how mainstream IR responds. The most familiar feminist work 'adds women' to existing frameworks. In the face of continued oppression of women as women, this is and remains a vital – even life-saving – contribution. Feminism, however, that goes no further than the 'adding women' project fails to advance feminisms' full critical and transformative implications. Much feminist work remains thus constrained in part because positivist commitments only recognize gender as an empirical (add women) but not an analytical category. This limitation then reproduces rather than complicates the dichotomy of male–female, and hence, other dichotomies, and leaves existing analytical frameworks in place. As one consequence, feminism can appear to be limited to advancing only 'women' (and, too often, elite women) into existing positions of power. This is a weakness insofar as the larger project, for many of us, is not simply to empower women but to transform oppressive *structures* in order to end the naturalized subordination of not only woman but also nature and 'others' denigrated as feminine.

Similarly, the marginalized status of feminists means that they cannot assume familiarity with their argumentation. A criticism of feminist IR is that it has not forged ahead with a research agenda. But this is due, in part, to the demands of writing for uninformed and resistant audiences. At this point in time, feminists cannot avoid the need, whenever engaging an IR audience, to devote inordinate attention to reviewing feminist arguments rather than getting on with new work and charting new directions. All critical interventions confront this dilemma, but it seems particularly acute in IR, where ignorance of, and resistance to, feminist scholarship is considerable. In sum, while there are no doubt weaknesses in the scholarship and vast improvements to be made, it is important to recognize the power of ideological, political and personal resistance to feminisms and how this affects what feminists themselves – given few numbers, marginalized locations, and scant resources – are structurally able to produce. One example is the recent development of a backlash against feminist IR. This not only misrepresents feminist contributions and fuels the tendency to ignore or dismiss feminist work. It also necessitates a response from feminists, who are again diverted from getting on with more 'serious' work.

Within this context, we can also specify problems with the work that has been produced. Here, as elsewhere, the strengths of feminist IR are also its weaknesses. Perhaps most glaring is the undeniable diversity and complexity of feminist IR. This poses a number of problems that feminists do and must continue to address. First, this diversity and complexity better corresponds to reality, but does not lend itself to easy comprehension and/or application. Feminists must be continually alert to the need for clear and accessible accounts. This is essential for increasing familiarity with feminist perspectives and securing support among a wider audience. At the same time, feminists must beware of simplifications that compromise the complexity that transdisciplinary, critical and postmodern analyses *must* engage. When speaking or writing to the mainstream, at this point there seems little choice but to strive for a balance between accessible review of unfamiliar arguments and stretching beyond that repetition to explore new terrain.

Second, clarity and coherence are especially important insofar as the development of gender-sensitive *policies* necessarily requires generalizations born of simplifications. To be relevant to policy debates and implementation, feminists must render their work contextually appropriate, and clarify relationships among feminist analyses and policy choices. As in IR more generally, the salience of these issues will vary according to particular authors' intentions and agendas. But the stakes for women – and all of us – are high, and feminist IR has a role to play in facilitating more effective and equitable policies.

Third, depending on the particular variation one is assessing, feminist IR can appear too radical and/or utopian – or in the IR context, too Idealist. The enormity of changes required to eliminate gendered hierarchies is all too likely to elicit a response of dismissal or paralysis. But this is a dilemma inherent to systemically transformative approaches, and cannot be 'resolved' in any simple sense. Rather, advocates of radical transformation must situate specific claims in terms of context and intention: Is the immediate objective to pose a previously unasked question? To justify a particular policy change by reference to a more encompassing feminist project? To explore horizons that can only come into focus once we go in search of them?

Conclusion

The growth of feminist IR marks a turning point in IR more generally. This turning point 'reflects' the interaction of empirical and analytical developments. The former include: the growth of women's movements worldwide and the effects of women's activism; the systemic feminization of poverty and its devastating effects on women, children and social reproduction; the shift to service economies and women as preferred workers; and systemic harms to women as effects of direct and structural violence through economic inequalities, environmental degradation, and armed conflicts. Analytical developments include: effects of the 'third debate' and dissenting voices within the discipline; challenges to conventional social theory and positivism across all disciplines; critical voices and alternative vantage points from diverse global locations; and feminist, postcolonial and postmodern critiques of reigning modes of thought and inquiry.

As the chapters of this book reveal, these interactive developments constitute a turning point in IR that evokes diverse images. As I have argued in this chapter, the image of 'a gendered global hierarchy' has no single author or simple meaning. It *can* be read as an empirical reference to the male-dominated activities that constitute IR theory and practice. Indeed, there is much to be learned – and unlearned! – from exploring even this (deceptively) simple observation. I have argued, however, that this would neglect what makes feminist IR singularly important and systemically transformative. It is rather the *interaction* of empirical and analytical insights, informed by a critique of foundational dichotomies as gendered, that renders feminist IR a powerful conceptual lens through which *all* of IR looks different. And seeing differently is not a luxury but a necessity for comprehending today's world politics.

CHAPTER 15

A 'Postcolonial World'?

Sanjay Seth[1]

The international environment changed decisively after the Second World War. Many processes served to reshape the political map of the world, but the most important, by far, was decolonization. From the 1940s through to the 1960s and beyond, there was a steady accession of new members to the world community of states, out of previous colonies – India and Pakistan, Indonesia, the two Vietnams, Ghana, Nigeria, Kenya, Uganda – the list goes on. Decolonization saw a largely European international society, one composed of a few leading states and their empires, and a number of lesser ones, transformed over time to one where the majority of nation-states in the United Nations General Assembly are from the continents of Asia and Africa. With decolonization, the world we inhabit changed fundamentally.

Or did it? For one could argue that while the size and even dynamic of international society had altered, its fundamental organizing principles, and its form, had not. As a system, international society continued to be a society of states, undergirded by the principle of sovereignty. One could argue that although the number of players changed, in more fundamental respects business went on as usual.

In this chapter I will suggest that a 'postcolonial' world is, in fact, radically different from its predecessor, and that this is so not only in that the world has changed, but even more so in that the very categories in and through which we think can now be reconsidered, and indeed, need to be rethought. 'Postcolonial theory' is the name sometimes given to a set of questions and a style of thought which are made possible by colonialism and its aftermath, and which seek to rethink, and redescribe, its own enabling conditions. In this essay I shall explore aspects of International Relations theory through the lenses of postcolonial theory; here postcolonialism offers a perspective or a vantage point for considering world politics at the beginning of the twenty-first century rather than, as with other essays in this volume, serving as a metaphor.

Since postcolonialism and its cognate, postcoloniality, are terms which have come into prominence only recently, and since in any case, as a recent introduction rightly observes, ' "postcolonialism" remains a diffuse and nebulous term' (Gandhi, 1998, p. viii), the first part of this essay provides a brief and highly individual account of the term, and some of the issues encompassed by it. The remainder of the essay takes up the question of whether international theory, which is by definition about a global system, is nevertheless in damaging ways Western and parochial; whether the valorization of the nation-state form mitigates this, by acknowledging and respecting cultural and other difference; and whether the difference acknowledged can be coded, and contained, in and by the nation-state form.

Postcolonialism

The 'post' in postcolonialism does not indicate the belief that colonialism is dead and buried, a matter of the past with no bearing on the present. Quite to the contrary, it is a form of periodization which aggressively signals the centrality of colonialism to the entire historical period after it. Postcolonialism is in part a historical claim, namely that the colonial encounter was a seminal event in modern history, and that it helped shape modernity. That is, this was not just an episode in another narrative such as the development of capitalism – but rather, like the industrial revolution and the Enlightenment, the colonial encounter was also decisive in the making of the modern world. It transformed not only the colonized, but also the colonizer. It did so not only by changing political configurations and economic patterns, by providing the loot and the markets necessary for the industrial revolution, and so on – but by shaping the very sense of self of colonizer and colonized, of West and East, and also by structuring the categories through which the world was seen and constructed.

Thus the 'post' in postcolonialism signifies not that colonialism is no longer salient, but rather that the effects of colonialism have shaped us and are shaping us still. Some of the ways in which this is so have been extensively discussed and documented, and hardly need a new term, such as postcolonialism, to describe them – for instance, the fact that gross economic and political inequalities between the first and third worlds exist, which are in significant measure the legacy of colonial exploitation, and are perpetuated through 'neo-colonial' means. Where postcolonialism has added something to our understanding – and here it appears as much a theoretical stance as a historical claim – is in drawing attention to the fact that the colonial encounter was also one with enduring effects in a whole series of domains, apart from the obvious economic and political ones; and that these were not unidirectional – it was not, as the historiography of colonialism has usually portrayed it, the non-West which was transformed, 'awakened' and so on, but also the colonizer whose imagination, sense of self and knowledge-practices were transformed in the course of the colonial encounter.

The research which goes under the name of postcolonialism is varied. Theoretical explorations of power, culture and identity which take the colonial moment and its aftermath as central have proved extremely suggestive, and influential (Bhabha, 1994; Spivak, 1990, 1999). Other works have sought to explore the impact of the colonial encounter on the Western imagination, as embodied in literature, or to outline the ways in which colonial domination was inscribed in and maintained through literary texts (Parry, 1972; Suleri, 1992; Perera, 1991; Boehmer, 1995). There are works examining the shaping, in and through the colonial encounter (McClintock, 1995; Stoler, 1995), of sexualities, and also of subjectivities (Fanon, 1970; Nandy, 1983). And there are studies of the way in which many of the forms of knowledge by which we seek to comprehend and describe the world – history and anthropology, for instance (Chakrabarty, 1992, 1998; Young, 1990; Duara, 1995; Prakash (ed.), 1995; Asad, 1973; Fabian, 1983; Wolfe, 1999) – were formed or inflected by the colonial encounter, and the implications of this for their practice today.

A feature of postcolonial explorations of this sort has been that they have sought to escape the binary oppositions in which the colonial encounter has been staged or represented, both by apologists for imperialism and sometimes by its critics. For postcolonial theorists neither view the colonial encounter as one in which the colonizer, whatever his motives, 'awakened' a slumbering East by disseminating knowledge, nor adopt the view that colonialism involved only brute exploitation and coercion. Relatedly, nationalism is seen neither as the inevitable outcome of 'the native' learning of liberty and self-determination from colonial schools, nor as the automatic and uncomplicated reflex of a people subjugated by foreigners. The problem has been that drawing attention to the 'cultural' dimensions of the colonial encounter has usually been the vocation of the apologist for imperialism, who has always been eager to point to the introduction of railways, schools, universities and 'scientific knowledge'. On the other hand, to ignore this aspect of the colonial encounter, and talk only of economic exploitation and political coercion, is to ignore an important aspect of it, as well as to implicitly, by omission, accept that this was in fact the 'good' side of colonialism. Postcolonialism seeks to escape the Scylla of seeing in colonialism only the dissemination of knowledge (with coercion and exploitation the unfortunate but incidental handmaidens of this central mission), and the Charybdis of seeing colonialism narrowly, seeing in it only power and inequality but not culture and the shaping of knowledge.

It does so in exemplary fashion in one of its seminal texts, Edward Said's *Orientalism*. Said draws upon the twin insights of Michel Foucault, that discourse shapes the world and is not just about the world, and that power does not contaminate knowledge, but rather that knowledge and power are inseparable. He puts this to service, characterizing Orientalism as 'a style of thought based upon an ontological and epistemological distinction made between "the Orient" and (most of the time) "the Occident"'. This discourse of Orientalism included poetical and other works of fiction, philology, political writings, art, and so on. What united this otherwise diverse range of literature and non-literary representations, according to Said, was that it was a way of 'knowing' and representing the Orient which was also, thereby, a way of dominating and ruling it. Orientalism, according to Said, was a way of 'dealing with [the Orient] ... by making statements about it, authorizing views of it, describing it, by teaching it, settling it, ruling over it... Orientalism [was/is] a Western style for dominating, restructuring and having authority over the Orient'. In Said's famous and influential formulation, then, it is not that there was colonial power on the one hand, and knowledge on the other, with the latter sometimes 'contaminated' by power. Rather, the very discourse of Orientalism was a form of power; to paraphrase Said, Orientalism is, rather than merely expresses, a will to understand, control and dominate.[2]

Western knowledge of the non-West, according to this claim – a claim which has been central to postcolonialism – was a form of power. It was so not because it was arrogant – because it assumed it was 'true' and other knowledges were false – for other knowledges, including non-Western ones, had done the same. Rather, this knowledge constituted an exercise of power over the non-Western world for two reasons. First, the new claims to knowledge coincided with a new and historically unparalleled capacity to enforce their writ. Simply put, Europe in the era of colonialism was able to insist that the knowledge it championed was the only true knowledge, because it was in a position to do so, and to crush or marginalize other knowledges. Second, the Enlightenment claim that it had discovered a new, scientific and universal mode of knowledge was qualitatively different from other claims to truth and universality. The most philosophically powerful and influential formulation of this claim sought to ground knowledge in the very structures of rationality, rather than in a philosophical anthropology and/or a conception of the good. This was a knowledge which claimed not only to be true, but declared itself to be deduced from nothing less than reason itself, rather than being grounded in the practices and conceptions of real historical communities. It could not thus be compared to the ideals and practices of other communities; Enlightenment reason did not see itself as on a par with other forms of knowledge. It was particularly dismissive of other claims to knowledge because it could not see or acknowledge that it too was, like all knowledges, a product of a history and a culture. The fact that Enlightenment reason was conceived to be grounded in the purity of a reason uncontaminated by history served to render this knowledge particularly and unusually blind to the relations of knowledge with history and with power, and yet obstinately insistent on its incontrovertible character.

Postcolonialism, then, foregrounds the connection between knowledge and power, and also between knowledge and forms of human community, of ways of being in the world. What is at issue here, it is important to emphasize, is much more than the 'cultural imperialism' and arrogance which were part and parcel of the colonial enterprise. For arrogance is an attitude, external to knowledge; it can be replaced by humility, without the form of knowledge itself being affected. What postcolonialism seeks to problematize and call into question, however, are the knowledges that accompanied and characterized colonialism and its aftermath. Postcolonialism also draws attention to the fact that all forms of knowledge are rooted in ways of being; that is, that ways of constructing and construing the world are always connected to ways of being-in-the-world. At the end of this essay I will return to this, and will suggest that the postcolonial critique has important normative or ethical ramifications. But for the moment, this introduction to the postcolonial critique of knowledge forms allows us to engage with one particular knowledge or discipline, that of International Relations.

Nation and Liberation

Let us begin with a paradox. It is a feature of the discipline of International Relations, suggests Rob Walker, that 'while grasping at a global or universal phenomenon, it does so almost entirely within one culturally and politically circumscribed perspective' (Walker, 1984a, p. 182). International Relations, like other modern disciplines, is very clearly, and quite demonstrably, an intellectual discipline which arose in the West, and which takes its intellectual bearings from landmarks in the Western intellectual tradition. That is, even though it purports to understand a global system, it remains a discipline uninflected by intellectual traditions other than those of the West from which it sprang.

Most practitioners of the discipline would acknowledge this – how could they but do so? – but would add a rider. This would stem from the discipline's notion of itself and what it does, and particularly from its epistemology, from its conception of the relation between the discipline and its object. For with some notable (and for the most part recent) exceptions, International Relations embraces an unrelentingly, almost grimly representational epistemology. More often than not, the discipline sees itself as describing the international order as it is, and discerning the underlying processes and logics which make it thus. It is this which has given the realist and neorealist strands dominant within the discipline much of their distinctive style and tone – the world weary 'we would 'twer otherwise but we simply calls 'em as we sees 'em' style. International Relations, in this version of it, can be neither guilty of arrogance nor capable of humility, for both are equally irrelevant for a discipline which seeks simply to portray the world as it is. And thus the International Relations practitioner might well defend the discipline by arguing that while it is indeed borne of European history and experience, so also is the international order. The fact that International Relations as a discipline constantly betrays its European origins is neither a problem nor a matter for apology, as the reality it seeks to describe is no longer limited to Europe, for Europe itself has become universal.

This is exactly what some International Relations theorists have argued. Hedley Bull and Adam Watson, for instance, point out:

> The present international political structure of the world – founded upon the division of the earth into separate states, their acceptance of one another's sovereignty, of principles of law regulating their coexistence and co-operation, and of diplomatic conventions facilitating their intercourse – is, at least in its most basic features, the legacy of Europe's now vanished ascendancy. (Bull and Watson, 1984a, p. 2)

And because it was 'Europe's ascendancy' which turned what was once a European wide system of organizing political relations into a global one, 'it is not our perspective but the historical record itself that can be called Eurocentric' (Bull and Watson, 1984a, p. 2).[3]

It is not International Relations the discipline which inappropriately and arrogantly generalizes from what is actually a parochial experience, but international society which has *in fact* generalized what was initially a Europe-specific experience. The spread of social and political modernity meant that Asian and African political communities began in important respects to resemble European ones, as 'domestic processes of political and social reform ... narrowed the difference between them and the political communities of the West' (Bull, 1984, p. 122). This facilitated their admission into the international system of states, which they demonstrated a keen desire to join. According to Bull and Watson (1984b, p. 433),

> The most striking feature of the global international society of today ... is the extent to which the states of Asia and Africa have embraced such basic elements of European international society as the sovereign state, the rules of international law, the procedures and conventions of diplomacy and international relations.

Thus not only has a European system become global – it has become so because it 'has been embraced by the non-European majority of states and peoples as the basis of their own approach to international relations' (Bull and Watson, 1984b, p. 435), non-European states which, moreover, 'manifest little if any wish to revert to the hegemonial or suzerain systems of states which prevailed outside Europe before the era of its expansion' (Bull and Watson, 1984b, p. 434).

In a moment I will return to the question of whether the globalization of an initially European system also renders European knowledge forms global. But it is first important to note that the process by which an international order, first confined to Europe, came to be globalized is a story of pillage, exploitation, violence, doctrines of racial superiority, and resistance of various sorts. Little of the conflict, drama and fundamental inequality of this is captured in the bland phrases of Bull and Watson, or indeed in most accounts of the origins and spread of the contemporary system of states. Phrases like 'embraced', 'admitted' and 'joined' function precisely to elide the realities of imperialism and colonialism, to make the globalization of Europe sound consensual rather than coercive, amiable rather than bloody. Nor is this all part of the past, an unfortunate episode buried and forgotten in the aftermath of decolonization. On the contrary, the existing international order continues to be deeply inequitable, and the wealthy – for the most part Western – nations continue to enrich themselves economically at the expense of the poorer peoples of the world.

Nevertheless, that the non-Western world has embraced the international order, even if not all aspects of it as currently instituted, does seem indisputable. And there is no denying that in most cases independent nationhood, and all the features and trappings associated with it – claims to sovereignty, to dignity and formal equality with other states, flags and anthems – were avidly sought. It is all this which makes the common narrative about the spread of the international system, of which Bull and Watson offer one version, sound plausible. The problem with the world order which had its origins in the West, according to this account, lay not in its Western origins but the fact that independent statehood and membership of this order was denied to the colonized. But once the excluded were admitted to the international order, with their own nation-states, this order became at once genuinely global and was also legitimated.

It will be noted that this account treats nationalism as the riposte of the colonized to their subordination, the realization of which provided the form and content of their liberation, in the form of independent statehood. This narrative assumes, in short, that nation and state are the instruments and the content of liberation. But what if they were but another form of tutelage?

Postcolonial theory has allowed us to pose this question, for it has engaged in a critique of nation and state, including – especially – the nation-state which emerged out of decolonization (see Chatterjee, 1986; Davidson, 1992; Duara, 1995). Such a critique has its historical-political, and intellectual, conditions of existence. The disenchantment which in many former colonies has followed upon decolonization runs sufficiently deeply in some places to have given impetus, not simply to critiques of governments and regimes, but to a questioning of the very desirability of the nation-state as the form through which self-governance, autonomy, self-respect and justice are to be pursued. Such writings have often been influenced by poststructuralist themes, especially an anti-essentialism which denies that identities (including national ones) are in any way natural or even stable, and also by poststructuralist critiques of the project of modernity, which have provided postcolonialism with some of the conceptual resources with which to question the desirability of the nation-state which is so integral a part of that modernity.

Critics have pointed, on the one hand, to the fact that for the colonized to assert themselves through nationhood (and also by seeking to become modern) may represent not an escape from but rather a continuation, even an intensification, of a moral-epistemological and political subordination to the West. For the state is not simply a form to which each people provides the content they wish; the nation-state presupposes (and helps to create) certain relations between authority and the people, between custom and law, knowledge and practice; presupposes certain forms of selfhood and community; and so on. The nation-state, in short, is not an empty container into which anything can be poured; it already has a content. This means that the nation-state cannot serve as the vehicle for expressing those aspirations which do not already accord with or 'fit' the frame of nation, state and modernity; and indeed, it may ill-serve as the vehicle for recovering and expressing what is autochthonous, rather than Western and derivative, about a political community and a culture. In this critical view, the postcolonial nation-state, rather than being the sign that an oppressed and scorned people have recovered their self-respect and found their place under the sun, may be but a further mark of the triumph of Western (in some versions, modern) categories and institutions.

Such critiques were less common – though not non-existent[4] – in the colonial period, because to criticize nationalism and the aspiration to statehood ran the risk of being politically associated with the colonial power. Today such critiques take the desirability of having got rid of the colonizer for granted. They are certainly not animated by nostalgia for a past of colonial domination – the critique of the nation is not an endorsement, even tacit, of colonialism, but rather an effort to retrieve and to imagine other forms of anti-colonialism. Critics often point to the many forms opposition to imperialism took – peasant revolts and millenarian movements, religiously inspired anti-colonial struggles, Gandhian movements and so on – by no means all of which were inspired by imaginings of state, nation and modernity. That historiography has tended to ignore or misinterpret anti-colonial struggles that were not nationalist is not because they were in fact of minor historical significance, but rather because they have either been assimilated to the history of nationalism, or else simply adjudged to be unimportant.[5] These may not always be recoverable as viable political projects today, and they may not, for that matter, be politically attractive: but to retrieve them helps us to imagine other forms of autonomy than 'national independence', other forms of selfhood than citizenship, and other forms of collective organization than the state.

If the nation-state form is not the inevitable and only outcome of anti-colonialism, and if it is not necessarily an adequate expression of the aspirations of the colonized, this has deeply unsettling implications for the argument that the expansion of the West, although originally imperialistic, ultimately provided the oppressed with the very tools for their liberation. It also thereby undermines the assumption that the international order is somehow legitimated by the fact that the formerly colonized sought to join this order. If the international order was not spontaneously chosen, but privileges certain forms of political community at the same time as it marginalizes or represses others, then the fact that the colonized also formed nation-states does not serve to justify an international political order characterized by states. Finally, it renders problematic the claim that the European intellectual origins of international relations in no way vitiates its analysis of what is a global, and not simply a Western, order.

Universal and Particular

Despite the above critique of the fashion in which the discipline of International Relations assumes that a set of categories and concepts of a particular history and provenance have universal relevance, it is nonetheless the case that International Relations theory, more than political theory, its 'domestic' counterpart, at least acknowledges the existence of difference. Indeed, while 'in the context of the state, Western social and political thought has pursued universalisms of one kind or another'; by contrast, 'international politics has been the realm where pluralism and relativism have remained the dominant values' (Walker, 1984b, p. 10). The ' "tradition of International Relations theory, with all its claims about necessities of state and the priority of power over ethics', Walker argues, 'is often articulated explicitly in opposition to a modernist reading of historical progress. Certain Nietzschean cadences, selectively heard and crudely harmonized with many other sceptical voices, are not difficult to detect in some of the more influential formulations of what a tradition of International Relations theory involves' (Walker, 1993, p. 30). Given this, International Relations may be guilty of wrongly assuming that its Western categories explain all, as I have argued above, but its very assumption that the world is composed of different states at least acknowledges and allows for the fact that these states embody different national cultures and forms of life. This, moreover, has real political effects –

for instance the principle of non-intervention is underpinned not simply by a pragmatic logic ('do unto others...'), but also takes the form of a moral injunction, that states should not intervene in the domestic affairs of other states. What underlies the 'should', according to Michael Walzer, is precisely a recognition and respect for particularity – acceptance that 'the survival and freedom of political communities – whose members share a way of life, developed by their ancestors, to be passed on to their children – are the highest values of international society' (Walzer, 1977, p. 254).

The tension between universal and particular is a very old one in Western thought, at least as old as Christianity and the tension between the claim that all Christians were members of a potentially universal Christendom, and the Pauline injunction to 'render unto Caesar his due'. It recurs in a variety of contexts in the modern era, an era which has simultaneously exalted the universal, and very often couched its claims in a political and ethical language which was universalist, and yet which has also been an age of 'proliferating autonomies', an age which has exalted the particularity of individual over community, and nation over humanity (see Seth, 1993, pp. 93–5). Each term has required the other, and only made sense when posited against the other, and in this sense they have not been opposites so much as old sparring partners. One of the most common and effective ways of negotiating this tension has been via a distinction between form and content, in which the form is universal while the content is particular and particularizing. Thus, we are *all* individuals, and the universality of this phenomenon becomes the basis for claims to equal dignity and so on; yet we are all *individuals*, and now the accent on 'individual' provides the basis for valuing autonomy and all that is necessary for expressing and realizing the self, and living life 'from the inside out'. Similarly, because the nation form is universal and not the special prerogative of any one state, all nations are equally entitled to respect, and must be formally equal in global forums. But because the international order is an order of so many *different* nations, each has a right to self-determination and to nurture its own unique form of life.

This typically modern way of negotiating and seeking to reconcile a potential tension proves, however, upon closer inspection, to be a way of domesticating or neutralizing particularity. Particularity appears as a sort of raw datum, rather than as an object of investigation; the fact that there are judged to be numerous such particularities (common in their uniqueness) means that the focus immediately shifts to the generality of the form and the means by which these numerous particularities may be subsumed under common rules. In political theory, the individual appears as a given, one whose choices and preferences and values must be aggregated (utilitarianism), or reconciled according to principles of justice, as in Rawlsian liberalism. In International Relations, difference, while it may get acknowledged, does not need to be explored; for the discipline, the important thing about the nation-states which are its basic units of analysis is their 'stateness', the fact that they are possessed of territory, that they seek to maximize their interests, occasionally go to war, and so on. In both political theory and International Relations, the particular content becomes the raw material of a theory which is about how particulars all become equally subsumed by rules, structures and procedures which are blind to their particularity. The individual in political theory, and the state-nation in International Relations, appear as particularities only briefly, before lending themselves to a formal theory, whether that be Rawlsian liberalism or neorealism.

This helps explain, too, how it is that International Relations theorists are frequently both statist and cosmopolitan.[6] Richard Ashley notes that theorists of what he terms the 'anarchy problematique', 'can be statists, on the one hand, and internationalists, on the other … they can be committed to the state as an agency of action and, at the same time, can define their values on a global plane' (1988, p. 240). That is, such theorists, while committed to the idea that the particularity represented by the state is the basic and untranscendable foundation of the international system, nonetheless locate their own values, commitments and research agenda at a level which does in fact transcend the interests and viewpoint of the state. The reason, of course, is that the particularity of states does not really matter; what matters is simply the fact of particularity, which then plays no further role in the analysis, which is more concerned with how the structures and rules of the system may be maintained. The 'nationness' of states does not, then, matter, and in this regard the conception that international theory escapes the homogenizing effects of other modernist disciplines, with their universalist presumptions and in-built conceptions of historical progress, is profoundly mistaken.

It is not just, however, that particularity is acknowledged only in order to be subsumed within the same. It is also that only one particularity is recognized; that here the opposite of universal is particular, rather than particulars. In fact, of course, difference always exceeds the form of the nation-state; and identities being composed not of pre-existent presence but constituted out of a play of differences, national identity itself is always unstable, something in need of regulation and enforcement, rather than a solid, given particular which is always and forever defiantly facing down would-be universals.

That socially significant differences cannot be confined simply to national ones should hardly need arguing, and yet this is precisely the assumption that international theory, for much of its history, has made, and indeed, insisted upon. International Relations has no warrant for coding all difference as national, and for assuming that the way difference enters the world and plays a role in it is through the nation-state, and yet this is precisely what its assumption that the state represents an irreducible and also untranscendable particularity amounts to. Why is this so, and what is the significance of the fact that international theory presumes that all difference can be represented as national difference?

Despite its self-image as a discipline – one that captures and re-presents what is 'out there' – here, as elsewhere, international theory clearly functions not simply as a way of describing the world but also as a way of seeking to order the world. The postcolonial – and also postmodern – critic would argue that, as with other modern ways of representing and seeking to understand the world, international theory privileges unity before difference and presumes a sovereign, trans-historical identity. As with other modern forms of power-knowledge, international theory seeks to 'manage' the potentially endless heterogeneity of the world; in the case of International Relations, by identifying/allowing only one form of difference, with the nation-state as its expression and – in both senses of the word – its 'container'.

But precisely because knowledge is not just a matter of knowing an object 'out there', but also a way of construing and constructing that object, the privileging of nation and state normalizes and authorizes certain expressions of particularity, and pathologizes others. It thereby also wittingly or unwittingly authorizes 'managing' difference so that it can be construed as national, and represented and contained by the state. Forms of difference which cannot be so represented – which exceed or are otherwise not homologous with the nation, and cannot be coded by the state – must be eliminated, or else remade so that they can be so coded. The assumption that this is in fact the principal form of identity is precisely what results in and legitimates efforts to 'force' a culture or political community into the mould of nation-state. Modernization and nation-building, those vast and often violent projects of modernity of which the state has been both means and end, in fact involve a high degree of social engineering, the coercive component of which increases proportionately according to the difficulty of fitting and forcing the particularity concerned into the mould of nationhood and statehood. Peasants have to be taught/forced to become Indians or Chinese; kinship, or caste, or the numerous other solidarities and forms of social organization to be found in the world have to give way to (or be subsumed by) citizenship; old public arenas must give way to new ones, and old rituals and practices of identity to the rituals of citizenship and statehood.

Conclusion

As it has proceeded, this essay has addressed paradoxes which revolve around the opposition between the universal and the particular, and which concern recognizing and dealing with difference. Questions such as these are at the heart of international relations, as a practice and as a discipline.

Thus, for instance, the critique of international theory often takes the form of counterposing a universal to the particular – for example, various forms of 'critical theory', seeking their inspiration and grounding in Kant, Marx or Habermas. It is yet another paradox of international theory that the 'radical' in international politics is often one who invokes some sort of universality to override national particularism (e.g., argues for enforceable universal human rights, for intervention where universal moral norms are violated, and so on), while in domestic politics the radical is frequently the one who argues that such universalisms are imperialistic, imposing upon indigenous peoples and minorities the particularistic moral conceptions of the majority.

I wish to conclude by suggesting that the danger lies not in the fact of international theory privileging the particularity of the nation. As I have argued above, this is only a seeming privileging, as the specificity of nations recedes the moment it is nominally acknowledged. The debate is set up as one between universal and (one) particular, between state-nation and world community, between local mores and universal morality. If these are the choices, we are surely damned, for we are then forced to choose between an unpalatable and frequently coercive particular and a 'universal' which invariably and necessarily, for reasons discussed early in this essay, turns out to be Western rather than universal.

These are not the only choices, however, even if they are the choices which some strands of international theory would allow us. At the beginning of this essay I observed that different forms of knowledge are linked to different forms of being. That is, the way in which peoples live and relate to each other and to the natural world is intimately bound up with the knowledge systems they produce. I will conclude by observing that even the rush to statehood in the era of decolonization did not efface other forms of organizing community and political life. Nor has the citizen yet become truly the only form the human can take. Other forms of selfhood, other ways of being in the world, and other ways of knowing the world still survive, despite modernization, nation-building and all the other projects and rituals of the modern. It is because of this that postcolonialism has something to say, and something that is politically and ethically important. Postmodernism, to which it is related, is still the modern age reflecting critically upon itself. Postcolonialism, however, arises out of the fact that there are still other ways of being in and seeing the world – not unaffected by the modern, but also not remade in its image – which offer us a vantage point on modernity which a deconstruction of its categories alone cannot offer. If postcolonialism offers a metaphor or image of the world at all, it is an image of numerous ways of being and seeing, far too varied to be coded and represented in the form of nation and state, and far too many for the alternatives of 'universal or particular' to even make sense. A postcolonial world, then, is one which cannot be adequately represented through the existing categories of Western thought. It is also one which poses a different order of political possibilities and ethical questions, possibilities and questions which push International Relations up to and beyond its limits.

CHAPTER 16

The 'End of Modernity'?

Roland Bleiker[1]

Proclaiming the end of things is a common rhetorical practice in the study of world politics. We have heard about the end of the Cold War, the end of the Westphalian state system, even the end of history. Some also believe that the all-encompassing historical period called modernity has given way to something else, a postmodernity, perhaps. In the latter case, though, the necrologists are often not those to whom this endism is usually ascribed. From a so-called postmodern perspective, the important task is not to hail the arrival of a new historical epoque but, rather, to search for ways through which we can understand and live modernity in more inclusive and dialogical ways. David Campbell, Michel Foucault, Paul de Man and Jean-François Lyotard are examples of presumably postmodern authors who remind us that modernity is already such an elusive phenomenon that the concept of postmodernity becomes nothing but a parody of the phantom it seeks to distance itself from. Indeed, the very idea of classifying historical periods can be seen as an obsession with ordering and controlling that is typically modern (Campbell, 1998b, pp. 212–13; Foucault, 1984a, pp. 248–9; de Man, 1986, p. 120; Lyotard, 1991, pp. 24–35).

While the conceptual contours of the postmodern will always remain elusive, the substantial issues that this image of world politics has brought to the forefront have clear and important implications. Critical engagements with modernity have emerged from a dissatisfaction with what Lyotard famously described as a long modern tendency to ground and legitimize knowledge in reference to a grand narrative, that is, a universalizing framework which seeks to emancipate the individual by mastering the conditions of life (Lyotard, 1979, pp. 7–9). Even when such a master narrative seems unquestionably desirable, it inevitably legitimizes and objectivizes certain interpretations and political agendas, thereby excluding everything that does not fit into its corresponding view of life. Authors who are said to represent a postmodern image of world politics grapple with the implications that emerge from the prevalence of master narratives in world politics. They challenge the way in which scientific discourses that have emerged from the Cartesian separation of object and subject mask the constituted dimensions of life. They engage prevalent thinking patterns so that we can see the world from more than one perspective, and that marginalized voices can be brought into the realm of dialogue. This search for epistemological tolerance and inclusion is as much political as it is philosophical. And its practical applicability is – needless to say – virtually unlimited. It is in this sense that, for instance, 'all feminisms can be thought of as postmodern' (Sylvester, 1994, p. 16).

The purpose of this essay is not to summarize the great variety of post-modern approaches to world politics. Several authors have already done so (see, for instance, Brown, 1994; Devetak, 1996). The main effort of this essay thus revolves around demonstrating how something termed postmod-ernism may work. From such a perspective the 'how' is as important as the 'is'. In fact, the 'how' becomes the 'is' insofar as the nature of something is identified primarily as the processes through which it works. The prime task of such an approach consists not of looking at modernity or postmodernity as metaphors of contemporary world politics, but of understanding – and acting upon – the more fundamental recognition that all forms of thought are metaphorical in nature. They cannot be anything else, for language itself is a series of metaphors through which we make sense of the world that sur-rounds us. And since we need language not only to communicate, but also to form our opinions of social phenomena, we inevitably think, live and politicize through a series of metaphors – that is, through forms of concep-tualizing that contain inevitable gaps between a representation of an event and the event itself.

Various implications follow from an approach that acknowledges the metaphorical nature of our understanding of world politics. At the begin-ning is perhaps the simple recognition that representation is an essential aspect of the political process. Political reality, F. R. Ankersmit stresses, 'is not first given to us and subsequently represented; political reality only comes into being after and due to representation' (1996, p. 47). What this means for an analysis of world politics is that before being able to move to any other question, one has to deal with how the representation has struc-tured the object it seeks to represent.

The concrete relevance of metaphor and representation for the study of world politics will be demonstrated through several examples, including the phenomenon of international terrorism. The essay shows not only that terrorism is a metaphor, but also, and more importantly, that the types of representations which are embedded in this metaphor are reflective of very particular perceptions of what terrorism is and how it ought to be dealt with. These perceptions have become objectified through existing linguistic practices even though they express very specific cultural, ideological and political values – values, one must add, that have come to circumvent the range of options available to decision makers who deal with the phenomenon of terrorism.

The practical dilemmas created by terrorism and other pressing contemporary political problems can be understood and addressed more adequately if one is aware of the forms of representation through which the issues in question have become what they are. To examine and deal with terrorism critically, for instance, is not to march towards it, but to first take a step backward and scrutinize the gaps that have opened up in the representations we have chosen to employ in order to deal with this phenomenon. Before asking 'what is to be done?' we must ask 'how have we arrived at the point where doing something means what it means?'. Expressed in other words, we have to inquire how a particular series of viewpoints of and responses to a terrorist incident has come to be perceived and accepted as reasonable.

These are some of the implications that emerge from an image of world politics that is usually associated with an 'end of modernity' metaphor. It is important to note that these implications contain clear ethical dimensions, even though, or, rather, precisely because they refuse to prescribe a particular set of values that would provide concrete guidelines about how to deal with a phenomenon like terrorism. From a postmodern perspective, ethics is a procedural issue. It revolves around the more fundamental processes through which one could deal with an issue in a fair and balanced way. Key to this process is the acceptance of difference and the search for ways through which difference can be redeemed dialogically. With this move emerges an image of multiplicities, of a fragmented world in which ethical conduct must take into account that no one position can capture the variety of perspectives from whence people experience life.

The Modern and the Postmodern as Metaphorical Images of World Politics

Before scrutinizing the practical implications of viewing politics as a series of metaphorical practices, it is necessary to contemplate how the modern and the postmodern have themselves turned into metaphors that shape the theory and practice of world politics. Modernity is generally understood to be the historical period that followed the Middle Ages. It emerged with the onset of the Renaissance in fifteenth-century Italy and spanned the centuries that followed. For many commentators, though, the key is not to look at modernity as a historical period or a set of institutions. Michel Foucault, for instance, stresses that modernity should primarily be seen as an attitude, 'a way of thinking and feeling', 'a mode of relating to contemporary reality'

(1984b, p. 39). Modernity, then, is the broad common theme that runs through a set of diverse discursive practices which, superseding and intersecting with each other, have come to constitute our contemporary consciousness.

To identify the key components of modernity is, of course, a near impossible task. The last 500 years have brought about changes that are more radical and far-reaching than virtually anything that had happened in human history before the advent of the Renaissance. From a philosophical point of view, however, one can, identify a few common traits that do exist across a variety of diverse phenomena. William Connolly, for instance, points out that while the waging of fierce intellectual debates emerged as a key feature of modernity, the range of these debates was not as boundless as it seemed at first sight. They all had a distinctive character. All, to a large extent, were framed by the recurring unwillingness to deal with what Nietzsche called 'the death of God', the disappearance, at the end of the medieval period, of a generally accepted world view that provided a stable ground from which it was possible to assess nature, knowledge, common values, truth, politics – in short, life itself. When the old theocentric world crumbled, when the one and only commonly accepted point of reference vanished, the death of God became the key dilemma around which modern debates were waged. Yet, instead of accepting the absence of stable foundations and dealing with the ensuing responsibilities, many prominent modern approaches embarked on attempts to find replacements for the fallen God (see Connolly, 1993). This quest has taken different shapes in various stages of the modern project. For Renaissance humanists, it centred on a sceptical and rhetorical belief in human agency and the virtue of 'men'. During the Enlightenment, it was trust in science and universal reason. For romantics, it was the belief in an aesthetics and a deified Self. For Marxists, it consisted of faith in history's teleological dimension.

The image that is usually associated with an end of modernity metaphor revolves around a variety of different attempts to break through such modern ways of grounding the world in Archimedean standpoints. But the actual meaning of the postmodern is far from clear. Indeed, the increasing sense of confusion in the proliferation of the postmodern leads Gianni Vattimo (1992, p. 1) to note that this term is so omnipresent and faddish that it has become almost obligatory to distance oneself from it. But Vattimo, and many others, nevertheless hold on. They view the postmodern as both a changing attitude and a fundamentally novel historical condition. They focus on cultural transformations that have taken place in the Western world and assume that we are witnessing 'a noticeable shift in sensibility, practices and discourse formations which distinguishes a postmodern set of assumptions, experiences and propositions from that of a preceding period' (Huyssen, 1984, p. 8). One could now go on and draw attention to the differences between those who speak of postmodernity (a new historical epoch) and those who embrace postmodernism (a new attitude towards modernity) (see Hutcheon, 1989; and Smart, 1993). But such is not the task of this essay. Rather, its purpose is to recognize the diversity that surrounds postmodern approaches. Indeed, if there is anything that unites them it is precisely the acceptance of difference. Whether or not the ensuing quest for inclusion constitutes a grand narrative itself, one that values and validates tolerance and diversity, is subject to debate – a debate that cannot be put to rest here.

To understand the practical implications of the end of modernity metaphor, it is perhaps more useful to leave terminological questions aside for a moment. The postmodern has become a highly contentious expression, one that is often used not by its advocates, but by polemicists that dismiss as relativist a variety of approaches that have very little in common except for the desire to break through totalizing forms of knowledge. Ankersmit offers an alternative and less polemical way of conceptualizing the issue. He still divides approaches to understanding contemporary politics into two main traditions, but he calls them mimetic and aesthetic. Mimetic theories presuppose the existence of a reality that can be represented as it is, and the effort of the theorist must thus consist of seeking forms of representation that are as authentic as possible. An aesthetic approach to politics, by contrast, assumes what Ankersmit (1996, especially Chapter 1) calls the 'brokenness' of political reality – the fact that there will always be a discrepancy between the represented and its representation.

The Politics of Metaphor

Some theoretical groundwork is necessary before the phenomenon of metaphor and representation can be explored in a practical context. One must first trace back the steps that make an acceptance of difference a compelling, even ethically necessary aspect of our understanding of world politics.

Metaphor is usually understood as 'the application of a name or descriptive term or phrase to an object or action to which it is imaginatively but not literally applicable' (*Oxford Dictionary*, 1995). To speak metaphorically, then, is to rely on tropes: practices of bestowing a word with a temporary meaning that differs from its usual significance. If I say 'I killed two birds with one stone' it is evident to everyone that I did not actually engage in an act of murder, but only borrowed the constellation of this visual image to express an activity of an imaginatively related but in essence fundamentally different nature. A trope thus consists of the tension between identity and difference, of the inevitable gap that opens up between a word's established place and its metaphorical appropriation. It is in the nature of this gap that the power and appeal of metaphor lies. The command of metaphor, Aristotle already believed, is by far the greatest thing, 'the mark of a genius' (Aristotle, 1948, XXII, p. 31). It is an ability that is usually associated with poets and philosophers, with writers who rely more on the power of creative images than on the type of realistic descriptions that usually characterize the works of, say, scientists or political analysts.

Although widely shared, this division between figurative and literal, fictional and realistic ways of speaking is largely misleading. No thought can be expressed without some form of representation. Nietzsche was one of the first authors to recognize that language cannot be anything other than a series of metaphors. Put simply, for Nietzsche, a person's intuitional perception creates an image, then a word, then patterns of words, and finally entire linguistic and cultural systems. Each step in this chain of metaphors entails interpretations and distortions of various kinds. When we look at things around us, Nietzsche illustrates, we think we know something objective about them, something of 'the thing in itself'. But all we have are metaphors, which can never capture an essence because they express the relationship between people and things (Nietzsche, 1982, pp. 42–7).

Because of his insights into language, Nietzsche is often regarded as the key turning point from modern to postmodern ways of thinking. A Nietzschean approach acknowledges that language and, indeed, knowledge itself is always metaphorical. No matter how insightful, how systematic, how apparently neutral a text or speech appears, it is always a form of representation that has chosen to structure its image of political reality through a particular series of metaphors. There is no neutral form of depicting the world that is somehow detached from the linguistic and social practices in which the speaker or writer is embedded.

Metaphors of Politics

Although all forms of speaking and writing are metaphorical, it is not always easy to recognize the political dimensions or even the very existence of these metaphors. After they have entered the vocabulary of everyday speech, metaphors often become so common that they start to appear as authentic representations of something termed reality. The process of forgetting that we have been conditioned by linguistically entrenched values largely camouflages the systems of exclusion that are operative in all speech forms. We become accustomed to our distorting metaphors until we 'lie herd-like in a style obligatory for all' (Nietzsche, 1982, p. 47). One way of recognizing this metaphorical – and thus also political – dimension of language is to leave familiar linguistic terrains and explore issues of metaphor in a different cultural context.

Consider the word a Korean man usually employs to refer to his own wife: *chip saram*. Literally translated this expression means 'house person'. For someone outside a Korean context it is rather obvious that *chip saram* is more than simply an objective description of a female person. It is an inherently political metaphor, one that represents a view of the world that assigns men and women fundamentally different societal roles. The political dimension of this metaphor lies in the tension between identity and difference, between the existence of a female person and the ways in which she is represented through language. Furthermore, it is also responsible for the sustenance of existing patriarchal practices. But for a Korean who hears and internalizes the word *chip saram* from early childhood on, the metaphor of 'house person' is not perceived as a metaphor. It is, quite naturally, seen as an authentic representation of an existing reality. This metaphorically embellished system of exclusion is then further entrenched through a range of grammatical structures. These semantic structures permit the expression of a societal consciousness in which metaphors like *chip saram* seem to lose their metaphorical dimensions because they appear natural in the context of a speech environment that has already objectified hierarchical representations of political realities.

The more one moves into familiar terrains, the more it becomes difficult to detect the political dimensions of tropes. Consider, just for an instance, one of the key metaphors of Cold War international relations, the notion of 'balance of power'. This political practice usually refers to a 'principle of international politics, whereby any state which threatens to increase its power becomes at once subject to increases in countervailing power from potential belligerents' (Scruton, 1983, p. 35). It is by and large around this metaphor that the 'free' Western world structured its 'defence' against the threat of Communism. The arms race is a product of a reciprocally perceived need to keep up with the other's strategic capacities. If the Soviet Union acquired a new generation of missiles, then the US had to follow suit in order not to endanger the precarious balance of power that guaranteed peace, or, rather, the absence of open war at a time when a nuclear confrontation could have annihilated the entire planet in seconds. Billions of dollars in defence spending have been justified in the name of this metaphor, and so have a variety of surrogate wars, from Vietnam to Nicaragua, that led to immense human suffering. But once the Soviet Union had crumbled it became evident that the balance that was supposed to be maintained at all costs had actually never existed. The Soviet Union had not only been, and this for quite some time, at the brink of economic and social collapse, but its actual military might was actually never quite what it appeared to be. Some of the massive missiles that were pompously displayed during annual military parades at Moscow's Red Square, for instance, turned out to be simulacrums: nothing more than empty shells. As recently released archival material has revealed, the Soviet Union never had the money or technology to build these missiles. Little did it matter, though, for the mere perception of these weapons, non-existent as they were, was enough to activate the balance of power metaphor and push the arms race up to the next higher level.

At the height of the Cold War the balance of power metaphor was, of course, not perceived as a metaphor. It was seen as a strategic reality, a situation that required not just urgent attention and action, but a certain kind of action. The range of options available to policy makers at the time was obscured and narrowed down by the fact that decision-making processes were taken based on Cold War thinking patterns that presented their representations of world politics as authentic images of political reality, rather than the metaphorical interpretation that they were. In retrospect, though, it has become obvious that these metaphorical practices contained strong political dimensions. Equally obvious is that the State has a certain interest in repressing the fact that politics is conducted and masked through a series of metaphors. The merit of ignoring representation, Ankersmit (1996, p. 55) stresses, 'is that it helps the state to make itself invisible, to obscure the nature and the extent of political power as much as possible and to assume without opposition the Leviathanistic dimensions that is has acquired in the course of the last two centuries'.

Representing International Terrorism: the Legitimate and Illegitimate Uses of Violence

In order to move away from the polemical discourses that surround the term postmodernism, this essay now explores issues of metaphor and representation from a practical point of view. It engages the phenomenon of terrorism in an attempt to illuminate the political and ethical dimensions that are entailed in accepting the brokenness and multiplicity of political realities. From such a perspective, photographic precision is not what is called for when representing and dealing with an entrenched political dilemma like international terrorism. From an aesthetic point of view the task is more akin to that of a painter who represents her object in ways that would allow us to view something familiar in a new light. It is through such forms of repainting and rethinking that innovative ways of dealing with old and seemingly irreconcilable dilemmas may emerge. Expressed in other words, the point is to acknowledge and explore, rather than to circumvent the inevitably metaphorical nature of representation.

The need for a critical re-evaluation of existing metaphors begins with the very concept of international terrorism. Nietzsche already knew how difficult it is to fix meanings to concepts: 'Only that which has no history can be defined' (Nietzsche, 1991, pp. 71–2). More than a century later, US decision makers came, although rather inadvertently, to a similar recognition when dealing with terrorism. Consider the following conversation between Ned Walker, Assistant to the Under-Secretary for Middle East Affairs at the US State Department, and Lee Hamilton, chairman of the Subcommittee on Europe and the Middle East. The conversation took place in the context of a committee discussion that dealt with talks between the US and the Palestine Liberation Organization (PLO) in the late 1980s and early 1990s:

Hamilton: Well, how do you define terrorism, do you define it in terms of non-combatants?

Walker: The State Department definition which is included in the terrorism report annually defines it in terms of politically motivated attacks on non-combatant targets.

Hamilton: So an attack on a military unit in Israel will not be terrorism?

Walker: It does not necessarily mean that it would not have a very major impact on whatever we were proposing to do with the PLO.

Hamilton: I understand that, but it would not be terrorism.

Walker: An attack on a military target. Not according to definition. Now wait a minute; that is not quite correct. You know, attacks can be made on military targets which clearly are terrorism. It depends on the individual circumstances.

Hamilton: Now wait a minute. I though that you just gave me the State Department definition.

Walker: Non-combatant is the terminology, not military or civilian.

Hamilton: All right. So any attack on a non-combatant could be terrorism?

Walker: Of course.

Hamilton: It certainly would include civilian, right?

Walker: Right.

Hamilton: But an attack on a military unit would not be terrorism?

Walker: It depends on the circumstances.

Hamilton: And what are those circumstances?

Walker: I do not think it will be productive to get into a description of the various terms and conditions under which we are going to define an act by the PLO as terrorism. (cited in Moon, 1997, pp. 3–4)[2]

It is not difficult to recognise from this evasive conversation that the 'circumstantial' dimensions of defining terrorism are also its political dimensions. It is also fairly clear that the issues at stake are not actually violence or the killing of civilians, for if they were, then a variety of official US actions, such as the American military involvement in Vietnam, Panama and the Persian Gulf, would undoubtedly have to be classified as acts of terrorism. The issues at stake, rather, have to do with who can legitimately employ violence to further certain political goals. 'What is described as terrorism by one group may be variously regarded as heroism, foreign policy, or justice by others' (Wardlaw, 1989, p. 5). It is more useful, then, to define terrorism, as Peter Chalk does, in a political way, as 'the systematic use of a particular type of *illegitimate* violence that is employed by *sub-state* actors as a means of achieving specific political objectives' (1998, p. 373; italics added).

The key to understanding terrorism does not lie with violence as such, but with the differences between legitimate and illegitimate uses of force. This division, in turn, is directly linked to issues of statehood and sovereignty. Max Weber famously described the state as a human community 'that claims the monopoly of legitimate use of physical force within a given territory' (Weber, 1991, p. 79). But the question of violence and legitimacy clearly goes beyond the territorial bounds of the sovereign state. At an international level, too, the state claims to have a certain right to the legitimate use of force. And it is out of this claim that the moral distinction between war (a legitimate act of violence perpetuated by a state) and terrorism (an illegitimate use of violence perpetuated by a non-state actor) emerges.

Civilian casualties that result from an inter-state war may be perceived as unfortunate, but such forms of 'collateral damage' are in themselves not enough to classify state-engendered violence towards civilians as terrorism. This terminology is reserved mostly for non-state actors. It is thus that a non-state organization, such as the PLO was in the 1980s, can attack a military target and its act of violence is likely to be labelled terrorism. The 'special circumstances' mentioned above by a US State Department official make such a political extension of the term possible. An attack on noncombatants, in State Department terms, thus includes attacks on 'military installations or on armed military personnel when a state of military hostilities does not exist at the site' (Badey, 1998, p. 92). It is thus that US soldiers walking in uniform through a foreign country could theoretically be classified as civilians.

The US government, by contrast, can present acts of violence against civilians as a politically and morally legitimate use of force. Consider, in addition to the above mentioned examples, the issue of land-mines, the terrorist weapon par excellence. Mines are not aimed at military installations – they kill or injure, rather indiscriminately, whoever steps on them. The numbers speak for themselves: over 20,000 people are killed or maimed each year by mine explosions. Most of the casualties are civilians who are killed or injured after hostilities have ended (United Nations Demining Database, 1999). Countries affected include Afghanistan, Angola, Bosnia, Cambodia, Croatia, Iraq, Mozambique, Nicaragua and Somalia. Not only have American companies produced and delivered a substantial amount of these mines, but the US government remains one of the few countries who refuse to sign an international convention that would prohibit the use, stockpiling, production and transfer of anti-personnel mines.[3] The strategic situation on the Korean peninsula, so the argument goes, makes land-mines an essential component in a defensive strategy against an attack from the Communist North. Little does it matter, it seems, that in an eventual post-Cold War era, Koreans will have to live in the midst of an indiscriminate and potentially disastrous terrorist killing machine: a more than 4 km-wide mine-infested strip of land, stretching all the way from the Yellow Sea to the Sea of Japan.

Representing International Terrorism: the Fundamentalist/Extremist Divide

To draw attention to the multiple, overlapping and contradictory relationships between legitimate and terrorist uses of force is not to vilify the US government, for a variety of other states pursue policies along exactly the same lines. The point is, rather, to examine how we have come to imbue certain acts of violence with legitimacy and how a greater awareness of this process may help us understand and address the human tragedies caused by violence.

Prevalent understandings of terrorism reflect distinct ideological, religious and even racial standpoints. These political dimensions are, again, camouflaged through a series of objectified metaphors. The concept of terrorism is not a reflection of some authentic phenomenon that takes place in the 'real world'. It is a form of interpretation, a political practice that usually revolves around a certain *Feindbild*: an image that depicts the contours of a threatening Other.

The Middle East – or, rather, the Arab component of it – is the stereotypical image of the terrorist Other, the one whose sense of identity, whose religious affinities and practices are so strange that they cannot be seen as anything other than a threat to the existing societal order. An example from the 'real' world may help to draw attention to this phenomenon and its consequential metaphorical dimension. Consider what is generally believed to be the worst ever terrorist attack undertaken on US soil: the bombing of the Alfred P. Murrah Federal Building in Oklahoma City on 19 April 1995. A total of 168 people died in the attack and hundreds of others were injured. Among the many revealing aspects of this tragic incident is the manner in which the search for the culprits took shape. In the following days, several Arab-American men were arrested. Various influential commentators, such as the columnist A.M. Rosenthal, drew an immediate link to 'Mideast Terrorism', even though there was no concrete evidence that could possible be used to advance such an interpretation (*New York Times* 21 April 1995, p. A31). The fact is, of course, that the Middle East had nothing whatsoever to do with the terrorist attack in Oklahoma. It was an entirely home-grown phenomenon. Timothy McVeigh, a US Army veteran, was later charged and found guilty of bombing the Federal Building. All detained Arabs had to be released. Moreover, various subsequent narratives of the incident conveniently erased this initial, ill-targeted search for the culprits. Three years after the incident, the *Washington Post*, for instance, narrates the search for culprits without any mention of the widespread initial resort to Arab enemy images. Rather, the narrative focuses only on the fact that McVeigh was arrested 90 minutes after the bombing, rather coincidentally, in a traffic-related offence, one must add. Post-factum one thus receives the rather misplaced impression of an efficient, objective and race-blind search for the culprits (see, for instance, 'Oklahoma Bombing Chronology', 1998).

While the rewriting of historical narratives is an easy and common political strategy, it is far more difficult to overcome a *Feindbild* that has been entrenched through a series of objectified metaphors. This is why even those who drew attention to the problematic blame that fell on Americans of Muslim faith and/or Arab descent were easily caught in the metaphorical dimensions of terrorism. A *New York Times* editorial, for instance, argued that the incident forced the US to look more closely at what was happening within its own borders, where 'evil is more difficult to acknowledge' (24 April 1995, p. A16). And yet, the metaphors chosen by the *New York Times* to rethink the phenomenon of terrorism clearly reflected the very same stereotypical images from which the editors sought to distance themselves.

The representational entrenchment of terrorism can, for instance, be seen in the widely used metaphorical distinction between 'extremism' and 'fundamentalism'. As in the *New York Times*, Arab terrorists are often depicted as 'Muslim fundamentalists' (21 April 1995, p. A26). A fundamentalist is, by definition, someone who derives his/her values from the core of a society, from its foundations. A fundamentalist represents, in a pure and crystallized way, all that this society is about – its essence, its core values, its vision of what is right and wrong. Fundamentalism is thus a metaphor that implicates not only the terrorist individual, but also the society whose fundamentals s/he represents. The fact is, of course, that most Arab terrorists are radicals whose actions do not necessarily reflect the opinions of the population at large. Even mainstream US magazines readily admit, at least at the level of rhetoric, that 'at no point do the basic texts of Islam enjoin terrorism and murder. At no point do they even consider the random slaughter of uninvolved bystanders' (Lewis, 1998, p. 19).

The political dimensions of metaphor become even more revealing when we contrast the fundamentalist description of Arab terrorists with those that are advanced when non-Arabs are implicated in a comparable incident. Timothy McVeigh is never portrayed as a fundamentalist. The *New York Times*, for instance, depicts him as a 'white extremist', as a criminal who has connections with other 'right-wing extremists' (*New York Times* 23 April 1995, p. I33; 24 April 1995, p. B8). This metaphor has a very different connotation: it portrays an individual who operates at the margins of life, a radical who in no way reflects the core values of a particular society. The metaphor of extremism thus creates a situation in which the society at large is absolved of responsibility. The fact is, of course, that McVeigh was much more of a fundamentalist than most Arab terrorists. Although a loner and social outcast, he is nevertheless a typical product of mainstream America. Not a radical, but a young white man who reflects the fundamentals of the American way of life: a man who fulfilled his patriotic military duties and was even awarded an official US government medal for it – the Bronze Star, given for 'valour and service during the Persian Gulf War' (*New York Times* 4 May 1995, p. A1.).

But the metaphorical construction of international terrorism created a linguistic and discursive environment in which McVeigh could easily be dismissed as an extremist. The society could thus, rather conveniently, avoid having to deal with a difficult and important issue: that fact that terrorism is also a home-grown phenomenon. It is a phenomenon that cannot simply be dealt with through a simplistic inside/outside metaphoric that absolves the Self from responsibility and puts all blame on to some stereotypically perceived antagonistic Other.

Conclusion: Towards an Ethics of Difference

The aim of this essay was to think through some of the images that are usually associated with an 'end of modernity' metaphor. The phenomenon of international terrorism has served to illustrate the implications that arise from applying such images to the study of world politics. An essay-length study is, of course, unable to deal with the phenomenon of terrorism in an exhaustive way. Neither can it possibly succeed in presenting the multitude of perspectives that are usually associated with a so-called postmodern approach to world politics. The point, rather, has been to illustrate *how* a postmodern approach may help us illuminate important aspects of world politics.

Politics and ethics are the spaces that open up between something that is, or takes place, in the world and the particular form of representation that is chosen to imbue these facts or events with meaning. This essay has thus presented issues of metaphor and representation as central to an adequate understanding and conduct of world politics. The ensuing need to rethink the political is far more important than trying to figure out whether we still live in a modern or already in a postmodern period. Indeed, notable exceptions notwithstanding, many so-called postmodern authors would, rather ironically, emphasize that we have hardly transgressed the discursive boundaries of modernity. If we should come to the end of anything, it is not the end of a historical period called modernity, but the end of a particular modern mode of thinking, a specific way of representing world politics. What ought to end, many postmodernists stress, is the compulsion to understand the world in its totality, as something that is not only coherent and rational, but also comprehensible through an all-encompassing gaze. 'God is dead', Nietzsche says, 'but...there may still be caves for thousands of years in which his shadow will be shown. – And we – we still have to vanquish his shadow, too' (Nietzsche, 1974, § 108, p. 167; translation altered). Although the medieval theocentric world view ceased to exist long ago, we still crave religious visions of the world, for forms of understanding that could anchor everything into one perspective, one truth, one God. For a postmodernist, the point is to accept the brokenness of political reality, the inherently political and exclusionary nature of the search for Archimedean foundations.

In the realm of terrorism, for instance, a postmodern perspective would seek to problematize how we have come to think about the issues in question. The point, then, is not to find an all-encompassing definition of terrorism and a corresponding set of globally valid guidelines about how to deal with the dilemmas in question. It is not to seek definitional clarity and lament, as some would do, the recurring inability to find a conceptual consensus about what terrorism actually is. The 'disabling impact' is not created by this 'never-ending definitional controversy', as a typically modern author would have us believe (Badey, 1998, p. 90). Of course, one could easily see that the absence of a universally valid description of terrorism makes it more difficult for states to justify the actions they undertake to fight terrorism. But are such forms of uncritical anti-terrorist engagements really the most adequate and effective strategies? Does a pragmatic definitional approach not miss out on the more fundamental point that it is precisely at the level of definition that politics happens and ethics is formulated?

To gain and retain the political tools that are necessary to fight a phenomenon like terrorism, one must not seek to end definitional controversy. Rather, the key lies in constantly questioning the manner in which existing definitional clarity may circumvent and hinder the search for innovative ways of dealing with existing dilemmas. Terrorism then becomes part of a wider problematique, one that is, as James Der Derian's insightful study shows, not limited to 'body-counts or a revolutionary threat to the states-system'. To understand what is at stake in terrorism one also has to look at this phenomenon as a legitimization crisis (Der Derian, 1992, pp. 80–1). It is part of a complex series of events that question the prevalent state-centric vision of global politics and the moral discourse that is intertwined with it. Whether or not this vision ought to be defended or discarded is open to debate, but the phenomenon of terrorism can hardly be understood and addressed without a form of critical engagement that makes this vision or a possible alternative to it an integral part of the political decision-making process.

From a postmodern perspective, an ethical approach to world politics is thus linked to a struggle with, and acceptance of, difference. Such a position comes out of knowledge that there are and always will be multiple perspectives, multiple truths and multiple Gods. To deny the existence of difference is a form of authoritarianism that inevitably excludes a variety of people and perspectives.

The search for such visions of heterogeneity is, of course, not easy. Neither can there be agreement on how a politics and ethics of difference should and would look. In some ways it is, at least for the purpose of this essay, less important to emphasize differences that have emerged between various so-called postmodern approaches to world politics than to understand their representational similarities. All of them, in one way or another, seek to redeem difference in a dialogical way. Out of this premise emerges a form of ethics that revolves, as Andrew Linklater (1998, p. 101) stresses, around the 'responsibility to engage others, irrespective of their racial, national and other characteristics, in open dialogue about matters which impinge on their welfare'.

Whether or not a postmodern redemption of difference is in itself based on some moral universalism, one that revolves around a Kantian respect for the individual, as Linklater points out (1998, especially pp. 48, 72), is subject to debate. Less contentious is the fact that we have a very long way to go until we reach the type of inclusive and dialogical politics that postmodernists advocate. Indeed, we may never get there at all, for the politics of metaphor will always seek to objectify a particular vision of the good life – and thus eclipse whatever does not fit into its prescriptions for the world. The best we can do, then, is retain an awareness of this process and understand politics not as a realm of facts and inevitabilities, but as a domain of contingencies. It is through representation that politics has emerged, and it is in the very same realm that new ways of addressing our daily problems, from the local to the global, from the mundane to the all-annihilating, may be found.

CONCLUDING CHAPTER

CHAPTER 17

The Future of World Politics

Jacinta O'Hagan and Greg Fry

The contemporary debate concerning the shape and possibilities of world politics, on which this volume has focused, is a debate about fundamentals. The protagonists have not focused on questions concerning the relative power of particular states, or on how particular international regimes can be bolstered, or on the fortunes of particular alliances – though there are debates elsewhere about such matters. To return to Gaddis's (1999) useful metaphor for contemporary social inquiry with which we began, their concern is rather with how to understand the 'geological' processes underlying the changing world order. The debate is driven by the view of many commentators that the world is not just going through rapid change, but rather, through radical transformation which calls into question all aspects of the way in which global society is ordered, and the meaning we should attach to that ordering. They see the end of the twentieth century not just as ending a long war, or even a century, but as being part of the ending of the modern period, or of the struggle between Enlightenment philosophies. Others see it primarily as the end of the Westphalian states' system, or as heralding the possibility of 'perpetual peace'. Even those disputing such transformation have felt it necessary to defend their 'business as usual' position at this 'geological' level given the strength of the challenge.

Such a debate is perhaps to be expected at the turn of a century, and indeed of a millennium, when arbitrary periodization takes on a semi-mystical quality and commentators are encouraged to think in *fin de siècle* terms. This questioning of fundamentals has also been encouraged by the end of the Cold War which, like the end of the other two major wars of the twentieth century, called forth an 'irresistible disposition to debate and reflect on the future of world order' (Falk, 1994: 476), a disposition which continued throughout the 1990s encouraged by the dramatic political, economic and technological developments of that decade.

The debate has centred on a quest to identify the essential feature of world politics from which all else follows. For many of the protagonists, this amounts to a search for the certainty of the Cold War era, where an East-West depiction seemed to provide a starting point for understanding, and for policy. This search for the 'metaphor for our times' has resulted, as we have seen, in the deployment of a series of dramatic images, each deployment occurring with an eye to what had gone before in this battle of sound-bite characterizations. Thus by 1996, Huntington (1996, pp. 31–35) was explicitly positioning his own 'clash of civilizations' in relation to Fukuyama's 'end of history' (1989), Goldgeier and McFaul's 'tale of two worlds' (1992), Mearsheimer's 'back to the future' (1991), Brzezinski's 'out of control'(1993), and Moynihan's 'pandaemonium'(1993). It is now common for authors to locate themselves in a debate framed, at the very least, by 'the end of history', the 'clash of civilizations', the 'coming anarchy', and 'globalization', and possibly a realist image of a 'world of states'.

The differences between these characterizations are, as we have seen, profound. In *Jihad vs McWorld* (1996), Benjamin Barber, speaking only of prominent understandings of world politics focused on 'globalization' or 'fragmentation', contends (p. 3) that 'the rival observers seem to consult different almanacs drawn from the libraries of contrarian planets'. He goes on to draw attention to the stark choices such understandings present: (p. 4):

> We are compelled to choose between what passes as 'the twilight of sovereignty' and an entropic end of all history; or a return to the past's most fractious and demoralising discord; to 'the menace of global anarchy', to Milton's capital of hell, Pandemonium; to a world totally 'out of control'.

Such differences in images of world politics matter when we appreciate that this is a debate which is watched closely by those who plan and manage global processes, who are looking for understandings of what we are 'in' in order to know what policies to pursue. It is a debate that is conducted in the accessible and influential domain between the policy world and academe. As powerful pictures representing influential ideas and frameworks, they can become as powerful as the various forms of Cold War imagery that preceded them in setting the parameters of debates and therefore influencing the understandings on which policy is built.

Our purpose has therefore been to clarify the theoretical assumptions underpinning these characterizations in order to establish a basis for intellectual, normative and political judgement about them. The survey of particular images presented by the contributors to this book goes a long way in presenting such a basis for judgement. There are two further important steps in clarifying what these pictures represent as a set of ideas and normative commitments. The first is to see how they compare in relation to the questions we raised about the fundamentals of world politics in the introductory chapter. These questions focus on whether global politics is undergoing transformation; on whether the world polity is to be seen as 'one world', 'two worlds', or many; on where political agency, community and identity are located; on forms of power; and on whether the global order is integrating or fragmenting. The second task is to explore the political and ethical issues that stem from the fact that the prominent characterizations of world politics, although universal in their claims, are predominantly images deployed in an American debate about US policy directions.

Contending Images and the Fundamentals of World Politics

Transformation?

The first question concerns whether the contemporary world order is to be seen as exhibiting continuities, at a fundamental level, with what we have known before or is undergoing radical change. The touchstone for most of these claims is that what is being transformed, or continued in the case of those denying transformation, is what George and Falk refer to in this volume as the Westphalian model: a system of self-regarding, sovereign territorial states co-existing in a situation of anarchy without a supreme authority.

We have seen a variety of answers to this question from those suggesting strong continuities and 'business as usual' to those seeing transformation of the entire system. At one end of the spectrum are the images of 'back to the future', a 'balance of power', and 'international society', which suggest strong continuity between the contemporary world order and the Westphalian model. As George demonstrates, while world politics is no longer bipolar, 'back to the future' continues to depict it pessimistically as manoeuvrings of autonomous power-seeking states pursuing self-interest. Richard Little highlights the continued salience of the concept of a 'balance of power' as a metaphor that describes the system and an explanation of how the system works, with the 'balance' seen as providing a mechanism that helps to maintain a form of stability within this order, if variously interpreted. Some suggest the United States is now the principal balancing agent, while others argue this unipolarity is neither likely to continue nor necessarily desirable, and that regional balances increasingly constitute a significant dimension of the overall world order. There is then considerable difference between 'back to the future' positions on how the 'balance of power' is changing, but agreement that whatever it is, it does not amount to radical transformation of the Westphalian system.

There are other images that depict continuities between past and present but which begin from a different idea of what the past represented. Those starting with a picture of past world politics as a gendered global hierarchy, or as a world of 'Islam and the West', or as one world capitalist system, do not see fundamental change as a result of the end of the Cold War or as a result of globalization. What they are seeing is a strengthening of this long-standing reality rather than a new departure. There are then very strange bedfellows depicting 'business as usual'.

This is also the case for those depicting a transformation in world order. They represent very different positions in their understanding of the nature of transformation and what is driving it. The 'end of history', for example, proposes that we see world order as having reached a point of conclusion in ideological evolution marked by the victory of the Western idea and expressed in the concept of the modern Western state. The West's victory in 'the battle for modernity' means that future institutional development will follow the model established by the West. In a more pessimistic tone, a 'world of tribes', a 'coming anarchy', 'ethnic cleansing' and a 'fragmenting world', depict change as movement back towards an earlier, more primitive and cruel world order with identity and community becoming more locally-based and less cosmopolitan in nature.

The image of 'neo-medievalism' suggests the emergence of a new form of order that echoes that of pre-Westphalian Europe. It is one that is less terri-torially bound and more complex, in many respects, with overlapping realms of authority in contrast to the perception that authority is effectively vested in the territorial state. World order is constituted by intersecting sets of economic, social and cultural forces, rather than simply focused on states and their cycles of warfare. Falk, however, is circumspect about whether the image of 'new medievalism' really represents the transformation in global order claimed for it, as it is largely based in the application of perceived developments in the European historical experience.

The other major depiction of transformation, and the most politically influential, is that of 'globalization'. It appears to presage the end of the Westphalian order based on the sovereign state and a move to one unified world. Clark suggests, however, that under closer examination, it appears that one of the most radical transformations that may be occurring is not the elimination of the state, but the transformation of the state itself.

There are other characterizations that imply transformation, but in fact demonstrate continuity. The 'clash of civilizations', for instance, at first glance appears to depict radical change in the actors and processes that determine world order. But closer examination reveals that, while the units of interaction have changed in this formulation (from states to civilizations), the image assumes strong continuity between the way civilizations are said to interact and the interaction of states in the traditional realist model of world order. It still presumes that the units are self-regarding, interacting in a condition of anarchy and seeking to maintain a balance of power; and envisages a role for great powers, and spheres of influence. Therefore this image presumes change in the construction of the identity of the actors, but not in the fundamental structure of world order.

These images present contending views on changes that are occurring in the actors, forces and structure of world politics. There are other depictions that imply that the transformation that is, or should be, occurring is that of the perceptions and assumptions that are brought to world politics. Peterson's work, for instance, suggests that an awareness of how the study and practice of world politics built upon constructed hierarchies of gender is a first step in beginning to change both practice and analysis. Furthermore, revealing how gendered hierarchies are constructed not only presents a more holistic account of world politics, but also assists in revealing and ultimately transforming other hierarchies and oppressive structures. Seth's discussion of the postcolonial perspective similarly seeks to reveal implicit hierarchies of power and knowledge built upon the colonial experience. Bleiker's essay suggests that, in part, this process of transformation and revelation is an aspect of the end of one mode of thinking and the acceleration of another. For Bleiker, the end of modernity can be taken to signal the end of a historical period, a change of eras. But from another perspective it can be taken to signal the change from one way of representing politics to another. By unsettling existing assumptions about world politics, Bleiker's work also suggests that we will in some important ways change world politics.

One World, Two Worlds or Many?

The second question concerns how the broad framework of world order should be envisaged. During the Cold War there was a bifurcation of world order into east and west, and north and south. Is the contemporary global order to be seen as comprising one world, two worlds or many? As part of this interest in how difference is imagined in the global polity, we are also interested in how the relationship between these imagined worlds is viewed. Much hinges on the answers to these questions including the moral basis of global society and the political basis of the right to participate.

The most powerful image of one world is contained in the family of depictions around globalization- including the 'end of sovereignty' and the 'borderless world'- and in the 'endangered planet' and other holistic, ecological images. Those envisaging one world in these depictions are those who see either ecological or globalization processes as universally positive. The 'balance of power' in many respects also suggests a deeply integrated world order, despite the existence of a 'world of states'. At the other end of the spectrum are those that see a highly diverse world order- the many worlds implied by fragmentation imagery- in the 'coming anarchy', or 'the world of regions'. It is also there in the form of globalization imagery which imagines the formation of hybrid cultures as a result of the differential impact of globalization in different parts of the globe.

Most characterizations, however, imply, or explicitly embrace, a 'two worlds' picture of world politics. They do so, however, for very different reasons and on very different bases. The 'end of history', while projecting that ultimately a single universal order will encompass all societies, depicts world politics as currently divided between the world of societies immersed in the violent processes of history, and the more peaceful and advanced societies that have attained the post-historical state. This bifurcation of world order is explicitly seen in Goldgeier and McFaul's 'Tale of Two Worlds' (1992) or Singer and Wildavsky's 'zones of peace' and 'zones of turmoil' (1993). Even the 'world of tribes', which at first looks like an image of many worlds in a fragmented global order, turns out to be primarily promoting a bifurcated world. It implies that the emergence of ancient tribal disputes indicates a divide between the civilized and the barbarian. The same is the case for the 'clash for civilizations' which at first looks like depicting six or seven civilizational worlds but is in the end seeing a West-non West struggle as the most dominant. The image of 'Islam and the West' of course also depicts a bifurcated world order. What all this suggests, then, is a clustering around the depiction of a bifurcated world of the West and the non-West, variously depicted as the civilized and barbarian, the rich and poor, the controllers and consumers of knowledge, the West and Islam, the stable and the chaotic, and the liberal democratic against the authoritarian.

It is notable that all of the 'two worlds' images implicitly or explicitly depict a hierarchical relationship between the two worlds. Keal's analysis of the 'international society' image reveals an inner and outer circle of membership, governed by different rules of legitimacy and norms of behaviour. He suggests that 'international society' can therefore be interpreted as supporting a hierarchical world order. Hierarchy is also critical to Peterson's discussion of how feminist perspectives understand world order. These hierarchies, she argues, privilege the masculine and denigrate the feminine but have, over time, become so naturalized that they are rarely seen or questioned. It is also, she argues, instrumental in reproducing other forms of global hierarchy linked to the denigration of peoples and practices associated with feminine qualities. Similarly, Seth argues that traditional conceptions that posit a universal order mask inequalities of power and the privileging of modern Western institutions and structures. For Seth, this structure of inequality that was established through colonialism continues to apply in spite of processes of decolonization. Peterson, Seth, and Bleiker all point to the need to deconstruct existing perceptions of order to understand the extent to which they are constructed in the interests of certain actors – Western, white, masculine, political elites – while marginalizing those of others.

One recurring basis of differentiation is that of levels of development. In the 'end of history', societies are distinguished by whether or not they have progressed to a post-historical state or continue to be 'mired' in the violent struggles for recognition and satisfaction that characterize historical evolution. In the 'age of regions', there is some sense that those societies that have reached ever-deeper levels of regional integration have somehow achieved a higher level of progress in an economic and political institutional sense. Sutherland also notes that some who deploy the image of an 'endangered planet' differentiate between the developed and underdeveloped world, either to portray developing societies as somehow less environmentally stable, or to suggest that environmental threats in the South are a product of its under-development at the hands of the North. However, while noting the different ecological conditions that apply to different regions and societies provides useful insights, Sutherland warns that a simple North /South differentiation can be overly simplistic obscuring a complex web of interests and relationships which exists across the world in respect of these issues.

Keal's discussion of 'international society' highlights significant strategies of differentiation implicated in the evolution of international law. Inclusion or exclusion in international society, he observes, was based on religion, then certain criteria based on social and political organization encapsulated in the phrase 'the standard of civilization'. More recently the criterion of legitimacy has been based not only on the external capacity to meet the obligations of a sovereign state, but also on the nature of domestic constitutions and practices. Differentiation in international society, therefore, appears to be based to a degree on standards of moral community, creating structures of difference not only between those inside and outside international society, but also a hierarchy within international society.

As with the criteria of progress and development in the economic fields, it seems that differentiation based on standards of institutional development parallels differences between Western and non-Western societies. The standard applied to other societies is invariably that achieved in modern Western societies. This suggests an interesting if often understated axis or differentiation based on race or culture.

In some of the images, differentiation based on racial or ethnic identity is, however, overt. This is the case in the images of the 'world of tribes' and the 'clash of civilizations', in which differentiation is based in the first case on ethnic identity, and in the second on cultural identity. In both images, these identities are innate and irreducible, and gaining primacy over alternative forms of political identity. Both images undermine aspirations towards coexistence. The 'clash of civilizations', in particular, suggests that differences between self and other are likely to produce conflict. Interestingly, however, the image suggests that while ethnicity and religion play a significant role in distinguishing cultures, the factors that distinguish them most are the norms and values that have evolved within particular civilizations. A 'world of tribes' also suggests there is an innate danger of conflict where different tribes or ethnic communities co-exist in proximate spaces. Mount's discussion of this image also brings to the fore other significant strategies of differentiation that are implicit in the discourse surrounding tribalism. These include differentiation between the civilized and the barbaric, the modern and the premodern, the progressive and the backward. This returns us to the sense of difference being linked and evaluated according to perceived levels of progress, one of the factors that can contribute to creating hierarchies of difference.

In a number of these images difference is associated with something seen as lesser than, or something threatening to, the self. For Seth and Bleiker, such associations can be related to a broader trends of homogenization that are part of the current of modern Western thought. Seth argues that while the discipline of International Relations has acknowledged the existence of difference in world politics, it domesticates difference, subjugating all difference into the concept of national difference, while states are perceived as essentially like units, a universal form in the international arena. The implication here is that failure to recognize and respect different forms of political community, values and identity provides a limited and exclusionary reading of world politics and is in itself an expression of dominance. Bleiker, Seth, and Peterson, and George in his critique of the 'back to the future' image, all argue that embracing rather than seeking to subjugate difference will enrich our understanding of world politics. Indeed, Bleiker argues that from a post-modern perspective, an ethical approach to world politics is linked to a struggle with, and acceptance of, difference.

Community, Identity and Agency

The third question on the fundamentals of world politics concerns the location of political community, identity and agency, a question spurred by the view of many commentators that the state is under siege as the primary site of community and political agency. The various images imply very different answers, some suggesting a continuation of a state-centric world; others suggesting a move in the loci of identity and agency to regions, civilizations, tribes, international institutions, transnational organizations, or, in the case of the 'new medievalism', a move to overlapping identities, loyalties and communities in a multi-layered world polity.

For many, the state remains the primary actor and locus of identity. Little, for instance, notes that the metaphor of the 'balance of power' is inextricably linked to the idea of a system of sovereign states. Keal notes that whilst conceptions of international society initially embraced individuals as actors, over time international society and international law which underpins it has effectively come to apply only to states. Not only do these images continue to view states as the most significant actors in world politics, they also continue to identify great powers as the most influential agents in this community. In the contemporary environment, the most powerful of these is the United States, but images such as the balance of power also acknowledge the influence wielded by other regional great powers, such as China, Russia and Japan.

As George's discussion makes clear, not only is the state the central actor in many conceptions, it is a particular kind of state – the self-interested modern Western territorial sovereign state – that is seen as the legitimate actor. Indeed, a number of the images allude to the hegemony of the West in world politics, implying that the West itself exercises some form of significant agency in contemporary world politics. This is very evident in the 'end of history' image, for instance, in which there is a very powerful sense of the West as an actor involved in the battle to direct the course of modernity. This raises the question of what sort of agency the West exercises? In some guises, it appears as an agglomeration of powerful states; in others as an economic system, an ideological locus or a normative community.

Other images debate the extent to which the agency of the state is diminishing in contemporary world politics. A 'borderless world' and 'new medievalism' both suggest that increasingly political agency will be less clearly linked with territory although, as Falk observes, the role of the state as the primary political actor has, perhaps, always been exaggerated. These images imply that the state's capacity and authority to control economic, but also to some extent political and social forces, including flows of information, is under attack from the rising capacity of other agents. These include transnational corporations and other market forces, international organizations and agents of global civil society, such as social movements, whose capacity to organize and operate is increasingly liberated by developments in technology and communications. These new agents, and the forces which they are products of, constrain and challenge the state in many ways. They challenge the state as the primary source of political identity and its monopoly of the legitimate use of force. Technological developments such as the internet induce a reconceptualization of space which has consequences for perceptions of identity and of power. Forces unleashed by the increased flexibility of global markets restrict the range of options available to states, creating new demands such as the need to maintain international competitiveness and the desire to retain the favour of investors of global capital.

However, while both Clark and Falk recognize the increased importance of new agents, like Pemberton, they are also wary of underestimating the continued salience of the state. Furthermore, Clark suggests that the diminishment of the state as an agent may in some respects be positive, but in others negative. States can be viewed as institutions which express the political preferences of their citizens, and afford some measure of protection to citizens from the negative impact of external forces. Clark asks us to consider the possibility that the state is not so much being superseded as itself experiencing transformation in response to the unleashing of the forces cited above. Similarly, Pemberton suggests that the concept of the sovereign state is perhaps not being surrendered so much as continuing to evolve. Falk agrees with commentators that the state no longer forms the sole focus of identity and that some sense of global citizenship is emerging, but suggests that we have yet to see the emergence of a truly cosmopolitan sense of identity.

Some of the images draw attention to the enhanced agency of existing actors and communities in world politics. The 'endangered planet', for instance, highlights the growing significance of transnational actors particularly non-governmental agencies and international organizations. Other images focus on the emergence of new agents. Advocates of the 'age of regionalism' suggest that regional organizations, institutions and alliances in the fields of economics, security and political coordination, are becoming a new locus of political power. Once again, its advocates vary on whether this new agent will supersede or supplement the state, act as an agent of the states which constitute each region, or even provide a forum for representing the interests and voice of non-state actors in civil society.

Two of the most dramatic images which suggest the emergence of new actors are the 'clash of civilizations' and the 'world of tribes'. The 'world of tribes' suggests that tribal communities are becoming increasingly prominent in world politics particularly in ethnic conflicts. The 'clash of civilizations' returns to the realm of earlier macro historians by suggesting that civilizations rather than states are the true agents of history. This does not mean that states are no longer significant actors in world politics, but that their interests and alliances are increasingly defined by cultural identity. What the 'world of tribes' and the 'clash of civilizations' are suggesting is that racial or cultural identities are becoming increasingly powerful as foundations for community. Some advocates of the 'age of regions' also imply that cultural identity provides a foundation for regional groupings, while the 'new medievalism' highlights the new prominence of those who stress the importance of religious identity as a foundation for community. All posit the political significance of forms of identity and community other than civic or national. However, as Mount's discussion suggests, these alternative forms of political community have not necessarily superseded the state as political agents. States still retain a powerful hold on political community. While ethnic groups, for instance, have now become prominent actors, a number of these movements seek legitimacy and voice in the form of the state

Other images, again, highlight not the emergence of new actors, but a heightened consciousness of the agency of actors which more traditional conceptions of world politics neglect. Thus Peterson argues that we need to transform our understanding of world politics by acknowledging the previously neglected agency of women. For Seth and Bleiker also, an important task is to denaturalize the assumptions that the state is the only legitimate form of political identity. These assumptions, they argue, marginalize a range of other forms of political agents. In fact, Seth argues that the primacy of the modern nation-state has been won by subsuming all other forms of difference into this sovereign, irreducible, trans-historical community. For Seth and Bleiker, the postcolonial and postmodern perspectives highlight, and therefore help to legitimate, alternative forms of community and agency in world politics, or what Seth calls other possible ways of being in the world.

Forms of Power

A fourth and related question concerns what conceptions of power are demonstrated in these various images. Traditionally in world politics, power is envisaged as geopolitical power, although implicitly this is always linked to some form of economic capacity. Such a concept is still fundamental to the images of 'back to the future' and the 'balance of power'. This form of capacity is embedded in a deeper structure of ideas in the 'end of history' image. In the image of 'international society', power entails not only capacity but also structural power as expressed through the institutions of the international community, and the ability to set the norms and rules. The 'clash of civilizations' also conceptualizes power as structural and sees the power to shape international norms and institutions as significant. However, Huntington maintains that the capacity to influence norms and values, so-called 'soft power', is always ultimately embedded in hard power, or material capacity.

What is clear in the contemporary debate between these depictions is the increased salience of forms of capacity and influence, other than conventional geopolitical power. In particular, economic power, and the capacity to project information and ideas, both enhanced by developments in technology and communications, have gained new prominence. These forms of power are not necessarily new, but have typically been viewed as subsumed in the broader capacity of states.

In some respects, the state draws its continued power from the widespread acceptance of states as the natural and legitimate location of power in world politics. This draws our attention to the contention of a number of authors that representation and knowledge themselves are significant forms of power. Sutherland stresses the importance of acknowledging the link between knowledge and power, that is power as expressed through the capacity to shape and legitimize certain discourses, or to portray certain representations as authentic, as natural and objective. Bleiker also makes this point, as illustrated by his discussion of terrorism and the debate about what constitutes the legitimate use of force. In this respect, imagery and power are deeply linked, since actors may be empowered by the acceptance of their perspective as authentic or legitimate in contrast to those conveyed by others. As Seth points out, power and representation are also linked in the way in which we construct both representations of others and ourselves. Seth argues the way in which we know and represent other peoples can in itself be a way of dominating or controlling them, and not merely an expression of that domination.

Such images suggest not necessarily a shift in the location of power in contemporary politics. Rather they seek to demonstrate how certain actors are empowered and others disempowered through language and representation. For Peterson, the representation of the feminine as lesser or weaker, and the privileging of the masculine is a subtle but widespread form of empowerment and disempowerment. These positions, then, suggest not a shift in the location, but in the perception of power.

Fragmentation and Integration

Finally, there is the question of the relative importance of the seemingly countervailing processes of integration and fragmentation in global politics, the relationship between them, and whether they are recent or longstanding forces. They feature prominently in the images associated with the 'borderless world' and the 'end of sovereignty' where the images suggest that globalization in contemporary world politics is distinguished by the rapidity and density of transactions in services, goods, information and capital prompting a transformation of world politics and the prominence of new actors. As seen from this perspective, the increased mobility of capital and investment in particular is producing new forms of pressure on states to enhance their attractiveness as locations for investment. The concept of globalization is particularly prominent in the areas of economics and technology, but Clark also indicates that this image is also relevant to the globalization of norms and ideas in areas such as environmental politics, migration and human rights. Similarly, the image of 'new medievalism' highlights that globalization is one of the forces effecting the transformation of political community.

The images present differing perceptions on whether globalization is a positive or a negative force. They also present contrasting views on what the driving force behind globalization is and, in particular, the degree to which states are simply subject to these forces, or the degree to which these forces are themselves generated and fostered by states. As Clark notes, this suggests that it may be misleading to draw a simple dichotomy between the growth of globalizing forces and a decline in state power. This assumption may mask an important symbiosis between the transformation of the state and globalizing forces.

In some respects, these images imply that there is something new about the processes of globalization. However, George argues that globalization is not necessarily a new force. Rather he identifies globalization as a contemporary expression of the longer term forces of modernization and Westernization that have shaped world politics for many centuries.

Some of the depictions suggest that globalization is part of an inexorable and positive process of development. Others see it more negatively as a further expression of hegemony that warrants and generates resistance at various levels of society. There is not only debate between the different images but also within interpretations of images. Both Pemberton and Clark, for instance, note that some see the 'borderless world' as heralding an incipient global society; others fear it presages a loss of a form of protection against the forces of global capitalism.

There is, then, considerable debate as to whether globalization is a positive or a negative force. There is also debate as to whether it is the dominant process in contemporary world politics, or whether the dominant process is that of fragmentation. For instance in Fry's discussion of the 'age of regionalism' image, certain interpretations of this image suggest that regionalism is a stepping stone to globalization, particularly in the area of trade, building towards a free market environment. Others, however, see regionalism as a form of resistance to globalization, particularly where globalization is seen as synonymous with the further promotion of Western hegemony. From this perspective, regionalism can be interpreted as a form of fragmentation rather than the building blocks of globalization. This is the interpretation that also emerges from the 'clash of civilizations' image.

The image in which fragmentation is most pronounced is that of the 'world of tribes'. This image is characterized by a sense of a world breaking into smaller, more localized units of identity, with the great multicultural empires loosing their integrity and cohesion. The 'endangered planet' is also an image that, at first glance, is very much focused on processes of fragmentation. In this case it is a physical fragmentation of the planet's environment, leading to political and social instability. But at another level, Sutherland's survey of the image suggests that strong positive trends of globalization of norms, value and association are being engendered by ecological crisis.

Mount notes that there is often a strong negative connotation associated with fragmentation. From some perspectives, however, it may be seen to be a positive process of re-empowerment. This suggestion emerges from Bleiker's discussion of the end of modernity. In fact, at a perceptual level, Bleiker argues that an acknowledgement of the 'brokeness of reality' is both necessary and desirable in order to achieve a more inclusive form of world politics. Bleiker recommends that we disaggregate the universalist perspectives that are necessarily exclusive and that reify and legitimize the positions of the powerful over others.

What emerges from the range of images is a sense of the interdependence of the processes of globalization and fragmentation. While the increased density of global transactions enhances relationships at certain levels, at others it generates forms of community and identity at a more local level. As Clark's discussion of globalization of capitalist structures indicates, one thing that globalization does not necessarily mean is homogenization. To simply see globalization as producing 'one world' masks the complexity of the current processes in world politics.

The Image-Makers

We now turn our attention to the image-makers. As we suggested at the outset, the normative and ethical commitments of the image-makers matter in understanding the images and the choices they represent. While the powerful images that have sway in the academic and policy community, and have formed the subject of this volume, are tremendously diverse, the image-makers are nearly all American, and certainly Western. That the most influential images of world politics should come from the United States is to some degree inevitable, given its prominence in world politics and in the production of knowledge. Nevertheless, this still leaves the question of whether and how this matters.

It is true that some images, such as 'international society' and the 'new medievalism', are more associated with British academia. It is also true that some American depictions have resonance elsewhere. The 'clash of civilizations', 'Islam and the West' and the 'balance of power', for example, do seem to have been embraced by some non-Western state elites. And the 'unipolar moment' is a benign form of a more threatening image of American hegemony common to some parts of the non-Western world. But broadly the American origin and Western circulation and promotion of these images does raise serious questions about the implications for universal claims implicit in them. It also raises questions about what gets left out of the debate.

It is not just that the image-makers may see the world from a particular world experience. Rather it is that many of the key image-makers are explicitly engaged in addressing the US foreign policy debate with the deployment of their images. While claiming a universal validity for their images as an understanding of world politics, they address concerns about what directions US foreign policy should take in an uncertain world. Friedman (1999), for example, concludes his book on globalization with a chapter on the way forward mainly directed to US policy makers; Barber (1996) suggests policy directions in his chapter on 'Securing Global Democracy'; Huntington (1996) ends up *The Clash* with advice to Western policymakers about foreign policy and also domestic policy; and Kaplan promotes 'proportionalism' as a 'realistic' approach to foreign policy in *The Coming Anarchy: Shattering the Dreams of the Post-Cold War* (2000). At the very least, this raises the issue Stanley Hoffmannn (1977: 59) posed about the study of International Relations up until the 1970s, which he described as an American social science tightly geared to the foreign policy concerns of the United States. For Hoffmann, the American study was too close to the 'fire' of American policy to claim to provide a science of international relations.

As a starting point we should note that although nearly all of these images are articulated by academics, commentators and political elites in the West and in the United States in particular, a number of the images also give voice to a broader community. The images of a 'balance of power', 'back to the future', a 'clash of civilizations' and the 'end of history' are all very closely associated with the US academic establishment but have also been taken up by sectors of government elsewhere in the West and, in some cases, the non-West. The slightly more abstract image of an 'international society' has evolved within the context of academic debates on the evolution of the system of states and institutions of international law, although the concept of international society is widely appealed to in political debates relating to international organizations, or transgovernmental and transnational activities and implicit in everyday discussions of world politics. However, as Keal notes, this image as it is currently constituted primarily gives voice to states and their interests, denying individuals, substate actors or indigenous peoples' legal personality.

The same point is made by Mount in his discussion of a 'world of tribes'. While there is now a widespread discourse that embraces multiculturalism and the rights of minority groups to self-determination, he notes that the institutions of international law and governance do not in effect recognize the voice of many of these substate actors. Sutherland's discussion of the image of an 'endangered planet', however, is more optimistic with regard to the range of actors given voice in this arena of governance. While traditional voices and interests are represented in the debate concerning the implications for security of environmental degradation, the image she discusses is one which has come to prominence through the activities of concerned environmental activists, lobby groups, transnational organizations and international organizations such as the UN and related agencies. She also notes that there has been some progress with regard to the respect being given to the views of indigenous peoples on issues relating to environmental management. The image of 'neo-medievalism' also implies that the loosening of state controls, particularly in the area of information and technology, provides opportunities for interest groups from the private sector and civil society to convey their ideas.

Seth, Bleiker and Peterson are focused on the goal of giving voice to groups and individuals previously marginalized in debates relating to global politics. Peterson, for instance argues that the feminist perspectives gives voice to women and their experiences. She emphasizes, however, that there is no single women's voice or perspective, but that it is important to listen to the views and experiences of a range of different women. Peterson, like Seth and Bleiker, suggest that allowing more voices to be expressed will enrich our understanding of world politics. However, despite the existence of images in the academic debate that may resonate with a broader community, the major images are of American origin and address American foreign policy dilemmas at the beginning of the twenty-first century. It therefore raises the very serious question of what different characterizations are excluded from the debate about the future shape and possibilities of global order, and to what extent the debate about future world order is an American foreign policy debate.

There is also a related issue that arises from the origin of these depictions. To appreciate this we need to reflect upon Edward Said's (1978b) influential injunction that to understand European images of the Orient, we need to understand that it tells us as much about the self-image of Europe as the Orient itself. This meant that images of the Orient, and the policies based on them, could be seen as much as products of changing self-identity in Europe as capturing changing realities in the Orient. In the case of the prominent contemporary depictions of world politics, they could be seen as reflecting a debate about who and what America is at the beginning of the twenty-first century. Huntington's image of a 'clash of civilizations' addresses not only the issue of how the West should conduct its relations with societies of a different cultural identity. It also expresses a deep disquiet with regard to the impact that multiculturalism and immigration are currently having upon the normative and cultural homogeneity of the United States. Huntington fears that the United States and the West in general is in danger of becoming riven by dangerous divisions. Kaplan's image of a 'coming anarchy' suggests that the environmental degradation and social fragmentation currently being experienced in Africa may augur things to come in the United States. Fukuyama's image of the 'end of history' is one that partly glosses over continuing inequities and problems in contemporary American societies in his depiction of the western liberal democratic state as the most satisfying form of society and the United States as a state unique in the degree to which it has assimilated people of diverse backgrounds into a society without sharply defined class or ethnic divisions (Fukuyama, 1992: 118). However, his vision of this society is ultimately permeated by the fear that ennui, bred by peace and prosperity, might ultimately drive individuals once more towards the bloody quest for glory. Saikal and Bleiker refer to the fear of Islam within American society that is reproduced as a prominent picture of global politics. Finally, Friedman (1999) and Barber (1996) advise on the need to 'democratize' globalization within the United States, as well as without.

In certain respects, then, these images of world politics are refracted through the prism of anxieties about contemporary American identity. We also noted that more broadly these can be seen as Western images of the future world polity. They either project a unified world polity based on Western ideas and practices, or a divided world of 'the West and the rest.' Carrying Said's point further, we suggest that these images can be seen as projections of various self-conceptions of the West, with the nature of the self-conception affecting the way the possible relationship between the West and other states and societies is pictured. The way Western policymakers in particular choose between these characterizations will therefore have important implications for relations within the global polity of the twenty-first century.

Notes and References

1 Contending Images of World Politics: An Introduction

1. This was less the case in the English School of International Relations where a more speculative and philosophically inclined approach kept alive a broader focus of International Relations theory (see Wight, 1991). Hedley Bull even argued that 'world politics' was the more appropriate name for the subject (Bull, 1972). Some American liberal scholars did try in the 1970s to make the case for a more complex pluralist world (Keohane and Nye, 1977) and used the term 'world politics' to depict this broader notion, but by the 1980s had retreated to a state-centric liberal institutionalism.
2. We are grateful to Spike Peterson for drawing our attention to this important distinction.
3. See, for example, Burton (1972, p. 77) and Mastanduno (1999, p. 19).
4. The fact that some contributors use a broader meaning (interchangeable with image) does not upset this purpose as long as the reader is aware that there is something special about images that employ the familiar to describe the unfamiliar. In fact, we had initially employed this broader usage of 'metaphor' ourselves. The workshop in which we first discussed these ideas was called 'Metaphors for our Time'.
5. Within the formal study of International Relations it is only John Burton and Kenneth Boulding (1956) to our knowledge that have attempted to think about the power of images. A former head of the Foreign Ministry in Australia turned international relations theorist, Burton (1972, p. 77-8) asserted that images (which he also called 'models') can be powerful in international policy. Consistent with this belief, he produced the image of a 'cobweb' to depict a pluralistic world society and to counter the influence of state-centric images. Kenneth Waltz's more famous use of images in *Man, The State and War* (1959) does not reflect upon the power of images. Waltz uses the term to refer to emphases in the theoretical understandings of the causes of war: one image emphasizing human behaviour; the second focusing on the internal structure of states, and the third emphasizing the international structure.
6. For the steps in adapting Said theoretically as an approach to theorising international relations in a policy setting see Fry (1997).

2   The 'End of History'?

1. The author would like to thank the members of the workshop on Metaphors for our Time: Contending Images of World Politics, held at the Australian National University in Canberra, April 1999, Ursula Vollerthun, and the editors, Greg Fry and Jacinta O'Hagan, for their comments.
2. Fukuyama may be credited with a certain prescience, in that the article was published before the fall of the Berlin Wall in November 1989.
3. The 'democratic deficit' in the European Union is often taken to refer to the weakness of the elected parliament in relation to the executive (the Council of Ministers and the Commission), but the term also refers to a more fundamental problem – namely, the perception, reflected in the low interest in elections to the European Parliament, that the European institutions, including the Parliament, are remote and virtually beyond popular control.
4. To mark the article's tenth anniversary, *The National Interest* published Fukuyama's 'second thoughts', together with several responses. In this article, Fukuyama maintained that none of the subsequent events or critiques had caused him to question his view that 'liberal democracy and a market-oriented economic order are the only viable options for modern societies' (1999a, p. 16). On the other hand, he now maintained that history would not come to an end so long as modern science has no end: indeed, new developments in science would abolish 'mankind as such' (p. 17).
5. Military dictatorships in Africa and Latin America proved unable to maintain their legitimacy in the face of the economic crises of the 1980s; the collapse of President Suharto's rule in Indonesia in 1998 provides a more recent example. It cannot be assumed that the ensuing democratic regimes will prove stable, but it also appears unlikely that any other regime can achieve durable support. For a general discussion of these issues, see Huntington (1991).
6. This, of course, is not the only function of elections. They determine who shall form the government; policy issues are often played down. However, when there are major well-defined policy differences the outcome of elections is accepted as decisive.
7. The first of these attracted sporadic attention in the Australian media; the author was informed of the second during a visit to Berlin in June 1999.
8. The author was shown the shelving devoted to new books during the previous two years, no more than about 20 per cent of that in the earlier 1990s.

3   'Back to the Future'?

1. There are a number of ways of illustrating that this is a perspective with a very flimsy grasp of (its own) historico-political reality. Indeed, even in its own (empiricist) terms its historical facts (for example, in regard to multi/bipolar systems) do not stand up to even rudimentary critical challenge (see Vasquez, 1998, chapter 12). In regard to the indisputable fact that we did not have nuclear war during the bipolar Cold War period and the view that, therefore, deterrence and nuclear threat theory worked, see a range of counter-propositional perspectives in the strategic and IR literature (for example, Booth (ed.), 1998; Lynn-Jones, 1991; Lebow and Stein, 1994, 1998; Vasquez, 1998; and MccGwire, 1985/6).

2. As Maynes (1995, p. 38) points out, Huntington's thesis in particular 'has shaped [US] foreign policy debates for the last few years'.
3. I do not seek here to put a full stop to memory, by providing an alternative real history to counteract the false one of Mearsheimer *et al*. Given that human history always involves interpretation there can be no ultimate Archemedian point from which to make such arbitrary judgement. This begs the question of why the critical historical perspective presented here should be regarded as any more credible than that it disputes. The answer, at least in the context of this chapter, is simple enough, because it takes into account a whole range of evidence, drawn from a range of sources and methodologies, all of which are ignored in 'back to the future' perspectives even while it claims universal insight for its perspective. In this sense my aim is to provide at least an adequate, if not ultimate body of knowledge on the issues at hand. And while the criteria of adequacy is itself a contestable category, I seek here to engage the 'back to the future' stance in relation to its own criteria of adequacy, truth, fact, relevance and credibility.
4. In the ex-Soviet context, as in the Balkans, the complexities are such that seizing the moment is always a risky business, but here surely the West must help the citizens of the old Soviet Union overcome the worst excesses of rapid Westernization in order that its more positive institutional and cultural features might take hold. It matters not whether one prescribes such activity as self-interested, what matters is that the violent images of the 'new pessimists' do not become self-fulfilling prophecies.
5. The condition of radical indeterminacy, in this context, is characterized by the acknowledgment that power relations are multifaceted and multilayered, contingent and fungible and therefore amenable to amelioration, communication and change. In regard to globalization it recognizes that for all the precision modelling of the corporate managers and their military-technocratic allies, the sheer scale and impact of the revolutions in technology, economics and productive forces will provoke various kinds of 'dysfunctional consequences'. In regard to democracy it recognizes that beyond the Schumpeterian obsession with elections and formal (US) models of elite-shuffling representative government, the keystone of democracy is that space where power is an absence rather than a predictable presence. Or, less obtusely, that space where power is not 'owned' (for example, by any individual, group, party system, sect, or religion) but where power is an indeterminate category within which genuine political debate and struggle can take place. On this, see Lefort (1988).

4   A 'Balance of Power'?

1. It seems very likely, however, that Guicciardini drew the idea from a manuscript written by Bernado Rucellai in the last decade of the fifteenth century (Nelson, 1943, p. 129).
2. I have discussed these two approaches to the balance of power in terms of adversarial and associative conceptions of balance. Here I have also attempted to link the terms to the idea of automatic and manual balances of power. This distinction is made by Claude (1962) and Jervis (1997).
3. One of the most interesting attempts to develop the normative dimension of the balance of power relates the balance of power to Rawls' theory of justice (1971). See Midlarsky (1983).

5 An 'International Society'?

1. The author wishes to thank Chris Reus-Smit for his helpful and penetrating comments on an earlier draft.
2. Oakeshott's distinction is between 'enterprise' association and 'civil' association.
3. This is a play on the title of Bull's 1980 article 'The Great Irresponsibles? The United States, The Soviet Union and World Order'.
4. This was a task Bull began to address in his Hagey Lectures delivered shortly before his death in 1985 (Bull, 1984b).

7 The 'End of Sovereignty'?

1. Walker comments:

   > The Theme of modernity as an era not only of rapid sociopolitical, economic and technological transformations but also of a new consciousness of temporality and the contingency of specifically modern experience, has been especially familiar since the late nineteenth century. In fact, much of the recent literatures on dynamics of late or postmodernity, as on late capitalism, may be read as a recovery and extension of ideas once associated with, say, Baudelaire, Bergson and Nietzsche as well as Marx. (Walker, 1995b, p. 314; Bergson, 1984, pp. 248-9, 307, 314, 342–3; see also Deleuze, 1988, p. 91 – Walker cites this work).

2. These are Bergson's expressions (see Bergson, 1984, pp. 208-11; Deleuze and Guattari, 1988, pp. 236-9, 386, 483-4, 573; see also Walker, 1993, p. 14).
3. Walker's choice of phrase echoes Bergson (see 1984, p. 197).
4. For a rich depiction of Newton and his work see Fauvel *et al.* (1988). Robert Wokler notes that the expression Enlightenment Project is a very recent invention (see 1998, p. 302). Philipp Frank, writing from Czechoslovakia in 1938 and concerned that mystical 'presentations of modern physics' could 'serve intellectual, and hence social, reaction and supply it with arms', explained that philosophical misinterpretations of modern science stemmed from confusing conceptual with linguistic identity:

   > The metaphysician ... looks upon the history of science as a struggle for or against his particular metaphysical theses. But this struggle has nothing to do with the development of science itself; it is merely a fight as to how human beings can express their private or collective wishes in such terms as also occur in the sentences of contemporary science. In this struggle the words may be combined into sentences according to rules incompatible with those of real scientific syntax. (1938, pp. 57-8)

5. See also Joseph Camilleri and Jim Falk who argue that the 'theory of a world partitioned into territorial domains ... is increasingly confronted by another equally long-standing perspective of a living planet as an integrated whole' (1992, p. 195).

6. I have taken this expression from Rorty. 'Their strategy [historicist thinkers] has been to insist that socialization ... goes all the way down' (1989, p. xiii).
7. Kuehls (1996, p. 30) writes that 'thinking society beyond sovereign territorial boundaries does not necessitate creating some kind of international governing body to encompass this global human population, but might suggest a smooth or rhizomatic social space... Thinking society beyond both sovereign territorial boundaries and species boundaries means taking into serious consideration the ambiguity, contingency, and diversity of life'.
8. These images and ideas are drawn from James (1971, p. 274-6, 283). See also James (1907, p. 79).
9. On Spengler's influence, see Liebert (1933, p. 34).
10. The notion of hyphenated loyalties comes from Laski (1916, p. 425).
11. I have borrowed this last expression from James (1897, p. 177).
12. This is Hans Kelsen's term (see 1961, p. 386).
13. For a discussion of this and historical examples, see Heyking (1928) and Bentwich (1934).
14. On the relation of sovereignty to natural law, see McIlwain (1933, p. 98). See also Vattel (1863, pp. 154-9) and Westlake (1910, I, pp. 319-20).
15. On this point, see Laski: 'We have to take the world of sense as we meet it, its losses and gains, its struggles and victories, and assume that ... it is a real world in space and time. We have to treat evil as genuine and not merely an appearance capable, otherwise, of being harmonized into good' (1925, p. 260; see also James, 1897, p. 61).

8   A 'New Medievalism'?

1. I read Thucydides, in contrast to realists and neorealists, as presenting Athenian decline as mainly an extreme example of imperial overstretch, but also as resulting from a decline in public morality that is severely aggravated by the deforming effects of demagogic manipulations of the Athenian democratic process. Such a tension in 'reading' most vividly surfaces in relation to whether the Melian Dialogue is understood as imparting the unconditional primacy of power in international relations or is taken as an expression of the corrupting impact of moral decline on the exercise of power. See Walzer (1977) for an influential instance of the mainstream reading.
2. Both the nuclear stalemate and the failures of interventionary diplomacy have produced such frustrations in the course of the last half-century. For an argument along these lines, see Falk (1997).
3. For consideration of this challenge, see Falk (1999a); for a more direct engagement with the allegedly anachronistic imagery of Westphalia, see Falk (1998).
4. Bull is also very definite that the medieval world was based on its Western Christian character, while the possibility of a new medievalism is conceived to be 'a modern and secular counterpart' that can be called medieval because it exhibits 'its central characteristic: a system of overlapping authority and multiple loyalty' (1977, p. 254).
5. It is true that terms such as 'neoclassical' or 'neoromantic' persist, but more to suggest their dependence on a preceding era than to identify their distinctiveness. No one has suggested that the emergent world order is in any way deriv-

ative from the medieval period; the usage is purely analogical, providing a historical analogy that discloses some important features of similarity.

6. Bull discusses, aside from new medievalism, a structure of authority that is of global scope that is 'a system but not a society', the disintegration of the societal dimensions of inter-state relations so that what exists is 'states but not a system', and world government (Bull, 1977, pp. 257-96). He emphasizes that he is engaging only in a thought experiment that is encouraged by the combination of integrative trends in Europe and certain aspirational goals of Europeanists, and thus introduces his inquiry with the carefully chosen words, 'We might imagine... ' such a new medievalism in this regional setting (p. 255). In fact, Bull is not enthusiastic about the prospect of a new medievalism as a secular reincarnation, and appears to doubt its superiority, pointing out that 'if it were anything like the precedent of Western Christendom, it would contain more ubiquitous and continuous violence and insecurity than does the modern states system' (p. 255).

7. Civil society advocates are also drawn to their 'construction' of medieval reality as sustaining transnational civic culture. For instance, Lipschutz (1992); for a more anarchistic reading by Lipschutz of global civil society, see Lipschutz (2000).

8. The prospect of satisfying cravings of 'nations' for 'self-determination' without necessitating the stressful shattering of existing 'states' is the main theme of Gottlieb (1993).

9. For a stress on the centrality of complexity as the empirical basis for the analogy, and its contrast with the simplicity of the modern statist reality, see Hirst and Thompson, (1995).

10. For comprehensive interpretations of the transforming impact of IT, see Castels (1995, 1996, 1997); a more one-sided, popularizing, yet still useful presentation is that of Negroponte (1995).

11. This has been the endeavour of the World Order Models Project for more than three decades. For its most recent effort to articulate normative potential in relation to humane governance, see Falk (1995a).

12. David Held has done seminal work, often in collaboration with Daniele Archibugi (see Held, 1995; see also Archibugi and Held (eds), 1995; Archibugi, Held and Köhler (eds), 1998).

13. Kung regards the idea of a Christian Europe as emphasizing exclusionary religious orientations and as working against inter-civilizational reconciliation that he regards as indispensable to any hope for a global ethic.

9 A 'Coming Age of Regionalism'?

1. I wish to thank John Ravenhill, Jacinta O'Hagan and Gavin Mount for their comments on this chapter.

2. Formerly National Security Adviser under Presidents Kennedy and Johnson, and author of the influential 'the stages of economic growth' thesis, Rostow was Professor of Economics and History at the University of Texas at Austin at the time of writing.

3. By 'regionalism' Rostow means the institutional links between contiguous states as in the idea of 'Europe' or 'Southeast Asia' rather than the development of sub-national loyalties within states. This is also the sense in which regionalism is used throughout this chapter.

4.   The term was coined by Wynne Russell of the Department of International Relations at the Australian National University (see Russell, 1998).
5.   Since the 1960s, in particular, there have been appeals to pan-nationalistic cultural identity in relation to African regionalism; in the evolution of Southeast Asian regionalism and the promotion by state elites of 'the ASEAN way'; in the Gulf Council and other Arab regionalist attempts; and in the South Pacific where Pacific Islanders promoted the concept of 'the Pacific Way'.
6.   There are, however, significant divisions within the economic profession between those sympathetic to regionalism, such as Bergsten (1994), and opponents such as Bhagwati (1994).

10   A 'Clash of Civilizations'?

1.   I would like to thank Greg Fry and Sanjay Seth for their helpful comments on this chapter.
2.   Russia suffered political instability with the demise of Gorbachev and the rise of Yeltsin, and pro-democratic, pro-nationalist and pro-communist forces battling for influence and support. Conflicts erupted in the former Soviet republics of Moldovia, Tadjikistan, Georgia and Azerbaijan.
3.   In his analysis, Huntington focused on interaction between eight major civilizations: Western, Islamic, Sinic, Japanese, Hindu, Slavic-Orthodox, Latin-American and 'possibly African'. He defined civilizations as 'the highest cultural groupings of people and the broadest level of cultural identity, short of distinction from other species' (Huntington, 1993a, p. 24).
4.   This does not prevent Huntington from advising Western powers to seek to cooperate with and even seek to co-opt members of sympathetic civilizations, such as Latin America, and to continue promoting the institutions that reflect its interests. However, a key element in his recommendations is the containment of the potentially most hostile civilizations, such as those of Islam and Confucius.
5.   Whilst there is some call for mutual comprehension in Huntington's work, it forms an extremely small part of his analysis. There are some five pages devoted to the topic in a 321-page book (Huntington, 1996).

11   A 'World of Tribes'?

1.   I would like to thank Greg Fry, Cindy O'Hagan, Jim George and the participants at the *Contending Images* workshop for their comments on earlier drafts. In keeping with the general dedication of this book, I would also like to thank Professor Jim Richardson for his guidance over the years.
2.   A common criticism of Huntington's model is that it is not very good at explaining why ethnic conflicts occur between peoples that share the same civilizational identity. The model also obscures the history of civilizational encounters with 'barbarian' entities.
3.   For example, Gurr (1993, 1994) has comprehensively demonstrated that the incidence and severity of ethnic conflicts have been steadily increasing since at least

the 1960s. He argues that the process of decolonization and postcolonial nation-alism has been a more important causal factor.

4. Contrast this with characterizations of national iconography of powerful and predatory animals such as the US 'eagle', the British 'bulldog' or the Russian 'bear'.

5. Wight identified four doctrines on barbarism: civilization has the right to expand itself; barbarians have no rights; barbarians may be exploited; and barbarians are not human (Wight, 1991, pp. 55-62).

6. Compare articles 1(2) and 2(7), *Charter of the United Nations*, 26 June 1945, San Francisco (see Franck 1992; Simpson, 1996).

7. *Agreement between the Republic of Indonesia and the Portuguese Republic on the Question of East Timor*, United Nations, New York, 5 May 1999.

12 'Islam and the West'?

1. This is a term which was used by the Jordanian Foreign Minister Abdel-Elah Khatib in a speech to the UN General Assembly in September 1999 (see *BBC News* 21 September 1999).

2. For a detailed discussion of the Soviet invasion, the Afghan Islamic resistance and US support, see Saikal and Maley (1991), Rubin (1995) and Roy (1986).

3. For details of the US-Israeli alliance and breakdown of grants and loans, see Mansour (1994).

4. On the significance of East Jerusalem for Muslims, see Tibawi (1969).

5. For a detailed discussion of this issue and America's operations in Pakistan and beyond, although containing some factual inaccuracies, see Cooley (1999, especially chapters 3, 5 and 9).

6. For good discussions of Pakistan's relations with the Taliban and America's role in it, see Rashid (1998) and Mackenzie (1998).

7. For a discussion of Islamic radicalism among the Palestinians, see Abu-Amr (1994).

8. This problem has continued to date to mar the US's approach to dealing with the Afghan conflict and the Taliban, as well as Taliban-related Islamic militancy in the region. For an analysis, see Khalilzad and Byman (2000).

9. To highlight this point, America's leading proponent of the 'clash of civilizations' thesis, Samuel Huntington, recently went so far as to describe the continuation of the conflict between the predominantly Muslim Chechnya and Christian Russia as 'one front among many in the contemporary global struggles between Muslim and non-Muslim peoples' (Huntington, 1999).

14 A 'Gendered Global Hierarchy'?

1. Masculinism refers to the *ideological* privileging of that which is associated with 'maleness'/masculinity (not limited to men) over that which is associated with 'femaleness'/femininity; masculinity–femininity is conventionally understood

as a dichotomy of mutually exclusive and exhaustive gender categories. Gender hierarchy describes a system of structural power that privileges men and masculinism over women. This privileging includes men's appropriation of women's productive and reproductive labour, men's control over women's bodies and regulation of their activities, and the promotion of masculinism to naturalize (depoliticize) this hierarchy.

2. See special issues of *International Studies Quarterly* (33, 3, 1989) and (34, 3 1990).

3. The follow-up to this special issue in 1988 (17, 3) was Grant and Newland, eds, (1991). Ten years later, another special issue was devoted to 'Gendering "The International" ' (27, 4, 1998).

4. For a recent overview and analysis of feminist IR, see True (1996).

5. In addition to the enormous literature on women/gender and development, feminist-IR books addressing IPE and globalization include Marchand and Parpart (1995), Pettman (1996), Boris and Prugl (eds), (1996), Bakker (ed.) (1994), Chin (1998) and Marchand and Runyan (eds), (2000).

6. As argued here, this distinction has been productive for feminist scholarship, but carries its own dangers insofar as it tends to essentialize sex as a biological given rather than insisting on both terms as social constructions.

15   A 'Postcolonial World'?

1. With thanks for their comments to the participants in a workshop convened to discuss draft chapters of this book; and thanks also to R.B.J. Walker and Joe Camilleri for comments on an earlier draft of this essay.

2. The outlines of Said's argument, and the passages quoted here, are to be found in Said (1978a).

3. This intellectual move is by no means atypical, or confined to International Relations. Chris Brown provides a good characterization of this style of argument, of which Bull and Watson provide one version: 'The effect of Western imperialism was to reshape the political, economic and social structure of the world, either by direct intervention or by creating a situation which ensured that the only way to resist intervention was to adopt European ways ... the logic of the argument ... [is thus] that universal conclusions can be drawn from initially European premises' (Brown, 1998, p. 342). See also Rengger (1989).

4. One of the most important and powerful was that of M. K. Gandhi, who called for a struggle against colonialism which was not necessarily a struggle for nationhood and modernity (see Parekh, 1999).

5. The most eloquent statement of this view is Guha (1982). See also Seth (1999).

6. See, for instance, the interesting remarks by Ashley (1988, pp. 238-40), on which I draw in this paragraph.

16   The 'End of Modernity'?

1. This essay develops ideas I first explored in slightly different contexts, most notably in Bleiker (1998, 2000). I am grateful to Jim George for drawing my atten-

tion to the balance of power metaphor, and to Tim Dunne for critically engaging a draft of this essay, and for being tolerant enough to suffer through my 'postmodern' approach to Australian roundabouts.

2. The State Department officially defines terrorism as 'premeditated, politically motivated violence perpetrated against noncombatant targets by subnational groups or clandestine agents usually intended to influence an audience' (United States Department of State, 1996, p. vi).

3. Note that between 1985 to 1996, the US produced more than 10 million new land mines – adding to a stockpile of an estimated 12–18 million (see Landmine Library, 1999).

Bibliography

Abu-Amr, Ziad (1994) *Islamic Fundamentalism in the West Bank and Gaza* (Bloomington, IN: Indiana University Press).

Acharya, Amitav (1999) 'Regionalism and the emerging world order: sovereignty, autonomy, identity' (Warwick: University of Warwick, paper delivered to the conference on After the Global Crises: What Next for Regionalism? 16–18 September).

Agathangelou, Anna M. and L. H. M. Ling (1997) 'Postcolonial Dissidence within Dissident IR: Transforming Master Narratives of Sovereignty in Greco-Turkish Cyprus', *Studies in Political Economy* 54: 7–37.

Ahmed, Akbar S. (1995) ' "Ethnic Cleansing": a Metaphor for our Time?', *Ethnic and Racial Studies* 18, 1: 1–25.

Ajami, Fouad (1993) 'The Summoning', *Foreign Affairs* 72, 4: 2–9.

Alagappa, Muthiah (1995) 'Regionalism and Conflict Management: a Framework for Analysis', *Review of International Studies* 21, 4: 359–87.

Albrow, M. (1996) *The Global Age: State and Society Beyond Modernity* (Cambridge: Polity Press).

Alexander, M. Jacqui and Chandra Talpade Mohanty (eds) (1997) *Feminist Genealogies, Colonial Legacies, Democratic Futures* (New York, NY: Routledge).

Anaya, S. James (1996) *Indigenous Peoples in International Law* (New York, NY: Oxford University Press).

Anderson, Kym and Richard Blackhurst (eds) (1992) *The Greening of World Trade Issues* (Ann Arbor, MI: University of Michigan Press).

Ankersmit, F. R. (1996) *Aesthetic Politics: Political Philosophy Beyond Fact and Value* (Stanford: Stanford University Press).

Apffel-Marglin, Frédérique and Stephen A. Marglin (1996) *Decolonizing Knowledge: From Development to Dialogue* (Oxford: Clarendon Press).

Appadurai, Arjun (1990) 'Disjuncture and Difference in the Global Cultural Economy', in Mike Featherstone (ed.), *Global Culture: Nationalism, Globalization and Modernity* (London: Sage).

Archibugi, Daniele and David Held (eds) (1995) *Cosmopolitan Democracy: an Agenda for a New World Order* (Cambridge, MA: Polity Press).

Archibugi, Daniele, David Held and Martin Köhler (eds) (1998) *Re-imagining Political Community* (Stanford, CA: Stanford University Press).

Aristotle (1948) *On the Art of Poetry*, translated by S. H. Butcher (New York, NY: the Library of Liberal Art).

Armstrong, David (1998) 'Globalization and the Social State', *Review of International Studies* 24, 4: 461–78

Arndt, H. W. (1993) 'Anatomy of Regionalism', *Journal of Asian Economics* 4, 2: 271–82; also appeared in 1994, in Ross Garnaut and Peter Drysdale (eds), *Asia*

Pacific Regionalism: Readings in International Economic Relations (Sydney: Harper Education).

Asad, Talal (1973) *Anthropology and the Colonial Encounter* (London: Ithaca Press).

Ashley, Richard (1987) 'The Geopolitics of Geopolitical Space: Toward a Critical Social Theory of International Politics', *Alternatives* 12, 4: 403–34.

Ashley, Richard (1988) 'Untying the Sovereign State: a Double Reading of the Anarchy Problematique', *Millennium* 17, 2: 227–62.

Axline, Andrew (ed.) (1994) *The Political Economy of Regional Cooperation: Comparative Case Studies* (London: Pinter Publishers).

Ayoob, Mohammed (1999) From regional system to regional society: exploring key variables in the construction of regional order (Canberra: Department of International Relations, The Australian National University, Fiftieth Anniversary Lecture, April).

Badey, Thomas J. (1998) 'Defining International Terrorism: a Pragmatic Approach', *Terrorism and Political Violence* 10, 1: 90–107.

Bahuguna, S. (1988) 'Chipko – the Peoples' Movement with a Hope for the Survival of Humankind', in Sahabat Alam Malaysia and the Asia-Pacific People's Environment Network (ed.), *Global Development and Environment Crisis: Has Humankind a Future?* (Penang, Malaysia: Sahabat Alam Malaysia [Friends of the Earth Malaysia]).

Bailey, Frederick G. (1977) *Morality and Expediency* (Oxford: Blackwell).

Bakker, Isabella (ed.) (1994) *The Strategic Silence: Gender and Economic Policy* (London: Zed Books).

Banac, Ivo (1993–94) 'Misreading the Balkans' (Review) *Foreign Policy* 93: 173–82

Bandarage, Asoka (1997) *Women, Population and Global Crisis: Political-Economic Analysis* (London: Zed Books).

Barber, Benjamin R. (1996) *Jihad vs. McWorld: How Globalism and Tribalism Are Reshaping the World* (New York, NY: Ballantine Books).

Barbier, Edward B., Joanne C. Burgess, Timothy M. Swanson and David W. Pearce (1990) *Elephants, Economics and Ivory* (London: Earthscan).

Barnett, Jonathon R. (1998) 'Environmental security: a critical examination and a human-centred reformulation' (Canberra: Australian National University, thesis submitted for the degree of Doctor of Philosophy).

Barney, Gerald O. (ed.) (1980–81) *The Global 2000 Report to the President – Entering the Twenty-first Century* (New York, NY: Pergamon Press, prepared by the Council on Environmental Quality and the Department of State).

Bartley, Robert (1993) 'The Case for Optimism: the West Should Believe in Itself', *Foreign Affairs* 72, 4: 15–18.

Barton, Thomas, G. Borrini-Feyerabend, A. de Sherbinin and P. Warren (1997) *Our People, Our Resources: Supporting Rural Communities in Participatory Action Research on Population Dynamics and the Local Environment* (Gland, Switzerland: IUCN).

Bartov, Omer (1996) *Murder in Our Midst: the Holocaust, Industrial Killing and Representation* (New York, NY: Oxford University Press).

Bauman, Zygmunt (1995) *Life in Fragments: Essays in Postmodern Morality* (Oxford: Blackwell).

Baumann, Miges, J. Bell, F. Koechlin and M. Pimbert (1996) *The Life Industry: Biodiversity, People and Profits* (London: Intermediate Technology Publications).

Baylis, John and Steve Smith (eds) (1997) *The Globalization of World Politics: an Introduction to International Relations* (Oxford: Oxford University Press).

Becker, Gary (1976) *The Economic Approach to Human Behavior* (Chicago: Chicago University Press).

Bell, Coral (forthcoming) 'Ethnicity, Territoriality, Tribalism and Warfare', in Coral Bell (ed.), *World Out of Balance: International Politics in the Twenty-first Century* (Sydney: Allen & Unwin).

Bentwich, Norman (1934) 'The League of Nations and Racial Persecution in Germany', *Transactions of the Grotius Society* 19: 75–88.

Bergson, Henri (1915) 'Life And Matter At War', *The Hibbert Journal* 14: 465–75.

Bergson, Henri (1984) *Creative Evolution,* translated by Arthur Mitchell, 1st edn 1911 (Lanham, MD: University Press of America).

Bergsten, C. Fred (1994) 'APEC and World Trade: a Force for Worldwide Liberalization', *Foreign Affairs* 73, 3: 20–6.

Berki, R. (1981) *On Political Realism* (London: J.M. Dent).

Bernstein, Alvin H. (1993) 'Ethnicity and Imperial Break-up: Ancient and Modern', *SAIS Review* 13, 1: 121–32.

Bhabha, Homi K. (1994) *The Location of Culture* (London and New York: Routledge).

Bhagwati, Jagdish (1994) 'Regionalism and Multilateralism: an Overview', in Ross Garnaut and Peter Drysdale (eds), *Asia Pacific Regionalism: Readings in International Economic Relations* (Sydney: Harper Education); first appeared in 1993, in Jaime de Melo and Arvind Panagariya (eds), *New Dimensions in Regional Integration* (Cambridge: Cambridge University Press).

Bigo, Didier (1994) 'Great debates in a small world: debates on international relations and their link with the world of security' (Washington, DC: Paper presented at the International Studies Convention, 28 March – 1 April).

Birnie, Patricia W. and Alan E. Boyle (1992) *International Law and the Environment* (Oxford: Clarendon Press).

Bleiker, Roland (1998) 'Retracing and Redrawing the Boundaries of Events: Postmodern Interferences with International Theory', *Alternatives* 23, 4: 471–97.

Bleiker, Roland (2000) *Popular Dissent, Human Agency and Global Politics* (Cambridge: Cambridge University Press).

Boehmer, Elleke (1995) *Colonial and Postcolonial Literature* (Oxford: Oxford University Press).

Booth, Kenneth (1998) 'The Cold War of the Mind' in Booth (ed.), *Statescraft and Security.*

Booth Kenneth (ed.) (1998) *Statecraft and Security: the Cold War and Beyond* (Cambridge: Cambridge University Press).

Boris, Eileen and Elisabeth Prugl (eds) (1996) *Homeworkers in Global Perspective* (New York, NY: Routledge).

Boulding, Kenneth (1956) *The Image: Knowledge in Life and Society* (Ann Arbor, MI: University of Michigan Press).

Boutros-Ghali, Boutros (1992) *Agenda for Peace: Preventive Diplomacy, Peacemaking, and Peace-Keeping* (New York, NY: United Nations).

Bozeman, Adda (1960) *Politics and Culture in International Relations* (Princeton, NJ: Princeton University Press).

Brady, Robert A. (1933) *The Rationalization Movement in German Industry: a Study in the Evolution of Economic Planning* (Berkeley, CA: University of California).

Braidotti, Rosi, Ewa Charkiewicz, Sabine Häusler and Saskia Wieringa (1994) *Women, the Environment and Sustainable Development: Towards a Theoretical Synthesis* (London: Zed Books in association with INSTRAW).

Brown, Chris (1994) ' "Turtles All the Way Down": Anti-Foundationalism, Critical Theory, and International Relations', *Millennium* 23, 2: 213–36.

Brown, Chris (1995) 'International Theory and International Society: the Viability of the Middle Way?', *Review of International Studies* 21, 2: 183–96.

Brown, Chris (1997) *Understanding International Relations* (London: Macmillan).

Brown, Chris (1998) 'The Modern Requirement? Reflections on Normative International Theory in a Post-Western World', *Millennium* 17, 2: 339–48.

Brown, Lester R. (1999) 'Feeding Nine Billion', in Lester R. Brown *et al.* (eds), *State of the World 1999: a Worldwatch Institute Report on Progress Toward a Sustainable Society* (New York, NY: W.W. Norton).

Brown, Michael E. (ed.) (1993) *Ethnic Conflict and International Security* (Princeton, NJ: Princeton University Press).

Brown, Michael E. (ed.) (1996) *The International Dimensions of Internal Conflict* (Cambridge, MA: MIT Press).

Brown, W. Jethro (1906) *The Austinian Theory of Law Being An Edition of Lectures, I, V, and VI of Austin's 'Jurisprudence', and of Austin's 'Essay on the Uses of the Study of Jurisprudence' with Critical Notes and Excurses* (London: John Murray).

Brzezinski, Zbigniew (1993) *Out of Control: Global Turmoil on the Eve of the Twenty-first Century* (New York, NY: Scribner).

Bull, Hedley (1972) 'International Relations as an Academic Pursuit', *Australian Outlook* 26, 3: 251–65.

Bull, Hedley (1977) *The Anarchical Society: a Study of Order in World Politics* (London: Macmillan and New York, NY: Columbia University Press).

Bull, Hedley (1979) 'Natural Law and International Relations', *British Journal of International Studies* 5, 2: 171–81.

Bull, Hedley (1980) 'The Great Irresponsibles? The United States, The Soviet Union, and World Order', *International Journal* 35, 3: 437–47.

Bull, Hedley (1984a) 'The Emergence of a Universal International Society', in Hedley Bull and Adam Watson (eds), *The Expansion of International Society* (Oxford: Oxford University Press).

Bull, Hedley (1984b) *Justice in International Relations*, the Hagey Lectures (Waterloo, Ontario: University of Waterloo).

Bull, Hedley (1992) 'The Importance of Grotius in the Study of International Relations', in Hedley Bull, Benedict Kingsbury and Adam Roberts (eds), *Hugo Grotius and International Relations* (Oxford: Clarendon Press).

Bull, Hedley and Adam Watson (1984a) 'Introduction', in Hedley Bull and Adam Watson (eds), *The Expansion of International Society* (Oxford: Oxford University Press).

Bull, Hedley and Watson, Adam (1984b) 'Conclusion', in Hedley Bull and Adam Watson (eds), *The Expansion of International Society* (Oxford: Clarendon Press).

Burton, John (1972) *World Society* (Cambridge: Cambridge University Press).

Bush, George (1991) 'Address to the Nation Announcing Allied Military Action in the Persian Gulf' (transcript of televised address, 16 January).

Buzan, Barry (1991) *People, States and Fear: an Agenda for International Security Studies in the Post-Cold War Era*, 2nd edn (London and New York, NY: Harvester Wheatsheaf).

Buzan, Barry (1993) 'The English School Meets American Theories', *International Organization* 47, 3: 327–52.

Buzan, Barry (1999) The emerging Asian security complex (Canberra: Department of International Relations, The Australian National University, Fiftieth Anniversary Lecture, March).

Buzan, Barry, C. Jones, and R. Little (1993) *The Logic of Anarchy* (New York, NY: Columbia University Press).

Caldecott, Leonie and Stephanie Leland (eds) (1983) *Reclaim the Earth: Women Speak Out for Life on Earth* (London: the Women's Press).

Camilleri, Joseph and Jim Falk (1992) *The End of Sovereignty? The Politics of a Shrinking and Fragmenting World* (Aldershot: Edward Elgar).

Campbell, David (1998a) *National Deconstruction: Violence, Identity and Justice in Bosnia* (Minneapolis: Minnesota University Press).

Campbell, David (1998b) *Writing Security: United States Foreign Policy and the Politics of Identity* (Minneapolis: University of Minnesota Press).

Camroux, David (1996) 'Huntington: Scénarios controversés pour le futur', *Etudes* juin: 735–46.

Carment, David (1993) 'The International Dimensions of Ethnic Conflict', *Journal of Peace Research* 30, 2: 137–50.

Carson, Rachel (1962) *Silent Spring* (Boston: Houghton Mifflin).

Carver, Terrell (1996) *Gender is Not a Synonym for Woman* (Boulder, CO: Lynne Rienner Press).

Castels, Manuel (1995, 1996, 1997) *The Information Age*, 3 volumes: *The Rise of the Network Society, The Power of Identity*, and *End of Millennium* (Cambridge, MA: Blackwell).

Cavalieri, Paola and Peter Singer (eds) (1994) *The Great Ape Project: Equality Beyond Humanity* (New York, NY: St Martin's Press).

Cerny, P. (1996a) 'What Next for the State?', in Eleonore Kofman and Gillian Youngs (eds), *Globalization: Theory and Practice* (London: Pinter).

Cerny, P. (1996b) 'International Finance and the Erosion of State Policy Capacity', in Philip G. Waltzummett (ed.), *Globalization and Public Policy* (Cheltenham, UK: Edward Elgar).

CGG (Commission on Global Governance) (1995) *Our Global Neighbourhood: the Report of the Commission on Global Governance* (Oxford: Oxford University Press, co-chairs: Ingvar Carlsson, Shridath Ramphal).

Chakrabarty, Dipesh (1992) 'Postcoloniality and the Artifice of History: Who Speaks for "Indian" Pasts?', *Representations* 37: 1–26.

Chakrabarty, Dipesh (1998) 'Minority Histories, Subaltern Pasts', *Postcolonial Studies* 1, 1: 15–29.

Chalk, Peter (1998) 'The Response to Terrorism as a Threat to Liberal Democracy', *Australian Journal of Politics and History* 44, 3: 373–88.

Charnovitz, Steve (1994) 'The World Trade Organization and Social Issues', *Journal of World Trade* 28, 5: 17–33.

Charnovitz, Steve (1995) 'Improving Environmental and Trade Governance', *International Environmental Affairs* 7, 1: 59–91.

Charnovitz, Steve (1997) 'A Critical Guide to the WTO's Report on Trade and Environment', *Arizona Journal of International and Comparative Law* 14, 2: 341–79.

Charvet, John (1992) 'The Idea Of An International Ethical Order', *Studies In Political Thought* 1, 2: 59–72.

Chatterjee, Partha (1986) *Nationalist Thought and the Colonial World: a Derivative Discourse?* (Delhi: Oxford University Press).

Chesneaux, Jean (1994) 'Ten Questions on Globalisation', *Pacifica Review* 6, 1: 87–93.

Chin, Christine B. (1998) *In Service and Servitude: Foreign Female Domestic Workers and the Malaysian 'Modernity' Project* (New York, NY: Columbia University Press).

Choucri, Nazli (1993) 'Multinational Corporations and the Global Environment', in Nazli Choucri (ed.), *Global Accord: Environmental Challenges and International Responses* (Cambridge, MA: the MIT Press): 205–53.

Clark, Ian (1989) *The Hierarchy of States: Reform and Resistance in the International Order* (Cambridge, UK: Cambridge University Press).

Clark, Ian (1997) *Globalization and Fragmentation: International Relations in the Twentieth Century* (Oxford: Oxford University Press).

Clark, Ian (1999) *Globalization and International Relations Theory* (Oxford: Oxford University Press).

Claude, Inis L. (1956) *Swords into Plowshares: the Problems and Progress of International Organizations* (New York, NY: Random House).

Claude, Inis L. (1962) *Power and International Relations* (New York, NY: Random House).

Claxton, Karl (1998) *Bougainville 1988–98: Five Searches for Security in the North Solomons Province of Papua New Guinea* (Canberra: Strategic and Defence Studies Centre, Australian National University).

Clegg, Stewart R. (1989) *Frameworks of Power* (London: Sage Publications).

Cody, Edward (1989) 'France Rules on Muslim Scarf Issue', *Washington Post* 28 November.

Cohen, Eliot A. (1996) 'A Revolution in Warfare', *Foreign Affairs* 75, 2: 37–54.

Cohn, Carol (1987) 'Sex and Death in the Rational World of Defense Intellectuals', *Signs: Journal of Women in Culture and Society* 12, 4: 687–718.

Cohn, Carol (1990) 'Clean Bombs and Clean Language', in Jean Bethke Elshtain and Sheila Tobias (eds), *Women, Militarism and War* (Savage, MD: Rowman and Littlefield).

Coker, Francis W. (1921) 'The Technique of the Pluralistic State', *American Political Science Review* 15, 2: 186–213.

Collinson, Sarah (1993) *Beyond Borders: West European Migration Policy Towards the 21st Century* (London: Royal Institute of International Affairs).

Comaroff, J. L. (1996) 'Ethnicity, Nationalism, and the Politics of Difference in an Age of Revolution', in Edwin N. Wilmsen and Patrick McAllister (eds), *The Politics of Difference* (Chicago: University of Chicago Press).

Commoner, Barry (1972) *The Closing Circle: Confronting the Environmental Crisis* (London: Jonathan Cape).

Condren, C. (1980) 'Marsilius and Machiavelli', in Ross Fitzgerald (ed.), *Comparing Political Thinkers* (Sydney: Pergamon Press).

Connolly, William E. (1993) *Political Theory and Modernity*, 1st edn, 1988 (Ithaca, NY: Cornell University Press).

Cook, Rebecca (ed.) (1994) *Human Rights of Women: National and International Perspectives* (Philadelphia: University of Pennsylvania Press).

Cooley, John K. (1999) *Unholy Wars: Afghanistan, America and International Terrorism* (London: Pluto Press).

Cox, Robert (1998) 'Civilizations and the 21st century: some theoretical considerations' (Vienna: ECPR/ISA Conference, September).

Cox, W. and C. Turrene Sjolander (1997) 'The Global Village and the Global Ghetto', in Kurt Burch and Rorbert A. Denemark (eds), *Constituting International Political Economy* (Boulder, CO: Lynne Rienner).

Craig, Gordon A. (1976) 'The United States and the European Balance', *Foreign Affairs* 55, 1: 187–98.

Cutler, A. Claire (1991) 'The "Grotian Tradition" in International Relations', *Review of International Studies* 17, 1: 41–65.

D'Amico, Francine and Peter R. Beckman (eds) (1995) *Women in World Politics: an Introduction* (Westport, CT: Bergin and Garvey).

Dalby, Simon (1992a) 'Ecopolitical Discourse: "Environmental Security" and Political Geography', *Progress in Human Geography* 16, 4: 503–22.

Dalby, Simon (1992b) 'Security, Modernity, Ecology: the Dilemmas of Post-Cold War Security Discourse', *Alternatives* 17, 1: 95–134.

Dalby, Simon (1996) 'The Environment as Geopolitical Threat: Reading Robert Kaplan's "Coming Anarchy" ', *Ecumene* 3, 4: 472–96.

Dalby, Simon (1998) 'Ecological Metaphors of Security: World Politics in the Biosphere', *Alternatives* 23, 3: 291–319.

Darian-Smith, Eve and Patrick Fitzpatrick (eds) (1999) *Laws of the Postcolonial* (Ann Arbor, MI: University of Waterloo).

Dauvergne Peter (1997) *Shadows in the Forest: Japan and the Politics of Timber in Southeast Asia* (Cambridge, MA: MIT Press).

David, S. R. (1998) 'The Primacy of Internal War', in Stephanie G. Neuman (ed.), *International Relations Theory and the Third World* (London: Macmillan).

Davidson, Basil (1992) *The Black Man's Burden: Africa and the Curse of the Nation–State* (London: James Currey).

de Man, Paul (1986) *The Resistance to Theory* (Minneapolis: University of Minnesota Press).

Deleuze, Gilles (1988) *Bergsonism*, translated by Hugh Tomlinson and Barbara Habberjam (New York, NY: Zone Books).

Deleuze, Gilles and Félix Guattari (1988) *A Thousand Plateaus: Capitalism and Schizophrenia*, translated by Brian Massumi (London: Athlone Press).

Deng, Francis M. (1993) *Protecting the Dispossessed: a Challenge for the International Community* (Washington, DC: Brookings Institution).

Der Derian, James (1992) *Anti-Diplomacy: Spies, Terror, Speed, and War* (Cambridge: Blackwell).

Deudney, Daniel (1992) 'The Mirage of Eco-war: the Weak Relationship Among Global Environmental Change, National Security and Interstate Violence', in Ian H. Rowlands and Malory Greene (eds), *Global Environmental Change and International Relations* (Basingstoke: Houndmills, and Macmillan in association with *Millenium: Journal of International Studies*).

Devetak, Richard (1996) 'Postmodernism', in Scott Burchill *et al.*, *Theories of International Relations* (New York, NY: St Martins Press).

Diamond, Irene (1994) *Fertile Ground: Women, Earth, and the Limits of Control* (Boston, MA: Beacon Press).

Diamond, Irene and Gloria Feman Orenstein (eds) (1990) *Reweaving the World: the Emergence of Ecofeminism* (San Francisco, CA: Sierra Club Books).

Diamond, Larry and Marc F. Plattner (1994) 'Introduction', in Larry Diamond and Marc F. Plattner (eds), *Nationalism, Ethnic Conflict, and Democracy* (Baltimore, MD: John Hopkins University Press).

Dibb, Paul (1995) 'Towards a New Balance of Power in Asia', *Adelphi Paper* 295.

Dicken, Peter (1992) *Global Shift: the Internationalization of Economic Activity*, 2nd edn (New York: Guilford Press).

Dobson, Andrew (ed.) (1991) *The Green Reader* (London: Andre Deutsch).

Duara, Prasenjit (1995) *Rescuing History from the Nation: Questioning Narratives of Modern China* (Chicago: Chicago University Press).

Dunne, Timothy and Nicholas J. Wheeler (eds) (1999) *Human Rights in Global Politics* (Cambridge: Cambridge University Press).

Dunne, Timothy (1998) *Inventing International Society: a History of the English School* (London: Macmillan).

Edwards, Michael and David Hulme (eds) (1996) *Beyond the Magic Bullet: NGO Performance and Accountability in the Post Cold War World* (West Hartford, CT: Kumarian Press).

Ehrlich, Paul R. (1970) *The Population Bomb* (New York, NY: Ballantine Books).

Ehrlich, Paul R. and Anne H. Ehrlich (1981) *Extinction: the Causes and Consequences of the Disappearance of Species* (New York, NY: Random House).

Ehrlich, Paul R. and Anne H. Ehrlich (1990) *The Population Explosion* (New York, NY: Simon & Schuster).

Ehrlich, Paul R., Anne H. Ehrlich and Gretchen C. Daily (1993) 'Food Security, Population, and Environment', *Population and Development Review* 19, 1: 1–32.

Eisenstein, Zillah (1996) *Hatreds: Racialized and Sexualized Conflicts in the 21st Century* (New York, NY: Routledge).

Elliott, Lorraine M. (1998) *The Global Politics of the Environment* (New York, NY: New York University Press).

Elshtain, Jean Bethke (1987) *Women and War* (New York, NY: Basic Books).

Elshtain, Jean Bethke and Sheila Tobias (1990) *Women, Militarism, and War* (Savage, MD: Rowman and Littlefield).

Elson, Diane (ed.) (1991) *Male Bias in the Development Process* (Manchester: Manchester University Press).

Enloe, Cynthia (1983) *Does Khaki Become You?* (Boston: South End Press).

Enloe, Cynthia (1990) *Bananas, Beaches and Bases: Making Feminist Sense of International Politics* (Berkeley, CA: University of California Press).

Enloe, Cynthia (1993) *The Morning After: Sexual Politics at the End of the Cold War* (Berkeley, CA: University of California Press).

Enzensberger, Hans Magnus (1994) *Civil War*, translated by Piers Spence and Martin Chalmers (London: Granta).

Esman, Milton J. and Shibley Telhami (eds) (1995) *International Organizations and Ethnic Conflict* (Ithaca, NY: Cornell University Press).

Esposito, John L. (1992) *The Islamic Threat: Myth or Reality?* (New York, NY: Oxford University Press).

Esty, Daniel C. (1994) *Greening the GATT: Trade, Environment, and the Future* (Washington, DC: International Institute for Economics).

Ethier, Wilfred J. (1998) 'The New Regionalism', *Economic Journal* 108, 449: 1149–61.

Evans, Gareth (1993) *Cooperating for Peace: the Global Agenda for the 1990s and Beyond* (St Leonards, NSW: Allen & Unwin).

Evans, Tony and Wilson, Peter (1992) 'Regime Theory and the English School of International Relations: a Comparison', *Millennium: Journal of International Studies* 21, 3: 329–52.

Fabian, Johannes (1983) *Time and the Other: How Anthropology Makes its Object* (New York, NY: Columbia University Press).

Fairbairn-Dunlop, Peggy (1994) 'Mother, Farmer, Trader, Weaver: Juggling Roles in Pacific Agriculture', in 'Atu Emberson-Bain (ed.), *Sustainable Development or Malignant Growth?: Perspectives of Pacific Island Women* (Suva, Fiji: Marama Publications).

Falk, Richard (1971) *This Endangered Planet: Prospects and Proposals for Human Survival* (New York, NY: Random House).

Falk, Richard (1987) *The Promise of World Order: Essays in Normative International Relations* (Philadelphia, PA: Temple University Press).

Falk, Richard (1993) 'The Making of Global Citizenship', in Jeremy Brecher, John Brown Childs and Jill Cutler (eds), *Global Visions: Beyond the New World Order* (Boston: South End Press).

Falk, Richard (1994) 'The Making of Global Citizenship', in B. Van Steenbergen (ed.), *The Condition of Global Citizenship* (London: Sage).

Falk, Richard (1995a) *On Humane Governance: Toward A New Global Politics* (Cambridge, UK: Polity Press).

Falk, Richard (1995b) 'Regionalism and World Order After the Cold War', *Australian Journal of International Affairs* 49, 1: 1–15.

Falk, Richard (1997) 'State of Siege: Will Globalization Win Out?' *International Affairs* 73, 1: 123–36.

Falk, Richard (1998) *Law in an Emerging Global Village: a Post-Westphalian Perspective* (Ardsley, NY: Transnational Publishers).

Falk, Richard (1999a) *Predatory Globalization: a Critique* (Malden, MA: Polity).

Falk, Richard (1999b) 'Hans Kung's Crusade: Framing a Global Ethic', *International Journal of Politics, Culture and Society* 13, 1: 59–77.

Fanon, Frantz (1970) *Black Skin, White Masks*, translated by Charles Lam Markmann (London: Paladin).

FAO (Food and Agriculture Organisation) (1996) *Rome Declaration on World Food Security and World Food Summit Plan of Action, 13–17 November 1996*, accessed from http://www.fao.org/

Fauvel, John, F. Flood, M. Shortland and Richard Wilson (eds) (1988) *Let Newton Be!* (Oxford and New York: Oxford University Press).

Fawcett, Louise (1995) 'Regionalism in Historical Perspective', in Fawcett and Hurrell (eds), *Regionalism in World Politics*.

Fawcett, Louise and Andrew Hurrell (eds) (1995) *Regionalism in World Politics: Regional Organization and International Order* (Oxford: Oxford University Press).

Flannery, Tim (1995) *The Future Eaters: an Ecological History of the Australasian Lands and Peoples* (Chatswood, NSW: Reed Books).

Foucault, Michel (1984a) 'Space, Knowledge, and Power', translated by C. Hubert, in P. Rabinow (ed.), *The Foucault Reader* (New York, NY: Pantheon Books).

Foucault, Michel (1984b) 'What is Enlightenment?', translated by C. Porter in P. Rabinow (ed.), *The Foucault Reader* (New York, NY: Pantheon Books).

Fowler, Cary and Pat Mooney (1990) *Shattering: Food Politics, and the Loss of Genetic Diversity* (Tucson, AZ: University of Arizona Press).

Franck, T. M. (1992) 'The Evolution of the Right of Self-Determination' (Amsterdam: Second Plenary Session at the 2nd International Law Conference: People and Minorities in International Law, 18–20 June).

Frank, Philipp (1938) *Interpretations and Misinterpretations of Modern Physics*, translated by O. Helemer and M. B.Singer (Paris: Hermann).

Friedman, Thomas L. (1999) *The Lexus and the Olive Tree* (New York, NY: Farrar, Straus, Giroux and London: HarperCollins).

Fry, Greg (1993) 'At the Margin: the South Pacific and Changing World Order', in Richard Leaver and J. L. Richardson (eds), *Charting the Post-Cold War Order* (Boulder, CO: Westview Press).

Fry, Greg (1997) 'Framing the Islands: Knowledge and Power in Changing Australian Images of the "South Pacific" ', *The Contemporary Pacific* 9, 2: 305–44.

Fukuyama, Francis (1989) 'The End of History?', *The National Interest* 16: 3–18.

Fukuyama, Francis (1992) *The End of History and the Last Man* (London: Penguin and New York, NY: Free Press).

Fukuyama, Francis (1999a) 'Second Thoughts: the Last Man in a Bottle', *The National Interest* 56: 16–33.

Fukuyama, Francis (1999b) 'Second Thoughts: the End of History 10 Years Later', *New Perspective Quarterly* 16, 4: 40–2.

Gaddis, John Lewis (1999) 'Living in Candlestick Park', *Atlantic Monthly* 283, 4: 65–77.

Gamble, Andrew and Anthony Payne (1996) 'Conclusion: the New Regionalism', in Gamble and Payne (eds), *Regionalism and World Order*.

Gamble, Andrew and Anthony Payne (eds) (1996) *Regionalism and World Order* (London: Macmillan).

Gandhi, Leela (1998) *Postcolonial Theory: a Critical Introduction* (St Leonards, NSW: Allen & Unwin).

Gedicks, Al (1993) *The New Resource Wars: Native and Environmental Struggles Against Multinational Corporations* (Boston, MA: South End Press).

George, Jim and Rodd McGibbon (1998) 'Dangerous Liasons: Neoliberal Foreign Policy and Australia's Regional Engagement', *Australian Journal of Political Science* 33, 3: 399–420.

George, Jim (1994) *Discourses of Global Politics: a Critical (Re)Introduction to International Relations* (Boulder, CO: Lynne Rienner).

Geras, Norman (1999) 'The View From Everywhere', in 'Forum on the Transformation of Political Community', *Review of International Studies* 25, 1: 139–74.

Gholz, Eugene, Daryl G. Press and Harvey M. Sapolsky (1997) 'Come Home America: the Strategy of Restraint in the Face of Temptation', *International Security* 21, 4: 5–48.

Gills, Barry and Joel Rocamora (1992) 'Low Intensity Democracy', *Third World Quarterly* 13, 3: 501–23.

Gilpin, Robert (1987) *The Political Economy of International Relations* (Princeton, NJ: Princeton University Press).

Gladstone, Jack A. (1995) 'The Coming Chinese Collapse', *Foreign Policy* 99: 35–52.

Goldgeier, James M. and Michael McFaul (1992) 'A Tale of Two Worlds: Core and Periphery in the Post-Cold War Era', *International Organization* 46, 2: 467–91.

Goldsmith, Edward *et al.* (1972) *A Blueprint for Survival* (Harmondsworth: Penguin, first appeared in *The Ecologist*, January 1972).

Goldstein, Judith and Robert O. Keohane (1993) 'Ideas and Foreign Policy: an Analytical Framework', in Judith Goldstein and Robert O. Keohane (eds), *Ideas and Foreign Policy: Beliefs, Institutions, and Political Change* (Ithaca, NY: Cornell University Press).

Gomez, A. (1999) *Radio Australia* (News Brief, Friday 10 September).

Gong, Gerrit W. (1984) *The Standard of 'Civilization' in International Society* (Oxford: Clarendon Press).

Gottlieb, Gidon (1993) *Nation Against State: a New Approach to Ethnic Conflicts and the Decline of Sovereignty* (New York, NY: Council on Foreign Relations).

Gottweis, Herbert (1998) *Governing Molecules: the Discursive Politics of Genetic Engineering in Europe and the United States* (Cambridge, MA: the MIT Press).

Graham, Frank (1970) *Since Silent Spring* (Boston: Houghton Mifflin).

Grant, Rebecca (1991) 'The Sources of Gender Bias in International Relations Theory', in Grant and Newland (eds), *Gender and International Relations*.

Grant, Rebecca and Kathleen Newland (eds) (1991) *Gender and International Relations* (Bloomington and Indianapolis: Indiana University Press).

Gray, John (1998) *False Dawn: the Delusions of Global Capitalism* (London: Granta Books).

Greaves, Harold R. G. (1931) *The League Committees and World Order: a Study of the Permanent Expert Committees of the League of Nations as an Instrument of International Government* (London: Oxford University Press).

Greider, William (1997) *One World, Ready or Not: the Manic Logic of Global Capitalism* (London and New York: Simon & Schuster).

Griffin, D. (1998–99) 'Agricultural Globalisation: a Threat to Food Security?', *Third World Resurgence* 100–101: 38–9.

Griffin, David Ray (ed.) (1990) *Sacred Interconnections: Postmodern Spirituality, Political Economy, and Art* (Albany, NY: State University of New York Press).

Groves, Denise (1998) 'India and Pakistan: a Clash of Civilisations?', *Washington Quarterly* 21, 4: 17–20.

Grugel, Jean and Wil Hout (1999) 'Regions, Regionalism and the South', in Grugel and Hout (eds), *Regionalism across the North–South Divide*.

Grugel, Jean and Wil Hout (eds) (1999) *Regionalism Across the North–South Divide: State Strategies in the Semi-Periphery* (London and New York: Routledge).

Guha, Ranajit (1982) 'On Some Aspects of the Historiography of Colonial India', in Guha (ed.), *Subaltern Studies I* (Delhi: Oxford University Press).

Guicciardini, Francesco (1966) *The History of Italy and History of Florence* (trans. C. Grayson) edited, abridged, and introduction by J. R. Hale (Chalfont St Giles, Bucks: Richard Sadler & Brown).

Gunningham, Neil and Peter Grabosky with Darren Sinclair (1998) *Smart Regulation: Designing Environmental Policy* (Oxford: Clarendon Press, and New York, NY: Oxford University Press).

Gurr, Ted Robert (1993) *Minorities at Risk: a Global View of Ethnopolitical Conflicts* (Washington, DC: US Institute of Peace Press).

Gurr, Ted Robert (1994) 'Peoples Against States: Ethnopolitical Conflict and the Changing World System', Presidential Address, *International Studies Quarterly* 38, 3: 347–77.

Haas, Ernst B. (1953) 'The Balance of Power: Prescription, Concept, or Propaganda', *World Politics* 5, 4: 442–77.

Haas, Ernst B. (1990) *When Knowledge is Power: Three Models of Change in International Organizations* (Berkeley, CA: University of California Press).

Haas, Peter M., Robert O. Keohane and Marc A. Levy (eds) (1993) *Institutions for the Earth: Sources of Effective International Environmental Protection* (Cambridge, MA: MIT Press).

Halliday, Fred (1994) 'International Society as Homogeneity', in Fred Halliday (ed.), *Rethinking International Relations* (Basingstoke: Macmillan).

Halliday, Fred (1995) *Islam and the Myth of Confrontation: Religion and Politics in the Middle East* (London: I.B. Tauris).

Han, Jongwoo and L. H. M. Ling (1998) 'Authoritarianism in the Hypermasculinized State', *International Studies Quarterly* 42, 1: 53–78.

Harding, Sandra (1986) *The Science Question in Feminism* (Ithaca, NY: Cornell University Press).

Harris, Stuart (1999) *The Asian Regional Response to Its Economic Crisis and the Global Implications* (Canberra, ACT: Working Paper 1999/4, Department of International Relations, Research School of Pacific and Asian Studies, The Australian National University).

Hartmann, Betsy (1995) *Reproductive Rights and Wrongs: the Global Politics of Population Control* (Boston, MA: South End Press).

Haugaard, Mark (1997) *The Constitution of Power: a Theoretical Analysis of Power, Knowledge and Structure* (Manchester: Manchester University Press).

Hekman, Susan (1987) 'The Feminization of Epistemology: Gender and the Social Sciences', *Women and Politics* 7, 3: 65–83.

Held, David (1995) *Democracy and the Global Order: From the Modern State to Cosmopolitan Governance* (Cambridge: Polity Press and Stanford, CA: Stanford University Press).

Held, David, Anthony McGrew, David Goldblatt, Jonathan Perraton (1999) *Global Transformations: Politics, Economics and Culture* (Oxford: Polity).

Helleiner, Eric (1994) *States and the Reemergence of Global Finance* (Ithaca: Cornell University Press).

Hettne, Björn and András Inotai (1994) *The New Regionalism: Implications for Global Development and International Security* (Helsinki: United Nations University World Institute for Development Economics Research).

Heyking, Baron (1928) 'The International Protection of Minorities – The Achilles' Heel of the League of Nations', *Transactions of the Grotius Society* 13: 31–51.

Hindmarsh, Richard, Geoffrey Lawrence and Jane Norton (eds) (1998) *Altered Genes: Reconstructing Nature: the Debate* (St Leonards, NSW: Allen & Unwin).

Hirsch, Herbert (1995) *Genocide and the Politics of Memory: Studying Death to Preserve Life* (Chapel Hill, NC: University of North Carolina Press).

Hirst, Paul Q. (1997) 'The Global Economy – Myths and Realities' *International Affairs* 73, 3: 409–25.

Hirst, Paul Q. and Grahame Thompson (1995) 'Globalization and the Future of the Nation-State', *Economy and Society* 24, 3: 408–42.

Hirst, Paul Q. and Grahame Thompson (1996) *Globalization in Question: the International Economy and the Possibilities of Governance* (Cambridge, UK: Polity Press).

Hoagland, K. Elaine and Amy Y. Rossman (eds) (1997) *Global Genetic Resources: Access, Ownership, and Intellectual Property Rights* (Washington, DC: Association of Systematics Collections).

Hobsbawm, Eric J. (1995) *Age of Extremes: the Short Twentieth Century, 1914–1991* (London: Abacus).

Hobsbawm, Eric J. (1996) 'Ethnicity and Nationalism in Europe Today', in Gopal Balakrishnan (ed.), *Mapping the Nation* (London: Verso).

Hoffmann, Stanley (1977) 'An American Social Science: International Relations', *Daedalus* 106, 3: 41–60.

Hoffmann, Stanley (1981) *Duties Beyond Borders: On the Limits and Possibilities of Ethical International Politics* (Syracuse, NY: Syracuse University Press).

Holden, Barry (ed.) (1996) *The Ethical Dimensions of Global Change* (Basingstoke: Macmillan Press).

Holdgate, Martin W. (1999) *The Green Web: a Union for World Conservation* (London: Earthscan).

Holsti, K. J. (1993) 'International Relations at the End of the Millennium', *Review of International Studies* 19, 4: 401–8.

Homer (1951) *The Iliad*, translated by Richmond Little (Chicago, IL: University of Chicago Press).

Homer-Dixon, Thomas F. (1999) *Environment, Scarcity and Violence* (Princeton, NJ: Princeton University Press).

Hoogvelt, Anki (1997) *Globalisation and the Postcolonial World: the New Political Economy of Development* (Basingstoke: Macmillan Press).

Horowitz, Donald L. (1985) *Ethnic Groups in Conflict* (Berkeley, CA: University of California Press).

Horowitz, Irving (1976) *Genocide: State Power and Mass Murder* (New Brunswick, NJ: Transaction).

Horsman, Mathew and Andrew Marshall (1994) *After the Nation-State: Citizens, Tribalism and the New World Disorder* (London: HarperCollins).

Hout, Wil (1999) 'Theories of International Relations and the New Regionalism', in Grugel and Hout (eds), *Regionalism Across the North–South Divide*.

Huang Yasheng (1995) 'Why China Will Not Collapse', *Foreign Policy* 99: 54–68.

Human Rights Watch (1995) *Playing the 'Communal Card': Communal Violence and Human Rights* (New York, NY: Human Rights Watch).

Hunter, James Davison (1991) *Culture Wars: the Struggle to Define America* (New York, NY: Basic Books).

Hunter, Shireen (1988) 'Iran and the Spread of Revolutionary Islam', *Third World Quarterly* 10, 2: 730–49.

Huntington, Samuel P. (1968) *Political Order and Changing Societies* (New Haven, CT: Yale University Press).

Huntington, Samuel P. (1991) *The Third Wave: Democratization in the Late Twentieth Century* (Norman, OK: University of Oklahoma Press).

Huntington, Samuel P. (1993a) 'The Clash of Civilizations?', *Foreign Affairs* 72, 3: 22–49.

Huntington, Samuel P. (1993b) 'If Not Civilisations, What? Paradigms of the Post-Cold War World – Response', *Foreign Affairs* 72, 5: 186–95.

Huntington, Samuel P. (1993c) 'The Ungovernability of Democracy' (Symposium) *American Enterprise* 4: 37.

Huntington, Samuel P. (1996) *The Clash of Civilisations and the Remaking of World Order* (New York, NY: Simon & Schuster).

Huntington, Samuel P. (1999) 'A Local Front of a Global War', *New York Times* 16 December.

Hurrell, Andrew (1995) 'Explaining the Resurgence of Regionalism in World Politics', *Review of International Studies* 21, 4: 331–58.

Hurrell, Andrew and Benedict Kingsbury (eds) (1992) *The International Politics of the Environment: Actors, Interests and Institutions* (Oxford: Clarendon Press).

Hurrell, Andrew and Ngaire Woods (1995) 'Globalisation and Inequality', *Millennium: Journal of International Studies* 24, 3: 447–70.

Hutcheon, Linda (1989) *The Politics of Postmodernism* (London: Routledge).

Huyssen, Andreas (1984) 'Mapping the Postmodern', *New German Critique* 33.

Hynes, H. Patricia (1989) *The Recurring Silent Spring* (New York, NY: Pergamon Press).

IBC Press Office (1999) 'Botanical Congress Issues Warnings', press release posted via consbio@u.washington.edu, 4 August.

ICDSI (Independent Commission on Disarmamant and Security Issues) (1982) *Report: Common Security: a Program for Disarmament* (New York, NY: Simon & Schuster, chair: O. Palme).

ICIDI (Independent Commission on International Development Issues) (1980) *Report: North–South: a Programme for Survival* (London: Pan Books, chair: W. Brandt).

Inoguchi, Takashi (1995) 'Dialectics of World Order: a View From Pacific Asia', in Hans-Henrik Holm and Georg Sorenson (eds), *Whose World Order?: Uneven Globalization and the End of the Cold War* (Boulder, CO: Westview Press).

IUCN Commission on Environmental Law (1995) Draft International Covenant on Environment and Development, of IUCN (Gland, Switzerland: prepared in cooperation with the International Council of Environmental Law, IUCN).

Jackson, Robert H. (1990) *Quasi-states: Sovereignty, International Relations and the Third World* (Cambridge: Cambridge University Press).

Jackson, Robert H. (1997) 'The Evolution of International Society', in Baylis and Smith (eds), *The Globalization of World Politics*.

James, Alan (1986) *Sovereign Statehood: the Basis of International Society* (London and Boston: Allen & Unwin).

James, William (1897) *The Will to Believe And Other Essays In Popular Philosophy* (New York, NY: Longmans, Green and Co.).

James, William (1907) *Pragmatism* (London: Longmans, Green and Co.).

James, William (1971) *A Pluralistic Universe*, edited by Ralph Barton Perry with an introduction by Richard J. Bernstein, 1st edn 1909 (New York, NY: Dutton).

Jervis, Robert (1997) *System Effects: Complexity in Political and Social Life* (Princeton: Princeton University Press).

Job, Cvijeto (1993) 'Yugoslavia's Ethnic Furies', *Foreign Policy* 92: 52–74.

Käkönen, Jyrki (1992) 'The Concept of Security: From Limited to Comprehensive', in Jyrki Käkönen (ed.), *Perspectives on Environmental Conflict and International Politics* (London: Pinter): 146–55.

Kant, Immanuel (1970) 'Perpetual Peace: a Philosophical Sketch', in Hans J. Reiss (ed.), *Kant's Political Writings* (Cambridge: Ca).

Kaplan, Robert D. (1994) 'The Coming Anarchy', *Atlantic Monthly* 273, 2: 44–76.

Kaplan, Robert D. (1996) *The Ends of the Earth: a Journey at the Dawn of the 21st Century* (New York, NY: Random House).

Kaplan, Robert D. (2000) *The Coming Anarchy: Shattering the Dreams of the Post-Cold War* (New York, NY: Random House).

Keal, Paul (1983) *Unspoken Rules and Superpower Dominance* (Basingstoke: Macmillan).

Keal, Paul (1995) ' "Just Backward Children": International Law and the Conquest of Non-European Peoples', *Australian Journal of International Affairs* 49, 2: 191–206.

Keck, Margaret E. and Kathryn Sikkink (1998) *Activists Beyond Borders: Advocacy Networks in International Politics* (Ithaca, NY: Cornell University Press).

Kegley, Charles W., Jnr and Eugene R. Wittkopf (1995) *World Politics: Trends and Transformation*, fifth edn (New York, NY: St Martin's Press).

Kelsen, Hans (1961) *General Theory of Law and State*, translated by Anders Wedberg (New York, NY: Russell).

Kennedy, Paul (1989) *The Rise and Fall of the Great Powers: Economic Change and Military Conflict from 1500–2000* (London: Fontana).

Keohane, Robert O. (1989) *International Institutions And State Power: Essays in International Relations Theory* (Boulder, CO: Westview).

Keohane, Robert O. and Joseph S. Nye (1977) *Power and Interdependence: World Politics in Transition* (Boston: Little, Brown).

Keohane, Robert O. and Marc A. Levy (eds) (1996) *Institutions for Environmental Aid: Pitfalls and Promise* (Cambridge, MA: MIT Press).

Keohane, Robert O. (ed.) (1986) *Neorealism and Its Critics* (New York, NY: Columbia University Press).

Khalilzad, Zalmay and Daniel Byman (2000) 'Afghanistan: the Consolidation of a Rogue State', *Washington Quarterly* 23, 1: 65–78.

Khan, Riaz Mohammad (1991) *Untying the Afghan Knot: Negotiating Soviet Withdrawal* (Durham, NC: Duke University Press).

Kirkpatrick, Jean J. (1993) 'The Modernizing Imperative: Tradition and Change', *Foreign Affairs* 72, 4: 22–4.

Klotz, Audie (1995) *Norms in International Relations: the Struggle Against Apartheid* (Ithaca, NY: Cornell University Press).

Knutsen, Torbjorn L. (1992) *A History of International Relations Theory: an Introduction* (Manchester: Manchester University Press).

Knutsen, Torbjorn L. (1999) *The Rise and Fall of World Orders* (Manchester: University of Manchester Press).

Kobrin, Stephen J. (1998) 'Back to the Future: Neomedievalism and the Postmodern Digital World Economy', *Journal of International Affairs* 51, 2: 361–86.

Kohli, Atul, Peter Evans and Theda Skocpol (1995) 'The Role of Theory in Comparative Politics: a Symposium', *World Politics* 48, 1: 1–49.

Korten, David C. (1990) *Getting to the 21st Century: Voluntary Action and the Global Agenda* (West Hartford, CT: Kumarian Press).

Krasner, Stephen (1995) 'Compromising Westphalia', *International Security* 20, 3: 115–52.

Krasner, Stephen (ed.) (1983) *International Regimes* (Ithaca, NY: Cornell University Press).

Krauthammer, Charles (1990/91) 'The Unipolar Moment', *Foreign Affairs* 70, 1: 23–33.

Krimsky, Sheldon and Roger P. Wrubel (1996) *Agricultural Biotechnology and the Environment: Science, Policy and Social Issues* (Urbana, IL: University of Illinois Press).

Kuehls, Thom (1996) *Beyond Sovereign Territory: the Space of Ecopolitics* (Minneapolis, MN: University of Minnesota Press).

Kung, Hans (1998) *A Global Ethic for Global Politics and Economics* (New York, NY: Oxford University Press).

Kuper, Leo (1981) *Genocide: its Political Use in the Twentieth Century* (New Haven, CT: Yale University Press).

Kurth, James (1994) 'The Real Clash', *The National Interest* 37: 3–15.

Laffey, John F. (1993) *Civilization and its Discontented* (Montreal: Black Rose).

Lake, D. A. and D. Rothchild (1996) 'Ethnic Fears and Global Engagement: the International Spread and Management of Ethnic Conflict' (San Diego, CA: University of California, Institute of Global Conflict and Cooperation, Policy Paper No. 20).

Lake, David A. and Patrick M. Morgan (eds) (1997) *Regional Orders: Building Security in a New World* (University Park, PA: Pennsylvania State University Press).

Landmine Library (1999) http: //www.vvaf.org/library/index.html (accessed Feb 2000).

Laski, Harold (1916) 'The Personality of Associations', *Harvard Law Review* 29: 404–26.

Laski, Harold (1925) *Grammar of Politics* (London: Macmillan).

Latour, Bruno (1993) *We Have Never Been Modern*, translated by Catherine Porter (Cambridge, MA: Harvard University Press).

Lawson, Stephanie (1996) 'Cultural Relativism and Democracy: Political Myths About "Asia" and the "West" ', in Richard Robison (ed.), *Pathways to Asia: the Politics of Engagement* (St Leonards, NSW: Allen & Unwin).

Layne, Christopher (1993) 'The Unipolar Illusion: Why New Great Powers Will Rise', *International Security* 17, 4: 5–51.

Layne, Christopher (1997) 'From Preponderance to Offshore Balancing: America's Future Grand Strategy', *International Security* 22, 1: 86–124.

Lebow, Richard Ned and Janice Gross Stein (1994) *We All Lost The Cold War* (Princeton, NJ: Princeton University Press).

Lebow, Richard Ned and Janice Gross Stein (1998) 'Nuclear Lessons of the Cold War', in Booth (ed.), *Statescraft and Security*.

Lefort, Claude (1988) *Democracy and Political Theory*, translated by David Macey (Minneapolis, MN: Minnesota University Press).

Lemkin, Raphaël (1944) *Axis Rule in Occupied Europe* (Washington, DC: Carnegie Endowment for Peace, Division of International Law).

Lewis, Bernard (1998) 'License to Kill: Usama bin Ladin's Declaration of Jihad', *Foreign Affairs* 77, 6: 14–19.

Liebert, Arthur (1933) 'Contemporary German Philosophy', *Philosophical Review* 42: 31–48.

Lindley, Mark F. (1969) *The Acquisition and Government of Backward Territory in International Law: Being a Treatise on the Law and Practice Relating to Colonial Expansion*, 1st edn 1926 (New York, NY: Negro Universities Press).

Linklater, Andrew (1998) *The Transformation of Political Community: Ethical Foundations of the Post-Westphalian Era* (Cambridge: Polity Press and Columbia, SC: University of South Carolina Press).

Lipschutz, Ronnie (1992) 'Reconstructing World Politics: the Emergence of Global Civil Society', *Millennium* 21, 3: 389–420.

Lipschutz, Ronnie (2000) *After Authority: War, Peace and Global Politics in the 21st Century* (Albany, NY: State University of New York Press).

Lipschutz, Ronnie D. with Judith Mayer (1996) *Global Civil Society and Global Environmental Governance: the Politics of Nature from Place to Planet* (Albany, NY: State University of New York Press).

Litfin, Karen (1994) *Ozone Discourses: Science and Politics in Global Environmental Cooperation* (New York, NY: Columbia University Press).

Little, Richard (1989) 'Deconstructing the Balance of Power: Two Traditions of Thought', *Review of International Studies*, 15, 2: 87–100.

Lohmann, Larry (1993) 'Resisting Green Globalism', in Wolfgang Sachs (ed.), *Global Ecology: a New Arena of Political Conflict* (London: Zed Books, and Halifax, Nova Scotia: Fernwood Publishing): 157–69.

Lorentzin, Lois Ann and Jennifer Turpin (1998) *The Women and War Reader* (New York, NY: New York University Press).

Lovejoy, Arthur O. (1936) *The Great Chain of Being: a Study of the History of an Idea* (Cambridge, MA: Harvard University Press).

Lynn-Jones, S. (1991) *The Cold War and After: Prospects for Peace* (Cambridge, MA: MIT Press).

Lyons, Gene and Michael Mastanduno (eds) (1995) *Beyond Westphalia?: State Sovereignty and International Intervention* (Baltimore: Johns Hopkins University Press).

Lyotard, Jean-François (1979) *La Condition Postmoderne: Rapport sur le Savoir* (Paris: Les Editions de Minuit).

Lyotard, Jean-François (1991) 'Rewriting Modernity', in *The Inhuman: Reflections on Time*, translated by Geoffrey Bennington and Rachel Bowlby (Stanford: Stanford University Press).

Maalouf, Amin (1984) *The Crusades Through Arab Eyes* (London: Al Saqi Books).

Mackenzie, Richard (1998) 'The United States and the Taliban', in William Maley (ed.), *Fundamentalism Reborn? Afghanistan and the Taliban* (London: Hurst).

Mahbubani, Kishore (1992) 'The West and the Rest', *The National Interest* 28: 3–12.

Mahbubani, Kishore (1993) 'The Dangers of Decadence: What the Rest can Teach the West', *Foreign Affairs* 72, 4: 10–14.

Malcolm, Noel (1994) *Bosnia: a Short History* (London: Macmillan).

Maley, William (1998) 'Interpreting the Taliban', in William Maley (ed.), *Fundamentalism Reborn? Afghanistan and the Taliban* (London: Hurst).

Mandel, Robert (1994) *The Changing Face of National Security: a Conceptual Analysis* (Westport, CT: Greenwood Press).

Manning, Charles A. W. (1962) *The Nature Of International Society* (London: Bell).

Mansour, Camille (1994) *Beyond Alliance: Israel in US Foreign Policy*, translated by James A. Cohen (New York, NY: Columbia University Press).

Marchand, Marianne H. and Anne Sisson Runyan (eds) (2000) *Gender and Global Restructuring: Sightings, Sites, and Resistances* (New York, NY: Routledge).

Marchand, Marianne H. and Jane L. Parpart (1995) *Feminism, Postmodernism, Development* (London: Routledge).

Marco, Gino J., Robert M. Hollingworth and William Durham (eds) (1987) *Silent Spring Revisited* (Washington, DC: American Chemical Society).

Mastanduno, Michael (1997) 'Preserving the Unipolar Moment: Realist Theories and the U.S. Grand Strategy after the Cold War', *International Security* 21, 4: 49–88.

Mastanduno, Michael (1999) 'A Realist View: Three Images of the Coming International Order', in T.V. Paul and John Hall (eds), *International Order and the Future of World Politics* (Cambridge: Cambridge University Press).

Maswood, Syed Javed (1994) 'The New "Mother of all Clashes": Samuel Huntington and the Clash of Civilisations', *Asian Studies Review* 18, 1: 17–21.

Mathews, Jessica Tuchman (1989) 'Redefining Security', *Foreign Affairs* 68, 2: 162–77.

Maynes, Charles William (1995) 'The New Pessimism', *Foreign Policy* 100: 33–45.

Mazarr, Michael (1996) 'Culture and International Relations: a Review Essay', *Washington Quarterly* 19, 2: 177–97.

MccGwire, Michael (1985/6) 'Deterrence: the Problem not the Solution', *International Affairs* 62, 1: 55–70.

McClintock, Anne (1995) *Imperial Leather: Race, Gender and Sexuality in the Colonial Conquest* (New York, NY: Routledge).

McCormick, J. (1989) *Reclaiming Paradise: the Global Environmental Movement* (Bloomington, IN: Indiana University Press).

McGlen, Nancy E. and Meredith Reid Sarkees (eds) (1993) *Women in Foreign Policy: the Insiders* (New York, NY: Routledge).

McGoldrick, Dominic (1996) 'Sustainable Development and Human Rights: an Integrated Conception', *International and Comparative Law Quarterly* 45, 4: 796–818.

McIlwain, Charles H. (1933) 'A Fragment on Sovereignty', *Political Science Quarterly* 48, 1: 94–106.

McLennan, A. D. (1997) 'Balance, Not Containment: a Geopolitical Take from Canberra', *National Interest* 49: 52–63.

McNeely, Jeffrey A. (1988) *Economics and Biological Diversity: Developing and Using Economic Incentives to Conserve Biological Resources* (Gland, Switzerland: IUCN).

McNeely, Jeffrey A. (ed.) (1995) *Expanding Partnerships in Conservation* (Washington, DC: Island Press).

Meadows, Donella H., Dennis L. Meadows and Jorgen Randers (1992) *Beyond the Limits: Confronting Global Collapse, Envisioning a Sustainable Future* (Post Mills, VT: Chelsea Green).

Meadows, Donella H., Dennis L. Meadows, Jorgen Randers and W. W. Behrens, III (1972) *The Limits to Growth: a Report for the Club of Rome's Project on the Predicament of Mankind* (London: Earth Island).

Mearsheimer, John (1990a) 'Back to the Future: Instability in Europe After the Cold War', *International Security* 15, 1: 5–56.

Mearsheimer, John (1990b) 'Why We Will Soon Miss the Cold War', *The Atlantic* 266, 2: 35–50.

Mearsheimer, John (1991) 'Back to the Future', in S. Lynn-Jones (ed.), *The Cold War and After: Prospects for Peace* (Cambridge, MA: MIT Press).

Mearsheimer, John (1994) 'Why We Will Soon Miss the Cold War', in P. Williams *et al., Classic Readings of International Relations* (Belmont, CA: Wadsworth Publishing).

Melucci, Alberto (1996) 'Nomads of the Present: Social Movements and Individual Needs in Contemporary Society' (an excerpt from the 1989 edition) in John Hutchinson and Anthony D. Smith (eds), *Ethnicity* (Oxford: Oxford University Press, an Oxford Reader).

Merchant, Carolyn (1995) *Earthcare: Women and the Environment* (New York, NY: Routledge).

Mestrovic, Stjepan G. (1993) *The Barbarian Temperament: Toward a Postmodern Critical Theory* (London: Routledge).

Mestrovic, Stjepan G. (1994) *The Balkanization of the West: the Confluence of Postcommunism and Postmodernism* (London: Routledge).

Midlasky, Manus I. (1983) 'The Balance of Power as a "Just" Historical System', *Polity* 16, 2: 181–200.

Mies, Maria and Vindanda Shiva (1993) *Ecofeminism* (Halifax, Nova Scotia: Fernwood and London: Zed Books).

Milner, Helen V. and Robert O. Keohane (1996) 'Internationalization and Domestic Politics: an Introduction', in Robert O. Keohane and Helen V. Milner (eds), *Internationalization and Domestic Politics* (Cambridge: Cambridge University Press)

Mische, Patricia M. (1989) 'Ecological Security and the Need to Reconceptualize Sovereignty', *Alternatives* 14, 4: 389–427.

Mittleman, James (ed.) (1996) *Globalization: Critical Reflections* (Boulder, CO: Lynne Rienner).

Moon, Kyoung-Hee (1997) Terrorism and the US invasion of Panama (Pusan: Pusan National University, mimeo).

Moran, M. (1994) 'The State and the Financial Services Revolution: a Comparative Analysis', in Wolfgang C. Muller and Vincent Wright (eds), *The State in Western Europe: Retreat or Redefinition?* (London: Frank Cass).

Morgan, Gareth (1997) *Images of Organization*, 2nd edn (Thousand Oaks, CA: Sage).

Moynihan, Daniel P. (1993) *Pandaemonium: Ethnicity in International Politics* (Oxford and New York, NY: Oxford University Press).

Mueller, J. (1989) *Retreat from Doomsday: the Obsolescence of Major War* (New York, NY: Basic Books).

Mugabe, John, Charles Victor Berber, Gudrun Henne, Lyle Glowka and Antonio La Vina (eds) (1997) *Access to Genetic Resources: Strategies for Sharing Benefits* (Nairobi: ACTS Press).

Murphy, David F. and Jem Bendell (1997) *In the Company of Partners: Business, Environmental Groups and Sustainable Development Post-Rio* (Bristol: Policy Press).

Muzaffar, Chandra (1994) 'The Clash of Civilisations or Camouflaging Dominance?', *Asian Studies Review* 18, 1: 9–16.

Myers, Norman (1979) *The Sinking Ark: a New Look at the Problem of Disappearing Species* (Oxford: Pergamon Press).

Myers, Norman (1996) *Ultimate Security: the Environmental Basis of Political Stability* (Washington, DC: Island Press).

Nandy, Ashis (1983) *The Intimate Enemy: Loss and Recovery of Self Under Colonialism* (Delhi: Oxford University Press).

Nardin, Terry (1983) *Law, Morality, and the Relations of States* (Princeton, NJ: Princeton University Press).

Nathanson, Charles E. (1988) 'The Social Construction of the Soviet Threat: a Study in the Politics of Representation', *Alternatives* 13, 4: 443–83.

Negroponte, Nicholas (1995) *Being Digital* (New York, NY: Knopf).

Nelson, Barbara J. (1989) 'Women and Knowledge in Political Science: Texts, Histories, and Epistemologies', *Women and Politics* 9, 2: 1–25.

Nelson, Ernest W. (1943) 'The Origins of Modern Balance-of-Power Politics', *Medievalia et Humanistica* 1: 124–42.

Neumann, Iver (1999) *Uses of the Other: 'The East' in European Identity Formation* (Minneapolis: University of Minnesota Press).

Nietzsche, Friedrich (1974) *The Gay Science*, translated by W. Kaufmann [1st edn, 1882] (New York, NY: Vintage Books).

Nietzsche, Friedrich (1982) 'On Truth and Lie in an Extra-Moral Sense', in W. Kaufmann (ed.), *The Portable Nietzsche* (New York, NY: Penguin Books).

Nietzsche, Friedrich (1991) *Zur Genealogie der Moral* (Frankfurt: Insel Taschenbuch).

Nisbet, Robert A. (1969) *Social Change and History: Aspects of the Western Theory of Development* (London: Oxford University Press).

Nussbaum, Martha C. (1996) 'Patriotism and Cosmopolitanism', in Martha C. Nussbaum, with respondents, *For Love of Country: Debating the Limits of Patriotism*, edited by Joshua Cohen (Boston: Beacon Press).

Nussbaum, Martha C. (1997) *Cultivating Humanity: a Classical Defense of Reform in Liberal Education* (Cambridge, MA: Harvard University Press).

Nye, Joseph (1971) *Peace in Parts: Integration and Conflict in Regional Organization* (Boston, MA: Little, Brown and Co).

O'Hagan, Jacinta (1995) 'Civilisational Conflict? Looking for Cultural Enemies', *Third World Quarterly* 16, 1: 19–38.

OECD (1996a) *Integrating Environment and Economy: Progress in the 1990s* (Washington, DC: OCED Publications and Information Center).

OECD (1996b) *Saving Biological Diversity: Economic Incentives* (Paris: Organisation for Economic Cooperation and Development).

Ohmae, Kenichi (1990) *The Borderless World: Power and Strategy in the Global Marketplace* (New York: HarperBusiness, 1990).

Ohmae, Kenichi (1995) *The End of the Nation State: the Rise of Regional Economies* (London: HarperCollins).

'Oklahoma Bombing Chronology' (1998) *Washington Post* http: //www. washingtonpost.com/wp-srv/national/longterm/oklahoma/stories/chron.htm (accessed Feb 2000).

Oliver, James K. (1982) 'The Balance of Power: Heritage of Interdependence and Transnationalism', *International Studies Quarterly* 26, 3: 373–96.

Ostrom, Elinor (1990) *Governing the Commons: the Evolution of Institutions for Collective Action* (Cambridge and New York, NY: Cambridge University Press).

Palan, Ronen P. (1994) 'State and Society in International Relations', in Ronen P. Palan and Barry Gills (eds), *Transcending the State-Global Divide: a Neostructuralist Agenda in International Relations* (Boulder, CO: Lynne Rienner).

Palmer, Norman D. (1991) *The New Regionalism in Asia and the Pacific* (Lexington, MA: Lexington Books).

Parekh, Bhikhu C. (1999) *Colonialism, Tradition and Reform: an Analysis of Gandhi's Political Discourse*, 1st edn 1989 (New Delhi and London: Sage).

Parry, Benita (1972) *Delusions and Discoveries: Studies on India in the British Imagination, 1880–1930* (London: Allen Lane).

Pasha, Mustapha Kamal and David L. Blaney (1998) 'Elusive Paradise: the Promise and Peril of Global Civil Society', *Alternatives* 23, 4: 417–50.

Payne, Anthony (1996) 'The United States and its Enterprise for the Americas', in Gamble and Payne (eds), *Regionalism and World Order*.

Payne, Anthony and Andrew Gamble (1996) 'Introduction: the Political Economy of Regionalism and World Order', in Gamble and Payne (eds), *Regionalism and World Order*.

Pearce, David and Dominic Moran (1994) *The Economic Value of Biodiversity* (London: Earthscan in association with IUCN).

Pearce, David and R. Kerry Turner (1990) *Economics of Natural Resources and the Environment* (Hemel Hempstead: Harvester Wheatsheaf).

Pearce, David W. and Jeremy J. Warford (1993) *World without End: Economics, Environment, and Sustainable Development* (New York, NY: published for the World Bank by Oxford University Press).

Pearce, David, Anil Markandya and Edward B. Barbier (1989) *Blueprint for a Green Economy: a Report for the UK Department of the Environment* (London: Earthscan).

Peet, Richard and Michael Watts (1993) 'Introduction: Development Theory and Environment in an Age of Market Triumphalism', *Economic Geography* 69, 3: 227–53.

Pepper, Stephen C. (1942) *World Hypotheses* (Berkeley, CA: University of California Press).

Perera, Suvendrini (1991) *Reaches of Empire: the English Novel from Edgeworth to Dickens* (New York, NY: Columbia University Press).

Peters, Julia and Andrea Wolper (eds) (1995) *Women's Rights, Human Rights: International Feminist Perspectives* (New York and London: Routledge).

Peterson, V. Spike (1992) 'Transgressing Boundaries: Theories of Knowledge, Gender, and International Relations', *Millennium: Journal of International Studies* 21, 2: 183–206.

Peterson, V. Spike (1997a) 'Seeking World Order Beyond the Gendered Order of Global Hierarchies?' in Robert Cox (ed.), *The New Realism: Perspectives on Multilateralism and World Order* (London: Macmillan).

Peterson, V. Spike (1997b) 'Whose Crisis? Early and Postmodern Masculinism', in Stephen Gill and James H. Mittelman (eds), *Innovation and Transformation in International Studies* (Cambridge: Cambridge University Press): 185–201.

Peterson, V. Spike (1999) 'Sexing Political Identity/Nationalism as Heterosexism', *International Feminist Journal of Politics* 1, 1: 21–52.

Peterson, V. Spike and Anne Sisson Runyan (1999) *Global Gender Issues*, 2nd edn, 1st edn 1993 (Boulder, CO: Westview Press).

Peterson, V. Spike and Laura Parisi (1998) 'Are Women Human? It's Not an Academic Question', in Tony Evans (ed.), *Human Rights Fifty Years On: a Radical Reappraisal* (Manchester: University of Manchester Press and New York, NY: St Martin's Press).

Pettman, Jan Jindy (1996) *Worlding Women: a Feminist International Politics* (New York, NY: Routledge).

Pfaff, William (1993a) *The Wrath of Nations: Civilization and the Furies of Nationalism* (New York, NY: Simon & Schuster).

Pfaff, William (1993b) 'Invitation to War', *Foreign Affairs* 72, 3: 97–109.

Philpott, Daniel (1995) 'Sovereignty: an Introduction and Brief History', *Journal of International Affairs* 48, 2: 353–68.

Pollard, A.F. (1923) 'The Balance of Power', *Journal of the British Institute of International Affairs* 2: 51–64.

Potter, Pitman B. (1943) 'Universalism Versus Regionalism in International Organization', *American Political Science Review* 37, 5: 850–62 .

Prakash, Gyan (ed.) (1995) *After Colonialism: Imperial Histories and Postcolonial Displacements* (Princeton, NJ: Princeton University Press).

Preece, Jennifer J. (1997) 'Minority Rights in Europe: From Westphalia to Helsinki', *Review of International Studies* 23, 1: 75–92.

Premdas, R. (1991) 'The Internationalization of Ethnic Conflict: Some Theoretical Explorations', in K. M. de Silva and Ronald J. May (eds), *The Internationalization of Ethnic Conflict* (London: Pinter).

Price, Richard and Christian Reus-Smit (1998) 'Dangerous Liaisons? Critical International Theory and Constructivism', *European Journal of International Relations* 4, 3: 259–94.

Princen, Thomas, Matthias Finger and with contributions by Jack P. Manno and Margaret L. Clarkdon (1994) *Environmenal NGOs in World Politics: Linking the Local and the Global* (New York, NY: Routledge).

Prins, Gwyn (ed.) (1993) *Threats Without Enemies: Facing Environmental Insecurity* (London: Earthscan).

Puchala, Donald (1997) 'International Encounters of Another Kind', *Global Society* 11, 1: 5–29.

Qian, Wenrong (1995) 'The United Nations and State Sovereignty in the Post-Cold War Era', *Pacifica Review* 7, 2: 135–46.

Rae, Heather and Reus-Smit, Chris (eds) (1996) *The United Nations: Between Sovereignty and Global Governance?* (Melbourne: Department of Politics, La Trobe University).

Raeburn, Paul (1995) *The Last Harvest: the Genetic Gamble that Threatens to Destroy American Agriculture* (New York, NY: Simon & Schuster).

Ramazani, R. K. (1986) 'The Impact of Khomeini's Iran', in Robert O. Freedman (ed.), *The Middle East After the Israeli Invasion of Lebanon* (Syracuse, NY: Syracuse University Press).

Ramazani, R. K. (1988) *Revolutionary Iran: Challenge and Response in the Middle East* (Baltimore, MD: the Johns Hopkins University Press).

Ranchod-Nilson, Sita and Mary Ann Tetreault (eds) (2000) *Women, States and Nationalism: At Home in the Nation?* (New York, NY: Routledge).

Randall, Vicky (1987) *Women and Politics: an International Perspective*, 2nd edn (Chicago: University of Chicago Press).

Rapaport, D. C. (1996) 'The Importance of Space in Violent Ethno-Religious Strife' (San Diego, CA: Institute of Global Conflict and Cooperation, University of California, Policy Paper No. 21).

Rashid, Ahmed (1998) 'Pakistan and the Taliban', in William Maley (ed.), *Fundamentalism Reborn? Afghanistan and the Taliban* (London: Hurst).

Rashid, Ahmed (1999) 'Afghan Terrorism and Pakistan', *The Nation* 8 October.

Rawls, John (1971) *A Theory of Justice* (Cambridge, MA: Bellknap Press).

Razavi, Shara (1997) 'Fitting Gender into Development Institutions', *World Development* 25, 7: 1111–25.

Reardon, Betty (1985) *Sexism and the War System* (New York, NY: Columbia University Teachers College).

Reed, David (ed.) (1996) *Structural Adjustment, the Environment and Sustainable Development* (London: Earthscan).

Reich, Robert B. (1991) *The Work of Nations: Preparing Ourselves for 21st-Century Capitalism* (New York, NY: A.A. Knopf).

Reid, Walter V., *et al.* (1993) *Biodiversity Prospecting: Using Genetic Resources for Sustainable Development* (Baltimore, MD: World Resources Institute).

Rengger, N. J. (1989) 'Incommensurability, International Theory and the Fragmentation of Western Political Culture', in John Gibbins (ed.), *Contemporary Political Culture* (London, Newbury Park and Delhi: Sage).

Renner, Michael (1996) *Fighting for Survival: Environmental Decline, Social Conflict and the New Age of Insecurity* (New York, NY: W.W. Norton).

Reuters Ltd (1998) 'Intel co-founder donates for biodiversity centre: J7U74467.htm'.

Reynolds, Henry (1982) *The Other Side of the Frontier: Aboriginal Resistance to the European Invasion of Australia* (Ringwood, Vic: Penguin).

Reynolds, Henry (1987) *Frontier: Aborigines, Settlers and Land* (Sydney, NSW: Allen & Unwin).

Reynolds, Philip A. (1975) 'The Balance of Power: New Wine in an Old Bottle', *Political Studies* 23: 352–64.

Rich, Bruce (1994) *Mortgaging the Earth: the World Bank, Environmental Impoverishment, and the Crisis of Development* (Boston, MA: Beacon Press).

Richards, Paul (1996) *Fighting for the Rain Forest: War, Youth and Resources in Sierra Leone* (London: Heinemann).

Roberts, Adam (1995) 'Communal Conflict as a Challenge to International Organization: the Case of Former Yugoslavia', *Review of International Studies* 21, 4: 389–410.

Robson, Peter (1993) 'The New Regionalism and the Developing Countries', *Journal of Common Market Studies* 31, 3: 329–48.

Rojas, M. (1999) 'The Biotrade Initiative: Programme for Biodiversity-based Development', *Biotechnology and Development Monitor* 38: 11–14.

Ronfeldt, David, John Arquilla, Graham E. Fuller, Melissa Fuller (1998) *The Zapatista 'Social Netwar' in Mexico* (Santa Monica, CA: Rand).

Rootes, Christopher (ed.) (1999) *Environmental Movements: Local, National and Global*, Special Issue, *Environmental Politics* 8, 1.

Rorty, Richard (1989) *Contingency, Irony, and Solidarity* (Cambridge: Cambridge University Press).

Rosecrance, Richard (1991) 'Regionalism and the Post-Cold War Era', *International Journal* 46, 3: 373–93.

Rosenau, James N. (1997) *Along the Domestic–Foreign Frontier: Exploring Governance in a Turbulent World* (Cambridge: Cambridge University Press).

Ross, Eric B. 1998, *The Malthus Factor: Population, Poverty and Politics in Capitalist Development* (London: Zed Books).

Rostow, W. W. (1990) 'The Coming Age of Regionalism', *Encounter* LXXIV, 5: 3–7.

Rotberg, Robert I. (ed.) (1996) *Vigilance and Vengeance: NGOs Preventing Ethnic Conflict in Divided Societies* (Washington, DC: Brooking Institution Press).

Rotberg, Robert I. and Thomas G. Weiss (eds) (1996) *From Massacres to Genocide: the Media, Public Policy, and Humanitarian Crises* (Washington, DC: Brookings Institute).

Roy, Olivier (1986) *Islam and Resistance in Afghanistan* (Cambridge: Cambridge University Press).

Rubin, Barnett R. (1995) *The Fragmentation of Afghanistan: State Formation and Collapse in the International System* (New Haven, CT: Yale University Press).

Rubin, Charles T. (1994) *The Green Crusade: Rethinking the Roots of Environmentalism* (New York, NY: the Free Press).

Rubinstein, Richard E. and Jarleth Crocker (1994) 'Challenging Huntington', *Foreign Policy* 96: 113–28.

Ruggie, John G. (1998) *Constructing the World Polity: Essays on International Institutionalization* (London: Routledge).

Runyan, Anne Sisson (1991) *Feminism, Peace, and International Politics: an Examination of Women Organizing Internationally for Peace and Security* (Ann Arbor, MI: University Microfilms International, American University, PhD dissertation, 1988).

Runyan, Anne Sisson (1992) 'The "State" of Nature: a Garden Unfit for Women and Other Living Things', in V. Spike Peterson (ed.), *Gendered States* (Boulder, CO: Lynne Rienner): 123–40.

Russell, S. (1996) *A History of WWF*, 3rd edn (Gland, Switzerland: WWF-World Wide Fund for Nature).

Russell, Wynne (1998) Emotion and hierarchy in international relations: 'identity diplomacy', Russian–Estonian relations, and the redefinition of 'Europe', 1991–1996 (Ebeltoft, Denmark: paper presented to the Danish Social Science Council workshop entitled Social Constructivism in European Studies, 25–28 June); see also, forthcoming, Identity diplomacy, diplomacy, hierarchy and emotion in international society: the Russian–Baltic competition to become 'European', 1991–1996 (Canberra: PhD thesis, Australian National University).

Russett, Bruce (1993) *Grasping the Democratic Peace: Principles for a Post-Cold War World* (Princeton, NJ: Princeton University Press).

Ryan, Stephen (1990) *Ethnic Conflict and International Relations* (Aldershot, Hants: Dartmouth).

Said, Edward (1978a) 'Introduction', in Said, *Orientalism*.

Said, Edward W. (1978b) *Orientalism* (London: Routledge & Kegan Paul).

Said, Edward W. (1994) *Culture and Imperialism* (New York and London: Vintage).

Said, Edward W. (1997) *Covering Islam: How the Media and the Experts Determine How We See the Rest of the World* (London: Vintage).

Saikal, Amin (1980) *The Rise and Fall of the Shah* (Princeton, NJ: Princeton University Press).

Saikal, Amin (1993) 'The West and Post-Khomeini Iran', *World Today* 49, 10: 197–200.

Saikal, Amin (1998) 'Afghanistan's Ethnic Conflict', *Survival* 40, 2: 114–26.

Saikal, Amin and William Maley (1991) *Regime Change in Afghanistan: Foreign Intervention and the Politics of Legitimacy* (Boulder, CO: Westview Press).

Salamé, Ghassan (1993) 'Islam and the West', *Foreign Policy* 90: 23–8.

Sánchez, Vincente and Calestous Juma (eds) (1994) *Biodiplomacy: Genetic Resources and International Relations* (Nairobi: ACTS Press).

Sands, Philippe (1993) 'Enforcing Environmental Security', in Sands (ed.), *Greening International Law*: 50–64.

Sands, Philippe (ed.) (1993) *Greening International Law* (London: Earthscan Publications).

Sato Seizaburo (1997) 'Clash of Civilizations or Cross-Fertilization of Civilizations?', *Japan Echo* October: 44–9.

Scarry, Elaine (1985) *The Body in Pain: the Making and Unmaking of the World* (New York, NY: Oxford University Press).

Schechterman, Bernard and Martin Slann (eds) (1993) *The Ethnic Dimension in International Relations* (Westport, CT: Praeger).

Scheffer, David J. (1992) 'Toward a Modern Doctrine of Humanitarian Intervention', *University of Toledo Law Review* 23, 2: 253–94.

Schlesinger, Arthur (1991) *The Disuniting of America: Reflections on a Multicutural Society* (New York and London: W.W. Norton and Company).

Schmidheiny, Stephan and Federico Zorraquin (1996) *Financing Change: the Financial Community, Eco-efficiency, and Sustainable Development* (Cambridge, MA: the MIT Press).

Schmidheiny, Stephan with the BCSD (Business Council for Sustainable Development) (1992) *Changing Course: a Global Business Perspective on Development and the Environment* (Cambridge, MA: MIT Press).

Scholte, Jan A. (1997) 'Global Capitalism and the State', *International Affairs* 73, 3: 427–52.

Schor, Juliet B. (1992) 'Introduction', in Tariq Banuri and Juliet B. Schor (eds), *Financial Openness and National Autonomy* (Oxford: Clarendon Press).

Scruton, Roger (1983) *A Dictionary of Political Thought* (London: Pan Books).

Seager, Joni (1993) *Earth Follies: Coming to Feminist Terms with the Global Environmental Crisis* (New York, NY: Routledge).

Seth, Sanjay (1993) 'Political Theory in the Age of Nationalism', *Ethics and International Affairs* 7: 75–96.

Seth, Sanjay (1999) 'Rewriting Histories of Nationalism: the Politics of "Moderate Nationalism" in India, 1870–1905', *American Historical Review* 104, 1: 95–116.

Shalom, S. (1999) 'Lesson and Hope From Kerala', Znet Commentary@tao.ca, 21 June: 1–4.

Shand, H. (1997) *Human Nature: Agricultural Biodiversity and Farm-based Food Security* (Ottawa, Ont: Rural Advancement Foundation International).

Shapira, Shimon (1988) 'The Origins of Hizbullah', *Jerusalem Quarterly* 46: 114–30.

Sharoni, Simona (1995) *Gender and the Israeli–Palestinian Conflict: the Politics of Women's Resistance* (Syracuse, NY: Syracuse University Press).

Shiva, Vandana (1986) 'Ecology Movements in India', *Alternatives* 11, 2: 255–73.

Shiva, Vandana (1988) *Staying Alive: Women, Ecology and Development* (India: Kali for Women and London: Zed Press).

Shiva, Vandana (1993a) *Monocultures of the Mind: Perspectives on Biodiversity and Biotechnology* (London: Zed Books and Penang: Third World Network).

Shiva, Vandana (1993b) 'The Greening of the Global Reach', in Wolfgang Sachs (ed.), *Global Ecology: a New Arena of Political Conflict* (London: Zed Books, and Halifax, Nova Scotia: Fernwood).

Simpson, Gerry J. (1996) 'The Diffusion of Sovereignty: Self-determination in the Post-colonial Age', *Stanford Law Journal of International Law* 32, 2: 255–86.

Singer, Max and Aaron Wildavsky (1993) *The Real World Order: Zones of Peace, Zones of Turmoil* (Chatham, NJ: Chatham House Publishers).

Slaughter, Anne-Marie (1997),'The Real World Order', *Foreign Affairs* 76, 5: 183–97.

Slaughter-Burley, Anne-Marie (1993) 'International Law and International Relations Theory: a Dual Agenda', *American Journal Of International Law* 87, 2: 205–39.

Smart, Barry (1993) *Postmodernity* (London: Routledge).

Smith, Anthony D. (1995) *Nations and Nationalism in the Global Era* (London: Polity).

Smith, Steve (1997) 'New Approaches to International Theory', in Baylis and Smith (eds), *The Globalization of World Politics*.

Snyder, Jack (1993) 'Nationalism and the Crisis of the Post-Soviet State', *Survival* 35, 1: 5–26.

Spengler, Oswald (1926) *The Decline of the West*, translated with notes by Charles F. Atkinson (New York, NY: Knopf).

Spengler, Oswald (1932) *Man and Technics: a Contribution to a Philosophy of Life* (London: Allen & Unwin).

Spivak, Gayatri (1990) *The Post-colonial Critic: Interviews, Strategies, Dialogues*, edited by Sarah Harasym (New York, NY: Routledge).

Spivak, Gayatri (1999) *A Critique of Postcolonial Reason* (Cambridge, MA: Harvard University Press).

Spretnak, Charlene (1997) *The Return of the Real* (Reading, MA: Addison-Wesley).

Sprout, Harold and Margaret Sprout (1971) *Toward a Politics of the Planet Earth* (New York, NY: Van Nostrand Reinhold).

Stamp, Patricia (1997) 'Pastoral Power: Foucault and the New Imperial Order', in Clare O'Farrell (ed.), *Foucault: the Legacy* (Brisbane, Qld: Queensland University of Technology): 564–70.

Stares, Paul B. (1996) *Global Habit: the Drug Problem in a Borderless World* (Washington, DC: Brookings Institution).

Steans, Jill (1998) *Gender and International Relations: an Introduction* (Cambridge: Polity Press).

Stein, A. (1983) 'Coordination and Collaboration: Regimes in an Anarchic World', in Stephen Krasner (ed.), *International Regimes* (Ithaca, NY: Cornell University Press).

Steiner, George (1975) *After Babel: Aspects of Language and Translation* (London: Oxford University Press).

Stiehm, Judith (ed.) (1983) *Women and Men's Wars* (Oxford: Pergamon Press).

Stienstra, Deborah (1994) *Women's Movements and International Organization* (New York, NY: St Martin's Press).

Stoler, Ann Laura (1995) *Race and the Education of Desire* (Durham and London: Duke University Press).

Storper, M. (1997) 'Territories, Flows, and Hierarchies in the Global Economy', in Kevin R. Cox (ed.), *Spaces of Globalization: Reasserting the Power of the Local* (New York, NY: Guilford Press).

Stowell, Ellery C. (1921) *Intervention in International Law* (Washington: John Byrne).

Strange, Susan (1990) 'The Name of the Game', in N. X. Rizopoulos (ed.), *Sea-Changes: American Foreign Policy in a World Transformed* (New York, NY: Council on Foreign Relations Press).

Strange, Susan (1996) *The Retreat of the State: the Diffusion of Power in the World Economy* (Cambridge: Cambridge University Press).

Suleri, Sara (1992) *The Rhetoric of English India* (Chicago: Chicago University Press).

Sutherland, Joe (1999) 'Stem Rust Discovered in Wheat in Uganda, Could Seriously Threaten Wheat Production Around the World', *Plant Breeding News*, 102.

Sylvan, Richard and David Bennett (1994) *The Greening of Ethics: From Human Chauvinism to Deep-Green Theory* (Cambridge: the White Horse Press and Tucson, AZ: University of Arizona Press).

Sylvester, Christine (1994) *Feminist Theory and International Relations in a Postmodern Era* (Cambridge: Cambridge University Press).

Synge, Hugh and Harry Townsend (eds) (1979) *Survival or Extinction: Proceedings of a Conference held at the Royal Botanic Gardens, Kew, entitled The Practical Role of Botanic Gardens in the Conservation of Rare and Threatened Plants, 11–17 September 1978* (Kew: Bentham-Moxon Trust, Royal Botanic Gardens).

Taylor, Paul (1990) 'Regionalism: the Thought and the Deed', in A. J. R. Groom and Paul Taylor (eds), *Frameworks for International Co-operation* (New York, NY: St Martin's Press).

Teeple, Gary (1995) *Globalization and the Decline of Social Reform* (Toronto: Garamond Press).

Tennant, Chris (1994) 'Indigenous Peoples, International Institutions, and International Legal Literature from 1945–1993', *Human Rights Quarterly* 16, 1: 1–57.

Tetreault, Mary Ann (1994) *Women and Revolution in Africa, Asia, and the New World* (Columbia, SC: University of South Carolina Press).

Thakur, Ramesh (1997) 'From National to Human Security', in Stuart Harris and Andrew Mack (eds), *Asia-Pacific Security: the Economics-Politics Nexus* (St Leonards, NSW: Allen & Unwin).

Thomas, Caroline (1992) *The Environment in International Relations* (London: the Royal Institute of International Affairs).

Thomas, S. M., M. Brady and J. F. Burke (1999) 'Correspondence: Plant DNA Patents in the Hands of a Few', *Nature* 399, 6735: 405–6.

Tibawi, Abdul Latif (1969) *Jerusalem: its Place in Islamic and Arabic History* (Beirut: Institute for Palestine Studies).

Tickner, J. Ann (1992) *Gender in International Relations* (New York, NY: Columbia University Press).

Tickner. J. Ann (1995) 'Re-visioning Security', in Ken Booth and Steve Smith (eds), *International Relations Theory Today* (Cambridge: Polity Press): 175–97.

Todorov, Tzvetan (1993) *On Human Diversity: Nationalism, Racism and Exoticism in French Thought*, translated by Catherine Porter (Cambridge, MA: Harvard University Press).

TRAC (Transnational Resource and Action Centre) (1999) 'Key United Nations Agency Solicits Funds from Corporations', http: //www.corpwatch.org, March.

True, Jacqui (1996) 'Feminism', in Scott Burchill and Andrew Linklater with Richard Devetak, Matthew Paterson, and Jacqui True, *Theories of International Relations* (London: Macmillan): 210–51.

Ullmann, Walter (1975) *Law and Politics in the Middle Ages: an Introduction to the Sources of Medieval Political Ideas* (London: Sources of History Limited).

UNDP (United Nations Development Program) (1995) 'Redefining Security: the Human Dimension', *Current History* 94, 592: 229–36.

UNEP (United Nations Environment Program) (1997) 'Global State of the Environment Report 1997: Executive Summary', see http: //www.unep. org/eia/geo1/exsum/.

UNEP (United Nations Environment Program) (1999) *Global Environment Outlook – 2000*, accessible at http: //www.unep.org/.

UNGA (United Nations General Assembly) (1997) *Resolution adopted by the General Assembly: S/19–2: Program for the Further Implementation of Agenda 21*, 19 September, UN Doc. A/Res/S-19/2.

United Nations (1972) *Report of the United Nations Conference on the Human Environment, Stockholm, 5–16 June*, UN Doc. A/Conf.48/14/Rev.1.

United Nations (1998a) *Arrangements and Practices for the Interaction of Non-govern-mental Organizations in all Activities of the United Nations System: Report of the Secretary-General, 10 July*, UN Doc. A/53/170.

United Nations (1998b) *Coordination of the Policies and Activities of the Specialized Agencies and Other Bodies of the United Nations System related to the Coordinated*

Follow-up to and Implementation of the Vienna Declaration and Programme of Action: Report of the Secretary-General, ECOSOC, 1 June, UN Doc E/1998/60.

United Nations (1998c) *Follow-up to and Implementation of the Beijing Declaration and Platform for Action: Report of the Secretary-General,* 20 January, UN Doc E/CN.6/1998/2.

United Nations (1999) 'Press Release: Mr. Annan's Speech: "A Compact for the New Century" ', accessed from http: //www.un.org.

United Nations Demining Database (1999) http: //www.un.org/Depts/Landmine/ (accessed Feb).

United States Department of State (1996) *Patterns of Global Terrorism: 1995* (Washington: Department of State Publications).

Vagts, Alfred (1941) 'The US and the Balance of Power', *Journal of Politics* 3, 4: 441–9.

Vagts, Alfred (1948) 'Balance of Power: Growth of an Idea', *World Politics* 1, 1: 82–101.

Van Creveld, Martin (1991) *The Transformation of War* (New York, NY: the Free Press).

van Kleeck, Mary (1931) 'Analysis and Review of the Congress', in Mary L. Fleddérus (ed.), *World Social Economic Planning: the Necessity for Planned Adjustment of Productive Capacity and Standards of Living* (The Hague: International Industrial Relations Institute).

Vasquez, J. (1998) *The Power of Power Politics: From Classical Realism to Neotraditionalism* (Cambridge: Cambridge University Press).

Vattel, Emerich De (1863) *The Law of Nations,* 1st edn 1758 (New York, NY: AMS).

Vattimo, Gianni (1992) *The Transparent Society,* translated by D. Webb (Baltimore: the Johns Hopkins University Press).

Vernon, Raymond (1971) *Sovereignty at Bay: the Multinational Spread of US Enterprises* (New York, NY: Basic Books).

Virilio, Paul (1986) *Speed and Politics,* translated by Semiotext (e) and Mark Polizzoti, 1st edn 1977 (New York, NY: Semiotext (e)).

Vogel, Joseph Henry (1994) *Genes for Sale: Privatization as a Conservation Policy* (New York, NY: Oxford University Press).

Wackernagel, Mathis and William E. Rees (1996) *Our Ecological Footprint: Reducing Human Impact on the Earth* (Gabriola Island, BC: New Society Publishers).

Waever, Ole (1995) 'Securitization and Desecuritization', in Ronnie D. Lipschutz (ed.), *On Security* (New York, NY: Columbia University Press): 46–86.

Wagner, R. Harrison (1993) 'What was Bipolarity?', *International Organization* 47, 1: 77–106.

Walker, R. B. J. (1984a) 'East Wind, West Wind: Civilizations, Hegemonies, and World Orders' in Walker (ed.), *Culture, Ideology and World Order* (Boulder and London: Westview Press).

Walker, R. B. J. (1984b) 'World Politics and Western Reason: Universalism, Pluralism, Hegemony', in Walker (ed.), *Culture, Ideology and World Order* (Boulder and London: Westview Press).

Walker, R. B. J. (1988) *One World, Many Worlds: Struggles for a Just World Peace* (Boulder, CO: Lynne Rienner Publishers).

Walker, R. B. J. (1993) *Inside/Outside: International Relations as Political Theory* (Cambridge: Cambridge University Press).

Walker, R. B. J. (1995a) 'From International Relations to World Politics', in Joseph A. Camilleri, Anthony P. Jarvis and Albert J. Paolini (eds), *The State in Transition* (Boulder, CO: Lynne Reinner).

Walker, R. B. J. (1995b) 'International Relations and the Concept of the Political', in Ken Booth and Steve Smith (eds), *International Relations Theory Today* (Cambridge: Polity Press).

Wallerstein, Immanuel (1974) *The Modern World System,* volumes 1 and 2 (New York, NY: Academic Press).

Walt, Stephen (1997) 'Building up New Bogeymen' (Review Essay) *Foreign Policy* 106: 177–89.

Waltz, Kenneth N. (1959) *Man, The State and War* (New York: Columbia University Press).

Waltz, Kenneth N. (1979) *Theory of International Politics* (Reading: Addison-Wesley).

Waltz, Kenneth N. (1993) 'The Emerging Structure of International Politics', *International Security* 18, 2: 44–79.

Walzer, Michael (1977) *Just and Unjust Wars: a Moral Argument with Historical Illustrations* (New York, NY: Basic Books).

Wardlaw, Grant (1989) *Political Terrorism: Theory, Tactic and Counter-Measures* (Cambridge: Cambridge University Press).

Warren, D. Michael, L. Jan Slikkerveer and David Brokensha (eds) (1995) *The Cultural Dimension of Development: Indigenous Knowledge Systems* (London: Intermediate Technology Publications).

Warren, Karen J. with Nisvan Erkal (eds) (1997) *Ecofeminism: Women, Culture, Nature* (Bloomington, IN: Indiana University Press).

Waters, Malcolm (1995) *Globalization* (London: Routledge).

Watson, Adam (1992) *The Evolution of International Societies: a Comparative Historical Analysis* (London: Routledge).

WCED (World Commission on Environment and Development) (1987) *Our Common Future* (Oxford: Oxford University Press, chair: Gro Harlem Brundtland).

Webb, Michael C. (1991) 'International Economic Structures, Government Interests, and International Coordination of Microeconomic Adjustment Policies', *International Organization* 45, 3: 309–42.

Weber, Cynthia (1999) *Faking It: US Hegemony in a 'Post-Phallic' Era* (Minneapolis, MN: University of Minnesota Press).

Weber, Max (1991) 'Politics as a Vocation', in H. H. Gerth and C. Wright Mills (eds), *From Max Weber: Essays in Sociology* (London: Routledge).

Weiss, Linda (1998) *The Myth of the Powerless State: Governing the Economy in a Global Era* (Cambridge: Polity Press in association with Blackwell).

Weiss, Thomas G. and Leon Gordenker (eds) (1996) *NGOs, the UN, and Global Governance* (Boulder, CO: Lynne Rienner Publishers).

Welch, David (1997) 'The "Clash of Civilisations" Thesis as an Argument and as a Phenomenon', *Security Studies* 6, 4: 197–216.

Wendt, Alexander (1999) *Social Theory of International Politics* (New York, NY: Cambridge University Press).

Westing, Arthur H. (1989) 'The Environment Component of Comprehensive Security', *Bulletin of Peace Proposals* 20, 2: 129–34.

Westing, Arthur H. (ed.) (1989) *Comprehensive Security for the Baltic: an Environmental Approach* (London: Sage).

Westlake, John (1910) *International Law*, 1st edn 1904 (Cambridge: Cambridge University Press).

Whitworth, Sandra (1994) *Feminism and International Relations: Towards a Political Economy of Gender in Interstate and Non-Governmental Institutions* (London: Macmillan).

Whitworth, Sandra (forthcoming) *Warrior Princes and the Politics of Peacekeeping* (Boulder, CO: Lynne Rienner).

Wight, Martin (1966a) 'Why is there no International Theory?', in Herbert Butterfield and Martin Wight (eds), *Diplomatic Investigations: Essays in the Theory of International Politics* (London: George Allen & Unwin).

Wight, Martin (1966b) 'The Balance of Power', in Herbert Butterfield and Martin Wight (eds), *Diplomatic Investigations: Essays in the Theory of International Politics* (London: Allen & Unwin).

Wight, Martin (1966c) 'Western Values In International Relations', in Herbert Butterfield and Martin Wight (eds), *Diplomatic Investigations: Essays in the Theory of International Politics* (London: George Allen & Unwin).

Wight, Martin (1977) *Systems Of States*, edited by Hedley Bull (Leicester: Leicester University Press).

Wight, Martin (1978) *Power Politics*, edited by Hedley Bull and Carsten Holbraad (Leicester: Leicester University Press).

Wight, Martin (1991) *International Theory: the Three Traditions*, edited by Gabriele Wight and Brian Porter (Leicester: Leicester University Press).

Wilkin, Peter (1997) 'New Myths for the South: Globalization and the Conflict between Private Power and Freedom', in Caroline Thomas and Peter Wilkin (eds), *Globalization and the South* (Basingstoke: Macmillan Press).

Wohlforth, William Curtis (1993) *The Elusive Balance: Power and Perceptions During the Cold War* (Ithaca: Cornell University Press).

Wokler, Robert (1998) 'The Enlightenment Project as Betrayed By Modernity', *History of European Ideas* 24, 4/5: 301–13.

Wolf, Eric R. (1982) *Europe and the People Without History* (Berkeley, CA: University of California Press).

Wolfe, Patrick (1999) *Settler Colonialism and the Transformation of Anthropology* (London and New York, NY: Cassell).

Wright, Moorhead (1975) *Theory and Practice of the Balance of Power 1481–1914: Selected European Writings* (London: Dent).

Wriston, Walter B. (1997) 'Bits, Bytes, and Diplomacy', *Foreign Affairs* 76, 5: 172–82.

Wyatt-Walter, Andrew (1995) 'Regionalism, Globalization, and World Economic Order', in Fawcett and Hurrell (eds), *Regionalism in World Politics*.

Young, Arthur P. (1933) *Forward From Chaos* (London: Nisbet).

Young, Crawford (ed.) (1993) *The Rising Tide of Cultural Pluralism: the Nation-State at Bay?* (Madison, WI: University of Winsconsin Press).

Young, Michael, Neil Gunningham, Jane Elix, Judy Lambert, Bruce Howard, Peter Grabosky and E. McCrone (1996) *Reimbursing the Future: an Evaluation of Motivational, Voluntary, Price-Based, Property Right, and Regulatory Incentives for the Conservation of Biodiversity*, Parts 1 and 2 (Canberra: Department of the Environment, Sport and Territories, Biodiversity Series, Paper No. 9).

Young, Oran R. (ed.) (1997) *Global Governance: Drawing Insights from the Environmental Experience* (Cambridge, MA: MIT Press).

Young, Robert (1990) *White Mythologies: Writing History and the West* (London and New York, NY: Routledge).

Younge, G. (1998) 'On a Journey Through Borders of Hate', *Guardian Weekly* (28 June): 24–5.

Yousaf, Mohammed and Mark Adkin (1992) *The Bear Trap: Afghanistan's Untold Story* (London: Mark Cooper).

Yuval-Davis, Nira (1997) *Gender and Nation* (Newbury Park, CA: Sage).

Zakaria, Fareed (1994) 'A Conversation with Lee Kuan Yew', *Foreign Affairs* 73, 2: 109–26.

Zalewski, Marysia and Jane Parpart (eds) (1998) *The 'Man' Question in International Relations* (Boulder, CO: Westview Press).

Zimmern, Alfred (1934) 'International Law and Social Consciousness', *Transactions of the Grotius Society* 20: 36–51.

Zolo, Danilo (1997) *Cosmopolis: Prospects for World Government* (Cambridge: Polity Press).

Index

absolutism, 100, 101
Afghanistan, 15, 164, 171–6 *passim*, 237
  see also Soviet Union
Africa, 44, 120, 152, 188, 204, 219, 260, 263n5, 269n5
Africa, Central, 25
Africa, North, 176
Africa, West, 34, 152
'age of regions', 251, 254, 257
  see also 'coming age of regionalism'
agency, 73, 118, 121–4, 125, 160, 252–5
aid, *see* development assistance
Algeria, 164, 171, 174
American Revolution, 21
anarchy, 34, 39, 40, 43, 91, 98, 106, 158, 246
  see also 'coming anarchy'
anarchy problematique, 224
Ankersmit, F.R., 228, 231, 234
apartheid, 27, 42
Arab-Israeli conflict, 168, 176
arms, 37, 129, 148, 153, 233, 234, 266n4
  see also nuclear weapons, weapons
ASEAN Regional Forum, 120, 129
Asia, 58, 122, 139, 140, 219
  see also Asia-Pacific region, Central Asia, East Asia, South Asia, Southeast Asia
Asia Pacific Economic Cooperation (APEC), 119, 122, 127, 128
Asia-Pacific region, 29, 120
Asian Development Bank, 190
Asian financial crisis, 122, 129, 141
Association of Southeast Asian Nations (ASEAN), 119, 121, 122, 139, 196
Australia, 29, 30, 194

authority, 5, 8, 92, 103, 106, 112, 115, 116, 267n6
  and civilizations, 138
  and gender, 206, 208
  and regionalism, 13, 118
  and the state, 61, 64, 68, 82, 248
  in Asia, 140
  in medieval Christianity, 110–11
  overlapping, 5, 12, 109, 110, 114, 121, 127, 162
Ayoob, Mohammed, 118, 121, 122, 126

'back to the future', 2, 11, 33, 34, 37, 38, 41, 42, 246, 259
  and differentiation, 252
  and power, 255
  and transformation of world politics, 247
'balance of power', 8, 73, 144, 247, 255, 259
  and the US, 48–9
  and world order, 2, 249
  as cause of war, 48
  as metaphor and myth, 6, 11–12, 52–9, 233–4
  in IR theory, 60
  metaphorical status of, 49–50
  mythical status of, 51–2
  shift in, 82, 141
Balkans, 33, 36, 37, 42, 144, 152
  see also Yugoslavia
Barak, Ehud, 175
barbarism, 151, 153, 156, 157, 158, 161
Bartley, Robert, 146–7
Beijer International Institute of Ecological Economics, 194